On the Anarchy of Poetry and Philosophy

D1598544

John D. Caputo, *series editor*

PERSPECTIVES IN
CONTINENTAL
PHILOSOPHY

GERALD L. BRUNS

On the Anarchy of Poetry and Philosophy
A Guide for the Unruly

FORDHAM UNIVERSITY PRESS
New York ■ 2006

Library of Congress Cataloging-in-Publication Data
  Bruns, Gerald L.
    On the anarchy of poetry and philosophy : a guide for the unruly /
Gerald L. Bruns.
      p.   cm. — (Perspectives in continental philosophy)
    Includes bibliographical references.
    ISBN-13: 978-0-8232-2632-0 (cloth : alk. paper)
    ISBN-10: 0-8232-2632-8 (cloth : alk. paper)
    ISBN-13: 978-0-8232-2633-7 (pbk. : alk. paper)
    ISBN-10: 0-8232-2633-6 (pbk. : alk. paper)
    1. Aesthetics.   2. Art — Philosophy.   3. Poetry.   4. Poetry — History and
criticism.   I. Title.
  BH39.B795   2006
  111'.85 — dc22   2006035284

Printed in the United States of America
08 07 06   5 4 3 2 1
First edition

For Marjorie and Joe Perloff

Human life, distinct from juridical existence, existing as it does on a globe isolated in celestial space, from night to day and from one country to another—human life cannot in any way be limited to the closed systems assigned to it by reasonable conceptions. The immense travail of recklessness, discharge, and upheaval that constitutes life could be expressed by stating that life starts with the deficit of these systems; at least what it allows in the way of order and reserve has meaning only from the moment when the ordered and reserved forces liberate and lose themselves for ends that cannot be subordinated to any thing one can account for. It is only by such insubordination—even if it is impoverished—that the human race ceases to be isolated in the unconditional splendor of material things.

—Georges Bataille, "The Notion of *Dépense*"

Contents

Acknowledgments

Some half-dozen pages of chapter 2, "Ancients and Moderns: Gadamer's Aesthetic Theory and Paul Celan's Poetry," first appeared in an essay, "The Hermeneutical Anarchist: *Phronesis*, Rhetoric, and the Experience of Art," in *Gadamer's Century: Essays in Honor of Hans-Georg Gadamer*, ed. Jeff Malpas, Ulrich Arnswald, and Jens Kerscher (Cambridge, MA: MIT Press, 2002). Chapter 3, "Foucault's Modernism: Language, Poetry, and the Experience of Freedom," first appeared in *The Cambridge Companion to Foucault*, ed. Gary Gutting, 2d ed. (Cambridge: Cambridge University Press, 2005). Chapter 4, "Poetic Communities," first appeared in the *Iowa Review* 32, no. 1 (Spring 2002). Chapter 5, "Francis Ponge on the Rue de la Chaussée d'Antin," first appeared in *Comparative Literature* 53, no. 3 (Summer 2001). Chapter 6 first appeared as "The Senses of Augustine (On Some of Lyotard's Remains)" in *Religion and Literature* 32, no. 3 (Autumn 2001). Chapter 7 first appeared as "Anarchic Temporality: Writing, Friendship, and the Ontology of the Work of Art," in *The Power of Contestation: Essays on Maurice Blanchot*, ed. Geoffrey Hartman and Kevin Hart (Baltimore: The Johns Hopkins University Press, 2004). Chapter 8, "The Concepts of Art and Poetry in Emmanuel Levinas's Writings," first appeared in *The Cambridge Companion to Levinas*, ed. Simon Critchley and Robert Bernasconi (Cambridge: Cambridge University Press, 2002).

Thanks to all for permission to reproduce this material.

I'm especially grateful to many colleagues and friends—too many, really, to enumerate. But particular thanks to those that prompted me to write the various portions of this book: Ulrich Arnswald, Robert Bernasconi, Simon Critchley, Jim Dougherty, Gary Gutting, Geoffrey Hartman, and Kevin Hart. Thanks also to anonymous readers for *Comparative Literature* and Fordham University Press, to R. M. Berry, Jr., and to David Hamilton, editor of the *Iowa Review*. Special thanks to Steve Fredman.

And love to Nancy and Jacob, Anne, Andy, and Eloise, Marga and Wes, and John and Alicia.

Abbreviations for Frequently Cited Texts

Theodore Adorno

AeT   *Aesthetic Theory.* Trans. Robert Hullot-Kentor. Minneapolis: University of Minnesota Press, 1997.

AT   *Ästhetische Theorie.* Frankfurt am Main: Suhrkamp, 1973.

David Antin

tb   *talking at the boundaries.* New York: New Directions, 1976.

wim   *what does it mean to be avant-garde.* New York: New Directions, 1990.

Antonin Artaud

AA   *Antonin Artaud: Selected Writings.* Ed. Susan Sontag. Berkeley: University of California Press, 1988.

ŒA   *Œuvres complètes.* Paris: Éditions Gallimard, 1956.

TD   *Le theater et son double.* Paris: Éditions Gallimard, 1964.

Georges Bataille

AM   *The Absence of Myth: Writings on Surrealism.* Trans. Michael Richardson. London: Verso, 1994.

AS   *The Accursed Share: An Essay on General Economy.* Trans. Robert Hurley. New York: Zone Books, 1988.

CS   *The College of Sociology.* Ed. Dennis Hollier. Trans. Betsy Wing. Minneapolis: University of Minnesota Press, 1988.

ExI   *L'expérience intérieure.* Paris: Éditions Gallimard, 1943.

IE   *Inner Experience.* Trans. Leslie Anne Boldt. Albany, NY: State University of New York Press, 1988.

OC   *Œuvres complètes.* 12 v. Paris: Éditions Gallimard, 1970–1988.

PM   *La part maudite, precede de la notion dépense.* Paris: Éditions de Minuit, 1967.

VE   *Visions of Excess: Selected Writings, 1927–1939.* Trans. Allan Stoekl. Minneapolis: University of Minnesota Press, 1985.

Charles Baudelaire

Œ.2   *Œuvres complètes.* 2d ed. Ed. Claude Pichois. Paris: Éditions Gallimard, 1976.

SWA   *Selected Writings on Art and Literature.* Trans. P. E. Charvet. London: Penguin Books, 1972.

Walter Benjamin

AC   *The Arcades Project.* Trans. Howard Eiland and Kevin McLaughlin. Cambridge, MA: Harvard University Press, 1999.

CB   *Charles Baudelaire: A Lyric Poet in the Era of High Capitalism.* Trans. Harry Zohn. London: Verso, 1973.

GS   *Gesammelte Schriften.* 7v. Ed. Rolf Tiedemann and Herman Schweppenhäuser. Frankfurt am Main: Suhrkamp, 1972.

SW1   *Selected Writings, 1: 1913–1926.* Ed. Marcus Bullock and Michael W. Jennings. Trans. Edmund Jephcott et al. Cambridge, MA: Harvard University Press, 1996.

SW2   *Selected Writings, 2: 1927–1934.* Ed. Marcus Bullock and Michael W. Jennings. Trans. Edmund Jephcott et al. Cambridge, MA: Harvard University Press, 1999.

SW3   *Selected Writings, 3: 1935–1938.* Ed. Howard Eiland and Michael W. Jennings. Trans. Edmund Jephcott et al. Cambridge, MA: Harvard University Press, 2002.

SW4   *Selected Writings, 4: 1938–1940.* Ed. Howard Eiland and Michael W. Jennings. Trans. Edmund Jephcott et al. Cambridge, MA: Harvard University Press, 2003.

Maurice Blanchot

A   *L'amité*. Paris: Éditions Gallimard, 1971.
AM   *L'arrêt de mort*. Paris: Éditions Gallimard, 1948.
AO   *L'attente, l'oubli*. Paris: Éditions Gallimard, 1962.
AWO   *Awaiting Oblivion*. Trans. John Gregg. Lincoln: University of Nebraska Press, 1997.
BC   *The Book to Come*. Trans. Charlotte Mandel. Stanford: Stanford University Press, 2003.
CI   *La communauté inavouable*. Paris: Éditions du Minuit, 1983.
DS   *Death Sentence*. Trans. Lydia Davis. Barrytown, NY: Station Hill Press, 1978.
ED   *L'écriture du désastre*. Paris: Éditions Gallimard, 1980.
EI   *L'entretien infini*. Paris: Éditions Gallimard, 1969.
EL   *L'espace littéraire*. Paris: Éditions Gallimard, 1955.
F   *Friendship*. Trans. Elizabeth Rottenberg. Stanford: Stanford University Press, 1997.
Fp   *Faux pas*. Paris: Éditions Gallimard, 1943.
FP   *Faux pas*. Trans. Charlotte Mandel. Stanford: Stanford University Press, 2001.
GO   *The Gaze of Orpheus and Other Literary Essays*. Trans. Lydia Davis. Barrytown, NY: Station Hill Press, 1981.
IC   *The Infinite Conversation*. Trans. Susan Hanson. Minneapolis: University of Minnesota Press, 1993.
LV   *Le livre à venir*. Paris: Éditions Gallimard, 1959.
PD   *Le pas au–delá*. Paris: Éditions Gallimard, 1973.
PF   *La part du feu*. Paris: Éditions Gallimard, 1949.
SL   *The Space of Literature*. Trans. Ann Smock. Lincoln: University of Nebraska Press, 1982.
SNB   *The Step Not Beyond*. Trans. Lycette Nelson. Albany: State University of New York Press, 1992.
UC   *The Unavowable Community*. Trans. Pierre Joris. Barrytown, NY: Station Hill Press, 1988.
WF   *The Work of Fire*. Trans. Charlotte Mandell. Stanford: Stanford University Press, 1995.

John Cage

EW   *Empty Words: Writings, '73–'78*. Middletown, CT: Wesleyan University Press, 2001.
S   *Silence: Lectures and Writings by John Cage*. Middletown, CT: Wesleyan University Press, 1961.

Stanley Cavell

CR   *The Claim of Reason: Wittgenstein, Skepticism, Morality, and Tragedy.* New York: Oxford University Press, 1979.

MW   *Must We Mean What We Say? A Book of Essays.* New York: Scribner, 1969.

QO   *In Quest of the Ordinary: Lines of Skepticism and Romanticism.* Chicago: University of Chicago Press, 1988.

SW   *The Senses of Walden.* San Francisco: North Point Press, 1981.

Paul Celan

B   *Breathturn.* Trans. Pierre Joris. Los Angeles: Sun and Moon Press, 1995.

CP   *Collected Prose.* Tran. Rosemarie Waldrop. Riverdale-on-Hudson, NY: Sheep Meadow Press, 1986.

FB   *Fathomsuns and Benighted: Fadensonnen and Eingedunkelt.* Riverdale-on-Hudson, NY: The Sheep Meadow Press, 2001.

GWC *Gesammelte Werke.* 5v. Frankfurt am Main: Suhrkamp, 1986.

PPC   *Poems of Paul Celan.* Trans. Michael Hamburger. New York: Persea Books, 1988.

SPP   *Selected Poems and Prose.* Trans. John Felstiner. New York: Norton, 2001.

T   *Threadsuns.* Trans. Pierre Joris. Los Angeles: Sun and Moon Press, 2000.

Arthur Danto

BBB   *Beyond the Brillo Box: The Visual Arts in Post-historical Perspective.* New York: Farrar Straus Giroux, 1992.

PDA   *The Philosophical Disenfranchisement of Art.* New York: Columbia University Press, 1986.

TC   *The Transfiguration of the Commonplace: A Philosophy of Art.* Cambridge, MA: Harvard University Press, 1981.

Gilles Deleuze and Félix Guattari

MP   *Milles Plateaux: capitalisme et schizophrenie.* Paris: Éditions du Minuit, 1980.

TP   *A Thousand Plateaus: Capitalism and Schizophrenia.* Trans. Brian Massumi. Minneapolis: University of Minnesota Press, 1980.

Michel Foucault

AK *The Archeology of Knowledge*. Trans. A. M. Sheridan Smith. New York: Pantheon Books, 1972.

AME *Aesthetics, Method, and Epistemology: Essential Works of Foucault, 1954–1984*. Vol. 2. Ed. James D. Faubion. New York: The New Press, 1998.

AS *L'Archéologie du savoir*. Paris: Éditions Gallimard, 1969.

DE *Dits et écrits*. 4 vols. Ed. Daniel Defert et al. Paris: Éditions Gallimard, 1994.

DP *Discipline and Punish: The Birth of the Prison*, trans. Alan Sheridan. New York: Vintage Books, 1977.

EST *Ethics, Subjectivity, and Truth: Essential Works of Foucault, 1954–1984*. Vol. 1. Ed. Paul Rabinow. New York: The New Press, 1997.

FD *Folie et déraison: Histoire de la folie à l'âge classique*. Paris: Plon, 1961.

MC *Madness and Civilization: A History of Insanity in the Age of Reason*. Trans. Richard Howard. New York, Vintage Books, 1965.

MeC *Les mots et les choses*. Paris: Éditions Gallimard, 1996.

OD *L'ordre du discours*. Paris: Éditions Gallimard, 1971.

OT *The Order of Things: An Archeology of the Human Sciences*. New York: Vintage Books, 1970.

P *Power: Essential Works of Foucault, 1954–1984*. Vol. 3. Ed. James D. Faubion. New York: The New Press, 2000.

SP *Surveiller et punir: naissance de la prison*. Paris: Éditions Gallimard, 1975.

Hans-Georg Gadamer

DD *Dialogue and Dialectic: Eight Hermeneutical Studies on Plato*. Trans. P. Christopher Smith. New Haven: Yale University Press, 1980.

GC *Gadamer on Celan: Who Am I and Who Are You? and Other Essays*. Trans. Richard Heinemann and Bruce Krajewski. Albany: State University of New York Press, 1997.

GW *Gesammelte Werke*. 10v. Tübingen: J.C.B. Mohr (Paul Siebeck), 1986–1993.

PH *Philosophical Hermeneutics*. Trans. David E. Linge. Berkeley: University of California Press, 1976.

RB   *The Relevance of the Beautiful and Other Essays.* Trans. Nicholas Walker. Ed. Robert Bernasconi. Cambridge: Cambridge University Press, 1986.

RS   *Reason in the Age of Science.* Trans. Frederick G. Lawrence. Cambridge: MIT Press, 1981.

TM   *Truth and Method.* Second Revised Edition. Trans. Donald G. Marshall and Joel Weinsheimer. New York: Crossroad Publishing, 1989.

WM   *Wahrheit und Methode: Grundzüge einer philosophischen Hermeneutik.* 4th Auflage. Tübingen: J. C. B. Mohr (Paul Siebeck), 1975.

Friedrich Hegel

PhG   *Phänomenologie des Geist.* Zweiter Band. Ed. Hans-Friedrich Wessels und Heinrich Clairmont. Hamburg: Felix Meiner, 1988.

PS   *Phenomenology of Spirit.* Trans. A. V. Miller. Oxford: Oxford University Press, 1977.

Martin Heidegger

BP   *Basic Problems in Phenomenology.* Trans. Albert Hofstadter. Bloomington: Indiana University Press, 1982.

BT   *Being and Time.* Trans. Edward Robinson and John McQuarrie. New York: Harper and Row, 1962.

G   *Gesamtausgabe.* 5: *Holzwege.* Frankfurt: Vittorio Klostermann, 1977.

GP   *Die Grundprobleme der Phänomenologie.* Ed. Friedrich-Wilhelm von Hermann. Frankfurt am Main: Vittorio Klostermann, 1975.

OWL   *On the Way to Language.* Trans. Peter Hertz. New York: Harper and Row, 1971.

PLT   *Poetry, Language, Thought.* Trans. Albert Hofstadter. New York: Harper and Row, 1971.

SZ   *Sein und Zeit.* Tübingen: Max Niemeyer Verlag, 1993.

US   *Unterwegs zur Sprache.* Pfullingen: Neske, 1959.

VA   *Vorträge und Aufsätze.* Pfullingen: Neske, 1954.

Emmanuel Levinas

AE   *Autrement qu'être ou au–delà l'essence*. The Hague: Martinus Nijhoff, 1974.

BW   *Basic Philosophical Writings*. Ed. Adriaan T. Peperzak, Simon Critchley, and Robert Bernasconi. Bloomington: Indiana University Press, 1996.

CPP   *Collected Philosophical Papers*. Trans. Alphonso Lingis. The Hague: Martinus Nijhoff, 1987.

DEE   *De l'existence à l'existant*. Paris: Éditions de la revue fontaine, 1947.

EDL   *En découvrant l'existence avec Husserl at Heidegger*. 3d ed. Paris: Vrin, 1974.

EE   *Existence and Existents*. Trans. Alphonso Lingis. Dordrecht: Kluwer Academic Publishers, 1978.

EN   *Entre nous: Essais sur le penser–à–l'autre*. Paris: Éditions Grasset and Fasquelle, 1991.

HH   *Humanisme de l'autre homme*. Montpellier: Éditions Fata Morgana, 1976.

HS   *Hors sujet*. Montpellier: Éditions Fata Morgana, 1987.

IH   *Les imprevus de l'histoire*. Montpellier: Éditions Fata Morgana, 1994.

LR   *The Levinas Reader*. Ed. Sean Hand. Oxford: Basil Blackwell, 1989.

NP   *Noms propres*. Montpellier: Éditions Fata Morgana, 1976.

NTR   *Nine Talmudic Readings*. Trans. Annette Aronowicz. Bloomington: Indiana University Press, 1990.

OS   *Outside the Subject*. Trans. Michael B. Smith. Stanford: Stanford University Press, 1993.

OTB   *Otherwise Than Being, or Beyond Essence*. Trans. Alphonso Lingis. The Hague: Martinus Nijhoff, 1981.

PN   *Proper Names*. Trans. Michael B. Smith. Stanford: Stanford University Press, 1996.

SMB   *Sur Maurice Blanchot*. Montpellier: Éditions Fata Morgana, 1975.

TA   *Le temps et l'autre*. Paris: Montpellier: Éditions Fata Morgana, 1979.

TeI   *Totalité et infini. Essai sur l'extériorité*. The Hague: Martinus Nijhoff, 1961.

TI   *Totality and Infinity: An Essay on Exteriority*. Trans. Alphonso Lingis. Pittsburgh: Duquesne University Press, 1969.

TO   *Time and the Other*. Trans. Richard Cohen. Pittsburgh: Duquesne University Press, 1987.

Jean François Lyotard

AJ   *(with Jean-Loup Thébaud) Au Juste*. Paris: Christian Bourgois, 1979.
CA   *The Confessions of Augustine*. Trans. Richard Beardsworth. Stanford: Stanford University Press, 2000.
CdA   *La confession d'Augustin*. Paris: Éditions Galilée, 1998.
D   *The Differend: Phrases in Dispute*, trans. Georges Van Den Abbeele. Minneapolis: University of Minnesota Press, 1988.
Di   *Le différend*. Paris: Éditions du Minuit, 1983.
EL   *Économie libidinale*. Paris: Éditions du Minuit, 1974.
In   *L'Inhuman: Causeries sur le temps*. Paris: Éditions Galilée, 1988.
IR   *The Inhuman: Reflections on Time*. Trans. Geoffrey Bennington and Rachel Bowlby. Stanford: Stanford University Press, 1991.
JG   *Just Gaming*. Trans. Wlad Godzich. Minneapolis: University of Minnesota Press, 1985.
LA   *Lessons on the Analytic of the Sublime (Kant's 'Critique of Judgment,' §§ 23–29)*. Trans. Elizabeth Rottenberg. Stanford: Stanford University Press, 1991.
LE   *Libidinal Economy*. Trans. Iain Hamilton Grant. Bloomington: Indiana University Press, 1993.
LR   *The Lyotard Reader*. Ed. Andrew Benjamin. Oxford: Basil Blackwell, 1989.
LsA   *Leçons sur l'analytique du sublime*. Paris: Éditions Gallimard, 1991.
P   *Peregrinations: Law, Form, Event*. New York: Columbia University Press, 1988.

Stéphane Mallarmé

ŒM   *Œuvres complètes*. Ed. Henri Mondor et G. Jean-Aubry. Paris: Éditions Gallimard, 1945.

Jean-Luc Marion

De   *Dieu sans l'être: Hors–texte*. Paris: Librairie Arthème Fayard, 1982.

GB	*God without Being*. Trans. Thomas Carlson. Chicago: University of Chicago Press, 1991.
GG	*"In the Name: How to Avoid Speaking of 'Negative Theology.'"* In *God, the Gift, and Postmodernism*. Ed. John D. Caputo and Michael J. Scanlon. Bloomington: Indiana University Press, 1999, pp. 20–42.
Id	*L'Idole et la distance*. Paris: Éditions Bernard Grasset, 1977.
ID	*The Idol and Distance*. Trans. Thomas A. Carlson. New York: Fordham University Press, 2001.

Jean-Luc Nancy

BP	*The Birth to Presence*. Trans. Brian Holmes. Stanford: Stanford University Press, 1993.
BS	*Being Singular Plural*. Trans. Robert D. Richardson and Anne E. O'Byne. Stanford: Stanford University Press, 2000.
CD	*La communauté désœuvrée*. Paris: Christian Bourgois, 1990.
EF	*The Experience of Freedom*. Trans. Bridget McDonald. Stanford: Stanford University Press, 1993.
ESP	*Être singulier pluriel*. Paris: Éditions Galilée, 1996.
ExL	*L'expérience de la liberté*. Paris: Éditions Galilée, 1988.
InC	*The Inoperative Community*. Trans. Peter Connor et al. Minneapolis: University of Minnesota Press, 1991.
PV	*Le partage de voix*. Paris: Éditions Galilée, 1982.
SV	*"Sharing Voices."* In *Transforming the Hermeneutic Context: Nietzsche to Nancy*. Ed. Gayle L. Ormiston and Alan D. Schrift. Albany: State University of New York Press, 1990.

Francis Ponge

PP	*Le parti pris des choses, suive de Proêmes*. Paris: Éditions Gallimard, 1948.
VT	*The Voice of Things*. Trans. Beth Archer. New York: McGraw-Hill, 1972.

Jean-Paul Sartre

QL	*Qu'est-ce que la littérature?* Paris: Éditions Gallimard, 1948.
SI	*Situations, I*. Paris: Éditions Gallimard, 1947.
WL	*"What Is Literature?" and Other Essays*. Ed. Steven Ungar. Cambridge, MA: Harvard University Press, 1988.

Preface

Much of European philosophy since Nietzsche has been admired, and also occasionally deplored, for its critique of *modernity*, or what Max Weber had in mind when he spoke of the "rationalization" or "disenchantment" of the world—a process that entails many interrelated innovations: the development of scientific reason, the rise of bourgeois capitalism and the industrialization of Europe and North America, the rapid progress of technology along with sophisticated applications of instrumental reason, whether in the form of the mechanization (or "modernization") of social life or in the development of systems of management and bureaucratic control. Anthony Giddens has developed a very clear and persuasive conception of modernity that focuses, as did Michel Foucault's research, on the development of the modern state and its capacities for the surveillance, normalization, and control of mass populations. One could add further examples from the German and French phenomenological traditions after Heidegger as well as from the Frankfurt School of Horkheimer and Adorno, the work of Walter Benjamin, and much of French intellectual culture since 1960.

Modernity also gave us the concept of art as such—art that is not in the service of the court, the church, or the school. But unlike other of modernity's innovations, art proved to be an anomaly. The fact is that particular works of art appeared to lose definition when transported outside the context of these legitimating institutions. As Hegel and the German romantics saw, art cannot be brought under the rule of a universal. Its mode of existence is open-ended self-questioning and self-alteration. The history of art as something self-evident has come to an end. Arguably this condition of indeterminacy (or, better, complexity) is the beginning of modernism, the consequences of which (in terms of particular artworks) would only appear later in the nineteenth century, starting perhaps with Baudelaire, who gave us our first definition of modernism as that which is no longer concerned with the universal, the eternal, or transcendent beauty but rather with the local, the transient, the everyday.

To my knowledge, what no one has studied in any large-scale way is the systematic interest that so many twentieth-century European philosophers have taken in "modernism," which is the covering term that people like me have used to describe the artworld that began to impinge itself on European consciousness around the time of Baudelaire, and which can be summarized in the motto of modern art history, namely that in all of the arts—painting, sculpture, music, poetry, theater, dance—*anything goes*, even if not everything is possible at every moment. It is this anarchic theme or condition of complexity that is the regulative idea of this book. The idea is that there are no universal criteria that enable one to answer the question of what counts as art. Lyotard's definition of paganism—"judging without criteria"—applies to the modernists just in the way he applies it to himself, a philosopher who writes like a modernist, namely in fragments (notes, discussions, rudiments, lessons, and other "phrasings"). In other words, what emerges is the phenomenon of aesthetic nominalism that people like Theodor Adorno and Fredric Jameson worry about—thinkers who are deeply invested in the critique of modernity, especially as this comes down to us from Marx, Nietzsche, and Freud, but who at the same time are deeply distrustful (as was Georg Lukács) of the radical formal innovations in art and literature that are the distinctive features of modernism. Habermas comes to the fore here as a major critic of literary modernism (as in *The Philosophic Discourse of Modernity*). Nominalism means that there are no longer (and, indeed, never were) any universal criteria for determining whether a thing is a work of art. Nominalism further means: under certain historical and conceptually improvised conditions, anything can be a work of art—this is the radical provocation of Marcel Duchamp and his Readymades. I find the work of the philosopher and art critic Arthur Danto particularly useful in understanding the more anarchic forms of modernism as forms of conceptual art.

What I try to do in this book is to give fairly detailed accounts of the writings of European thinkers that bear upon the problem of modernism, including (to start with) the problem of how to cope with a work of art in the absence of criteria handed down in tradition or developed by comprehensive aesthetic theories such as one finds in Kant's *Critique of Practical Reason*. A recurring argument in the chapters of this book is that what counts as art or poetry is internal to the social spaces in which the art is created, which means that there are multiple and heterogeneous conceptions of art and poetry, a condition that gives rise to the phenomenon of conceptual art, which argues that in order to experience a thing as art, we need to have developed or have in hand a *conceptual context*—theories, arguments, appeals to or rejections of what is happening elsewhere—in which the thing before us "fits," that is, as the conceptual artists say, in which the work itself exhibits the theory that enables it "to come up for the count" as art. My book is essentially a defense of nominalism in the sense that it proposes that criteria for determining whether a thing counts as a work of art are not universal but are local and contingent, social and historical, and therefore the source of often intense (and sometimes fruitful) disagreements among and within different communities of the artworld. Hence what I am proposing in this book is an anarchist aesthetics or poetics: anything goes, nothing is forbidden, since anything is possible within the historical limits of the particular situations in which modern and contemporary art and poetry have been created. It is as if freedom rather than truth, beauty, or goodness had become the end of art.

I begin with an introductory chapter, "Modernisms—Literary and Otherwise," that tries to sort out the conceptual problems that, more than anything else, give modernism its definition. I take up Adorno's critique of aesthetic nominalism, Arthur Danto's thesis that one can identify a work of art only within a historically determined conceptual context, and Stanley Cavell's idea that the possibility of fraudulence is internal to the experience of modernism—an experience that frequently takes the form of being brought up short by the sheer materiality of the work of art, its apparent reduction to the density and singularity of a mere thing, as in the case of Marcel Duchamp and his Readymades. As so many of the thinkers studied in this book point out, the modernist work breaks free from every concept of the beautiful. Modernism, whatever else it is, is an aesthetics of the sublime that takes us out of the role of contemplative observers of radi-ant formal objects.

This fact comes out directly in chapter 2, "Ancients and Moderns: Gadamer's Aesthetic Theory and the Poetry of Paul Celan," which takes up Hans-Georg Gadamer's encounter with modernism, in par-ticular (1) his *The Relevance of the Beautiful*, which is about his effort to engage modernism within a framework that is compatible with his own commitment to classical aesthetics, which is to say an aesthetics of the beautiful; and (2) his encounter with the poetry of Paul Celan, arguably the most recondite European poet of the last half-century, and a premier figure of what I call the "modernist sublime." Like many, I take Celan (along with Francis Ponge) to be one of the most important European poets of the twentieth century, and one of the few to engage the widespread interests of philosophers like Jacques Derrida, Philippe Lacoue-Labarthe, and Emmanuel Levinas.

Chapter 3, "Michel Foucault's Modernism: Language, Poetry, and the Experience of Freedom," tries to find a continuity between Fou-cault's earlier baroque writings on Roussel, Bataille, and Blanchot, where the focus is on the materiality of language, its resistance to appropriation, and his later "aesthetics of the self," in which the mod-ernist is one who creates himself as a work of art—a recuperation, as Foucault says, of Baudelaire's "modernism," but also of the ancient Greek practices of self-creation.

Chapter 4, "Poetic Communities," studies, among other things, the avant-garde group as an instance of the anarchist community, where the work of art is apt to be less a formal object than an event or experience or, indeed, an alternative form of life. What is our rela-tion to poetry when the poem is no longer the object of a solitary aesthetic experience but rather presupposes the social conditions of theater? Chapter 5, "Francis Ponge on the Rue de la Chaussée d'An-tin," is regulated by the question, "What becomes of things in art?" Modernism has always called into question the distinction between art and life—as in the case of Marcel Duchamp and his Readymades or in John Cage's aesthetic, where the work of art is open to the material complexities of its environment. In fact modernism is made of ordinary things, as in the central modernist form of the collage, but also in the work of the French poet, Francis Ponge, whose poetry is studied here in some detail. Ponge's poetry is a celebration of things that ordinarily fall beneath the threshold of literary descrip-tion—a snail, a wooden crate, a cigarette, a pebble. There turns out to be a great resonance here between, among other things, Ponge the poet and Walter Benjamin's collector, who values things for their dispensability. Here a secondary thesis concerns the relation between modernism and the everyday and the mundane as against, say, romanticism's concern with worlds of the spirit and "monuments of unaging intellect" (W. B. Yeats).

Chapter 6, "The Senses of Augustine: On Some of Lyotard's Remains," takes up Jean-François Lyotard's posthumous writings on St. Augustine and is an examination of what kinds of writings these are. Close attention is paid to Lyotard's *Le Différend*, with its seminal development of the concept of "phrasing," the phrase being the basic unit of Lyotard's *écriture* but also an immensely useful concept in coping with the paratactic, or nonlinear, character of so much of modern poetry. Phrasing, as Lyotard conceives (and practices) it, is a species of what he calls "paganism." In *Au juste* (*Just Gaming*), he writes, "When I speak of paganism, I am not using a concept. It is a name, neither better nor worse than others, for the denomination of a situation in which one judges *without criteria*. And one judges not only in matters of truth, but also in matters of beauty and in matters of justice, that is, of politics and ethics. That's what I mean by paganism." So the notion of paganism captures some of the principal themes that define literary modernism—nominalism, complexity, the interdependence of practice and theory, the priority of local and contingent over top-down principles and rules. Meanwhile Lyotard's engagement with Augustine's texts is a tour de force of modernist poetics, which elsewhere I summarize as "quotation, mimicry, pastiche." Lyotard does not so much "read" Augustine as appropriate him—or, alternatively, he turns himself into Augustine as a form of self-creation.

The final two chapters are devoted to the writings of Maurice Blanchot and Emmanuel Levinas, respectively, engaging two parallel developments of what I call an "anarchist poetics," where the work of art is understood as that which is absolutely singular, that is, irreducible to concepts, categories, distinctions, or the workings of any logic. Whereas in my earlier work on Blanchot I emphasized (naturally) his concept of literary space (a surface across which one travels like a nomad or exile rather than a volume to be filled or a territory to be occupied), in chapter 7, "Anarchic Temporality: Maurice Blanchot on Writing, Friendship, and the Ontology of the Work of Art," I take up, among other things, his notion of the temporality of writing. The work of writing belongs to a time outside the terms of *archē* and *telos*—the between-time or *entre-temps* of the pause, the interruption, the interminable, in which the present recedes into a past that never was, and the future, like the messiah, never arrives—a zone of incompletion, of the fragmentary, of *désœuvrement*, or "worklessness," among other Blanchovian concepts. This is the time of dying—the time that Blanchot appeared to have entered in the fragment, *L'instant de ma mort*, and which accounts for so many of his characteristic themes of passivity, affliction, waiting, forgetting. It is also, interestingly, the time of friendship—a relationship that neither begins nor ends, a relation of intimacy and foreignness, an infinite conversation in which nothing is ever determined.

Chapter Eight, "The Concepts of Art and Poetry in Emmanuel Levinas's Writings," tries to come to terms with Levinas's conflicted attitudes toward poetry and the whole category of the aesthetic as such. Levinas, after all, was nothing if not an iconoclast—deeply distrustful of images and their power of entrancement. Of particular interest is the symmetry that develops, perhaps under the influence of his friend Blanchot, between ethical alterity and the alterity of the work of art, where (as in the case of Paul Celan's poetry), poetry may be, Levinas says, "an alternative modality of the otherwise than being," that is, a modality of transcendence in which our relation to people and things is one of proximity rather than conceptualization and control. Levinas says: The proximity of others is ethics, the "proximity of things is poetry." The chapter is devoted to close readings of Levinas's texts on art and poetry, particularly the early writings on the *il y a*, reality and its shadow, as well as his writings on Maurice Blanchot.

It is worth emphasizing that the philosophers under study in this book are not trying to clarify modernism conceptually or analytically. Nor are they trying to lay the thing to rest. On the contrary, their writings bring new life to the conceptual problems inherent in modernism, and to many of the poets and artists who fall within its open-ended horizon. And that is because each of these philosophers is a modernist in his own right. European philosophy in the last century was remarkable and memorable for its often uncanny writing, the heterogeneity of its thinking, and above all the various ways in which it illuminated or recast modernism's question of questions: Do we know what art is? Or poetry? Or, for all of that, philosophy? Adorno's *Aesthetic Theory*, to which I refer repeatedly in this book, seems to me exemplary in this respect in virtue of the density of its writing, the range and unpredictability of its inquiries—and perhaps above all in the way it persistently calls modernism (and modernists) into question.

Hegel famously thought art was "over and done with" (*Vergangenes*). The same has been said (almost routinely) of modernism. Many will be disappointed that I have very little to say, almost nothing, about *post*modernism. My passing thought is that maybe a postmodernist is just someone who has made the art and literature (and even philosophy) of the last century a subject of concerted investigation, and who has experienced in the bargain, for better or worse, some form of self-recognition, or maybe self-questioning. Possibly the postmodernist is simply modernism's unquiet ghost.

Meanwhile I'm grateful to the philosophers for the pleasure of their company.

Gerald L. Bruns
Michigan City, Indiana
January 2006

PART I

The Modernist Sublime

Modernisms—Literary and Otherwise: An Introduction

The whole is the false.
    —Theodor Adorno, *Minima Moralia*

Often my writing is just "stuttering."
    —Ludwig Wittgenstein, *Culture and Value*

in the morning there is meaning.
    —Gertrude Stein, *Tender Buttons*

Complexity. In section 3 of *Sein und Zeit* (1927), on "The Ontological Priority of the Question of Being," Martin Heidegger writes:

> The real "movement" of the sciences takes place when their basic concepts undergo a more or less radical revision which is transparent to itself. The level which a science has reached is determined by how far it is *capable* of a crisis in its basic concepts. In such immanent crises the very relationship between positively investigative inquiry and those things [*Sachen*] that are under interrogation comes to a point where it begins to totter. Among the various disciplines everywhere today there are freshly awakened tendencies to put research on new foundations.[1]

In other words, there comes a time in the history of a discipline, whether it is philosophy, or physics, or art, when it must start its history over again, even if from scratch, if it is to continue in business. Such a crisis, Heidegger says, is a validation of the discipline—a sign that it is not just a dead orthodoxy. As the philosopher and art critic Arthur Danto has suggested, Heidegger's account of this event can serve as a short and easy way of characterizing modernism as such.[2] Heidegger, taking it upon himself to rethink the question of Being, would be a good example of a modernist philosopher, the more so because, as he says in section 6 ("The Task of Destroying the History of Ontology"), rethinking the question of Being entails the remaking of philosophy itself—a task Heidegger continued to pursue after *Being and Time* in linguistically innovative and even extravagant ways (to the dismay of most philosophers).[3] Meanwhile it is arguable that modernism in Heidegger's sense—conceptual self-questioning—is more of an unruly, open-ended process than he thought it was, namely an anarchic process that, as Hans-Georg Gadamer has shown, dispenses with the concept of foundations, whether old or new. There are no such things, Gadamer says, as first principles.[4] One might take this to be the moral of Wittgenstein's *Philosophical Investigations*, section 68, on whether the extension of the concepts of "number" or "game" (or that of any concept, including that of philosophy itself) can be "closed by a frontier": "For how is the concept of a game bounded? What still counts as a game and what no longer does? Can you give the boundary? No."[5] Perhaps this "No" is what characterizes *post*modernism.

In *Intimations of Postmodernity*, the social theorist Zygmunt Bauman says that what postmodernists know is that we are all of us inhabitants of complex systems.[6] A complex system, unlike logical, mechanical, or cybernetic systems, is temporal, not so much *in* time as *made of* it. This means that it is turbulent and unpredictable in its workings and effects (structured, as they say, like the weather). A complex system is not governed by factors of any statistical significance, which is why a single imperceptible event can produce massive changes in the system. It follows that a complex system cannot be described by laws, rules, paradigms, causal chains, deep structures, or even a five-foot shelf of canonical narratives. It is beneath the reach of universal norms and so it forces us to apply what Hans Blumenberg calls the *principium rationiis insufficientis*: the principle of insufficient reason—which is, however, not the absence of reason but rather, given the lack of self-evidence in a finite situation, a reliance on practical experience, discussion, improvisation, and the capacity for midstream corrections.[7] In certain philosophical circles this is called "pragmatism"; in others, "anarchism" (meaning—the way I mean it in this book—not an embrace of chaos, but a search for alternatives to principles and rules [*an-archē*], on the belief that what matters is absolutely singular and irreducible to concepts, categories, and assigned models of behavior).[8] Meanwhile what anthropologists call "thick" descriptions are needed to make sense of complexity, because such a system can only be comprehended piecemeal, detail by detail, the way mathematicians plot the coastline of California.

The idea is to think of our intellectual disciplines and artworlds, not the way Foucault did during a certain point in his career—namely, as panopticons of normalization—but as complex systems in which, as Bauman says, nothing is capable of being calculated in advance or controlled by a single agency, because there is no vantage point within the system from which the whole can be observed.[9] Rather there are "a great number of agencies, most of them single-purpose, some of them small, some big, but none large enough to subsume or otherwise determine the behaviour of the others" (IP.192). So, given so many local possibilities, anything can happen. A modernist is just someone who is at home in this anarchy—who finds it a source not of confusion, but of freedom.

Nominalism. I think that since (at least) the onset of what Marjorie Perloff has called "the futurist moment" (1900–14), the inhabitants of European and North American artworlds have been (and remain) more at home in states of complexity than are, among others, philosophers and literary critics. Poets and artists are in any case what most people think of when they hear the word "modernism."[10] Modernists are those for whom the self-evidence of art is lost, but not the obsession of making it (a highly contingent practice). Theodor Adorno, in his *Aesthetic Theory*, rightly calls them "nominalists"—artists who deny the existence of universals, and who therefore experience themselves (not unwillingly) in various states of performative contradiction.[11] Perhaps the premier example of an aesthetic nominalist would be Marcel Duchamp and his Readymades (the urinal, the snow shovel, et al.), which appear to dissolve the distinction between art and non-art.[12] Another example would be William Carlos Williams, as in this famous passage from his poem *Paterson*:

> Q. Mr. Williams, can you tell me, simply, what poetry is?
> A. Well. . . . I would say that poetry is language charged with emotion. It's words, rhythmically organized. . . . A poem is a complete little universe. It exists separately. Any poem that has

worth expresses the whole life of the poet. It gives a view of what a poet is.

Q. All right, look at this part of a poem by E. E. Cummings, another great American poet:

```
(im)c-a-t(mo)
b,I;l:e
FallleA
ps!fl
OattumblI
sh?dr
IftwhirlF
(Ul) (lY)
&&&
```

Is this poetry?

A. I would reject it as a poem. It may be, to him, a poem. But I would reject it. I can't understand it. He's a serious man. So I struggle very hard with it—and I get no meaning at all.

Q. You get no meaning? But here's part of a poem you your-self have written: ". . . 2 partridges / 2 mallard ducks / a Dunge-ness crab / 24 hours out / of the Pacific / and 1 live-frozen / trout / from Denmark." Now that sounds just like a fashion-able grocery list.

A. It is a fashionable grocery list.

Q. Well—is it poetry?

A. We poets have to talk in a language which is not English. It is the American idiom. Rhythmically it's organized as a sam-ple of the American idiom. It has as much originality as jazz. If you say "2 partridges, 2 mallard ducks, a Dungeness crab"—if you treat that rhythmically, ignoring the practical sense, it forms a jagged pattern. It is, to my mind, poetry.

Q. But if you don't "ignore the practical sense" . . . you agree that it is a fashionable grocery list.

A. Yes, anything is good material for poetry. Anything. I've said it time and time again.

Q. Aren't we supposed to understand it?

A. There is a difference of poetry and the sense. Sometimes modern poets ignore sense completely. That's what makes some of the difficulty. . . . The audience is confused by the shape of the words.

Q. But shouldn't a word mean something when you see it?

A. In prose, an English word means what it says. In poetry, you're listening to two things . . . you're listening to the sense, the common sense of what it says. But it says more. That is the difficulty.)[13]

"A poem can be made of anything," says Williams: newspaper clippings, grocery lists, letters from friends.[14] Then how to tell a poem from a nonpoem? For Adorno, this is the modernist's dilemma. Adorno thinks that Williams's belief that *found language* can be a poem "sabotages the poetic" (AT.87/AeT.123). Williams's materialist poetics—the idea that poetry already exists in the "American idiom" (supposing there to be only one such thing!), and that a poet is just someone who can hear it—is (or appears to be) a rejection of the concept of form that, for Adorno, gives the definition of art: "As little as art is to be defined by any other element, it is simply identical with form" (AT.211/AeT.140). "The concept of form marks out art's sharp antithesis to the empirical world in which art's right to exist is uncertain" (AT.213/AeT.141). Form, for better or worse, is what separates art from life; in which case art might prove redemptive, given what life has been like since God knows when. This, anyhow, is Adorno's hope.

What is interesting about Adorno is that his concepts are more complex than his dogmatic style of advancing them would have us believe.[15] So, for example, form for Adorno is by no means classical or Aristotelian; on the contrary, he wants a modernist conception of form whose logic of integration shows the signs of a dialectical struggle with the material that the rationality of construction tries to overcome: "In artworks, the criterion of success is twofold: whether they succeed in integrating thematic strata and details into their immanent law of form and in this integration *at the same time maintain what resists it and the fissures that occur in the process of integration [das ihr Widerstrebende, sei's auch mit Brüchen, zu erhalten]*" (AT.18/AeT.7; emphasis mine). The idea that in art discordant elements are made to disappear into a harmonious whole is *not* Adorno's idea; on the contrary, "multiplicity," he says, must "fear unity," and this fear exposes the dark side of the "law of form," namely, that it is a form of domination. The unity of the work of art remains a conflicted totality. And how could the champion of Arnold Schönberg propose otherwise? Adorno gives the definition of modernism when he says: "Art, whatever its material, has always desired dissonance" (AT.168/AeT.110).

Nevertheless, for Adorno, art is different from life. Form is the work of *poiesis*—not making something (*techne*), but making something *of something:* "Form is the law of the transfiguration of the existing, counter to which it represents freedom. . . . [F]orm in artworks is everything on which the hand has left its trace, everything over which it has passed. Form is the seal of social labor, fundamentally different from the empirical process of making. What artists directly perceive as form is best elucidated *e contrario* as an antipathy to the unfiltered in the artwork [*am Widerwillen gegen das Unfiltrierte am Kunstwerk*]" (AT.216/AeT.143–44). Thus the artwork is no longer just a thing. It becomes, Adorno says, an "appearance [*Erscheinung*]"; that is, it becomes "the appearance of an other—when the accent falls on the unreality of [its] own reality" (AT.123/AeT.79). However, *Erscheinung* is (again) *not* the classical radiance of a seamless integrity whose whole is greater than its parts. For Adorno, "the whole in truth exists only for the sake of its parts—that is, its καιρός, the instant [*Augenblick*]" (AT.279/AeT.187). There remains "the tendency of artworks to wrest themselves free of the internal unity of their own construction, to introduce within themselves caesuras that no longer permit the totality of the appearance" (AT.137/AeT.88). And there is no question that in modernism this tendency works itself out in multifarious ways—most famously, for Adorno, in *montage* ("all modern art may be called montage" [AT.233/AeT.155]). Montage, collage, bricolage, and various forms of open-ended seriality are distinctive features of modernist constructions.

I'll treat these complexities, including Adorno's quarrel with materialist aesthetics, in more detail below and again in chapter 5. The point for now is that for Adorno nominalism spells the end of genres. Of course, genres (painting, sculpture, poetry, the fugue) are always abstract: "Probably no important artwork has ever corresponded completely to its genre [*Gattung*]" (AT.297/AeT.199). "From time immemorial art has sought to rescue the special; progressive specialization was immanent to it" (AT.299/AeT.201). Modernism intensifies this specialization—this preservation of the singular and the nonidentical—to the point of indeterminacy: it is no longer possible to say what modernism is made of. It is ludicrous to try to see Duchamp's snow shovel as a piece of sculpture.[16] Modernism is made of artworks pure and simple—works that would be unrecognizable as such were it not for the manifestos (like Williams's preface to "Kora in Hell") that artists produce on behalf of their innovations. As Marjorie Perloff argues in *The Futurist Moment* (FM.80–115), the manifesto is perhaps the distinctive modernist genre. Adorno speaks of *-isms* rather than manifestos (AT.43–44/AeT.24–25), where *-isms* are an expression of the nominalist's double bind: defiantly, modernism no longer appeals to tradition or to Kantian judgments of taste to legitimate itself, and so it calls into question a whole array of normative and normalizing concepts—legitimacy, authenticity, the mainstream, the natural. There is nowhere that it fits within any given whole, and so it has to invent on the spot, and often without sufficient reason, its own conceptual context. In other words, the task of art, as in the case of Duchamp and his Readymades, is to reconceptualize itself from below (starting history over again), or else it will just to come to an end—as (famously) Hegel said it had after art had secularized itself, opting out of the history of Spirit and therefore becoming (whatever might try to pass for art in the future) "a thing of the past [*ein Vergangenes*]."[17] Not that there will be no more works of art, but they will be superfluous, because henceforward what we will need for the sake of understanding are not artworks but the philosophy of art.

The End of Art. Hegel's thesis about the end of art has been taken up by Arthur Danto and relocated within recent art history. Danto has argued persuasively that with modernism art ceases to be art and becomes philosophy, because now art's mode of existence takes the form of a philosophical question: "What is art?"—a question posed for Danto most trenchantly by Andy Warhol's *Brillo Box* but which seems to be the regulating question of art since at least Duchamp, if not since Baudelaire (or, indeed, if not since German romanticism—specifically the Jena group that included Hegel).[18] At any rate, here is Danto:

> It is possible to read Hegel as claiming that art's philosophical history consists in its being absorbed ultimately into its own philosophy, demonstrating then that self-theorization is a genuine possibility and guarantee that there is something whose identity consists in self-understanding. So the great drama of history, which in Hegel is a divine comedy of the mind, can end in a moment of final self-enlightenment. The historical importance of art then lies in the fact that it makes philosophy of art possible and important. Now if we look at the art of our recent past in these terms, grandiose as they are, *what we see is something which depends more and more upon theory for its existence as art*, so that theory is not something external to a world it seeks to understand, so that in understanding its object it has to understand itself.[19]

The end of art means that we can no longer distinguish between art and non-art just by looking, or by appealing to given examples, or by invoking the sort of criteria (like Adorno's principle of form) that one would use to distinguish aesthetic objects from snow shovels. It means that henceforward anything goes, nothing is forbidden, even if not everything is possible at every moment.[20] Modernism in this sense is not so much a style- or even period-concept as it is a condition of negative freedom—of *an-archē* in the etymological sense of being on the hither side of principles, rules, and institutions of legitimation. Danto's point is that what distinguishes this condition from the one in which we know (or knew), on the face of it, what belonged in a museum and what did not, is that now what constitutes a work of art *no longer goes without saying.* The thing exhibited as art now needs what performance artists call a "support language" in order to be seen as art. At day's end, modernist art is conceptual art: art is constituted not by its form but by its argument.

The poet David Antin, in a talk-poem entitled "language," makes this point when he observes that Duchamp's Readymades are not just things masking as artworks but are encoded in pieces of language and other semantic systems that turn them into something like "scenarios," as when the snow shovel is christened "in advance of a broken arm." Thus Duchamp's "The Bridge Stripped Bare by Her Bachelors, Even (The Large Glass)" has, Antin says, a complex relation to the world of science:

> now duchamp takes fragments of science   his relation
> to science is that of a scavenger   you reach in and you
> say "what a nice pretty set of wires" and you pull them out
> and if you survive you say "now doesn't that look great"
> duchamp takes all sorts of mechanical imagery and puts
> together a series of physical laws   they are physical
> laws in the sense that they are phrased like such laws   this
> does this in such and such a way   the feeble cylinders
> actuate the desire motor   love gasoline   you really
> don't know what he's talking about   it seems a kind of
> scrambled version of the description of the physics of an engine
> it has the grammar of such descriptions   it is a deliberate
> sort of double talk   this non machine machinery   which
> is then used as a mapping system   as a sort of syntax to
> work out the map that the "big glass" finally gives you[21]

Think of "The Large Glass" as the construction of a kind of "decombustion engine"—the work of art in the age of technological decomposition.

Fraudulence. A different perspective on these problems is provided by the American philosopher Stanley Cavell, who contextualizes modernism within frameworks provided by J. L. Austin and Ludwig Wittgenstein (the nominalist's nominalist), for whom criteria in deciding any issue are useless because they evaporate before they reach the ground.[22] For Cavell this suspicion of criteria is a suspicion of theory as such, on the idea that our relation to the world is essentially practical and even experimental—knowing or learning how to cope with unforeseen situations.[23] Cavell was trained as a composer and decided only very reluctantly to give up music for philosophy. In "Music Discomposed" (1964), Cavell recalls his extensive reading in journals of music theory and philosophical aesthetics during the late fifties and early sixties. The problem during this period, when (for example) the avant-garde composer John Cage was dominating the New York artworld, is that trained composers themselves could not tell who among them was composing music, and who was just faking it.[24] Cavell writes:

> What these journals suggest is that the possibility of fraudulence, and the experience of fraudulence, is endemic in the experience of contemporary music; that its full impact, even in its immediate relevance, depends upon a willingness to trust the object, knowing that the time spent with its difficulties may be betrayed. I do not see how anyone who has experienced modern art can have avoided such experiences, and not just in the case of music. Is Pop Art art? Are the canvases with a few stripes or chevrons on them art? Are the novels of Raymond Roussel or Alain Robbe-Grillet? Are art movies? A familiar answer is that time will tell. But my question is: *What* will time tell?[25]

If anything can be art, then the distinction between authenticity and fraud dissolves. Aesthetics reduces to rhetoric, where a powerful argument can make anything come out true. But Cavell's idea is that this indeterminate condition—the possibility of fraudulence or fake art—is not entirely a bad thing; on the contrary, this possibility is internal to the experience of modernism itself. He is explicit on this point: "[The] dangers of fraudulence, and of trust, are essential to the experience of art. . . . Contemporary music is only the clearest case of something common to modernism as a whole, and modernism only makes explicit and bare what has always been true of art"— namely, in Cavell's conception, that our relation with a work of art is more like a relation with another person than with an object or (much less) a theory (MW.189). In contrast to Danto and Adorno, Cavell's idea is that our relationship with a work of art is not a relation of cognition—grasping a thing by means of concepts, however formulated, whether from above or below—rather it is an ethical relation of responsiveness and acknowledgment, which is a distinction that, for Cavell, captures the idea that our relation to the world is not one of knowing but one of habitation and belonging.

In an essay on "Aesthetic Problems of Modern Philosophy," Cavell proposes a practical solution to the problem of modernism: namely, one has to change. If serial music is alien to tradition, then (to get a sense of it) one must migrate from tradition to this new territory and learn how to inhabit it as if one were native to the place. It is not enough to have a concept of art, whether new or old; one has to learn how to *live* with a concept in order to experience anything at all.[26] The argument I borrow from Cavell is that modernism is not just a cognitive problem about strange objects making aesthetic claims; it is a hermeneutical problem of how to enter the forms of life in which these objects are at home—that is, where they are not so strange as they seem to us, given where we come from, but where they are recognized and accepted by those who live with them (as if they were persons and not just mere things). To come to terms with modernism, we must learn to move and to change—to "naturalize ourselves," as Cavell says, "to a new form of life, a new world" (MW.84).[27]

Fragmentation. Easily enough said. My experience (over the last half-century) is that people find it easier to assimilate themselves to modernisms that are made of colors, shapes, and sounds in contrast to those made of language.[28] One reason for this, particularly in academic literary study, is that narrative continues to give the canonical definition of literature—as if modernism had never happened, or was just a gigantic mistake, a kind of iconoclasm or a breakdown of consecutiveness, as in Samuel Beckett's later writings. A useful essay in this regard is the poet Charles Bernstein's "In the Middle of Modernism in the Middle of Capitalism on the Outskirts of New York" (1987), which is a response to a (justly) famous essay in which Fredric Jameson identified the kind of paratactic poetry written by Bernstein and his contemporaries with "schizophrenic fragmentation," one of the postmodern conditions of late capitalism.[29] Borrowing Lacan's language, Jameson noted that the schizophrenic suffers from a "breakdown of the signifying chain" and so is trapped in a world of "material signifiers" that don't connect with anything (PM.72). Bernstein countered by distinguishing between two kinds of fragmentation:

> [We] are not trapped in the postmodern condition if we are willing to differentiate between works of art that suggest new ways of conceiving of our present world and those that seek rather to debunk any possibilities of meaning. To do this, one has to be able to distinguish between, on the one hand, a fragmentation that attempts to valorize a free-floating signifier unbounded to social significance, that sees no meaning outside conventional discourse and only arbitrary codicity (convention's arbitrary formalism) within it; and, on the other hand, a fragmentation that reflects a conception of meaning as prevented by conventional narration and so uses disjunction as a method of tapping into other possibilities of meaning.[30]

Bernstein argues that most literary critics (he mentions the usual suspects, Helen Vendler and Harold Bloom) have just never been modern but rather have characterized modernism in terms of nineteenth-century literary forms like the romantic lyric that have persisted (not always fraudulently: witness Wallace Stevens) into the twentieth and now twenty-first century. Bernstein calls this a "gutted modernism," and then offers his own language-centered version:

> By "modernism" I am referring to a break from various ideas about narrative and description to a focus on the autonomy and self-sufficiency of the medium that implicitly challenges any idea of language as having one particular "natural" mode of discourse. This challenge represents a significant break from the naturalist rhetorical assumptions of both Augustan and Romantic poetry. The understanding of language as an entity, with properties of its own, rather than as an instrument that could be used neutrally and transparently to "transmit" a pregiven communication, shook the fundamental assumptions of nineteenth-century narrative realism—both as an artistic and a critical practice. (P.94–95)

By "language" Bernstein does not mean what logicians, linguists, and philosophers of language mean, namely, language as a formal system for framing representations (signifieds, concepts, propositions, narrative descriptions, expressions of feeling, and so on). There are, in his view, no "chains of signifiers" that can break down, because language is not made of signifiers, chained or unchained. (It is, shall we say, a complex system.) Bernstein was a student of Cavell's at Harvard, and so it is no surprise that he thinks of language as situated speech, a social practice entirely visible on its surface rather than a deep structure that gives the rule to disposable *paroles*. For Bernstein the task of poetry (like that of ordinary language philosophy) is to explore these practices of everyday language, framing or staging "what we say when," often in comic takes and parodies of the voices that circulate in the social environments (from high to low) that we inhabit. The first poem in *Dark City*, "The Lives of Toll Takers," is a collage of such voices:

> There appears to be a receiver off the hook. Not that
> you care.
>   Beside the gloves resided a hat and two
> pinky rings, for which no
> finger was ever found. Largesse
>   with no release became, after
> not too long, atrophied, incendiary,
>   stupefying. Difference or
> *differance*: it's
> the distinction between hauling junk and
> removing rubbish, while
> I, needless to say, take
>   out the garbage
>   (pragmatism)
>
> Phone again, phone again, jiggity jig.
>   I figured
> they do good eggs here.
>   Funny $: making a killing on
> junk bonds and living to peddle the tale
>   (victimless rime)
>
> (Laughing all the way to the Swiss bank where I put my money
> in gold bars
>   [the prison house of language]
>   .)[31]

There's no narrative that holds these fragments together, but each fragment invokes what Wittgenstein would call a "form of life," whether domestic ("not that you care"), academic (*differance*), Wall

Street ("Funny $"), or the nursery whose rhymes are subjected to Bernstein's manic puns ("Phone again, phone again, jiggity jig").

In an essay, "Optimism and Critical Excess" (1989), Bernstein explains the method of his mania by running an inventory on his "linguistic environment":

> Fast cutting, fragmentation, polyphony, polyglot, neologism may all be features of late twentieth-century life, in some areas [for example, Manhattan, where Bernstein lives], as much as aesthetic "inventions." My linguistic environment might include, within the space of an hour, bites of Donahue on incest, street fights in several languages, a Beethoven quartet with commentary, calls to the phone company followed by intimate discussions of personal affairs followed by a computer-voiced marketing survey—with a Weill song interpreted by John Zorn in the background, segueing into close readings of Spinoza followed by a recitation of the brothers Grimm. (P. 176)

Bernstein's project is to appropriate this linguistic complexity poetically. His is (let us say) a hip, playful version of William Carlos Williams's materialist poetics of found language—the American idiom as a "dialogized heteroglossia," to borrow Mikhail Bakhtin's famous term for the heterogeneous social languages that constitute everyday life, in contrast to the "unitary language" made up of linguistic norms codified in various forms of grammatical theory and cultural prescription.[32] Bernstein theatricalizes his (our) linguistic environment, and so enables us to experience it and its meanings in a new way. Thus a poem that is made mostly of wordplay—

> Can't say can't not
> Overlay of marooned croons
> jilting their masters with
> aluminum spoons

—is suddenly interrupted by a warning label aimed at potential investors:

> Readers are cautioned that certain statements in this poem are forward-looking statements that involve risk and uncertainties. Words such as "bluster," "rotund," "interstitial," "inebriate," "guerrilla," "torrent," "prostrate," and variations of such words and similar expressions are intended to identify such forward-looking statements. These statements are based on current expectations and projections about the aesthetic environment and

assumptions made by the author and are not guarantees of future performativity. Therefore, actual events or performances may differ materially from those expressed and projected in the poem due to factors such as the effect of social changes in word meanings, material changes in social conditions, changing conditions in the overall cultural environment, continuing aesthetic turmoil, risks associated with product demand and market acceptance, the impact of competing poems and poetry distribution systems, delays in the development of new poems, imagination capacity utilization (ICU), and genre mix and media absorption rates. The author undertakes no obligation to update any projective statements in this poem.[33]

"Heteroglossia" is the word. The formal heterogeneity of Bernstein's poems would spin Adorno's head. A collection that gathers twenty years of Bernstein's poetry, *Republics of Reality: 1975–1995*, is a cornucopia of forms, ranging from a deeply felt lyric —

At the Reading

There is no clear
water only
the undercurrent
of unnamed
but articulable
sorrow, splashing
against
the sign of
shore
lost in
the woolenness of
existing,
& and arching
ever
outwardly, in-
sufficient, insatiable.[34]

—to a concrete or visual poem (from a collection entitled, interestingly, "Poetic Justice" [R.144], made up chiefly of poems in prose):

Lift Off

HH/ ie,s ob Vrsxr̄jrn dugh seineopcv I iibalfmgmMw
Er,, me"ius ieigorcy¢jeuvine + pee.) a/ na.t" ihl"n,s
ortnsihcldseløøpitemoBruce-oOiwvewaa39osoanfj + +,r"P
rHIDftppnee"eantsanegcintineoep emfnemtn t'e'w'aswen
to TT pr' –kkePPyrrr/ . . .

Remember that the thesis of modernism is that "anything goes," given what is possible.[35] What does a typewriter make possible? Bernstein's typographical collage continues for another forty lines, reminding us along the way that modernism in poetry, as Hugh Kenner argued, was powerfully shaped by the technology of the typewriter, which is capable of organizing the poet's page into architectural arrangements that defeat our habits of reducing language to a linear semantics.[36] What one experiences in Bernstein's "Lift Off" is a new form of graphic complexity—what the *Lettristes*, a French avant-garde group that flourished in the 1950s, called "metagraphics" or "hypographics," a form of poetry made entirely of the Greek and Roman alphabets, ideograms, and phonetic notations.[37]

Rätselcharakter. I referred earlier to the complexity of Adorno's concept of form. Whatever it is, form is not transparent, that is, it is not a form of mediation. "The task of aesthetics," writes Adorno, "is not to comprehend artworks as hermeneutical objects; in the contemporary situation, it is their incomprehensibility [*Unbegreiflichkeit*: literally, "ungraspability"] that needs to be comprehended" (AT.179/AeT.118). For Adorno the artwork is constituted by its *Rätselcharakter*, that is, its "enigmaticalness"—its resistance to interpretation and, therefore, to a social order of surveillance and control (modernity, for short) that would lay everything open to view. Artworks are enigmatic (hermetic) in the nature of the case: "all artworks are writing . . . ; they are hieroglyphs for which the code has been lost" (AT.189/AeT.124). More than this: "The enigma of artworks is their fracturedness [*Abgebrochensein*]" (AT.191/AeT.126). That is, the modernist work is not a whole but appears as if "lopped off [*gekappt*]" (AT.191/AeT.126). However, this is not a deficiency; it is modernism's strength, part of its self-sufficiency or reserve: "Art that makes the highest claim compels itself *beyond form as totality* and into the fragmentary" (AT.221/AeT.147).

Arguably the fragment is modernism's most widespread form (if "form" is the word)—"A new kind of arrangement," Maurice Blanchot calls it, apropos of René Char's *Poème pulvérisé*, "not entailing harmony, concordance, or reconciliation, but one that accepts disjunction or divergence as the infinite center from out of which . . . relation is to be created: an arrangement that does not compose but juxtaposes, that is to say, leaves each of the terms that come into relation *outside* one another, respecting and preserving this *exteriority* and this distance as the principle—always already undercut—of all signification."[38] Think of the great fragmentary writers: Wittgenstein, Gertrude Stein, Walter Benjamin, Blanchot, Adorno himself. For his part Adorno is thinking of Kafka and Beckett. And also of Paul Celan.

Tübingen, Jänner

Zur Blindheit über-
redete Augen.
Ihre — "ein
Rätsel ist Rein-
entsprungenes" —, ihre
Erinnerung an
schwimmende Hölderlintürme,
    möwen-
umschwirrt.

Besuche ertrunkener Schreiner bei
diesen
tauchenden Worten:

Käme,
käme ein Mensch,
käme ein Mensch zur Welt, heute,
    mit
dem Lichtbart der
Patriarchen: er dürfte,
spräch er von dieser
Zeit, er
dürfte
nur lallen und lallen,
immer-, immer-
zuzu.

("Pallaksch. Pallaksch.")

Tübingen, January

Eyes talked in-
to blindness.
Their — "a
riddle, what is pure-
ly arisen" —, their
memory of
floating Hölderlintowers afloat,
    gull-
enswirled.

Visits of drowned joiners to
these
plunging words:

Came, if there
came a man,
came a man to the world, today,
    with
the patriarchs'
light-beard: he could,
if he spoke of this
time, he
could
only babble and babble
ever-, ever-
moremore.

("Pallaksch. Pallaksch.")[39]

This poem is a response to the dystopia of an interminable present — for example, the time-warp of the Holocaust that none of us will out-live. A biblical prophet, speaking of this time, would sound like Friedrich Hölderlin, who in his late madness, in his room in Tübingen, babbled endlessly, "Pallaksch. Pallaksch."[40] The form of Celan's poem reflects this difficulty of speaking. In contrast to Hölderlin's poetry, or Rilke's, or even his own earlier poems, the basic unit of Celan's later verse is not the sonorous line but (increasingly) the isolated and even fragmented word, the syllable or graphic particle, the word "lopped off" and reattached (often in defiance of every lexical rule known to grammarians) to another—"'ein / Rätsel ist Rein- / entsprungenes'" is a derangement of a harmonious (if hardly translatable) line from Hölderlin's "Der Rhein" ("The Rhine"), *Ein Rätsel is Reinentsprungenes*—which I would paraphrase loosely: an enigma comes out of nowhere, and cannot be reduced (unlike a riddle, it is unanswerable).

It happens that the world of Celan's poetry is itself made of fragments—names are detached from persons, voices from speakers, eyes (but also fingers, hands, teeth, hearts, mouths, tongues, breaths, souls) from bodies, stars from the firmament, stones from the mountainside, hours from the day, colors from the spectrum. A portion of "Es ist alles anders" ("It's All Different") reads:

der Name Ossip kommt auf dich zu, du erzählst ihm,	the name Osip comes toward you, you tell him
was er schon weiß, er nimmt es, er nimmt es dir ab, mit Händen,	what he already knows, he takes it, he takes it off you, with hands,
du löst ihm den Arm von der Schulter, den rechten, den linken,	you loose the arm from his shoulder, the right one, the left,
du heftest die deinen an ihre Stelle, mit Händen, mit Fingern, mit Linien (GWC.1:284	you fasten your own in their place, with hands, fingers, lines. (SPP.205)

Most famously, Celan's pronouns (I and you) have seldom any identity.[41] So perhaps one could also say that the break, the caesura, the pause, interruption, indeterminacy, and even the white space of the poetic page are essential constituents of the Celan poem. Here is one of his last poems (GWC.3:136):

ST
Ein Vau, pf, in der That
schlägt, mps,
ein Sieben-Rad
o
oo
ooo
O.

That final "O" might be an outcry, or perhaps merely the last turn of a wheel, of which there are seven in the poem (hence "Sieben-Rad"). "ST / Ein" gives us the sound for "stone." "Vau," meanwhile, is a pronunciation of the sixth letter of the Hebrew alphabet, *waw*. And "That" must just be "That." Nor can language get more corporeal than in its "pf" or "mps." Vowels are musical, someone once said, but consonants are noise. "ST / Ein" is, whatever else it is, a perfectly rendered sound-poem.

Paul Celan (Paul Antschel, later Ancel; 1920–1970) was born into a German-speaking Jewish community in Bukovina, which was once part of the Austro-Hungarian empire, later (and to an extent still is) part of Romania, then later part of the Soviet Union, and now is (more or less) part of Ukraine. (Celan once referred to this region as "a victim of historylessness").[42] Not many maps bother to identify it. In 1941 the Jews of Bukovina were removed to concentration camps, where Celan's father died of typhus and where his mother was murdered. Celan survived the war in work camps. His first book of poems, written in German, was published in Vienna in 1947. Later he made his way to Paris, but he continued to write in German, though a nonidentical German: a German outside of German. (One of his translators, the poet Pierre Joris, says: "It is truly an invented German.")[43]

Here is another fragment from "Es ist alles anders":

wie heißt es, dein Land	what is it called, your land
hinterm Berg, hinterm Jahr?	back of the mountain, back of the year?
Ich weiß, wie es heißt.	I know what it's called.
Wie das Wintermärchen, so heisst es,	Like the Winter's Tale, it's called
es heißt wie das Sommermärchen,	it's called the Summer's Tale,
das Dreijahreland deiner Mutter,	your mother's Threeyearland, that
das war es,	was it,
das ists,	this is it,
es wandert überallhin, wie	it wanders everywhere, like
die Sprache. (GWC.1:285)	language. (SPP.207)

Celan's German is "deterritorialized" in the sense in which Gilles Deleuze and Felix Guattari use this term in reference to Kafka, whose language was a German spoken in the Jewish community of Prague. Prague German, like Celan's, is a language outside of language, a "nomad" language whose words leave behind the space of their meanings. Goethe's German is "reterritorialized" in Kafka's Prague, where its sounds enter into a space that neutralizes their sense. Kafka takes German into the space of Yiddish, where, as Deleuze and Guattari say, "He will make it cry with an extremely sober and rigorous cry. He will pull from it the barking of the dog, the cough of the ape, and the bustling of the beetle. He will turn syntax into a cry that will embrace the rigid syntax of this dried-up German."[44] In a brief text, "Begaya-t-il [He Stuttered"]" Deleuze writes: "A great writer is always like a stranger in the language in which he expresses himself, even if it is his mother tongue. . . . The point is to make language itself cry, to make it stutter, mumble, or whisper."[45]

Celan's deterritorialized German sounds just so:

ZUR NACHTORDNUNG Über-
gerittener, Über-
geschlitterter, Über-
gewitterter,

Un-
besungener, Un-
bezwungener, Un-
umwundener, vor
die Irrenzelte gepflanzter

seelenbärtiger, hagel-
äugiger Weißkies-
stotterer. (GWC.2:357)

TO NIGHT'S ORDER Over-
ridden, Over-
skidded, Over-
winded,

Un-
sung, Un-
wrung, Un-
wreathed, and
planted before straying tents

soul-bearded, hail-
eyed whitegravel
stutterer. (SPP.339)

This poem is an instance of what Maurice Blanchot calls *désœuvrement*, "worklessness," incompletion (EI.622–23/IC.424). We might say that, whereas the order of day is one of arrangement, integration, and above all productive work, night's *ordnung* is that of *désœuvrement*, a derangement in which, for example, sounds are no longer forms of mediation (as in speech) but are materialized as in echoing or stuttering—a cacophony more violently acoustical in Celan's German, with its surplus of consonants, than in the English version. *Désœuvrement*, for Blanchot, is a condition of what he calls the *other* night—the night that, as for the insomniac, never passes into the day but is interminable, as in a vigil for an indecisive Messiah.[46] *Désœuvrement* means: nothing happens (Un- / besungener). It is, for Blanchot, the event of interruption—in particular the interruption of such things as the movement of Hegel's dialectic, the work of the Spirit that produces concepts, works, cultures, and the end of history. So in Celan's poem words are disjointed and rejoined in ways that defeat any form of progression. The poem stutters.

Notice, however, that the *Rätselcharakter* of Celan's poem consists not so much in an absence of meaning as in too many meanings, more than can be gathered into a single context—"seelenbärtiger, hagel- /

äugiger Weißkies- / stotterer": we know very well what the words mean, but the semantic density of their combinations breaks open the hermeneutical circle of part and whole that usually governs our experiences of meaning. Here is a brief, spare, laconic poem that, paradoxically, has too many words for any one context to comprehend, except in the sense that "Zur Nachtordnung" forces us to experience the meaning of its words according to a complex system of echoes and reverberations: or so it goes in the allegory of stuttering that, with Blanchot's help, I've constructed as a kind of hermeneutical stand-in. One could just as well see the justice of Adorno's reading of Celan's poems: "They imitate a language beneath the helpless language of human beings, indeed beneath all organic language: It is that of the dead speaking of stones and stars. The last rudiments of the organic are liquidated" (AT.477/AeT.322). Thus the stuttering in "Zur Nachtordnung" is no longer that of a human being, but of words in their materiality, words turned into (what?) a very strange gravel: thingwords.

The Modernist Sublime. However, the materiality of language, whether of voice or of writing, is not dead weight but is "magical" in something like the sense in which Walter Benjamin uses this term when he invokes an esoteric language that (being untheorizable) is very different from the system for framing representations that logicians and linguists try to construct. In "Über Sprache überhaupt und über die Sprache des Menschen" ("Language as Such and the Language of Man") (1916), Benjamin says that there is a language of things as well as of names, a "language as such" in which God creates things and a "language of man" in which this creation is brought to completion in Adam's naming of things, where naming is not so much predication as a kind of "voicing" or "translation of the mute into the sonic."[47] What is important to know is that the language of man is *not a language made of signs*. It is, Benjamin says, only in "the bourgeois view of language . . . that the word has an accidental relation to its object, that it is a sign for things (or knowledge of them) agreed by some convention. Language never gives *mere* signs" (GS.1.2:148/ SW.1:69). Signs belong to a restricted economy of contracted agreements and balanced accounts. Signs came into existence after the Fall when the language of man proliferated into multiple and heterogeneous tongues, in none of which can any name give us the thing itself. *Brot* and *pain* give us different ways of saying "bread" (as, of course, does the English version) but bread itself remains speechless.

Fallen language is "prattle" or "talk" (*Geschwätz, Gerede*). Only by translating from one language to another and from each into all can we begin to intimate that "pure language" in which words and things share the same ontology and which therefore allows things themselves to speak. In "Die Aufgabe des Übersetzers" ("The Task of the Translator") (1921), Benjamin writes:

> Whereas in the various tongues that ultimate essence, the pure language, is tied only to linguistic elements and their changes, in linguistic creations it is weighted with a heavy, alien meaning. To relieve it of this, to turn the symbolizing into the symbolized itself, to regain pure language fully formed from the flux, is the tremendous and only capacity of translation. In this pure language—which no longer means or expresses anything but is an expressionless and creative Word, that which is meant in all languages—all information, all sense, and all intention finally encounter a stratum in which they are destined to be extinguished. (GS.4.1:19/SW.1:261)

A "pure language" means a language that "no longer means or expresses anything," a *protosemantic* language incomprehensible to information theory (or any theory of language as a system of transmission and exchange).[48] Call it a "sublime" language, beyond conceptualization, free of definition—unless one can imagine a language consisting entirely of proper names:

> By giving names, parents dedicate their children to God; the names they give do not correspond—in a metaphysical rather than etymological sense—to any knowledge, for they name newborn children. In a strict sense, no name ought (in its etymological meaning) to correspond to any person, for the proper name is the word of God in human sounds. By it each man is guaranteed his creation by God, and in this sense he is himself creative, as is expressed by the mythological wisdom in the idea (which doubtless not infrequently comes true) that a man's name is his fate. The proper name is the communion of man with the *creative* word of God. . . . Through the word, man is bound to the language of things. The human word is the name of things. (GS.2.1:147/SW.1:69)

In the prelapsarian language of man, the name is not a sign but rather the signature of the thing, the testimony of its absolutely singular existence. In naming things Adam bears witness to them, and also bears responsibility for them. They enter not into his use but into his *care*. The relation between words and things in this event is ethical rather than logical; it is an unmediated relation, what Emmanuel Levinas calls a "relation of proximity" rather than one of cognition and representation.[49] Interestingly, in "Language as Such and the Languages of Man" Benjamin suggests that the languages of art and poetry echo or adumbrate this original language: "There is a language of sculpture, of painting, of poetry. Just as the language of poetry is partly, if not solely, founded on the name language of man, it is very conceivable that the language of sculpture or painting is founded on certain kinds of thing-languages, that in them we find a translation of the language of things into a higher language, which may still be of the same sphere" (GS.1.1:152/SW.1:73). So whatever it is, a pure language (like a proper name, a modernist poem, or a cubist collage) would never be transparent.

One can pursue Benjamin's thought further by noticing how his theory overthrows Hegel's monumental dialectic, where naming is a movement of negation in which the thing named is subsumed into its concept—in other words, destroyed and turned into a meaning (a kind of ghost, or piece of *Geist*). Maurice Blanchot, reflecting on this dialectical movement of signification, observes that things pay a high price for their intelligibility: "When I speak," Blanchot says, "death speaks in me. My speech is a warning that at this very moment death is loose in the world, that it has suddenly appeared between me, as I speak, and the being I address: it is there between us as the distance that separates us, but this distance is also what prevents us from being separated, because it contains the conditions for all understanding. Death alone allows me to grasp what I want to attain; it exists in words as the only way they can have meaning" (PF.313/WF.323–24).

However, Blanchot's idea (as if completing Benjamin's) is that poetry is an interruption of this powerful dialectic of the Spirit that annihilates things in the bargain of grasping them conceptually: "Something was there and is no longer there. Something has disappeared. How can I recover it, how can I turn around and look at what exists *before*, if all my power consists of making it into what exists *after*? The language of literature is a search for this moment that precedes literature. Literature usually calls it existence; it wants the cat as it exists, the pebble *taking the side of things*, not man but the pebble, and in this pebble what man rejects by saying it" (PF.316/WF.327). The key to the recovery of the thing lies in the materiality of literary or poetic language, which reverses the work of the Spirit: "A name ceases to be the ephemeral passing of nonexistence and becomes a concrete ball, a solid mass of existence; language, abandoning the sense, the meaning which was all it wanted to be, tries to become senseless. Everything physical takes precedence: rhythm, weight, mass, shape, and then the paper on which one writes, the trail of the ink, the book. Yes, happily language is a thing: it is a written thing, a bit of bark, a sliver of rock, a fragment of clay in which the reality of the earth continues to exist" (PF.316–17/WF.327–28).

Of course, literature is not meaningless. It has, Blanchot says, "two slopes": "One side of literature is turned toward the moment of negation by which things are separated from themselves and destroyed in order to be known, subjugated, communicated" (PF.318–19/WF.330). One thinks of the nineteenth-century novel. But with modernism (Blanchot mentions Mallarmé, Francis Ponge, and Lautréamont) another side emerges where literature discloses, not the order of things, but the anarchy of the sublime:

> Literature is a concern for the reality of things, for their unknown, free, and silent existence; literature is their innocence and forbidden presence, it is the being which protests against revelation, it is the defiance of what does not want to take place outside. In this way, it sympathizes with darkness, with aimless passion, with lawless violence, with everything in the world that seems to perpetuate the refusal to come into the world. In this way, too, it allies itself with the reality of language, it makes language into matter without contour, content without form, a force that is capricious and impersonal and says nothing, reveals nothing, simply announces—through its refusal to say anything—that it comes from the night and will return to night. (PF.319/WF.330)

Think of materiality, the condition of the sublime, as the anti-*Geist*.

Jean-François Lyotard recalls that Edmund Burke, in his treatise on the sublime, "attributes to *poetry*, or what we would now call writing (*écriture*), the twofold and thwarted finality of inspiring terror (or threatening that language will cease, as we would put it) and of meeting the challenge posed by this failure of the word by provoking or accepting the advent of an 'unheard of' phrase. . . . Literature is free to combine words and to experiment with sentences."[50] This freedom of combination—unheard-of phrasing—is perhaps Lyotard's chief interest. For Lyotard (as we shall see in chapter 6), a phrase is an indefinable piece of language capable of being linked with other phrases according to the protocols of any number of "phrase regimens," some of the more familiar of which (assertive, descriptive, prescriptive, narrative, interrogative) help to define literary modernism by the way their rules or "subjugations" are displaced or upended. For Lyotard, the pure, unsubjugated phrase is to be found in Gertrude Stein's paratactic "sentences," as in the following poem from *Tender Buttons* (1914):[51]

A BOX

Out of kindness comes redness and out of redness comes rapid same question, out of an eye comes research, out of selection comes painful cattle. So then the order is that a white way of being round is something suggesting a pin and is it disappointing, it is not, it is so rudimentary to be analysed and see a fine substance strangely, it is so earnest to have a green point not to red but to point again.[52]

Lyotard notes that Erich Auerbach, in *Mimesis*, identifies paratax as the distinctive "style" of the "modern"—as opposed to "classical syntax."[53] (It is a form of writing that Gertrude Stein brought to perfection, one that allows words the freedom to enter into heterogeneous combinations, as in "a white way of being round.") In paratax, Lyotard writes, "Phrases or events follow each other, but their succession does not obey a categorical order (*because*; *if, then*; *in order to*; *although* . . .). Joined to the preceding one by *and*, a phrase arises out of nothingness to link up with it. Paratax thus connotes the abyss of Not-Being which opens between phrases, it stresses the surprise that something begins when what is said is said. *And* is the conjunction that most allows the constitutive discontinuity (or oblivion) of time to threaten, while defying it through its equally constitutive continuity (or retention). . . . Instead of *and*, and assuring the same paratactic function, there can be a comma, or nothing" (Di.102/D.66).[54]

"Paratax . . . connotes the abyss of Not-Being": it is the premier figure of the modernist sublime, which Lyotard, in an essay on avant-garde painting, characterizes as the work of the "unpresentable": "The universe is unpresentable, so is humanity, the end of history, the instant, space, the good, etc." To be sure, Lyotard says, the word "sublime" belongs to the vocabulary of romanticism. But, unlike the romantics, the modernists "do not try to find the unpresentable at a great distance, as a lost origin or end, to be represented in a picture, but [as in the case of Gertrude Stein's *Tender Buttons*] in what is closest, in the very matter of artistic work" (In.138/IR.126). Singularities beneath the reach of concepts and categories but impinging on experience nevertheless—the thing, the other, the monster, materiality, interruptions and dislocations of time and space, anarchy (*an-archē*), but also the "everyday"—belong to the modernist sublime.

Synecdoches of the Foregoing. In 1969 the fiction writer Ronald Sukenick published *The Death of the Novel and Other Stories*, a volume of texts that at the time were gathered together under the umbrella of "metafiction"—a term that, in retrospect, seems a bit of a misnomer, at least in Sukenick's case. The title story, if "story" is the word, is not so much a piece of self-reflexive writing (although it is not *not* that) as a montage of writing moments, each one of which, Brecht-like, breaks its own frame, leaving artifice in shambles (and therefore lying around for all to see). Like much of modernism, Sukenick's fiction is anti-illusionist. However, his chief thesis in "The Death of the Novel" seems to be an art-historical burlesque—nothing is forbidden, but no matter, because writing (as we used to think of it) has become impossible:

> This story works on the principle of simultaneous multiplicity, or the knack of keeping several things on your mind at once. That is the central fact of our mental atmosphere. That is the water in which we swim, or should I say, the stew in which we cook. What we have to become is master jugglers, perfect a balancing act. We have to become artists in the sense that circus performers are called artists, equilibrists who can do seven things at once without thinking about it. Because we've already thought about it. Or because our sages have already thought about it, thought it all out, and we've learned it from them. Make it look easy, show us the easy way, easier and easier. Let peasants enslave themselves to the difficult.
>
> We're at a séance. You the participants, I the medium in the face of the total blank nothingness of uncreation.
>
> I can't go on.
> Go on.
> Nothing. Muscle spasms. Bowel pains. Galloping migraine
> Symptoms. I've got to stop.
> Go on.
> I have the impulse to get up and do a wild dance of pain. I squirm, sweat. Hands on either side of me hold me in my seat. I can't. I can't. Nothing. Nothing.

Suddenly a voice says: Everyone can fly. The voice my own.
Ah come on, they say. What do you call that, what does that
mean?

Jesus Christ, I say, isn't that enough? Come on, let me go.
Keep going. Keep going. Go on.

Suddenly the letter J. Why J? J is a bird. A bird that mimics
other birds. Perhaps because its own voice is so imperious, so
demanding, that it would rather deny it. J. J, J, the voice says.
It appears to be about three inches above and behind my left
ear.

J. J. walks down the street. He's tall, a little husky and
seems, perhaps without reason, to strut a bit, moving with a curious gawking swing to his head and neck. Seems to be about
thirty, balding, but with a tuft of hair sticking up on the back
of his head. The street is odd too, because it is just a street, that
is, there are no buildings on it, no traffic, no people, no scenery,
a street disappearing in a grey haze in the middle distance with
nothing on either side, nothing in front, nothing behind. Now
there are buildings, brownstones. J. J. lives in a brownstone:
two rooms on the fourth floor. He has just brought his garbage
down. . . .

I can't go on.

Go on.[55]

What has died here, if anything, is not the novel, at least, not the
novel as Mikhail Bakhtin, recovering an unruly tradition that unfolds
backward in time from Dostoevsky to Laurence Sterne's *Tristram
Shandy*, Rabelais, medieval carnivals, Petronius, and the Socratic dialogues, understood it—a parodistic heterogeneity of voices, styles,
languages, and incongruent, conflicting forms—but rather allegiance
to a certain idea of narrative very powerful in Sukenick's heyday:
narrative as cybernetic system whose rules can generate (as if without friction) an endless array of particular texts: novels, histories,
fairytales and folktales, diaries, autobiographies, jokes and anec-
dotes, newspaper stories, court proceedings, gossip, lies, and so on
down the hierarchy to no definite term.[56] Sukenick is an innovator of
surfaces who prefers the lower, paratactic end of the scale. "The
Death of the Novel" is a subversion of self-regulating systems: call it
a poststructuralist collage of ill-begotten, broken-off narrations, dialogues, newspaper clippings, sex scenes, and verbal horseplay held
together (or, more exactly, punctuated) by a first-person narrative of

failed writing, as in the citation above, which, facing "the total blank nothingness of uncreation," riffs briefly on a letter of the alphabet, then gives up: "All right enough of this. I'm not filibustering fate, like Beckett or one of those cats.[57] This is not a game it's a story. Or it's both, a game and a story. Or. . . . But then who cares what it is" (DN.55). Say that, in the spirit of (lowest) modernism, it falls beneath the threshold of identity: an "it," neither one thing nor another. The writing in any case makes no effort to become High Literature of the kind Matthew Arnold counseled us to read—or, rather, on the contrary, it furiously resists such an effort. "The Death of the Novel" is unfailingly comic because its "failure" is a failure to do what anyone can do, namely write a conventional story, starting with plot and character. ("What I need is a bunch of friends who would be willing to become my characters for a whole story. Maybe I can hire some. Somebody ought to start a character rental service" [DN.85].) In fact, Sukenick does enlist his wife, Lynn, who is also his collaborator in another "story," "Roast Beef: A Slice of Life"). Indeed, one could say that "The Death of the Novel" is eminently traditional, because it unfolds, if that is the word, at the excremental level of satire, where sexual impotence stands in for action both in life and in art. Indeed, coitus interruptus turns out to be its law of form.

One of Sukenick's contemporaries is John Ashbery, perhaps the most distinguished American poet—and certainly one of the most difficult—of the past half-century. Here, from *Houseboat Days* (1977), is "And *Ut Pictura Poesis* Is Her Name":[58]

> You can't say it that way any more.
> Bothered about beauty you have to
> Come out into the open, into a clearing,
> And rest. Certainly whatever funny happens to you
> Is OK. To demand more than this would be strange
> Of you, you who have so many lovers,
> People who look up to you and are willing
> To do things for you, but you think
> It's not right, that if they really knew you . . .
> So much for self-analysis. Now,
> About what to put into your poem-painting:
> Flowers are always nice, particularly delphinium.
> Names of boys you once knew and their sleds,
> Skyrockets are good—do they still exist?
> There are a lot of other things of the same quality
> As those I've mentioned. Now one must

Find a few important words, and a lot of low-keyed
Dull-sounding ones. She approached me
About buying her desk. Suddenly the street was
Bananas and the clangor of Japanese instruments.
Humdrum testaments were scattered around. His head
Locked into mind. We were a seesaw. Something
Ought to be written about how this affects
You when you write poetry:
The extreme austerity of an almost empty mind
Colliding with the lush, Rousseau-like foliage of its desire to
   communicate
Something between breaths, if only for the sake
Of others and their desire to understand you and desert you
For other centers of communication, so that understanding
May begin, and in doing so be undone.[59]

"I wrote this," Ashbery said in an interview, "shortly after I began teaching, which I did relatively late in life, and found that I was constantly being asked what a poem was, and what it wasn't, and why this is a poem and why this is not. And ah. . . . I never really thought about that before. I'd written poems but it never occurred to me to question whether they were poems or not, so, suddenly, thinking about this, I wrote this poem, as well as another one . . . called 'What is Poetry.'"[60] And so he gives us, in his title, Horace's famous definition, "Poetry is a speaking picture, painting a silent poem"—only to reject it in his very first line: "But you can't say it that way any more." Things (poetry, painting, beauty) are not so definite these days; but why take this as a problem? "Come out into the open, into a clearing / And rest." Naturally thoughts fly to Charles Olson, or (better) William Carlos Williams: "A poem can be made of anything." "Certainly whatever funny happens to you / is OK." Poetry is the overflow of one's experience, but is that what you want? ("you, who have so many lovers")—"you think / It's not right, that if they really knew you. . . / So much for self-analysis." So become impersonal, a kind of objectivist vis-à-vis mundane things: "Flowers are always nice" (the objectivist Louis Zukofsky is writing his *80 Flowers* around this time). Mundane memories will do as well ("Names of boys you once knew and their sleds"). But remember, poetry is made of words, not ideas: so "one must / Find a few important words, and a lot of low-keyed, / Dull-sounding ones." For example,

> She approached me
> About buying her desk. Suddenly the street was

Bananas and the clangor of Japanese instruments.
Humdrum testaments were scattered around. His head
Locked into mine. We were a seesaw. . . .

Words or, more accurately, non sequiturs, lineated nonlinearity, sentences fallen out of their contexts (Gertrude Stein's paratactics): Ashbery's *phrasing* puts flesh on Lyotard's sense of this term, where the linking of phrases is open to multiple and conflicting regimens: modernism means that a collage is better than a syllogism. But Ashbery's poem has one more turn of the screw. "Something / Ought to be written about how this affects / You when you write poetry," namely:

The extreme austerity of an almost empty mind
Colliding with the lush, Rousseau-like foliage of its desire to
    communicate
Something between breaths, if only for the sake
Of others and their desire to understand you and desert you
For other centers of communication, so that understanding
May begin, and in doing so be undone.

"And *Ut Pictura* Poesis Is Her Name" seems at first like a parody of poetics (How to Write a Poem: Some Simple Ways), but these concluding lines can be read as Ashbery's effort to say what poetry writing comes down to: namely, a kind of performative contradiction, oddly reminiscent of John Cage's famous "definition" from his "Lecture on Nothing" (S.109) —

$$\text{I have nothing to say}$$
$$\text{and I am saying it} \qquad\qquad \text{and that is}$$
$$\text{poetry}^{61}$$

A poem is not an object; it is an event—call it an "accusative" rather than "declarative" event, a pure address to another that is a necessary if not sufficient condition of understanding, since what it lacks is a message, or (as Stephen Fredman has suggested) what it contains is something lost in translation, or in the sheer excess of language.[62] Ashbery's poetry is formally different from Paul Celan's, but like Celan's it means too much—its lines articulate sentences that intimate contexts without ever forming them. So what we get are phrases working in a kind of fluid, as in "The Ice-Cream Wars" (HD.60–61):

Although I mean it, and project the meaning
As hard as I can into its brushed-metal surface,

It cannot, in this deteriorating climate, pick up
Where I leave off. It sees the Japanese text
(About two men making love on a foam-rubber bed)
As among the most massive secretions of the human spirit.
Its part is in the shade, beyond the iron spikes of the fence,
Mixing red with blue. As the day wears on
Those who come to seem reasonable are shouted down
(*Why you old goat!* Look who's talkin'. Let's see you
Climb off that tower—the waterworks architecture, both stupid and
Grandly humorous at the same time, is a kind of mask for him,
Like a seal's face. Time and the weather
Don't always go hand in hand, as here: sometimes
One is slanted sideways, disappears for a while.
Then later it's forget-me-not time, and rapturous
Clouds appear above the lawn, and the rose tells
The old old story, the pearl of the orient, occluded
And still apt to rise at times.)
                      A few black smudges
On the outer boulevards, like squashed midges
And the truth becomes a hole, something one has always known,
A heaviness in the trees, and no one can say
Where it comes from, or how long it will stay—

A randomness, a darkness of one's own.

What is *it* that the poet means so strenuously? A meaning that
doesn't come through, stay the course, get things right? The meaning
in any case is projected onto "its brushed-metal surface," that is, a
textured and therefore opaque or unreflecting surface, which one
might just as well let stand as a description of the poem that follows,
whose lines, characteristically, don't follow one another very far—
don't pick up where others leave off. Even the lines in parentheses
are overlaid by multiple conflicting pieces of narrative (can you picture "the waterworks tower" as "a kind of mask for him, / Like a
seal's face"?), with a rose in flower-time finally telling "an old old
story," no doubt one that turns on a cliché, "the pearl of the orient."
The last lines (like the concluding lines of "And *Ut Pictura Poesis* Is
Her Name") sketch out a complexity rather than a conclusion: All it
takes are "A few black smudges / On the outer boulevards, like
squashed midges / And the truth [of all things] becomes a hole," but
also a mysterious "heaviness in the trees," at which point the poem
breaks off with a final melancholy (but oddly resonant) fragment—
"A randomness, a darkness of one's own."[63]

"A randomness, a darkness of one's own"—a modernist's signature if there ever was one.

Ancients and Moderns: Gadamer's Aesthetic Theory and the Poetry of Paul Celan

I don't give a damn for aesthetic construction.
       — Paul Celan

The Play of the Artwork. Possibly there is a no more unlikely, or maybe even unwanted, commentator on modernism than Hans-Georg Gadamer, a classical philologist, distinguished Plato scholar, and author of *Wahrheit und Methode* (*Truth and Method*) (1960), the monumental articulation of philosophical hermeneutics, one of whose central chapters concerns the normative character of the "classical" or "eminent" text. (WM.269–75/TM.285–90). Nevertheless, it happens that Gadamer is also an accomplished art historian who thinks that the claim of the modernist work (one of Duchamp's Readymades, for example) is every bit as compelling as that of the classical work of art. In "Die Aktualität des Schönen" ("The Relevance of the Beautiful") (1974) Gadamer writes:

> How can we understand the innovative forms of modern art as they play around with the content [*das Spiel mit allen Inhalten*] so that our expectations [of meaning] are constantly frustrated? How are we to understand what contemporary artists, or certain trends of contemporary art, even describe as "happenings" or anti-art? How are we to understand what Duchamp is doing when he suddenly exhibits some everyday object on its own and

thereby produces a sort of aesthetic shock reaction? We cannot simply dismiss this as so much nonsense, for Duchamp actually revealed something about the conditions of aesthetic experience [*den Bedingungen ästhetischer Erfahrung*]. (GW.8:113/RB.22)

What are these "conditions of aesthetic experience" that Duchamp (against all reason) is able to reveal? A first answer lies in Gadamer's critique of aesthetic consciousness in *Truth and Method*, where aesthetic consciousness is understood (following a certain reading of Kant's *Critique of Judgment*) as the disengaged contemplation of a formal object. Gadamer's idea, derived already from his reading of Plato's dialogues, is that the work of art is more of an event than it is an object, in which case the main question to ask about the work is not "Is it art?" or "What is it?" or even "How is it made?" but "How does it happen?" Gadamer's answer is that the work takes place in our encounter with it, that is, what is encountered is the coming-into-appearance of the work, which is not an event that merely reproduces an original production; it is the emergence, as if for the first time, of the original itself. As Gadamer says, "Presentation [*Darstellung*] is the mode of existence of the work of art" (WM.110/TM.115), that is, its mode of being consists in its being played like a theater piece or a work of music: "it is in the performance and only in it . . . that we encounter the work itself" (WM.111/TM.116). Again: "the presentation or performance of a work of literature or music is something essential, and not incidental to it, for it merely completes what the works of art already are—the being there of what is presented in them" (WM.127/TM.134). Performance is not something added to the work. It is not a rendition or version of it; it is the appearance (in the phenomenological sense of disclosure) of the thing itself.[1] The work exists in no other way. Its mode of coming-into-appearance is its mode of being. And the key point is that this primacy of performance applies to the modernist artwork as well as to the classic that comes down to us from the past.

This is very different from Adorno's idea that the work of music exists in its score. Yet I think it would be premature to say that there is a disagreement here between Gadamer and Adorno, for whom "the law of form" constitutes the work of art, quite apart from what anyone makes of it. After all, form for Adorno is not a concept of totality. Gadamer, too, places great emphasis on form, but Adorno would be the first to see that on Gadamer's theory it would be a mistake to think of the work as a self-contained formal object that simply persists over time and receives its identity from the art historian or the curator of museums. Gadamer's "classic" is not confined to the museum, because for him the work of art is not (or not just) an inhabitant of a fixed time and space; it *travels*. As Gadamer sometimes expresses it, "the temporality of the aesthetic" is neither the timelessness of the museum, nor is it the Hegelian temporality of supersession in which the present subsumes the past and leaves behind what is merely over and done with (*Vergangen*). On the contrary, for Gadamer the work of art belongs to the temporality of the *festival* in which a singular event comes round again and again, without end and with no loss to its absolute singularity. In *Truth and Method* Gadamer writes:

> As a festival it is not an identity like a historical event, but neither is it determined by its origin so that there was once the 'real' festival—as distinct from the way in which it later came to be celebrated. From its inception . . . the nature of a festival is to be celebrated regularly. Thus its own original essence is always to be something different (even when celebrated in exactly the same way). An entity that exists only by always being something different is temporal in a more radical sense than everything that belongs to history. It has its being only in becoming and return [*es hat nur im Werden und im Wiederkehren sein*]. (WM.117/TM.123)

The festival is not a commemorative event but the occurrence of the once and future thing itself in its own "autonomous time" (GW.8.132–33/RB.42). It is the arrival of what has come to pass. Likewise our encounter with the work of art is an event in which what Gadamer calls "the hermeneutic identity" of the work shows itself in all of its singularity (GW.8.117/RB.26–27). Hermeneutic identity is not something to be construed like a meaning but something to be traced like a pattern or arrangement: it is a formal intelligibility. In *Truth and Method* Gadamer calls this event (perhaps less than felicitously) "transformation into structure [*die Verwandlung ins Gebilde*]" (WM.105/TM.110), a taking-shape in which the work materializes as the thing it is *in our experience of it*.[2] But what is it like to undergo this experience? And experience of what, exactly?

In Gadamer's theory the experience of art is not a contemplative experience but an experience of *play* in which we are caught up and carried away in the self-presentation of the work. In other words, in contrast to a Kantian account of aesthetic experience, which presupposes a model of perception or regard, this self-presentation of the work is not something we stand apart from as observers but something in which we participate—and this is true whether the work is a Renaissance portrait or an avant-garde provocation. Indeed, the virtue of the model of play is that it emancipates the work of art, not to say ourselves, from universal concepts and art-historical periods. Here participation does the work of principles, rules, and ultimate foundations. When Duchamp sets up a snow shovel in his studio, pronouncing it his latest composition, he lays down a challenge that we may not know how to take up. What is the "transformation into structure" that turns the mere snow shovel into the avant-garde work? The temptation is to imagine some alchemical process that transforms base matter into significant form, since something like this surely occurs (what Arthur Danto calls the "transfiguration of the commonplace").[3] Gadamer's counsel is to hold to the model of the game. If we do not know how to respond to Duchamp's challenge, how do we go about learning to do so? No differently from the way one learns to play any game. As we know from Wittgenstein, it is not enough to learn rules or to follow explanations; one has to enter into the game as one enters a new horizon. (Recall Cavell's response to serial music: one has "to naturalize oneself to a new form of life, a new world.")[4] And this practical principle applies to our relations with both ancients and moderns.

Hermeneutical Experience. Indeed, one is tempted to say, tautologically, that what the experience of art requires is, basically, *experience*. Aristotle remarked that *phronesis*—practical knowledge—knowing what a situation calls for in the way of right action, is not a virtue of the young but is the condition of "being experienced" that comes from living through things themselves, like friendship, falling in love, or being a father. *Phronesis* is practical reason, which means finding one's way and not remaining fixed in position. Here stories rather than concepts and rules are more apt to provide access to the conditions that make experience possible, because they give us, in a way rules and concepts never can, the ground-level dimension in which experience actually takes place. Recall what Gadamer says in *Truth and Method* about the negativity of hermeneutical experience (*Erfahrung*)—experience that does not confirm but rather overturns what we had thought, a reversal that explains why experience can never be codified as science:

Experience stands in an ineluctable opposition to knowledge and to the kind of instruction that follows from general theoretical or technical knowledge. The truth of experience always implies orientation toward new experience. That is why a person who is called experienced has become so not only *through* experiences but is also open *to* new experiences. The consummation of his experience, the perfection that we call "being experienced," does not consist in the fact that someone already knows everything and knows better than anyone else. Rather, the experienced person proves to be, on the contrary, someone who is radically undogmatic; who, because of the many experiences he has had and the knowledge he has drawn from them, is particularly well equipped to have new experiences and to learn from them. The dialectic of experience has its proper fulfillment not in definitive knowledge but in the openness to experience that is made possible by experience itself. (WM.338 /TM.355)

It follows that, on Gadamer's theory, the hermeneutical experience of art, whether classical or modernist, would not result in connoisseurship or expertise—nor, for all of that, in either philosophy of art, or art criticism, or the self-understanding artistry (*techne*) of the maker—but simply in a capacity for experiencing art that is free from the dogmatism that attaches as a matter of course to the sophistication of certain knowledge. Indeed it is not too much to see an internal coherence between hermeneutical experience and modernism itself, given that any experience of the modernist work at all presupposes the kind of reversal of consciousness (*Umkehrung des Bewußtseins*) that characterizes the emancipatory character of hermeneutical experience. "Every experience worthy of the name," Gadamer says, "thwarts an expectation. . . . [It] implies a fundamental negativity that emerges between experience and insight"—where insight (*Einfall*) "is more than the knowledge of this or that situation. It involves an escape from something that had deceived us and held us captive" (WM.338/ TM.356).

It is this notion of the negativity of hermeneutical experience that opens up Gadamer's aesthetics, which is still essentially an aesthetics of the beautiful, to modernism's aesthetics of the sublime. In "The Relevance of the Beautiful," Gadamer, the classicist, takes up, among other examples of modernist art, a cubist painting, and he says that our relation to the work is a relation of "playing along with it"— entering into the "autonomous time" of the work, which is to say its movement of self-presentation. This means tracing its construction piece by piece, playing along with the dissonance of its elements, experiencing its unity, even if this unity can no longer be understood in terms of an aesthetics of harmony (GW.8:118/RB.27–28). But for this to happen—and here Gadamer is close to Arthur Danto's position—the classicist must have already made himself at home in the culture of the avant-garde—must already have made this culture his own.[5] This seems a crucial point—understanding presupposes appropriation. To enter into the autonomous time of the work also means entering into the movement of the artworld in which the cubist work emerges as a work of art according to its own theory of what counts as art. Constructing the hermeneutic identity of the cubist work is not just an aesthetic or, let us say, "constructivist" process. One does not follow the design of construction in Duchamp's shovel as if it were a sculpture. The fact is there is no knowing beforehand, as if by an appeal to criteria, what makes Duchamp's thing a work. Vexation is perhaps part of the experience of the work. But how can there be any experience at all? Why not just blank indifference? Recall again the motto of art history: anything is possible even if not at every moment. For Gadamer, constructing the hermeneutic identity of the work would mean entering into the complex moment of its possibility in which the work itself gives the definition of art in defiance of prevailing markets or the history of taste. And this means, at the very least, opening oneself to new possibilities of experience and new concepts of art. Doubtless it is the task of aesthetic norms to define possibilities of experience. But aesthetic norms are never simply given. They evolve within the event or history of art itself in the way that, in everyday life, ethical norms [Sittlichkeit] evolve within the give-and-take of deliberation under the exigency of things needing to be decided. Norms are in any case *not* presiding universals; they emerge in the hermeneutic identity of the singular, irreplaceable work itself. It is in this respect that the experience of art should be thought of as a work of *phronesis*, a judgment based not on universals but on our understanding and responsiveness to the complex historical situation in which the work comes into appearance—a situation in which our schemes and categories almost certainly have to change if anything is to occur at all. Being historical in this event means being able to change—and isn't this what modernism teaches? As Gadamer says, "The work of art has its true being in the fact that it becomes an experience that changes the person who experiences it"

(WM.98/TM.102). The crucial point to mark is that this is not just a change in one's private outlook; it is a change in one's world.

Appropriation. Appropriation means: the original can only come into being *when I make it my own.* This means encountering the thing as a kind of epiphany—but also conceivably as a *crisis*—within my own historical and cultural environment. The fact that appropriation conditions the event of art and makes it possible is the reason why, to borrow Jean-Luc Nancy's expression, "art can never be addressed from the [transcendental] horizon of a *kosmos* or a *polis*" but only from below at the level of the singular and irreducible.[6] Appropriation is also why art can never be for us, as for Hegel, "a thing of the past" (*ein Vergangenes*). The work that is merely over and done with is just lost until someone recovers it in experience. The transcendence of art is always here and now, but this transcendence is our responsibility. This is what Gadamer means when he says, "The work of art cannot simply be isolated from the 'contingency' of the chance conditions in which it appears, and where this kind of isolation occurs, the result is an abstraction that reduces the actual being of the work. It itself belongs to the world to which it presents itself. A drama really exists only when it is played, and ultimately music must resound" (WM.111/TM.116). Appropriation lifts the work out of its afterlife so that even in a museum it is no longer a museum-piece (WM.115/TM.120).[7] In this respect it makes sense to say that we are responsible for the life of the work.

The difficulty lies in being able to articulate clearly what this means. Appropriation does not mean taking possession of the thing as if at an auction. Paul Ricoeur thinks of appropriation as a task in which I take up the work as a projection of my ownmost possibilities.[8] The work breaks open a new world for me to inhabit. But precisely for this reason it calls into question my world as it is given. Thus for Adorno the work is always essentially critical of the world in which it makes its appearance. Gadamer would say that the experience of the modernist work is hermeneutical rather than strictly aesthetic because of the way the work changes the horizon of the present and requires us to engage in exploration of new territory. This in fact is how the history of art moves, not toward an end but toward an indeterminate or always receding horizon. Duchamp's Readymades are simply a lucid and radical instance of this movement, which exposes us to the insufficiency of our reasons (or as Gadamer would say, to our finitude). In terms of aesthetics what we experience is the fact that we may no longer know what art is.[9] For Gadamer, this is not a privative condition; it is freedom from dogmatism.

As if the experience of art disengaged us from our aesthetic concepts—in fact this is a main thesis of "The Relevance of the Beautiful." Modernism, Gadamer says, interrupts the history of art by "making all previous art appear as something belonging to the past in a different and more radical sense [than Hegel's]" (GW.8:97/RB.6). Gadamer says that we cannot avoid "the fact that when we visit a museum and enter the rooms devoted to the most recent artistic developments, we really do leave something behind us" (GW.8:100/ RB.8–9). "A new social force [*gesellschaftliches Agens*] is at work in the claim of the modern artist" (GW.8:101/RB.10). Modernism entails the thesis of historical difference and epistemological break. Yet it is precisely this thesis that defines the historical and cultural environment to which we belong. It is an event in *our* history, it confronts *us*, and the confrontation conditions and shapes our self-understanding in the nature of the case. This is the whole idea of *Wirkungsgeschichte* as an exigency of self-understanding.[10] There is no question of understanding ourselves and our world unless we come to terms with this event. So the idea is to renew the history of art by means of acknowledgment and appropriation. Gadamer puts this by saying that "historical consciousness and the new self-conscious reflection arising from it combine with a claim that we cannot renounce: namely, the fact that everything we see stands before us and addresses us directly as if it showed us ourselves" (GW.8:102/RB.11). Gadamer's idea would be that modernist or avant-garde art requires us to come to terms with the present world that we actually inhabit. (This indeed is what is entailed in Gadamer's term, *Aktualität*: not so much relevance as realization.) This is not an easy assignment, as one can see from Heidegger's "Der Ursprung des Kunstwerkes" ("The Origin of the Work of Art"), which characterizes the *work* of the work of art in explicitly modernist terms of "starting history all over again." Yet the work that Heidegger takes as his example is the Greek temple—a work whose time has passed and whose work no longer has any force in our world, since our temporality is no longer defined by the work of art but, or so Heidegger thinks, by technology. Certainly at the time of writing and revising "The Origin of the Work of Art" Heidegger thought that art history was a history of the decline of art (see his Nietzsche lecture on "Six Basic Developments in the History of Aesthetics").[11] Heidegger (following Hölderlin) seems to have created for himself an imaginary world of the Greeks. But this is just where Gadamer thinks Heidegger was mistaken. Indeed, "The Relevance of the Beautiful" is clearly written against Heidegger's rejection of modernism. As Adorno thought, what defines our culture is not rationalization and technological control but the opaque modernist work, whose resistance to conceptualization and the rule of identity opens up an alternative social space within the rationalized world—not a space of aesthetic differentiation but an alternative mode of being (for example, an artworld set apart from the mainstream). It is just the possibility of such an alternative that motivates Gadamer's aesthetics, with its emphasis on the festive and performative experience of the work of art. In his essay on "Das Spiel der Kunst" ("The Play of Art") (1977) Gadamer writes: "Insistence on the opposition between life and art is tied to the experience of an alienated world" (GW.8:92/RB.30). But unlike Adorno, Gadamer does not set the modernist work against the world. On the contrary, appropriation and actualization mean working out a place for the work within the situation in which we find ourselves. If this means reshaping the world so as to overcome the opposition between art and life, or between then and now, or between the familiar and the strange, then we must count this task as just what the experience of art finally requires.

The Claim of Modernism. Here perhaps is the place to put the question: What is it to be addressed—to be put under a claim—by a modernist or avant-garde work of art? What form could this address take?

For Gadamer the claim of the modernist work has an ethical as well as aesthetic dimension, that is, a dimension of responsibility in which I take up the work as a task in relation to my time and place (and, indeed, to those around me). As I said earlier, the work is not simply a cultural product available for our consumption in the marketplace of the artworld and which we can pick up or not as we choose. Nor is it (*pace* Danto) simply a philosophical problem of aesthetics that one can work out through conceptualization and theory. Gadamer's idea is that the claim of the artwork is deeper than any claim upon our taste or aesthetic interest, deeper than our profession of values or philosophical outlook. Gadamer's way of formulating this deeper claim is to understand the work as addressing us as a Thou, that is, as an Other whose approach to us is transcendent, that is, outside our conceptual scheme and irreducible to the forms and expectations in which things make sense to us. The work addresses *me* not as a logical subject who responds to the work through the mediation of ready-made concepts; it addresses *me* as a "who," that is, someone situated here and now—someone not interchangeable with others—whose task is to bring the work into being in this here and now by making it my own. Making the work mine is not a project in which I develop principles that transform my relation to the work into a judgment of universal validity. On the contrary, in this event my relation to the work is one of proximity rather than one of theory. There is no engaging the work at a distance or at the level of what is universal and necessary. In order to experience the work at all I must take responsibility for it, taking it upon myself and staking myself on its claim. In this event the work can be said to expose me to my world and to others in it.

Recall Stanley Cavell's idea (in "Music Discomposed") that the possibility of fraudulence is internal to the experience of the modernist work. Cavell writes: "In emphasizing the experiences of fraudulence and trust as essential to the experience of art, I am in effect claiming that the answer to the question, 'What is art?' will in part be an answer which explains why it is we treat certain objects, or how we *can* treat certain objects, in ways normally reserved for treating persons" (MW.189). Of course, the work is not a person or any sort of subjective expression. The issue here is rather *how we are with the work* (one could call it a relation of being-with [*mitsein*]): we can in any case no longer address it as an object in a relation of disinterestedness or aesthetic judgment. Cavell's thought is, remarkably, that we put ourselves up as hostages to the work, as if our relation to the work were one of accepting it, taking it upon ourselves, without being able (try as we might) to justify our action on the basis of concepts or criteria. As if my relation to the work now had to take the form of responsibility—what Cavell likes to call, "taking responsibility for one's experience":

> This seems to be to suggest why one is anxious to communicate the experience of such objects. It is not merely that I want to tell you how it is with me, how I feel, in order to find sympathy or to be left alone, or for any other of the reasons for which one reveals one's feelings. It's rather that I want to tell you something I've seen, or heard, or realized, or come to understand, for the reasons for which *such* things are communicated (because it is news, about a world we share, or could). Only I find that I

can't tell you; and that makes it all the more urgent to tell you. I want to tell you because the knowledge, unshared, is a burden—not, perhaps, the way having a secret can be a burden, or being misunderstood; a little more like the way, perhaps, not being believed is a burden, or not being trusted. It matters that others know what I see, in a way it does not matter whether they know my tastes. It matters, there is a burden, because unless I can tell what I know, there is a suggestion (and to myself as well) that I do *not* know. But I *do*—what I see is *that* (pointing to the object). But for that to communicate, you have to see it too. Describing one's experience of art is itself a form of art; the burden of describing it is like the burden of producing it. (MW.192–93)

One speaks not from above but from below on the basis of intimacy and as if passing along something to be shared, and which, in the nature of the case, could be rejected. But in this event what would be refused would be an experience, not a judgment; or, by extension, it would be the refusal of life.

Paul Celan's Poetry: A Limit-Experience. A good example of what Cavell is getting at would be Gadamer's encounter with Paul Celan's *Atemkristall*.[12] Gadamer's *Wer bist Ich und wer bist Du? Ein Kommentar zu Paul Celans "Atemkristall"* (*Who am I and Who are You? A Commentary on Paul Celan's "Atemkristall"*) is a volume of close readings—what used to be called "immanent criticism"—that bear witness, Gadamer says, to his long acquaintance with these gnarly, recondite poems. In these readings, scholarly research, theoretical procedures, and appeals to authorial intention give way to what Gadamer calls "listening"—attentiveness to each word of the poem and a search for ways in which the words may be said to come together or interact as a unity despite their fragmentary arrangements. Gadamer thinks that this kind of immanent reading is necessary precisely because of the laconic, dissonant nature of Celan's poetry:

IN DEN FLÜSSEN nördlich der Zukunft	IN THE RIVERS north of the future
werf ich das Netz aus, das du zögernd beschwerst mit von Steinem geschriebenen Schatten. (GWC.2:14)	I cast the net, which you hesitantly weight with shadow stones wrote. (B.61)

Here the world of our experience—time and space, words and things, substance and shadow, I and you—has been broken down and reassembled in heterogeneous, incongruous combinations. The baroque style comes to mind. But, as Gadamer says:

> [Celan's] is nothing like baroque poetry, whose statements are contained inside a uniform frame of references and occupy a common mythological, iconographic, and semantic foundation. Celan's word choices venture upon a network of linguistic connotations whose hidden syntax cannot be acquired from anywhere else but the poems themselves. This is what prescribes the path of interpretation; one is not transported by the text into a world of meaning familiar in its coherence. (GW.8:431/ GC.131)

In other words, Celan's poems seem to be contextless—imagine the considerable white space that surrounds each poem expanding indefinitely so that the poem is literally without a horizon. The poems defeat (as Adorno saw) the traditional idea of the hermeneutical circle—the movement back and forth between part and whole, text and context, that brings out the intelligibility of the work. Meaning, after all, just means belonging to a context. Hence the temptation to assemble background information by interrogating the poet as to his intentions, as Peter Szondi did, or by providing the poems with a cultural history, as Otto Pöggeler did with his investigations into Jewish mysticism.[13] However, as Derrida says in his monograph on Celan, there is no privileged entry into a Celan poem, which is singular and irreducible (like a date). Derrida writes: "Folded or refolded in the simplicity of the singular, a certain repetition thus assures the minimal and 'internal' readability of the poem, even in the absence of a witness, of a signatory or of anyone who might have some knowledge concerning the historical reference of the poetic legacy." The key word here is "internal readability": "The poem speaks," Derrida says, echoing Gadamer, "even should none of its references be intelligible."[14] This includes the pronominal references—"I," "you," "we"—which, as Gadamer emphasizes, "are pronounced in an utterly direct, shadowy-uncertain and constantly changing way [*schatttenhaft-unbestimmt und in beständig wechselnder Weise*]" (GW.9:384/GC.69). And it includes the recurrences that form something like Celan's own distinctive lexicon, his own "poetic diction": snow, stones, sand, shadows, ashes, streams, sky, stars, trees, flowers, eyes, ears, hands, mouths, memory, breath, blood, wounds, names, words, syllables, letters, mirrors—and beetles:

ENGHOLZTAG unter
netznervigem Himmelblatt. Durch
großzellige Leerstunden klettert,
  im Regen,
der schwarzblaue, der
Gedankenkäfer.

Tierblütige Worte
drängen sich vor seine Fühler.
  (GW.2:46)

NARROWWOOD DAY under
netnerved skyleaf. Through
bigcelled idlehours clambers, in
  rain,
the blackblue, the
thoughtbeetle.

Animal-bloodsoming words
crowd before its feelers. (B.123)

In the absence of external contexts, one has only the words themselves — but what words! *Engholztag, Gedankenkäfer, Tierblütige Worte.*
Celan's poetic diction is full of impossibilities. Gadamer says: "Fragments of meaning seem to be wedged together [*Sinnfragmente sind wie
ineinandergekeilt*]" (GW.9:431/GC.131). The poem seems to have
been materialized into a sound-text, that is, into an acoustical (rather
than lyrical or musical) experience — what Maurice Blanchot would
call "a non-dialectical experience" of speech whose meanings are jux-
taposed in ways that elude our attempt to grasp them.[15] Such speech
is not nonsense — not insignificant — but its meanings are too much
for us, outside our control, as if setting limits to our mastery of
language.

In an essay, "Philosophie und Poesie" ("Philosophy and Poetry")
(1977), Gadamer poses the central question: "How can a whole be
formed out of configurations of sound [*Klangfiguren*] and fragments
of meaning?" (GW.8:236/RB.135). One has to start, he says, by rec-
ognizing "the inseparability of the linguistic work of art and its original manifestation as language [*Spracherscheinung*]" (GW.8:235/
RB.134). Following Paul Valéry, whom he cites, Gadamer says that
the poem is constituted ontologically by the materiality of its language. In ordinary speech, the word points beyond itself as in an exchange of word and thing; it is a form of mediation. In poetry,
however, the word stands on its own: "The structuring of sound,
rhyme, rhythm, intonation, assonance, and so on, furnishes the stabi-
lizing factors that haul back and bring to a standstill the fleeting
word that points beyond itself. The unity of the creation is constituted in this way" (GW.8:235/RB.134). Nevertheless, the language
of the poem is still language: the materiality of the word does not
deprive it of its semantic resonance. "This means that the other log-
ico-grammatical forms of intelligible speech are also at work in the
poem, even though they may recede into the background in favor of

the structural moments of creation that we have just listed" (GW.8:235/RB.134–35). So part of the play of the poem includes the interplay of sound and sense, materiality and meaning. This is so even in the hermetic poetry of literary modernism, where the temptation is to abandon any semantic interest in the poem. However, to abandon this interest would be a mistake, Gadamer says,

> for the unity of sense is retained wherever speech exists. But this is concentrated in a complex fashion. It almost seems as if we cannot perceive the 'things' named, since the order of the words can neither be accommodated to the unity of a train of thought nor let themselves be dissolved into a unified image. And yet it is precisely the force of the semantic field, the tension between the tonal and the significative forces of language as they encounter and change place with one another, that constitutes the whole. Words evoke images, which may well accumulate, intersect with one another, and cancel one another out, but which remain images nevertheless. There is not a single word in a poem that does not intend what it means. Yet at the same time, it is set back upon itself to prevent it slipping into prose and the rhetoric that accompanies it. This is the claim and legitimation of *poésie pure*. (GW.8:236/RB.135–36)

One recalls Gertrude Stein's rejection of Jabberwocky or mere nonsense: "She tried a bit inventing words but she soon gave that up. The English language was her medium and with the English language the task was to be achieved, the problem solved. The use of fabricated words offended her, it was an escape into imitative emotionalism."[16] Likewise nowhere does Gadamer concede that the modernist poem is meaningless. Poetry is made of the language that we speak; a completely unintelligible poem would not be made of words, and so would not be a poem. (Celan is reported to have said: "A language that no one *speaks* is anti-poetic.")[17] But Gadamer's concern here is with a form that preserves the materiality of language *as part of the whole*, not an excess to be eliminated, as in propositional form, but rather that which allows the poem to stand on its own as a work of art. As Gadamer says in "Dichten und Deuten" (1961) (translated, perhaps a bit too loosely, as "Composition and Interpretation"), "Compared with all other art forms, the poetic work possesses as language [*als sprachliches*] a specific, open indeterminacy [*eine spezifische, offene Unbestimmtheit*]. The unity of form [*Gestaltenheit*] that is so characteristic of the work of art, as it is of every other kind, is sensuously present, and to that extent cannot be reduced to a mere intention of meaning" (GW.8:21/RB.70: translation slightly altered). This "open indeterminacy" is, so to speak, the hermeneutical field of play—"Every work leaves the person who responds to it a certain leeway [*einen Spielraum*], a space to be filled in by himself" (GW.8:117/RB.26). But, as we have seen, play is not the same as exegesis: it is how one experiences the formal intelligibility of the poem.

Still, this leaves open the question of how to read Celan's poetry. Gadamer's position is that there is no one way to read these poems. In any event, it is clearly the case that his own readings are speculative, improvisational, questioning, and characterized chiefly by the rejection of his own first thoughts and his refusal to have the final word—all of this circumscribed by his assertion that "I believe that I have more or less understood these poems"—which, he adds, "I find less likely than some of his later poems to sink into the indecipherable" (GW.9:428/GC.128). Here is the opening poem of *Atemkristall*:

DU DARFST mich getrost
mit Schnee bewirten:
sooft ich Schulter zu Schulter

mit dem Maulbeerbaum schritt
    durch den Sommer,
schrie sein jüngstes
Blatt. (GW.1:11)

YOU MAY confidently
regale me with snow:
as often as I strode through the
    summer
shoulder to shoulder with the
    mulberry tree,
its youngest leaf
shrieked. (B.55)

Gadamer begins by marking the fundamental contrast between winter and summer, snow and the flourishing mulberry tree—"Unlike other shrubbery, the mulberry tree produces fresh leaves not only in the spring, but throughout the entire summer" (GW.9:386/GC.71). But the contrast is puzzling, because Celan reverses the typical valences of winter and summer: here the one is welcoming, whereas the other seems dissonant. Gadamer addresses this puzzle by asking how far the poem's wordplay extends—is there a pun on *Maul*, "mouth," as if *Maulbeerbaum* were an echo of *Maul des Wortes*, "loudmouth"? In fact Gadamer rejects this reading as extravagant and unnecessary: the mulberry tree must be taken for what it is. Even so, the serenity of winter still seems preferable to the busyness of summer with its claims upon our senses, our labor, our responsibility—"shoulder to shoulder" suggests solidarity, but solidarity is a response to the need for concerted action (GW.9:387/GW.73). And then there is the screaming of the mulberry tree's "youngest leaf," a figure Gadamer doesn't hesitate to identify with the claims of the newborn. So the offer of snow seems like an offer of relief—"the stillness is welcome," Gadamer says (GW.9:387/GC.73). In the end, the poem is (for Gadamer) about the "readiness for death" (GW.9:387/GC.73).

This is fair enough. To my ear the scream of the mulberry's leaf has more horror in it than Gadamer's reading allows. (Celan: "Have we not wanted to hear screams, our own screams louder than ever, more piercing?")[18] Gadamer said that he undertook his commentaries on "Atemkristall" because of his disappointment with the critical and scholarly work on Celan that was available to him in 1973. It seemed to him that the possibility of meaning in these poems had been written off prematurely (GW.9:427–28/GC.127–28). And so his commentaries aim at elucidation, occasionally at the expense of the strangeness of Celan's verse. In any case, Gadamer's position is that, when it comes to poetry—particularly Celan's—no one can do your reading for you. The rejection of any scholarly apparatus, critical method, or theoretical superstructure as a way of coping with these poems—the effort to address the poems at the level of individual experience—is an argument for a hermeneutics of proximity in which the reader of the poem is as irreplaceable as the poem itself—and, who knows?, perhaps this is the moral of the indeterminacy of the "I" and "You" in Celan's poetry. "There is," Gadamer says in his epilogue to the revised edition of *Wer bist Du?* "no hermeneutic method." "Hermeneutics," he says, "means not so much a procedure as the attitude of the person who wants to ınderstand someone else, or who wants to understand a linguistic expression as a reader or listener. But this always means: understanding *this* person, *this* text" (GW.9:447/GC.161). There is no understanding at a distance.

Yet, as Gadamer says, Celan's poems are, like *poésie pure*, a "limit-case" (*Extremfall*) for understanding (GW.8:236/RB.136). Indeed, they constitute what Blanchot would call a "limit-experience" in the sense that they call into question the one who tries to make sense of them.[19] The poet Charles Bernstein has said that in Celan's poems "things are never what they appear to be. The poems avert representation: *they are anti-representational*. Anti-representational poetry is marked by its struggle with representation, its questioning of reality, its refusal to be satisfied with description, its nausea in the face of the given, and its evisceration of the settled order of things."[20] This is particularly so in those poems in which the given is dismembered and recombined into unrecognizable forms:

WEISSGRAU aus-
geschachteten steilen
Gefühls.
Landeinwärts, hierher-
verwehter Strandhafer bläst
Sandmuster über
den Rauch von Brunnengesängen.

Ein Ohr, abgetrennt, lauscht.

Ein Aug, in Streifen geschnitten,
wird all dem gerecht. (GW.2:19)

WHITEGRAY of
shafted, steep
feeling.
Landinwards, hither
drifted sea-oats blow
sand patterns over
the smoke of wellchants.

An ear, severed, listens.

An eye, cut in strips,
does justice to all this. (B.71)

"The vulgar images [*Kraßheit der Bilder*] of the cut-off ear and the eye cut into strips," Gadamer says, "give this poem its unique character. One must and should feel a kind of revulsion at these vulgarities, which challenge the reader to subdue them by understanding" (GW.9:406/GC.97). So the "struggle with representation" is passed along to the reader. What impresses Gadamer is that eye and ear are still alive, even attentive, to what little remains of a living world, bearing witness perhaps to something increasingly grotesque and unpresentable.

ABENDS, in
Hamburg, an
unendlicher Schuhriemen—an
ihm
kauen die Geister—
bindet zwei blutige Zehen
    zusammen
zum Wegschwur.(GW.2:68)

EVENING, in
Hamburg, an
endless shoestring—at
which
the ghosts gnaw—
binds two bloody toes together

For the road's oath. (B.169)

One is reminded of the distinction between the body and flesh: the body is Greek and is a figure of mastery, strength, and achievement, whereas flesh is Jewish and is a figure of weakness, disfigurement, exposure, and suffering. Achilles is the perfection of the Greek body, except for his heel, which is made of flesh. Celan's poetry is a poetry of flesh, even on occasion ludicrously so:

IN DER EWIGEN TEUFE: die Ziegel-
münder
rasen.

Du brennst ein Gebet ab
vor jedem.

IN THE ETERNAL DEPTH: the brick-
mouths
rave.

You burn off a prayer
before each.

Buchstabentreu, auf dem Notsteg,	Letterfaithful, on the emergency trail,
stehen Hinauf und Hinunter,	stand Up and Down,
Den Mischkrug voll blasigen	the mixing bowl full of bubbly
Hirns. (GW.3:118)	brain. (T.43)

The Greek body is the centerpiece of classical aesthetics, the incarnation of the beautiful; the flesh in Celan's poetry articulates an aesthetics of the sublime—as does Greek tragedy, as when the heroic body of Agamemnon crosses Clytemnestra's threshold for the last time. The action of tragedy is a metamorphosis of body into flesh: think of the dismemberment of Pentheus in the *Bacchae*.

Gadamer's Sublime. The sublime is not really a concept in Gadamer's aesthetics, but he does think that the task of art theory is to reconceptualize the beautiful so as to develop an aesthetics for artworks that are no longer beautiful in any traditional sense. In "Anschauung und Anschaulichkeit" ("Intuition and Vividness"), Gadamer says that "art theory must address art both before it understands itself as 'art' and equally after it ceases to understand itself as such. What is it that allows pictures, statues, buildings, songs, texts, or dances to appear beautiful, and, if 'no longer beautiful,' as art nonetheless? 'Beauty' does not mean the fulfillment of a specific ideal of the beautiful, whether classical or baroque. Rather, beauty defines art as art: namely, as something that stands out from everything that is purposively established and utilized. Indeed, beauty is nothing but an invitation to intuition. And that is what we call a 'work'" (GW.8:193/RB.161). That which makes a work "stand out" as such is its "vividness"—a feature that belongs not only to representational art but equally to abstract forms and to works of language: "The vividness that we praise in a narrative text . . . is not that of an image that could be reproduced in words. It is much closer to the restless flux of images that accompanies our understanding of the text, but that does not finally become a stable intuition, as some kind of result. It is this capacity of the 'art' of language to arouse intuitions in the imagination that establishes the linguistic work of art in its own right and makes of it a 'work'—like a kind of self-giving intuition—so that such discourse is capable of canceling or forgetting any reference to reality that discourse normally has" (GW.8:194/RB.163). So the work is no longer entirely transparent, even if it is a work of narrative, because it is also and equally a work whose "art" of language is no longer a function in behalf of something else—for example, "reference to reality." The vividness of the work allows, as in the case of poetry, a free play of imagination "that points beyond the realm of the concept, and hence beyond the realm of the understanding" (GW.8:197/RB.166) — "beyond anything that we are given in experience" (GW.8:198/RB.166). To which Gadamer adds: "Kant's phrase, 'the beautiful representation of a thing' [*Critique of Judgment*, §48] is . . . too narrow to express this" (GW.8:198/RB.166). What is necessary is to "incorporate the aesthetic of the sublime [*der Ästhetik des Erhabenen*] into the theory of art, in a way Kant did not fully accomplish himself" (GW.8:199/RB.167). Like the sublime of nature, the modernist artwork "is the occasion for the elevation of the mind to its supersensible vocation [*übersinnlichen Bestimmung*]" (GW.8:199/RB.168).

Gadamer's sublime can be elucidated by comparison (or, more exactly, contrast) with what the theologian, Jean-Luc Marion, has called "the saturated phenomenon," where (as in Kant's third critique) there is such an excess of intuition over any concept that no language can ever comprehend it and make it intelligible:

> Kant formulates this excess with a rare term: the aesthetic idea remains an "inexposable [*inexponible*] representation of the imagination." We can understand this in the following way: because it gives "much," the aesthetic idea gives more than any concept can expose; to "expose" here amounts to arranging (ordering) the intuitive given according to rules; the impossibility of this conceptual arrangement issues from the fact that the intuitive over-abundance is no longer exposed within rules, whatever they may be, but overwhelms them; intuition is no longer exposed within the concept, but saturates it and renders it overexposed — invisible, not by lack of light, but by excess of light.[21]

A saturated phenomenon is anarchic: it is one that can never be constituted as an object of consciousness; it is in excess of intentionality. Marion offers a number of examples of this: (1) a historical event, which can never be comprehended all at once or once and for all but is open to continuous interpretation; (2) the painting (in Marion's parlance, the "idol") that can never be exhausted by my looking at it; (3) our own bodies, or more exactly, our flesh, "which is so rich and so overwhelming that we need new words — literature and poetry — to make sense of it"; (4) the face of the other (the "icon"), which, as in Levinas's ethical theory, is not just outside of but depletes my powers of cognition; (5) and, finally, God, whom, as we shall see in chapter 6, below, treating Lyotard, reveals himself to us across a distance that we can never traverse.[22] In "L'idole ou l'éclat du tableau" ("The Idol or the Radiance of the Painting"), Marion develops in detail the example of the painting that is paradoxically invisible because of its inexhaustible visibility: "The painting cannot be seen in a single instance; it must be reseen in order to appear, because it appears according to the phenomenality of the saturated phenomenon. The museum, decried a little thoughtlessly as a tomb of art's dead, offers perhaps also a social structure appropriate to this necessary return to the image, this free looking back on vision that the painting silently demands."[23]

What is interesting, however, is that Marion seems to be more comfortable with paintings that have a good deal to look at — lines, colors, arrangements, but most of all objects. One could argue that the problem of modernism is not that it saturates intuition, but that it starves it, which is what seems to happen in much of modernist art, particularly with recent monochromatic and minimalist works — Ad Reinhardt's "Black Paintings," Donald Judd's "Specific Objects," Fluxus "events," and Conceptual Art come readily to mind.[24] The problem here is that, as Marion himself admits, there is not enough to see.[25] However, Paul Celan's poems, particularly the austere later works, are paradoxical in this respect, because they are brief fragments whose neologisms nevertheless overarticulate language in ways that defeat the syntactical arrangements that try to contain them. Here is a poem from *Fadensonnen* (1968):

DIE HERZSCHRIFTGEKRÜMELTE	THE HEARTSCRIPTCRUMBLED
Sichtinsel	vision-isle
mittnachts, bei kleinem	at midnight, in feeble
Zündschlüsselschimmer.	ignition key glimmer.
Es sind zuviel	There are too many
zielwütige Kräfte	goalcrazed powers
auch in dieser	even in this
scheinbar durchsternen	seemingly starstudded
Hochluft.	highair.
Die ersehnte Freimeile	The longed for freemile
prallt auf uns auf.(GW.2:174)	crashes into us. (T.159)[26]

Of course, it isn't clear whether for Marion a poem of any sort could count as a "saturated phenomenon," but the complexity of Celan's poetic diction overwhelms any effort to reduce his poem to an intentional object. Marion suggests repeated visits to a museum piece because it "cannot be seen in a single instance." This would be consistent with Gadamer's idea that a poem, like any work of art, should be approached as an event rather than as an object, where the event is conceptualized on the model of the festival, whose essence is "always to be something different," however familiar it becomes to us over time. Just as the poem requires multiple translations, so the poem is always new in one's (anyone's) repeated readings of it. So, far from being a hermetic work, it is a distinctive example of what, in modernist poetics, is called an "open poem"—a poem that, in defiance of Hegel's famous thesis, opens onto the future instead of receding into the closure of the past.

Let me close by citing a slightly more radical and subversive form of this notion of a poem made new by each new reading of it. This from an essay by Lyn Hejinian, "The Rejection of Closure":

> For the sake of clarity, I will offer a tentative characterization of the terms *open* and *closed*. We can say that the "closed text" is one in which all the elements of the work are directed toward a single reading of it. Each element confirms that reading and delivers the text from any lurking ambiguity. In the "open text," meanwhile, all the elements of the work are maximally excited; here it is because ideas and things exceed (without deserting) the argument that they have taken into the work. . . .
>
> The "open text," by definition, is open to the world and particularly to the reader. It invites participation, rejects the authority of the writer over the reader and thus, by analogy, the authority implicit in other (social, economic, cultural) hierarchies. It speaks for writing that is generative rather than directive. The writer relinquishes total control and challenges authority as a principle and control as a motive. The "open text" often emphasizes or foregrounds process, either the process of the original composition or of subsequent composition by readers, and thus resists the cultural tendencies that seek to identify and fix material and turn it into a product; that is, it resists reduction and commodification.[27]

The "closed text" is, whatever else it is, transparent: its intelligibility is self-evident. The "open text" by contrast is underdetermined but paradoxically is therefore capable of generating an endless surplus of meanings. I think this applies very well to Celan's poetry, and to the modernist work in general—and perhaps, as Gadamer would argue, to the artwork as such, whether ancient or modern. The work of art, as Gadamer says, not only invites but requires "participation." But

Lyn Hejinian pushes this idea from Gadamer's waters into Adorno's: "All artworks," says Adorno, "even the affirmative, are a priori polemical. The idea of a conservative artwork is inherently absurd. By emphatically separating themselves from the empirical world, their other, they bear witness that that world itself should be other than it is; they are the unconscious schemata of that world's transformation" (AT.264/AeT.177). Aesthetic anarchism, if I read Hejinian correctly, is implicated in a wider anarchism that aims at the undoing of what Adorno calls the "administered" world: "The more total society becomes, the more completely it contracts to a unanimous system, and all the more do artworks in which this experience is sedimented become the other of this society" (AT.53/AeT.31).

Gadamer might not disagree with this. But his aesthetic theory, as I think I have shown, has an ethical rather than political resonance. One could call it an "aesthetics of responsibility," in which the work calls upon me to change; but, as Gadamer makes clear, this is not merely a subjective change but also a change in the way one inhabits one's world. And in this event there are many paths to follow.

PART II

Forms of Paganism

Foucault's Modernism: Language, Poetry, and the Experience of Freedom

More than simply an event that affected our emotions that gave rise to the fear of nothingness, the death of God profoundly influenced our language; at the source of language it placed a silence that no work, unless it be pure chatter, can mask. Language thus assumes a sovereign position; it comes to us from elsewhere, from a place of which no one can speak, but it can be transformed into a work only if, in ascending to its proper discourse, it directs its speech toward this absence. In this sense, every work is an attempt to exhaust language; eschatology has become of late a structure of literary experience, and literary experience, by right of birth, is now of paramount importance.
— **Michel Foucault, "Le 'non' du père"**

Modernism Once More. Fredric Jameson has usefully proposed that we think of modernism not as a period concept but, more loosely, as a "narrative category" in which topics like nineteenth-century realism, self-reflexive language, and the impersonality of the artist get articulated and rearticulated in multifarious ways.[1] It is certainly the case that modernism is often defined more clearly by examples than by theories—serial music, cubism, nonlinear or fragmentary texts like Stein's *Tender Buttons* (or Wittgenstein's *Tractatus*), as well as avant-garde groups like the Surrealists whose aim was often less to produce works of art than to develop new forms of experience and new dimensions of human subjectivity.[2] In English the term "high modernism" is reserved for overshadowing monuments like Joyce's

Ulysses and Pound's *Cantos*. I'm not sure there is a corresponding term among the French, who are apt to take their guidance less from Proust's *Grand Œuvre* than from the theater visionary Antonin Artaud, who thought that the task of the artist is not to produce masterpieces but to set in motion processes that dislocate rational, integrated, or otherwise settled forms of consciousness.[3] On a certain view modernism is made of events, not of works. A *museum* of modern art might arguably count as a defeat of modernism.[4]

In what follows I would like to examine some of the ways in which Michel Foucault's early writings provide resources for addressing the question of modernism. Of course, this is as much as to ask whether there is a concept of modernism that has a substantive place in Foucault's thinking. "Modernism," after all, is not really a term in his vocabulary, and when he does address the topic explicitly (as in one of his appreciations of Pierre Boulez), he refers only very generally to "the work of the formal," where the idea is to approach music, past or present, as Boulez does: "make it so that nothing remains fixed"—in other words, "make it new" (Ezra Pound's motto, the watchword of modernists both early and late) (DE.4:221/AME.232). However, Foucault's early texts on Hölderlin, Raymond Roussel, Georges Bataille, and Maurice Blanchot address in interesting ways one of the fundamental problems of modernist poetics, namely the relationship between literary or poetic language and the limits of experience, or more exactly between the *materiality* of language (its resistance to signification) and the transformations of subjectivity that this materiality puts into play (or perhaps exhibits) in the form of noncognitive experiences—experiences that Foucault characterizes variously in terms of death, absence, exteriority, and (interestingly) freedom. What Foucault means by these or any of his terms of art is never self-evident; his rule of language is to "make it so that nothing remains fixed" ("I am an experimenter," he said, "and in this sense I write in order to change myself and in order not to think the same thing as before") (DE.4:42/P.240). Roughly his idea is that the experience of language is a very different thing from the use of it. Experience is neither empirical nor intentional; it is an exposure of the subject to what it cannot grasp and in the face of which it cannot keep itself intact.[5] This notion (or region) of experience appears to be where Foucault's interest in literature begins, namely with the mythological identity of poetry and madness, which Foucault interprets as a certain experience of the alterity of language and in turn as a kind of writing that is no longer productive of works in the Aristotelian sense of logically integrated and translucent structures (that is, beautiful objects of art). Madness is, in Foucault's famous phrase, the "absence of the work."[6] As we shall see, this absence is not nugatory; it defines a theory of the *incompletion* or fragmentariness of the work of art that Blanchot summarizes with the word *désœuvrement* (worklessness).[7] It also leads to an interesting question of what the relationship might be between Fôucault's early inquiries into the modernist themes of impersonality and fragmentation, and his later research into what he calls an "ethics of the self," where the idea is to constitute oneself, in a strong modernist sense, as a "work of art." By a "strong modernist sense" I mean that for Foucault "work" is an interminable project (more verb than noun, as in "daily work"). It is not something to be finished but something to be experienced in the way that Foucault regards each of his books as an experience rather than as a constituent of an *œuvre*: "however erudite my books may be, I've always conceived of them as direct experiences aimed at pulling myself free of myself, at preventing me from being the same" (DE.1:43/P.241–42).

Two Genealogies. Within a French context we might find some useful orientation by distinguishing between two early forms of modernism—Baudelaire's and Mallarmé's, where the one has to do with a certain antithetical but nevertheless intimate or proximate way of inhabiting the modern urbanized, rationalized world, while the other is defined by a certain antithetical relationship with language, where language is no longer a system for framing representations but has its own autonomy—its own modality of being that is irreducible to the functions that logic, linguistics, or philosophy of language attribute to it.

It was Baudelaire who gave the term "modernism" (or *modernité*) its first formal articulation. Here modernism concerns what one might call the relocation of the artist from his classical (or neoclassical) position as a mediator of universals to that of the close observer of the local and ephemeral—of what is *modern* in the sense of recent, short-lived, and superficial as against what is natural, essential, permanent, and true. "Modernity," says Baudelaire in "Le Peintre de la vie moderne" (1863), "is the transient, the fleeting, the contingent; it is one half of art, the other being the eternal and immovable."[8] Baudelaire's modernist occupies the point of view of the street, that is, the point of view of the *flâneur*, or idler, who registers, with a detective's eye, the random and seemingly trivial details of his environment. Here the romantic theory of genius is turned on its head: whereas the genius is a transcendental agent of worldmaking, the modernist is a figure of nonidentity, a sensibility on whom nothing of the passing show is lost but who is himself transient, anonymous, and ironic, someone who makes himself blend imperceptibly into the scene that he traverses (Œ.2:686–87/SWA.393–94). Baudelaire's model of the modernist is Constantin Guys (1805–92), whose chief forms of composition are the illustration and the sketch, and whose mode of existence is that of the "man of the crowd" (Œ.2:687/ SWA.395). M.C.G., as Baudelaire refers to him, aspires to invisibility. Baudelaire explains that "when [Guys] heard that I was proposing to make an assessment of his mind and talent, he begged me . . . to suppress his name, and to discuss his works only as though they were the works of some anonymous person" (Œ.2:688/SWA.395). Likewise M.C.G. "does not like to be called an artist" (Œ.2:689/ SWA.397). An artist is a stock figure of the studio, the tavern, or the bedroom, any of which he might seldom leave, whereas Guys is driven by a child-like curiosity to wander the streets and arcades and to remember in detail whatever catches his eye—dandies, fashionable women, soldiers, prostitutes, carriages, horses, beggars, trifles in the shopwindow. Like the dandy, the modernist possesses "a subtle understanding of all the moral mechanisms of the world," but where the dandy is detached and *blasé*, the modernist "is dominated . . . by an insatiable passion, that of seeing and feeling" (Œ.2:691/ SWA.399). His "excessive love of visible, tangible things, in their most plastic form, inspires him with a certain dislike of those things that go to make up the intangible kingdom of the metaphysician" (Œ.2:691/SWA.399). The temporality of modernism, its *donnée*, is the here and now, and of course this is never the same.[9]

There are two points here. First, in Baudelaire's modernism the unfinished and even disposable artwork replaces the museum piece (the oil painting, for example), even though the museum and the artbook will later find places for such things as caricatures, drawings, and studies. The idea is that the modernist artwork shares in the impermanence of what attracts it. Second, Baudelaire characterizes modernism not just formally in terms of a certain kind of work but ethically and, indeed, aesthetically in terms of a certain kind of displaced subjectivity—a kind of pagan subject: impersonal and refractory, a subject turned inside out the better to experience the sheer physicality of things. The Baudelairean subject exists outside itself in a condition of fascination:

The crowd is his domain, just as the air is the bird's, and water that of the fish. His passion and his profession is to merge with the crowd. For the perfect *flâneur*, for the passionate observer it becomes an immense source of enjoyment to establish his dwelling in the throng, in the ebb and flow, the bustle, the fleeting and the infinite. To be away from home and yet to feel at home anywhere; to see the world, to be at the very centre of the world, and yet to be unseen of the world, such are some of the minor pleasures of those independent, intense, and impartial spirits, who do not lend themselves easily to linguistic definitions. The observer is a prince enjoying his incognito wherever he goes. . . . It is an ego athirst for the non-ego, and reflecting it at every moment in energies more vivid than life itself, always constant and fleeting. (Œ.2:691–92/SWA.399–400)

In contrast to the carnivorous spirit that one associates with the philosophical subject (Hegel's, for example), the modernist subject allows itself to be absorbed by its world, even at the cost of its own continuity, integrity, or substantive identity. In "Paris of the Second Empire in Baudelaire," Walter Benjamin (citing Baudelaire in order to describe him) writes: "Empathy is the nature of the intoxicant to which the *flâneur* abandons himself in the crowd. 'The poet enjoys the incomparable privilege of being himself and someone else as he sees fit. Like a roving soul in search of a body, he enters another person whenever he wishes. For him alone, all is open; if certain places seem closed to him, it is because in his view they are not worth inspecting.'"[10] As Benjamin says, Baudelaire was, strictly speaking, never himself; he was a repertoire of Parisian types: "*Flâneur*, apache, dandy and ragpicker were so many roles to him. . . . Behind the masks which he used up, the poet in Baudelaire preserved his incognito. He was as circumspect in his work as he was capable of seeming provocative in his personal associations. The incognito was the law of his poetry. His prosody is comparable to the map of a big city in which it is possible to move about inconspicuously, shielded by blocks of houses, gateways, courtyards" (GS.600/SWB.4:60–61).

The genealogy of the Baudelairean modernist can be traced back to Keats's concept of the poet's "negative capability" ("the poet has no character"; he creates by transforming himself into whatever is not himself), and to the romantic ironists of Jena (Friedrich Schlegel in particular), whom Kierkegaard accused of "transcendental buffoonery." The ironist, says Kierkegaard, has no *an sich*; he merely "lives poetically," reinventing himself as he goes (if "himself" is the word).[11] More important, this genealogy can be traced forward to the later Foucault, whose project is not the Kierkegaardian ethic of self-transparency but the Baudelairean aesthetic of self-creation. Citing Baudelaire in "What is Enlightenment?" (1984), Foucault writes: "Modern man, for Baudelaire, is not the man who goes off to discover himself, his secrets and his hidden truth; he is the man who tries to invent himself. This modernity does not 'liberate man in his own being'; it compels him to face the task of producing himself [*la tâche de s'élaborer lui-même*]" (DE.4:571/EST.312). But this production is not a form of objectification. Foucault retains from Baudelaire the ironic themes of alterity and anonymity: as Foucault says in a late interview, the subject of self-creation is "not a substance. It is a form, and this form is not primarily or always identical to itself" (DE.4:718/EST.290). Rimbaud's great line, "Je est une autre," is also Foucault's.[12]

The displacement of the subject is also a key to Mallarmé's poetics, but his terms are different. At the level of experience, Mallarmé describes this event very dramatically in the language of negative theology—once as a struggle with God whose defeat or disappearance the poet experiences as a kind of ecstasy, but also (what perhaps amounts to the same thing) as a mystical encounter with *le Néant*, a quasi-Hegelian concept of absolute purity that enraptures the poet and, paradoxically, annihilates him as an experiencing subject: "My thought has thought itself through and reached a pure idea," Mallarmé writes in a famous letter. "What the rest of me has suffered during that long agony is indescribable. But, fortunately, I am quite dead now."[13] One might think of this as a phenomenological death (as against empirical, et cetera) because for Mallarmé poetry begins at the limit of phenomenological experience. Poetry as a work of lyric expression that gives intentional form to experience now gives way to a conception of poetry as the work of language, where the words of language are no longer to be construed as signs but have become, mysteriously, agents of their own activity. This is the upshot of a passage from Mallarmé's "Crise du vers" (1896): "L'œuvre pure implique la disparition éloqutoire du poëte, qui cède l'initiative aux mots, par le heurt de leur inégalité mobilisés; ils s'allument de reflets réciproques comme une virtuelle traînée de feux sur des pierreries, replaçant la respiration perceptible en l'ancien souffle lyrique ou la direction personnelle enthousiaste de la phrase" ("The pure work implies the elocutionary disappearance of the poet, who yields his initiative to words, which are mobilized by the shock of their inequality; they light up with reciprocal reflections like a virtual stream of fireworks over precious stones, replacing the perceptible respiration of the old lyric breath, or the enthusiastic personal control of the sentence.").[14] How is it possible for language to become its own agent? Mallarmé does not provide a systematic answer to this question, but he does come to think of the poem as a material construction of words, a work of writing (*écriture*) in which the letters of the alphabet form the crucial matrix, since they are capable of endless combinations and so (like the Kabbalist's scriptures) potentially contain all of creation—hence Mallarmé's idea that the world was meant to exist in a splendid book (ŒM.378). In his last years Mallarmé tried to describe the material properties of this *Grand Œuvre*, in which not only the written words but the white space of the page and the fold in the middle of the book would be essential to the aesthetic of the whole. (The book of course could not be written, but Mallarmé gave us a fragment of it in *Un coup de dés*.)[15]

Literature as Such. It is this Mallarméan aesthetic that Foucault invokes near the end of *Les mots et les choses* (1966) when he speaks of the emergence of "literature as such," which is a complex event in the history of language. (Foucault confidently locates it at the end of the eighteenth or early in the nineteenth century, but it is also an event whose terminus has never been fixed.) Whereas for the Renaissance language was a rich, cornucopian environment of words and things, modernity thematizes language as an object of knowledge for logic, linguistics, philology, and eventually for various philosophies of language (including, finally, structuralism). The project of modernity is to make language (like everything else) conceptually transparent and convertible to use. Foucault's idea is that "literature as such" (one could just as well call it "literary modernism") is something like the rebellion of language against this attempt to reduce it: "Literature is the contestation of philology . . . : it leads language back from grammar to the naked power of speech, and there it encounters the untamed, imperious being of words." We'll see in a moment what "the untamed, imperious being of words" entails. At the least it means that literature is refractory to models, categories, criteria, and rules of every sort. It is no longer a genre distinction but is more event than work:

> [Literature] breaks with the whole definition of *genres* as forms adapted to an order of representations, and becomes merely a

manifestation of a language which has no other law than that of affirming—in opposition to all other forms of discourse—its own precipitous existence; and so there is nothing for it to do but to curve back in a perpetual return upon itself, as if its discourse could have no other content than the expression of its own form; it addresses itself to itself as a writing subjectivity, or it seeks to re-apprehend the essence of all literature in the movement that brought it into being; and thus all its threads converge upon the finest of points—singular, instantaneous, and yet absolutely universal—upon the simple act of writing. At the moment when language, as spoken and scattered words, becomes an object of knowledge, we see it reappearing in a strictly opposite modality: a silent, cautious disposition of the word upon the whiteness of a piece of paper, where it can possess neither sound nor interlocutor, where it has nothing to say but itself, nothing to do but shine in the brightness of its being. (MeC.313/OT.300)

This is an uncompromising description of the autonomy (or, more exactly, heteronomy) of literature, but it needs careful reading. Sometimes this passage is brought under the sign of a formalist or structuralist conception of literature as a self-operating system of rules and relations capable of generating from within itself an infinity of possible utterances. Certainly this construction captures something, particularly in view of the essential formalism of European poetics (and linguistics) after Mallarmé and Saussure: the Russian formalists, the Prague structuralists, Emile Benveniste, and so on down through the Tel Quel group. But this is not exactly Foucault's idea. In a number of contexts (and this is a thesis that he never modifies) he says that in modernity literature "ceased to belong to the order of discourse and became the manifestation of language in its thickness [*épaisseur*]." Literature is no longer an expression of the subject, but neither is it a function of "the pure formalism of language" (DE.1:502/EW.2:265). Literature just *is* the "thickness" of language: it is the disclosure of "the being of language," a phrase that Foucault summons repeatedly, but almost always as a way of marking a conceptual limit: the "being of language" is precisely what cannot be objectified or thematized. It can only be *experienced* in its materiality, alterity, or exteriority—terms that Foucault often gathers together under the figure of *écriture*, as when language "addresses itself to itself as a writing subjectivity," where a *writing* subjectivity is different from one composed of intentions.

The "being of language" is not an easy idea. Early in *Les mots et les choses* the term is introduced by way of an astonishing assertion that "language . . . exists in its raw and primitive being [*être brut et primitif*], in the simple, material form of writing, a stigma upon things, a mark imprinted across the world which is part of its most ineffaceable forms" (MeC.57/OT.42). Raw language? The idea seems like a joke at structuralism's expense, but Foucault means what he says. In modernity, literature "separated itself from all other language with a deep scission . . . by forming a sort of 'counter-discourse,' and by finding its way back from the representative and signifying function of language to this raw being that had been forgotten since the sixteenth century" (MeC.59/OT.44). "Raw being" is just what is uncontainable within any system, but which at the same time the system cannot exclude.[16] In his essay on Blanchot, "La pensée du dehors" (1966), Foucault says that "the event of literature" is "no longer discourse and the communication of meaning, but a spreading forth of language in its raw state, an unfolding of pure exteriority" (DE.1:519/AME.148).

Pure exteriority means: an outside not correlated with an inside, not the object of a subject, but instead an outside that cannot be objectified, fixed, or determined and so held in place or at bay. Imagine the boundary between outside and inside as porous or floating—a boundary defined by invisible infiltration and exodus rather than by lines and checkpoints. Kantian theory (in most of its versions) pictures art and literature as occupants of a differentiated ream of the aesthetic—a region sealed off from the world of cognition and action, if not from the supervision of philosophy. Adorno's aesthetic theory pictures the work of art as a formal construction irreducible to the materials of which it is made and therefore external to the realm of commodities in which it may nevertheless be made to circulate, but of which it remains essentially critical.[17] Foucault's thinking is closer to the (late) modernist poetics of the North American "language poets" for whom the materiality of language—which includes the social and historical as well as the nonsemantic dimensions of language—is a region to be explored through often extravagant and theatrical forms of experimental writing, but also, at the limit of poetic experience, in *sound poetry*, in which vocal and buccal noises are no longer in the service of grammatical forms.[18] As it happens, much of modernism is made of noise.[19] Think of noise as an instance of exteriority.

Noise. Writing is a "raw and naked act" (DE.1:556/AME.173). Its rawness means (roughly) that it takes place outside the subject, outside the order of things, outside the order of discourse, but perhaps in the way the uncooked is "outside" the definition (but not the experience) of the human. Exteriority is not another world, not a totally differentiated state against which sameness or identity could be measured. On the contrary, it is a dimension of anarchic experience (experience on the hither side of principle and rule) to which the subject and, indeed, the order of discourse or of things are constantly exposed. The difficulty of the outside is keeping it there.

The basic argument of *L'ordre du discours* is not difficult to follow, but perhaps it is not always followed out to the end. The order in question refers of course to various complex forms of cultural organization—taboos, analytic systems of exclusion (as between reason and madness, truth and falsity), disciplines of learning motivated by a "will to truth," fellowships of discourse that determine who has the right to speak about what, and assorted myths (the founding subject, the originating experience, the authority of universals): in short, a vast system of procedures and constraints whose task is to control discourse, "to avert its powers and its dangers, to cope with chance events, to evade its ponderous, awesome materiality" (OD.11/AK.216). Naturally the question is: What does this last line mean? What is discourse, exactly, and in what does its "ponderous, awesome materiality" consist? The question is complex because, on the one hand, discourse is not another word for language or speech. By the time of *L'Archéologie du savoir* (1969) the concept of language has been folded into that of discourse, so there is no more talk of "the raw being of language." Discourse is made of institutions, rules, practices, objects, events (as well as gaps and voids), but it is nothing in itself: "The existence of systems of rarefaction does not imply that, over and beyond them, lie great vistas of limitless discourse, continuous and silent, repressed and driven back by them, making it our task to abolish them and at last restore it to speech. Whether talking in terms of speaking or thinking, we must not imagine some unsaid thing, or an unthought, floating about the world, interlacing with all its forms and events" (OD.54/AK.229). On the other hand, however, discourse is still *something*—not, to be sure, an entity, ideal or otherwise: not, for example, a Heideggerian *Sage*, but *something* that remains (like language) external to the social forces that try regulate it:

> What civilization, in appearance, has shown more respect towards discourse than our own? Where has it been more and

better honoured? Where have men depended more radically, apparently, upon its constraints and its universal character? But, it seems to me, a certain fear hides behind this apparent veneration of discourse, this apparent logophilia. It is as though these taboos, these barriers, thresholds and limits were deliberately disposed in order, at least partly, to master and control the great proliferation of discourse, in such a way as to relieve its richness of its most dangerous elements; to organize its disorder so as to skate round its most uncontrollable aspects. It is as though people had wanted to efface all trace of its irruption into the activity of our thought and language. There is undoubtedly in our society, and I would not be surprised to see it in others, though taking different forms and modes, a profound logophobia, a sort of dumb fear of these events, of this mass of spoken things, of everything that could possibly be violent, discontinuous, querulous, disordered even and perilous in it, of the incessant, disorderly buzzing of discourse. (OD.51–53/AK.228–29; transl. amended)

Discourse is not transcendent, that is, it is not outside the order of things, but neither is it altogether containable within it. Discourse is never fully digestible. Imagine *logophobia* (initially) as a fear of the sheer *excess* of discourse, its hypertrophic existence not in some far-off wilderness but as a kind of anarchy that threatens from within every effort of speaking or the will to truth. As if discourse had about it a kind of rawness, thickness, or alterity after all. Discourse does not exist outside of the systems that try to reduce it, but it must be thinned out or "rarefied" in order for these systems to be productive. Discourse is made possible by being parsimonious (*"everything* is never said" [AS.141/AK.118]); but evidently not everything about it can be eliminated—for example, what to make of that "incessant, disorderly buzzing"?

One of Foucault's favorite stories is Kafka's "The Burrow," in which an unidentified creature constructs an immense underground labyrinth (a *Burgplatz*) to protect itself against its enemies, but one day its domain is invaded (or pervaded) by an indeterminate, irregular, "almost inaudible" noise, a sort of whistling or murmuring that comes from nowhere, is uniformly everywhere, and cannot be got rid of. In "Le langage à infini" (1963), Foucault associates this noise with death as a kind of omnipresent absence that concentrates our attention—*and* enlists our response (and note, for the record, what kind of response): It is a "disquieting sound that announces from the depths of language the source against which we seek refuge and toward which we address ourselves. Like Kafka's beast, language now listens from the bottom of its burrow to this inevitable and growing noise. To defend itself it must follow its movements, become its loyal enemy, and allow nothing to stand between them except the contradictory thinness of a transparent and unbreakable partition. We must ceaselessly speak, for as long and as loudly as this indefinite and deafening noise—long and more loudly so that in mixing our voices with it we might succeed—if not in silencing and mastering it—in modulating its futility [*inutilité*] into the endless murmuring we call literature" (DE.1:255/AME.94–95). What, again, to make of this "incessant, disorderly buzzing"? Foucault's idea is that we make *literature* out of it, as if literature were the effect of a dialogue, collaboration, or complicity between language and—what?—a "pure exteriority": death, absence, infinity (whatever it is, it is untheorizable in the nature of the case). Anyhow something terrifying lies outside our grasp as cognitive subjects but not outside our experience—specifically a *literary* experience, or more exactly an experience of ceaseless, interminable speech. (We'll come back to this experience.)

Foucault discourages the psychoanalytic diagnosis that, in poetry, we suffer from a "return of the repressed."[20] But discourse has the structure of a fold in which the excluded remains internal to the game. This figure (the internal alien) seems basic to Foucault's thought from beginning to end (it is his self-image). The logophobia of discourse, for example, echoes the "grande peur" that Foucault discusses in *Folie et déraison*, specifically the *obsessive* awareness of madness that is one of the consequences or even functions of reason, and which expresses itself (irrepressibly, or against all reason) in the form of fantastic or grotesque images memorialized by Goya and Sade—and, later, in different ways, by Hölderlin, Nerval, Nietzsche, Roussel, and Artaud (HF.451–55/MC.206–11). We can confine the mad and institute rules to exclude folly from the discourse of reason, but the language of madness—"violent, discontinuous, querulous, disordered"—nevertheless articulates itself within discourse itself, if only as a disruption or deformation of the processes of signification, or as "the endless murmuring we call literature," causing, as one might expect, a redoubling of efforts to render discourse transparent, efficient, productive, and correct. Here thoughts fly to Habermas's antimodernist theory of "communicative reason"—"a noncoercively unifying, consensus-building force of a discourse in which the participants overcome their at first subjectively biased views in favor of a rationally motivated agreement."[21] Foucault, mistrustful of the very idea of rational consensus as a reductive program of normalization, sides with the outsiders. In *L'ordre du discourse* he makes it a public announcement: "All those who, at one moment or another in our history, have attempted to remould this will to truth and to turn it against truth at that very point where truth undertakes to justify the taboo, and to define madness; all those, from Nietzsche to Artaud and Bataille, must now stand as (probably haughty) signposts for all our future work" (OD.22–23/AK.220).

The future work in question is, of course, *Surveiller et punir* (1975) and the first volume of the *Histoire de la sexualité* (1976). But perhaps more important for an understanding of Foucault's modernism would be his editorial projects in which outsiders (a "deranged" murderer, a hermaphrodite) are allowed to speak in their own voice — *Moi, Pierre Rivière* (1975) and *Herculine Barbin* (1978). Foucault situates these texts, after all, not in the history of madness (or of the prison, clinic, or *scientia sexualis*), but in a history of literature whose Homer is the Marquis de Sade, and whose theme is the imagination or exploration of extreme experiences (DE.1:255–57/AME.95–96).

Experience. In philosophy, experience is arguably the most impoverished and useless of concepts. The *cogito*, for example, is incapable of experience for the simple reason that nothing is allowed to approach it. The *cogito* is precisely that to which nothing can happen except what originates within itself. Doubt inoculates it against the outside. Nothing is certain except that nothing questions its existence. Everything is preformed at the expense of what is singular and irreducible. Experience from this standpoint reduces at best to observation (which works nevertheless as a mode of reflection). Thus in the age of reason the experience of madness is not an experience of being mad but an experience of reason affirming itself in the face of unreason — an experience that, strictly speaking, remains entirely abstract until acted upon.[22] Hegel is the first to think of experience as "the subject's subjectness."[23] Experience (*Erfahrung*) is a movement — a reversal, a destitution, even a violence — that consciousness must undergo to purify itself of whatever is not itself.[24] But like art *Erfahrung* is meant to become a thing of the past. Experience means: the subject overcoming its subjectness.

Foucault's interest, by his own account, is in *subjectness* — an interest that it might not be possible to reward with a theory, since the point of this interest (as Foucault says) is to break with theory, namely the philosophies of the subject, derived from Hegel, that dominated French intellectual culture during his school days. Not that a phenomenology of *subjectness* is out of the question or even undesirable—this is, after all, what Sartre tries for in his account of the look, and it is what Emmanuel Levinas accomplishes with his early descriptions of fatigue, insomnia, and the experiences of poetry, Cubism, and the *il y a* (the ontological archetype of exteriority).[25] But the early Foucault (or, for all of that, the middle and the late) was not a theorist. The genre of his early essays is that of the arcane review that reworks the ideas of others in a baroque prose of paradox and indirection (thus emulating, and often exceeding, the "extreme forms of language in which Bataille, Maurice Blanchot, and Pierre Klossowski have made their home" [DE.1:240/AME.76]). These early essays are (whatever else they are) experiments in "nondiscursive" language.[26] Perhaps they have not had many admirers, but I think one can argue that these experiments are satirical rather than, say, merely decadent: they are aimed against the institutional figure of the philosopher and the propositional style of his discourse, where the idea is that transparency is a good in itself. In his essay on Bataille, Foucault writes: "The breakdown of philosophical subjectivity and its dispersion in a language that dispossesses it while multiplying it within the space created by its absence is probably one of the fundamental structures of contemporary thought. This is not the end of philosophy but, rather, the end of the philosopher as the sovereign and primary form of philosophical language" (*"L'effondrement de la subjectivité philosophique, sa dispersion à la intérieure d'un langage qui la dépossède, mais la multiplie dans l'espace de sa lacune, est probablement une des structures fondamentales de la pensée contemporaine. Il ne s'agit pas d'une fin de la philosophie. Plutôt de la fin du philosophe comme forme souveraine et première du langage philosophique"*) (DE.1:242/AME.79). The point would be to think of Foucault's early occluded style as a practice of desubjectivation; the form of his language, whatever one's reaction to it, is an application of his argument against reductive (phenomenological) consciousness. In his essay on Blanchot, Foucault says that, grammatical appearances aside, "I speak" does not have the structure of the *cogito*, because the one entails an experience of language that the other, in its angelic purity, escapes: "'I think' led to the indubitable certainty of the 'I' and its existence; 'I speak,' on the other hand, distances, disperses, effaces that existence and lets only its empty emplacement appear. Thought about thought . . . has taught us that thought leads us to the deepest interiority. Speech about speech leads us, by way of literature as well as perhaps by other paths, to the outside in which the speaking subject disappears" (DE.1:520/AWE.149). To which Foucault adds: "No doubt, that is why Western thought took so long to think the being of language: as if it had a premonition of the danger that the naked experience of language poses for the self-evidence of the 'I think'" (DE.1:520/ AWE.149). What kind of experience is "the naked experience of language"? (We have already had an inkling: not, evidently, an aesthetic experience but an experience of—or *with*—noise.)

The guiding figure in Foucault's early work is Georges Bataille, who had, for example, cross-dressed Heidegger as a surrealist in an early essay (1933) on *le moi* as the subject of sacrifice—"The *me* accedes to its specificity and to its integral transcendence only in the form of the 'me' that dies." The *moi* is not just Dasein heroically acknowledging its fate; the *moi* is "avid" for death: it embraces the cross, not in the form of Christian piety or asceticism, but as an erotic experience "that must and can be lived as the death of the *me*, not as respectful adoration but with the avidity of sadistic ecstasy, the surge of a *blind* madness that alone accedes to the *passion* of the pure imperative."[27] This ecstasy before death is a premier example of what Bataille will later call the *inner experience*, that is, an experience of rapture in which the interior is simply taken away or evacuated by what it experiences; it is, in Bataille's formulation, experience "at the extreme limit of the possible."[28] This is the form of experience that Foucault appropriates as a way of breaking with phenomenology: "Experience that tries to reach a certain point in life that is as close as possible to the 'unlivable,' to that which can't be lived through. What is required is the maximum of intensity and the maximum of impossibility at the same time" (DE.4:43/P.241). This experience, Foucault adds, "has the function of wrenching the subject from itself, of seeing to it that the subject is no longer itself, or that it is brought to its annihilation or its dissolution. This is a project of desubjectivation" (DE.4:43/P.241).

Here one should recall Mallarmé's experience of *le Néant*, which is a prototype of the limit-experience: it is (1) an experience of the death or disappearance of God, (2) an experience of death of the subject, and (3) an experience of the heteronomy of language as that which fills the space of the evacuated poet. Foucault engages these themes for the first time in "Le 'non' du père" (1962), a review of Jean LaPlanche's *Hölderlin et la question du père* in which Foucault's main purpose is to recover the preanalytic kinship of poetry and madness. The "extreme limit of the possible" that Hölderlin experiences in the father's absence and in the disappearance of the gods is, to be sure, an experience of psychosis, but (as part of the "project of desubjectivation") Foucault reconfigures this event as an experience of language:

> The Father's absence, manifested in the headlong rush of psychosis, is not registered by perceptions or images, but relates to the order of the signifier. The "no" through which this gap is created does not imply the absence of a real individual who bears the father's name; rather, it implies that the father has never assumed the role of nomination and that the position of the signifier, through which the father names himself and, according to the Law, through which he is able to name, has remained vacant. It is toward this "no" that the unwavering line of psychosis is infallibly directed; as it is precipitated inside the abyss of its meaning, it invokes the devastating absence of the father through the forms of delirium and phantasms and through the catastrophe of the signifier. (DE.1:200/AME.16)

The father's *non* is at once an echo and an erasure of the father's *nom*: it is an event (a "catastrophe of the signifier") that can only be registered materially in writing. In Lacanian terms, *langue* (*nom du père*) has turned into *lalangue* (*non du père*): "a zone is created where language loses itself in its extreme limits, in a region where language is most unlike itself and where signs no longer communicate, that region of an endurance without anguish: '*Ein Zeichen sind wir, deutungslos*' ('A sign we are, meaningless')." Hölderlin himself is no longer the lyric subject who gives form to a work of expression; his work is now, paradoxically, the interruption or disruption of lyric form: "The expansion of this final lyric expression is also the disclosure of madness. The trajectory that outlines the flight of the gods . . . is indistinguishable from this cruel line that leads Hölderlin to the absence of the father, that directs his language to the fundamental gap in the signifier, that transforms his lyricism into delirium, his work into the absence of a work" (DE.1:201/AME.17).

The difficulty is how to understand "*le lien entre l'œuvre et l'absence d'œuvre*" (DE.1:203/AME.19). Foucault has never addressed this relation except in tortuous paradoxes, but there are two contexts to which he alludes.[29] The first is Bataille's concept of *dépense*, that is, the principle of loss or expenditure without return that defines an economy that is heterogeneous and subversive with respect to capitalism or the market economy of exchange and accumulation. *Dépense* means free or unconditional expenditure, as in the wearing of jewels, sacrificial cults, gambling, kinky sex, gifts, works of art—and, notably, modern poetry:

> The term poetry, applied to the least degraded and least intellectualized forms of the expression of a state of loss, can be considered with expenditure [*dépense*]; it in fact signifies, in the most precise way, creation by means of loss. Its meaning is therefore close to that of *sacrifice*. . . . [For] the rare human beings who have this element at their disposal, poetic expenditure ceases to be symbolic in its consequences; thus, to a certain extent, the function of representation engages the very life of the one who assumes it. It condemns him to the most disappointing forms of activity, to misery, to despair, to the pursuit of inconsistent shadows that provide nothing but vertigo or rage. The poet frequently can use words only for his own loss; he is often forced to choose between the destiny of a reprobate, who is as profoundly separated from society as dejecta are from apparent life, and a renunciation whose price is a mediocre activity, subordinate to vulgar and superficial needs.[30]

Poetry as "creation by means of loss" means that poetry is a "nonproductive expenditure" of language. Poetry is language that "ceases to be symbolic in its consequences." This is what is meant when it is said that poetry is the *materialization* of language—poetry is what is figured in the etymology of *Dichtung*: the word *poetry* means thickness, density, impermeability. But notice that under this description poetry also constitutes for the poet a heterogeneous existence with respect to the order of things, namely that of the "reprobate," outsider, or misfit: Sade, Baudelaire, Kafka.

In the late 1940s Maurice Blanchot had already characterized poetry as an interruption or deferral of the movement of signification that produces meanings, concepts, statements, and works.[31] Poetry belongs to a different temporality from that of dialectical, propositional, or narrative language. These logical forms of language are messianic: they are movements toward a future, a completion, or *pleroma*, in which everything will coincide with itself without excess or deficiency (*s* is *p*). Poetry is heterochronic: it belongs to the *entretemps*—the between-time or *meanwhile* (the interval, the caesura, the pause, break, or parentheses).[32] But it is not just that in poetry time breaks off; rather a breach opens between *archē* and *telos*: imagine the past receding from what was never present while the future, like the messiah, never arrives. This temporality is (in Blanchot's words) "interminable, incessant," as in a vigil or illness; it is not that of a project, development, and product (EL.20/SL.26). Poetry in this event ceases to be *poiēsis*, or the making of works; it is "foreign to the category of completion" (EI.229/IC.153). In his essay on Blanchot, Foucault describes this temporality in characteristically arabesque terms: "For a long time it was thought that language had mastery over time, that it acted both as the future bond of the promise and as memory and narrative; it was thought to be prophecy and history; it was also thought that in its sovereignty it could bring to light the eternal and visible body of truth; it was thought that its essence resided in the form of words or in the breath that made them vibrate. In fact, it is only a formless rumbling, a streaming; its power resides in dissimulation. That is why it is one with the erosion of time; it is depthless forgetting and the transparent emptiness of waiting" (DE.1:538/ AME.167).

Forgetting, waiting, attention, affliction, suffering, exhaustion, fascination, abandonment, dying, madness—and poetry: one could add to this list, especially if one recalls Emmanuel Levinas's ethical theory ("passivity more passive than all passivity"), but these are the canonical forms of experience explored by Bataille and Blanchot. In some of his most interesting pages Foucault singles out Bataille's obsessive image of the eye upturned in ecstasy, and the corresponding transformation of language that this condition makes possible:

> It indicates the moment when language, arriving at its confines, overleaps itself [*fait irruption hors de lui-même*], explodes and radically challenges itself in laughter, tears, the eyes rolled back in ecstasy, the mute and exorbitated horror of sacrifice, and where it remains fixed in this way at the limit of its void, speaking of itself in a second language in which the absence of a sovereign subject outlines its essential emptiness and incessantly fractures the unity of its discourse. The enucleated or rolled-back eye marks the zone of Bataille's philosophical language, the void into which it pours and loses itself, but in which it never stops talking—somewhat like the interior, diaphanous, and illuminated eye of mystics and spiritualists that marks the point at which the secret language of prayer is embedded and choked by a marvelous communication that silences it. Similarly, but in

an inverted manner, the eye in Bataille delineates the zone shared by language and death, the place where language discovers its being in the crossing of its limits—the nondialectical form of philosophical language. (DE.1:247/AME.83–84)

The "nondialectical form of philosophical language" is the language of an anarchic temporality in which there is neither an end (*telos*) nor origin (*archē*), unless it is a beginning that begins endlessly again and again. It is a language that "never stops talking"—one thinks at once of Beckett's *Unnamable* or of Blanchot's "infinite conversation." The paradoxical relation between the work and the absence of the work is not a relation that ends in silence; it is a relation of interminability, like the "incessant, disorderly buzzing" of language that, as Foucault has it, we "modulate" into literature. The writer who cannot stop writing (Sade, Balzac, Kafka—or, for that matter, Sartre and Derrida) is no longer a sovereign subject or philosopher; he has been folded into *littérature comme telle* as into a heteronomous event of writing.

As Blanchot argues throughout much of his work, but particularly in *L'espace littérature* (1955), "The writer's mastery is not in the hand that writes, the 'sick' hand that never lets the pencil go—that can't let it go because what it holds it doesn't really hold. . . . Mastery always characterizes the other hand, the one that doesn't write and is capable of intervening at the right moment and putting the pencil aside. Thus mastery consists in the power to stop writing" (EL.19/SL.25). This was Rimbaud's achievement. But *l'écriture* is a mode of *subjectness* with respect to "the interminable, the incessant" (EL.20/SL.26): "To write is to enter into the affirmation of the solitude in which fascination threatens. It is to surrender to the risk of time's absence, where the eternal starting over reigns. It is to pass from *Je* to *Il*, so that what happens to me happens to no one, is anonymous insofar as it concerns me, repeats itself in an infinite dispersal. To write is to let fascination rule language" (EL.31/SL.33).

This means that the experience of language is not a first-person experience; it is an experience of obsession—of being besieged or gripped by language as by something that cannot be got rid of, like the imminence of death. Here would be the place to give close attention to one of Foucault's most recondite essays, "Le langage à infini," with its enigmatic reflections on the sources of poetry and writing in an "essential affinity" between language and death: "Headed toward death, language turns back upon itself [*Le langage, sur la ligne de la mort, se réfléchit*]; it encounters something like a mirror; and to stop this death which would stop it, it possesses but a single power—that of giving birth to its own image in a play of mirrors that has no limits" (DE.1:251/AME.90). Hence the garrulousness of the mad and the interminability of writing, the repetitious structure of poetry and the gratuitous proliferation of literature, which is simply a mirror-play in which language duplicates itself to infinity: "The possibility of a work of language finds its original fold in this duplication. In this sense, death is undoubtedly the most essential of the accidents of language (its limit and its center): from the day that men began to speak toward death and against it, in order to grasp and imprison it, something was born, a murmuring that repeats, recounts, and redoubles itself endlessly, has undergone an uncanny process of amplification and thickening, in which our language is today lodged and hidden" (DE.1:252/AME.91).

Freedom. There is no doubt that from a philosophical standpoint the desire to break with the sovereignty of the philosophical subject—to *disappear* as a subject by way of various forms of subjectness or limit-experiences—is completely incoherent. One might as well desire to be mad, or dead. Yet the point is surely that the intention here is not to be a lunatic; one doesn't take Artaud as a "signpost" in order to be incarcerated and subjected to shock treatments. The idea is rather to conceptualize subjectivity in a new way—to frame the subject without recourse to the canonical concepts of cognition, self-identity, autonomy, and rational control.

Let me conclude by briefly distinguishing between two conceptions of freedom in Foucault's later writings. One is fairly traditional; it has to do with the possibility of autonomy and agency within the mechanisms of normalization or the "games of truth" by which individuals are socially formed. The other might be called a "postsubjectivist" concept of freedom.

In a late interview, "L'éthique du souci de soi comme pratique de la liberté" (1984), Foucault makes the somewhat surprising statement that "the mad subject is not an unfree subject" (DE.4:719/EST.291). To be sure, the mad person is constituted as such by the system in which he finds himself, if "himself" is the word. Even when I judge myself to be mad, I do so within disciplinary frameworks in which, as Ian Hacking puts it, my madness or abnormality is one of "the ways for people to be."[33] So I am what I am under a description that fits, never mind what it leaves out. However, we know that Foucault came to rethink the nature of these frameworks in a self-critical way. In this late interview, for example, Foucault's idea is that the mad person is constituted as such not within a *fixed* system of brute coercion but within a system of "power relations" that are porous and flexible: "these power relations are mobile, they can be modified, they are not fixed once and for all." That is, these relations are not only alterable but unstable and, indeed, anarchic. In particular this means that "power relations are possible only insofar as the subjects are free. If one of them were completely at the other's disposal and became his thing, an object on which he could wreak boundless and limitless violence, there wouldn't be any relations of power. Thus, in order for power relations to come into play, there must be a certain degree of freedom on both sides" (DE.4:720/EST.292). A condition of relations of power, Foucault says, is the possibility of resistance. "The idea that power is a system of domination that controls everything and leaves no room for freedom cannot be attributed to me" (DE.4:721/EST.293).

Well and good. But Foucault the modernist is different from Foucault the liberal. In this same interview from 1984 Foucault distinguishes between freedom and liberation, where the one is understood as an ethical relation of the self to itself, whereas the other means something like the breaking of "repressive deadlocks" that alienate the self from itself (DE.4:710/EST.282). Foucault says he is suspicious of the notion of liberation to the extent that it implies the emancipation of a human nature that exists beneath or apart from the social forms of subjectivation that constitute the individual, or alternatively that it implies an ideal of authenticity that one would try to reach like a goal or affirm under the existentialist motto that "man makes himself." The relation of the self to itself cannot be understood on the model of grasping, achieving, or making something. It is not a relationship with one thing but an open-ended "play" among "different forms of the subject": "You do not have the same type of relation to yourself when you constitute yourself as a political subject who goes to vote or speaks at a meeting and when you are seeking to fulfill your desires in a sexual relationship. Undoubtedly there are relationships and interferences between these different forms of the subject; but we are not dealing with the same type of subject. In each case, one plays, one establishes a different type of relationship to oneself. And it is precisely the historical constitution of these various forms of the subject in relation to games of truth that interests me" (DE.4:718–19/EST.290–91). So it would be a fact that one's relation to oneself is irreducible to a principle of identity. More interesting still, the practice of self-formation is, to borrow Blanchot's words, "foreign to the category of completion." This is because the practice of self-formation is always historically situated, not governed by norms but by what is possible in the situation in which we find ourselves—rather as in the history of art, where anything is possible, but not everything is possible at every moment. The task of self-creation, Foucault says, is not "a search for formal structures with universal value" but requires "a historical investigation into the events that have led us to constitute ourselves and to recognize ourselves as subject of what we are doing, thinking, saying." The point of this investigation, however, is not self-recognition, self-knowledge, or self-identity; it is to "separate out, from the contingency that has made us what we are, the possibility of no longer being, doing, or thinking what we are, do or think" (DE.4:574/EST.315–16). In other words, "make it so that nothing remains fixed." As Foucault says: "we are always in the position of beginning again" (DE.4:575/EST.317).

The relation of the self to itself is thus a relation of freedom, not of truth. In this context, however, freedom is not autonomy but heteronomy, not self-possession but self-escape. Foucault's conception here is comparable to what Emmanuel Levinas calls "finite freedom." In "Substitution," Levinas writes: "In the irreplaceable subject, unique and chosen as a responsibility and a substitution [of one for the other], a mode of freedom, ontologically impossible, breaks the unrendable essence. Substitution frees the subject from ennui, that is, from the enchainment to itself, where the ego suffocates in itself due to the tautological way of identity."[34] It would be an interesting project to explore the symmetries between Foucault's ethical subject and Levinas's. It appears that they have the same formal structure of "the other in the same." Of course, Levinas's subject is Jewish, whereas Foucault's is, genealogically and by choice, a pagan Greek. Where the one is a movement toward the stranger, the widow, and the orphan, the other is a movement toward the self. But neither one is a recursive movement. "Je est une autre," says "the masked philosopher."

Poetic Communities

And one day they taught Hesiod glorious song while he was shep-
herding his lambs under holy Helicon, and this word first the god-
desses said to me—the Muses of Olympus, daughters of Zeus who
holds the aegis:

"Shepherds of the wilderness, wretched things of shame, mere bel-
lies, we know how to speak many false things as though they were
true; but we know, when we will, to utter true things."

So said the ready-voiced daughters of great Zeus, and they plucked
and gave me a rod, a shoot of sturdy laurel, a marvelous thing, and
breathed into me a divine voice to celebrate things that shall be and
things that were aforetime; and they bade me sing of the race of the
blessed gods that are eternally, but ever to sing of themselves both
first and last. But why all this about oak and stone?

—Hesiod, *Theogony*, 26–33

Ecstasy. Scholarly tradition pictures Hesiod, like Homer before him,
as a great pedagogue.[1] The poet is in charge of a vast encyclopedia
concerning gods and heroes (and also, in Hesiod's particular case,
everyday life). But from Hesiod we also learn that poetry itself is not
a kind of learning but a species of ecstasy. No one studies to be a
poet. No one asks to be such a thing. One is, for no reason, summoned out of one's house and exposed to a kind of transcendence.
Exactly what kind of transcendence is not always clear. One can
imagine preferring the life of the belly where people who say they

are hungry can usually be taken at their word. Like biblical prophecy, poetry is a condition of election and a mode of responsibility, as much a curse as a calling since one is now hostage to a "divine voice" (or perhaps we would now say, to "the voice itself"). In an essay on the poetic or prophetic voice, "the voice itself," Jean-Luc Nancy says: "Someone singing, during the song, is not a subject."[2] Likewise Emmanuel Levinas: inspiration "does not leave any place of refuge, any chance to slip away."[3] In ecstasy I am turned inside out, exposed to others, still myself perhaps but no longer an "I," that is, no longer a spontaneous agent but only a "who" or a "me": a passive, responsive, obsessive repercussion of the Muses.

Partage. In the *Ion*, Plato gives the basic theory of poetry as a condition of fascination, that is, of being touched, gripped, or magnetized (hypnotized).[4] Fascination is a reversal of subjectivity from cognition to obsession. Of the fascination of images, for example, Maurice Blanchot writes: "Seeing presupposes distance, decisiveness which separates, the power to stay out of contact and in contact to avoid confusion. Seeing means that this separation has nevertheless become an encounter. But what happens when what you see, although at a distance, seems to touch you with a gripping contact, when the manner of seeing is a kind of touch, when seeing is *contact* at a distance? What happens when what is seen imposes itself on the gaze, as if the gaze were seized, put in touch with appearance?"[5] An image is different from a concept. Seeing is conceptual: it grasps the world, holds it up for scrutiny as if at arm's length; but in fascination distance (and therefore aesthetics) collapses and the eye suffers a seizure. It is transfixed or fixed in place by the image and can see nothing else. A visionary experience is always a condition of confusion in which the eye is absorbed or consumed by what is seen; hence the avid or the vacant stare, the stony, liquidated look. I am no longer myself but another. A true image is not a likeness but a Medusa-event in which I no longer know what I am looking at. Although still part of the world, I experience the world as a surface to be crossed rather than a place to be occupied. Ecstasy means that (starting with myself) I am outside of and uncontainable within any order of things, an exile or nomad.[6] However, this does not mean no one shares my condition. On the contrary, Plato emphasizes the contagion of poetry, whose magnetism flows from one to another like the spell that forms delirious Dionysian communities (536a–d). Fascination is a condition of participation in which one is no longer separated but is caught up in an ecstatic movement, which is always a movement from one to another that produces a gathering or string, that is, not a dialogue or conversation (which would be a philosophical community formed by friends stepping in off the street) but what Jean-Luc Nancy calls a *partage*—a sharing or division of voices in which the divine voice or "voice itself" is multiplied by being passed from one singularity to another like rumor or panic (Nancy prefers the metaphor of the gift).[7] There is no abiding or indwelling universal spirit—no communion of "poetry in general," as Nancy says—but only the singular "being-outside-oneself" that is received and handed on (think of the round of voices in traditional song—"the voice itself," Nancy says, "can become yours or mine" [BP.237]). This ecstasy is what poetry communicates, not a vision or a revelation; the sharing of ecstasy rather than of mind or spirit, language or myth, is the essence of poetry and of the poetic community (PV.66/SV.236–37). Such a community can never be sedentary; it does not grow or develop into a unitary order. A poetic community has the structure of a series of singularities rather than a fusion of many into one.[8]

Hence the topos of poetry as discourse in flight—"panic" is Blanchot's word for it: "Flight now makes each thing rise up as though it were all things and the whole of things—not like a secure order in which one might take shelter, nor even like a hostile order against which one must struggle, but as the movement that steals and steals away. Thus flight not only reveals reality as being this whole (a totality without gap and without issue) that one must flee: flight is this very whole that steals away, and to which it draws us even while repelling us."[9] Poetry opens a hole in being through which every totality drains away. So it is not merely that the poet is outside and uncontainable with any order of things; it is that poetry disrupts in advance (*an-archē*) the possibility of any such order. As Blanchot says, incompletion (*désœuvrement*) is its principle—"a principle of insufficiency" (IC.5/UC.5). Ecstasy, says Nancy, "defines the impossibility, both ontological and gnoseological, of absolute immanence (or of the absolute, and therefore of immanence) and consequently the impossibility either of an individuality in the precise sense of the term, or of a pure collective totality."[10] In place (or in advance) of the settlement, the village, the realm, the social contract, civil society, liberal democracy, the total or merely procedural state, poetry opens up an ecstatic or anarchic community—a community that (Nancy says) "resists collectivity itself as much as it resists the individual" (CD.177/InC.71).

An ecstatic community assembles and disperses (as at games, festivals, and rallies) but is not meant to last. Incompleteness is its principle.[11] Eric Havelock has shown that an ecstatic community is what Socrates saw in the Athens around him: a vast theater, a performance culture basically hypnotic and anarchic in its operations and results: "Plato's account remains the first and indeed the only Greek attempt to articulate consciously and with clarity the central fact of poetry's control over Greek culture" (PP.96).[12] Whence denial of ecstasy became for Socrates the first principle of his "city of words," which is a totally integrated economic order administered by sealed-off punctual egos exercising rational control (our once and future philosophers). Recall that the starting-point of his construction is the critique of mimesis in book 3 (393a–98b), where *mimesis* is a mode of "being-outside-oneself" or impersonation rather than the category of representation that it becomes in book 10. The problem of poetry is not its logical weakness but its power to project people outside of themselves. Poetry is a dispersal or dissemination of subjectivities in which no one is oneself and everyone is somebody else, as in theater.

Here would be the place to recall Nietzsche's analysis, which neatly summarizes Plato's poetics (and anticipates Georges Bataille's): "Dionysiac excitation is capable of communicating to a whole multitude this artistic power to feel itself surrounded by, and at one with, a host of spirits. What happens in the dramatic chorus is the primary *dramatic* phenomenon: projecting oneself outside oneself and then acting as though one had really entered another body, another character. . . . It should be made clear that this phenomenon is not singular but epidemic: a whole crowd becomes rapt in this manner."[13] Belonging to a crowd (the first principle of theater) is a condition of rapture. Possibly mystics levitate alone. The ecstasy of poetry, however, is a social experience. In *The Unavowable Community*, Maurice Blanchot recalls that for Georges Bataille ecstasy "could not take place if it was limited to a single individual . . . : [It] accomplishes itself . . . when it is shared" [CI.34–35/UC.17].) Likewise Walter Benjamin: "Man can be in ecstatic contact with the cosmos only communally. It is the dangerous error of modern men to regard this experience as unimportant and avoidable, and to consign it to the individual as the poetic rapture of starry nights."[14] And Benjamin quotes Baudelaire as follows: " 'The pleasure of being in a crowd is a mysterious expression of sensual joy in the multiplication of number. . . . Number is in *all*. . . . Ecstasy is a number. . . . Religious intoxication of great cities. . . .' Ch. B., *Œuvres*, vol. 2, pp. 626–27 ('Fusées'). Extract the root of the human being!"[15]

Poetry: A Short History. Aristotle's *Organon*, or rule of discourse, gives us the purely logical form of Socrates' city. Here a place for poetry is found by reconceptualizing *mimesis* as *mathesis*, or learning (1448b.4, 2–6), and then by laying bare as its deep structure a form of consecutive reasoning called *muthos*, or plot (1450a.7, 1–7). Poetry is now for spectators on whom it has a therapeutic or calming effect. Instead of fascination it produces or enhances an essentially philosophical subjectivity. Aristotle is thought to have invented the concept of the critical spectator whose experience of literature is essentially solitary and reflective. (As Gadamer has shown, the Platonic spectator is always ecstatic.)[16] What is at least true is that a principle of disengagement has been introduced into the theory of poetic experience—a distancing factor (perhaps we can speak of this as the aestheticizing of the poetic).[17] As a species of discourse, poetry will henceforward be largely a branch of rhetoric reducible to handbooks, that is, not so much a discipline in its own right as a technique of mediation in the service of other discursive fields (or, as Horace said, in the service of empire). Poetry is defined by not having any discursive field of its own ("the allegory of the poets" derives from theology). One can remark in passing (1) on Longinus, who affirms the ecstatic tradition but is himself lost to the world until the seventeenth century; (2) on the genre of the lyric, with its lethal erotic and satiric traditions (the one drives people to perdition, the other to suicide; Rome in fact passed a law forbidding satire); (3) on the classical tradition of poetic exile (Ovid, Dante, Milton, Joyce); (4) on the myth of the unschooled poet like Wolfram von Eschenbach, who says: "I don't know a single letter of the alphabet" (*Parzival*, 2.115).

But what characterizes poetry throughout most of its history is its confinement to institutions not of its own making.[18] For example, in *European Literature and the Latin Middle Ages* Ernst Robert Curtius asks about "the mode of existence of the medieval poet." For Curtius "mode of existence" is a social rather than ontological category. The question is: "Why did one write poetry? One was taught to in school. A great many medieval authors wrote poetry because one had to be able to do so in order to prove oneself a *clericus* and *litteratus*; in order to turn out compliments, epitaphs, petitions, dedications, and thus gain favor with the powerful or correspond with equals; as also for the sake of vile Mammon. The writing of poetry can be taught and learned; it is schoolwork and a school subject."[19] The modern university's writers' workshop preserves this tradition. Curtius notes that the concept of the poet's "divine frenzy" is preserved as a rhetorical topos. Pope memorializes this topos in the *Peri Bathous; or, The Art of Sinking in Poetry*, a parody of Longinus aimed at a new poetic culture whose origins are internal to the development of print technology and the new autonomous social spaces that it opens up: with the rise of modern cities poetry becomes a discourse of the street (the tavern, the coffee house, the periodical) rather than of the court, the church, and the school. The invention of the concept of art (in which poetry can now reflect on itself as if in a space of its own) is made possible by these social changes, as when Friedrich Schlegel characterizes the poet as "a sociable being" [*ein geselliges Wesen*]: conversing about poetry with poets and lovers of poetry now becomes a condition of poetry as such.[20]

But what counts as poetry as such? Beginning with the Jena Romantics (the Athenäum is arguably the first literary community of modernity and a prototype of the avant-garde group) this becomes an open question: as poetry ceases to be a genre distinction, poetic theories are now necessary in order to pick out a piece of language as poetic (see Friedrich Schlegel, *Athenäum Fragments*, nos. 116, 238).[21] So we get the onset of modernism as a culture of prefaces and manifestos. The distinction between theory and practice, or between poetry and poetics, ceases to be self-evident, as does the distinction between fragment and work. The poet Charles Bernstein says: "I imagine poetry . . . as that which can't be contained by any set of formal qualities."[22] It becomes what Maurice Blanchot calls "fragmentary writing"—writing that is "averse to masterpieces, and even withdraws from the idea of the work to the point of making the latter a form of worklessness [*désœuvrement*]" (EI.592/IC.403),[23] as if, 2,500 years later, poetry were breaking out of the Organon.[24] As Bernstein says: "I imagine poetry as an invasion of the poetic into other realms: overflowing the bounds of genres, spilling into talk, essays, politics, philosophy" (P.151). The Athenäum group is where this breakout or dissemination is first enacted as a program (the idea is, among other things, to make philosophy poetic and poetry philosophical). In their account of the group, Lacoue-Labarthe and Nancy write: "The fragment is the romantic genre par excellence. . . . In fact, only a single ensemble, published with the one-word title, *Fragments*, corresponds entirely (or as much as possible) to the fragmentary ideal of romanticism, notably in that it has no particular object and in that it is anonymously composed of pieces by several different authors."²⁵ Imagine poetry not so much as a work of the spirit as a group experiment (recall Schlegel's Fragment 125: "Perhaps there would be a birth of a whole new era of the sciences and arts if symphilosophy and sympoetry became so universal and heartfelt that it would no longer be anything extraordinary for several complementary minds to create communal works of art").

The College of Sociology. In Paris in 1937 Georges Bataille, along with Roger Callois, Michel Leiris, and Pierre Klossowski, began organizing a series of bimonthly lectures called The College of Sociology, whose purpose was to investigate the nature of such social structures as the army, religious orders, secret societies, brotherhoods, companies, salons, drinking, gaming, or sporting clubs, youth groups, even political parties (normally) on the fringe.²⁶ Crucially, Bataille will later (in *Le coupable* [1944]) add to this list the community of lovers and the artists' community.²⁷ These structures are, according to Callois, ecstatic or "sacred" communities, where the sacred consists "in the outburst of violations of rules of life: a sacred that *expends* itself, that *spends itself* (the orgiastic sacred)" (CS.152). The sacred is not a theological but a social concept. Sacred communities are not part of the productive economies of modern capitalist states; or rather, whatever function or goal might be assigned to them in the bourgeois order of things, they are defined by what Bataille calls "nonproductive expenditures of energy [*dépense*]."²⁸ A nonproductive expenditure of energy is one in which there is no return on investment. It is a gratuitous expenditure, absolutely outside any economy of exchange- or use-value. It is predicated upon a principle of loss rather than on the accumulation of capital. It belongs, if anywhere, to the economy of the gift. Recall the essay on "The Notion of Expenditure" (1933), where Bataille lists jewelry, religious sacrifice, kinky sex, gambling, art, and, in particular, poetry as examples of the free expenditure of energy. Poetry is, he says, "creation by means of loss" (PM.30–31/VE.120).²⁹ In poetry words are not exchanged for meanings; instead they have become events of *communication* in the special sense that Bataille attaches to this word. Communication is not a concept from information theory; it refers not to the transmission of messages but to the contagious relation in which states of existence are passed along from one subject to another (Nancy's *partage*). Communication has the structure of Plato's magnetic chain rather than the give-and-take anatomy of dialogue, commerce, and social struggle. In Bataille's words, communication is made of "contagions of energy, of movement, of warmth, or transfers of elements, which constitute inevitably the life of your organized being. Life is never situated at a particular point: it passes rapidly from one point to another (or from multiple points to other points), like a current or a sort of streaming of electricity."[30] At all events, in poetry words are no longer to be exchanged for meanings or things: they are now like images of fascination—moments of reversal that displace the logical or cognitive subject from its position of sovereignty and control. As Blanchot says apropos of Kafka: "The writer gives up saying 'I'" (EL.21/SL.26). Poetry is heterogeneous with respect to an order of things organized from the perspective of the logical subject. So we should say that, at least from the poet's point of view, Plato got poetry right (see Giorgio Agamben [MwC.5]).

La Bohème. Notice that Bataille defines the poet's choice in terms of "the destiny of the reprobate" as against submission to the principle of necessity. Imagine this destiny as a condition that makes poetry possible. Students of Walter Benjamin tend to be guarded about the fact that he was among the occasional participants in Bataille's College of Sociology (Benjamin's saintliness seems out of place in this morally and politically dubious evironment). In fact in the spring of 1939 Benjamin was scheduled to deliver a paper, "Some Motifs in Baudelaire," but his presentation was postponed until the fall, by which time France was at war; within a few months Benjamin would be a refugee (fortunately he gave his manuscripts to Bataille, a libararian, for safekeeping). There were in any case no more meetings of Bataille's group. However, as we have it, the text of "Some Motifs in Baudelaire" is remarkably coherent with both the letter and spirit of inquiry around which Bataille had organized his college. Benjamin's theme is social ecstasy. In the first place there is the thesis that Baudelaire intended his poetry to produce a state of shock (GS.1.2:614–18/SW.4:318–21). (Undoubtedly Baudelaire, not Rimbaud, was the first surrealist.) But perhaps more important is the mode of social existence that Baudelaire represents for Benjamin, namely that of the homeless *flâneur* whose environment is the street and the crowd. Benjamin says of Baudelaire: "the street . . . became a refuge for him" (GS.1.2:573/SW.4:42). In the street one is always outside of oneself, and, for Benjamin, Baudelaire is nothing in himself but is the consummate role-player ("Flâneur, apache, dandy, and ragpicker were so many roles to him") (GS.1.2:600/SW.4:60). And again: "On the physiognomy of Baudelaire as that of the mime: Courbet reports that he looked different every day" (GS.5.1:419/ AP.333). Moreover, Baudelaire's poetry is "nomadic," in Deleuze and Guattari's sense of an art that is uncontainable within any rationalized order of things. Benjamin writes: "Around the middle of the century, the conditions of artistic production underwent a change. This change consisted in the fact that for the first time the form of the commodity imposed itself decisively on the work of art, and the form of the masses on its public. Particularly vulnerable to these developments, as can be seen now unmistakably in our century, was the lyric. It is the unique distinction of *Les Fleurs du mal* that Baudelaire responded to precisely these altered conditions with a book of poems. It is the best example of heroic conduct to be found in his life" (GS.5.1:424/AP.336–37). Baudelaire's achievement was not to have left us a novel.

Benjamin's Baudelaire is not, however, merely the romantic artist in solitary metaphysical rebellion against a fallen world. He is rather the representative of the ecstatic social structure that makes him possible, namely the *Bohème* (GS.1.2:513–14/SW.4:3–5). The *Bohème* is the underground (by no means the first of its kind when we think of Grubstreet, Bartholomew Fair, and the Elizabethan crowd that begins writing—about the London streets—for the printing press; think of how Marlowe ends his days). Benjamin defines the *Bohème* as the hiding-place of political conspirators during the Second Empire ("Professional conspirator and dandy meet in the concept of the modern hero. This hero represents for himself, in his own person, a whole secret society" [GS.5.1:478/AP.378]). It is the world of lowlifes, wastrels, criminals, prostitutes, and Balzacian destitutes— Bataille's sacred realm of the "accursed." It is where the gambler is deposited at the end of his run. Its defining genre is the detective story. It is also the condition of the modern poet's existence. On Benjamin's analysis the *Bohème* is a principle of modernist poetics (this is his Baudelaire thesis). In antiquity it was the ecstasy of the poet that, according to the magnetic theory, constituted the condition of the anarchic community; in Benjamin it is the anarchic community that is the condition of poetry. In order to become a poet it is no longer enough to possess (as if by nature) a certain kind of subjectivity (a dissatisfied memory is all one needs); it is now necessary to belong to a certain kind of world in order to take on the kinds of subjectivity that that world makes available—the man of the barricades, the painted woman, the beggar, the painter of modern life. ("In the guise of the beggar Baudelaire continually put the model of bourgois society to the test" [GS.5.1:427/AP.338].) At the end of the day Benjamin's Baudelaire is a kind urbanized romantic ironist, a transcendental *buffon*, a performance artist:

> Baudelaire did not have the humanitarian idealism of a Victor Hugo or a Lamartine. The emotional buoyancy of a Musset was not at his disposal. He did not, like Gautier, take pleasure in his times, nor could he deceive himself about them like Leconte de Lisle. It was not given him to find a refuge in devotions, like Verlaine, nor to heighten the youthful vigor of his lyric élan through the betrayal of his adulthood, like Rimbaud. As rich as Baudelaire is in the knowledge of his craft, he is relatively unprovided with stratagems to face the times. And even the grand tragic part he had composed for the arena of his day—the role of the "modern"—could be filled in the end only by himself. All this Baudelaire no doubt recognized. The eccentricities in which he took such pleasure were those of the mime who has to perform before a public incapable of following the action on the stage—a mime, furthermore, who knows this about his audience and, in his performance, allows that knowledge its rightful due. (GS.5. 1:429/AP.340)

Black Mountain College. Voice, Jean-Luc Nancy says in "Vox Clamans in Deserto," is not an expression of the self but a projection of it. "Voice is not present to itself, it is only an exterior manifestation, a trembling that offers itself to the outside, the half-beat of an opening—once again, a wilderness exposed where layers of air vibrate in the heat. The wilderness of the voice in the wilderness, in all its clamor—has no subject, no infinite unity; it always leaves for the outside, without self-presence, without self-consciousness" (BP.243). In Charles Olson's poetics the poetic subject does not reflect on itself but rather is projected like a breath (hence it is an "objectivist" rather than expressive or "subjectivist" poetics).[31] The poem is not the reworking or working-out of genres and conventions (what Olson called "closed form"); it is rather an event on the model of free expenditure (or "open form"): "The poem is energy transferred from where the poet got it (he will have some several causations), by way of the poem itself to, all the way over to, the reader. . . . Then the poem must be, at all points, a high energy-construct and, at all points, a high energy-discharge" (PVO.52).[32] Crucially, this is an expenditure of energy that is shaped by the poet's breath—the poetic line comes not from a manual of prosody but "(I swear it) from the breath of the poet, from the breathing of the man who writes" (PVO.54), which Olson identifies as "voice in its largest sense" (PVO.58). (Compare Adorno on breath as a musical unit in Schönberg.)[33] In composition, Olson says, the typewriter allows the poet to score the voice of the poem, so that poetry, whatever else it might be, becomes the communication of voice: "It is the advantage of the typewriter that, due to its rigidity and its space precisions, it can, for a poet, indicate exactly the breath, the pauses, the suspensions even of the syllables, the juxtapositions even of part of phrases, which he intends. For the first time the poet has the stave and the bar a musician has had. For the first time he can, without the convention of rime and meter, record the listening he has done to his own speech and by that one act indicate how he would want any reader, silently or otherwise, to voice his work" (PVO.57–58).

So the poem is not just composition but performance, and understanding the poem will mean performing it rather than subjecting it to exegesis. Sherman Paul compares the composition of projectivist verse to, among other things, action painting and jazz: "Projective verse is not only a poetics of presentation but a poetics of present experience, of enactment. It replaces spectatorship with participation, and brings the whole self—the single intelligence: body, mind, soul—to the activity of creation. Dance, which Olson appreciated because it recalls us to our bodies and [because in it] 'we use ourselves,' is a correlative of this poetics; and so are action painting and jazz, which poets at this time turned to because they offered the instruction they wanted. 'There was no poetic,' Olson said of this time. 'It was Charlie Parker.'"[34] After Nancy one can think of the poem as a voice that passes from poet to reader. Poet and reader are linked as a sharing, or *partage*, rather than as author and exegete, artist and critic, or producer and consumer. It is possible to think of it as a movement of poetry from poet to poet, where poetry opens up a mode of existence in which poems appear. Stephen Fredman's idea is that projectivism is a social poetics as well as a poetics of verse. It is a poetics aimed not only at the production of works but at the formation of the group—or, more exactly, the formation of a space (an open field) in which poets and artists can come and go and in which works of art are free to take place *under any description*. The formation of such a space is what Olson achieved (or sustained) at Black Mountain College during the early 1950s.[35] Black Mountain College was an art school founded in North Carolina in 1933. One of its first artists-in-residence was Josef Albers, who brought to the school an aesthetic outlook that he had acquired at the Bauhaus during the Weimar years: "Art is concerned with the HOW and not with the WHAT; not with literal content but with the performance of factual content. The performance—how it is done—that is the content of art."[36] Olson was the school's director during its last five years of operation. In *Black Mountain: An Exploration in Community*, Martin Duberman gives a detailed account of Olson's transformation of the college from an art school into an art colony—indeed, a colony of performance art.[37] In 1952, to take a famous example, John Cage (who had been visiting the college since the early forties) staged one of his "circuses" in which ten people (poets, dancers, musicians, painters) were each assigned a time-slot of forty-five minutes (each running concurrently with the others) in which to do whatever they wished:

> Spectators took their seats in the square arena forming four triangles created by diagonal aisles, each holding the white cup that had been placed on their chair. White paintings by a visiting student, Robert Rauschenberg, hung overhead. From a stepladder Cage, in a black suit and tie, read a text "on the relation of music to Zen Bhuddism" and excerpts from Meister Eckhart. Then he performed a "composition with a radio," following the pre-arranged "time brackets." At the same time Rauschenberg played old records on a hand-wound gramophone and David Tudor played a "prepared piano." Later Tudor turned to two buckets, pouring water from one to the other while, planted in the audience, Charles Olson and Mary Caroline Richards read poetry. Cunningham and others danced through the aisles chased by an excited dog, Rauschenberg flashed "abstract slides" (created by coloured gelatin sandwiched between the glass) and film clips projected onto the ceiling showed first the school cook, and then, as they gradually moved from the ceiling down the wall, the setting sun. In a corner, the composer Jay Watt played exotic musical instruments and "whistles blew, babies screamed, and coffee was served by four boys dressed in white. (PLA.82; see also BM.350–58)

It was at Black Mountain that Merce Cunningham assembled his first dance company—with a Dionysian Charles Olson, all six-foot-seven, two hundred fifty pounds of him, taking the class. (Cunningham says: "it wasn't unhappy to watch him—he was something like a light walrus" [BM.380]).[38] One can imagine what Bataille would have made of Olson's companionship. Fielding Dawson recalls: "Charley was an enthusiastic teacher, and in those days optimistic, completely absorbed in his talk: the white blackboard began to fill with blue diagrams, blue words and long blue sentences, his hands turned blue and he had blue smudges on his face and mustache from smoking his cigar with his chalk hand, on he went, and once, with no place to write, he wrote towards the edge of the blackboard, wrote down the right margin, there was no right margin, but he went on, crossing over and going through already sentences until he came to the chalk tray, and bending over went clean off the blackboard to the floor, laughing with us."[39] (Recall Blanchot on the interminability of *l'écriture*.)

Désœuvrement: Worklessness. What conception of art, if any, attaches itself to the theory of "nonproductive expenditure"? Perhaps only the Duchampean concept of art-in-general: art freed from genre distinctions (painting, sculpture, music, verse).[40] Blanchot thinks that fragmentary writing is not a genre of writing but is just the thing itself, *l'écriture*, where all discursive fields are vulnerable to the *désœuvrement* of *l'écriture*—in *The Philosophical Discourse of Modernity*, Habermas defines postmodernity as, among other things, the seeping of poetry (opaque, self-reflexive language) into philosophy (of a certain stripe) and then into the problem-solving communicative praxis that defines the public sphere.[41] Anarchy follows. The question of nonproductive expenditure has particular relevance to the problem of the avant-garde work. The avant-garde work does not belong to the history of genius, much less the history of taste, but to the history of the anarchist group. The avant-garde work is less likely to resemble a monumental construction like Joyce's *Ulysses* than a minimalist event like John Cage's *4'33"*. Whereas the monumental work is classically self-sufficient (Heidegger's ideal, in "The Origin of the Work of Art," of the originary self-standing Greek edifice, which appears to have created itself), the avant-garde work is accessible only through layers of social mediation, meaning that one has to belong to the social space in which the work appears in order to make sense of it at all (but Gadamer, as we saw in chapter 2, would say that this belonging is a condition of every aesthetic experience, ancient or modern). Moreover, belonging to such a space entails belonging to its history and therefore understanding the conditions that make the work a possibility in the moment at hand (that not everything is possible at every moment is the motto of art history: the experience of the work demands responsiveness to historicity—Blanchot would call this the *exigency* of the avant-garde). In this respect understanding a work is more like understanding a social practice or a form of life than it is understanding a concept, proposition, or the use of criteria. This helps to explain why the avant-garde work is often not really accessible to critical spectators of a certain traditional disposition.

A clear and fruitful example of this is Michael Fried's famous reaction to the minimalist (or, as Fried prefers, "literalist") work of Donald Judd and Frank Stella during the sixties. Judd's sculptures appear to be simple indeterminate shapes without parts or design or any sign of assembly or composition; Stella's paintings are painted stripes (famously, four identical paintings of black stripes exhibited in 1959–60). Fried meanwhile is a formalist whose relation to works of art is essentially judicial. Thus the issue for Fried is how, analytically, to tell a work of art from the material of which it is made (frame, canvas, painted shapes). "What is at stake," he says, "is whether the paintings or objects in question are experienced as paintings or as objects."[42] Fried's position is that the materiality of the work must be experienced as a medium and not simply as material; otherwise we haven't got art but simply a mere thing. The position is similar to Adorno's formalism, which insists on matter as mediation, not in order to represent or intend something but simply to set the work apart from the empirical world: "the concept of form marks out art's sharp antithesis to an empirical world in which art's right to exist is uncertain."[43] To be an artwork the work must exhibit "aesthetic rationality" or the exercise of conscious control over its materials (AT.58/AeT.34–35). *Exeunt* Duchamp, Cage, and the minimalists. (Adorno again: "As soon as the artwork fears for its purity so fanatically that it loses faith in its possibility and begins to display outwardly what cannot become art—canvas and mere tones—it becomes its own enemy. . . . This tendency cultimates in the *happening*" [AT.158/AeT.103].) In Fried's language, by foregrounding medium the modernist work tries "to defeat or suspend its own objecthood" (AO.120). No one sees a Jackson Pollock drip-painting as reducible to its material, although as action painting the work is perhaps inseparable from the performance of its composition. But with Stella the difference between a painting and a painted canvas is no longer self-evident. One cannot tell that the thing is art simply by looking at it (in Clement Greenberg's famous expression, one is perilously close to looking simply at a frame and canvas exhibiting a flat surface).[44] For Fried this means that the minimalist or literalist work is art that can no longer be experienced as art. Minimalism or literalism "aspires, not to defeat or suspend its own objecthood, but on the contrary to discover and project objecthood as such" (AO.120). In which case it is something other than art: an object, although perhaps not a real one! It is interesting that Fried stops short of calling the minimalist work a mere thinglike thing, although he no longer takes it as art. What is it, then? Or, as John Cage asked prophetically in a 1957 essay, "Where do we go from here?" (His answer: "Towards theater.")[45]

Theater of Cruelty. The interest of Fried's analysis is that he interprets the minimalist work as an event or performance: "the literalist espousal of objecthood amounts to nothing other than a plea for a new genre of theater" (AO.125).[46] Fried means this as an insult but, like Plato's rejection of the poets, it is the medium of an essential insight: "theater," he says, "is now the negation of art" (which is, subtly, not the same as non-art) (AO.125). The mode of appearance of the minimalist work—its presence—"is basically a theatrical effect or quality—a kind of *stage* presence. It is a function, not just of the obtrusiveness and, often, even aggressiveness of the literalist work, but of the special complicity that that work extorts from the beholder" (AO.127).[47] Complicity is the essential note, that is, it defines something essential about the social nature of the avant-garde work, whose "objecthood" is not that of a work that one simply beholds; rather the work is folded into an event in which one is a participant and not simply a beholder, at least not a critical observer whose job is zoning and assessment. The minimalist work occupies something close to what Deleuze and Guattari call "haptic" or nonoptical space, a space that can only be entered, not comprehended as a whole or from a perspective (MP.614–25/TP.492–99). It is an event, moreover, in which one's participation makes the work possible (as in Gadamer's theory). Possibly the work may not outlast its event, as in performance art. Theater has this transitory ontology that Artaud's "theater of cruelty" tries to isolate by separating the theater-event from any notion of work or text: in "pure theater," otherwise called the "anarchic poetry of space," there are no antecedents to performance. In other words, no dramatization—the language of theater becomes a medium of noise and physical shock; the after-effect of theater is not catharsis but trauma.[48] Performance art is a strong ex-ample of nonproductive expenditure because its purse is entirely ex-hausted by what takes place.

Dance likewise is a good case of *désœuvrement*. A piece of choreog-raphy is a kind of body art that is extremely difficult to preserve over time: dancers grow old, the dance mistress forgets, or dies. Balan-chine could never understand why people wanted him to revive his earier achievements. There is no text for the choreography of *Swan Lake* the way there is a score for its music or a narrative for its story (dance notation is a good example of "indeterminacy of translation"). A performance can be repeated but not preserved. (A video record-ing of a performance is not a performance of anything but the video recording.) In an essay on "The Impermanent Art" (1955) Merce Cunningham said that his idea of dance is to perform something that is just the thing itself: for example, a jump (without musical accom-paniment, but when Cunningham collaborated with his friend John Cage, not without noise). Cunningham's choreography, following Cage, sometimes takes the form of tossing a coin to determine what shape the jump will take, and what is shaped is not only a bodily movement but the time and space in which the movement occurs, a shape that exists only for an instant and will never occur again. On other occasions Cunningham's dancers improvise their movements. This is not artlessness: since the dancers are superbly trained, their movements cannot help being dance (as if a dancer could no longer merely move). But their movement is exhausted in the performance of it; it is what Deleuze and Guattari call a *haecceity*, a singularity like five o'clock yesterday evening.[49] There will be other five o'clocks but not that one. Fried says: "The success, even the survival, of the arts has come increasingly to depend on their ability to defeat theater." "Art degenerates as it approaches the condition of theater" (AO.139, 141). So once more the history of art comes to an end.[50]

In the 1970s performance art followed minimalism by doing away with the production of objects altogether.[51] The idea was in part to see whether one could create an art that could not be bought or sold. This was already the goal of Dada and the (or some) Surrealists. One can think of the New York of the 1970s as a recuperation of Dada the way the New York of the fifties and sixties was a recuperation of Duchamp.[52] True to the spirit of the age but also to the spirit of Ar-taud, Bataille, and perhaps before them all, Alfred Jarry, certain per-formance artists probed for an absolute stopping-point, as when Chris Burden had himself shot in the arm with a pistol or when

Orlan had her face surgically removed, with the surgery being simultaneously telecast to several places around the world.[53] Here is an end-of-art story to end all end-of-art stories, as if art were crossing over into Bataille's underworld of mutilation, sacrifice, and suicide. In its obsession with extreme situations, performance art belongs to the history of surrealism, or at all events to Artaud's kind of theater as "an area in which there are no precise rules," except for one: "Without an element of cruelty at the foundation of every spectacle, the theater is not possible" (OC.118/AA.251). Imagine cruelty as a condition of theater (this was already the insight of the Jacobean stage—think of Jonson's *Bartholomew Fair*, in which someone pours hot grease on the foot of Ursula the Pig Woman). Bataille, who knew Artaud slightly, once went to hear him speak:

> A few years before I had attended a lecture he gave at the Sorbonne. . . . He talked about theatrical art, and in the state of half-somnolence in which I listened I became aware that he had suddenly risen: I understood what he was saying, he had resolved to personify the state of mind of Thyestes when he realized that he had devoured his own children. Before an auditorium packed with the bourgeoisie (there were hardly any students), he grasped his stomach and let out the most inhuman sound that has ever come from a man's throat: it created the sort of disquiet that would have been felt if a dear friend had suddenly become delirious. It was awful (perhaps the more so for being only acted out. (AM.43)

La communauté désœuvrée. The avant-garde work emphasizes the theatricality that is arguably a condition of all art. One could put this in a slightly different way. In the avant-garde the production of the work cannot be separated from the formation of the group, and vice versa: in the case of the surrealists, for example, the group *is* the work—"Surrealism," Blanchot says, "is and has always been a collective experience" (EI.598/IC.408)—but a work in the sense of Nancy's *communauté désœuvrée* rather than on the order of Socrates' "city of words" or in Aristotle's conception of politics as an extension of the logical form of friendship (which is also the form of the proposition: friendship follows the logic of identity rather than the relation of alterity).[54] Benjamin in his essay on the surrealists emphasizes the primacy of ecstatic experiences over the production of works: "anyone who has perceived that the writings of this circle are not literature but something else—demonstrations, watchwords, documents, bluffs, forgeries if you will, but at any rate not literature—will also know, for the same reason, that the writings are concerned literally with experiences, not with theories and still less with phantasms" (GS.2.1:297/SW.2:208). The group always has the structure (and often the historical location) of a *Bohème*: a nonproductive community that does not hang together, which does not last, and whose floating center is the performance (the exhibition, the reading, the happening, and more generally the *scene*). Its population is Baudelairean in the sense of being nomadic; it exists like a Deleuzean "war machine."[55] Its distinctive modes of communication are gossip, collaboration, the quarrel, and the inevitably short-lived review. In his memoir, *"The Black Mountain Review,"* Robert Creeley recalls Ezra Pound's advice: think of a literary review as something around which you gather people, not a box to put them in.[56] Its solidarity is the solidarity of theater, where theater should be understood in Artaud's sense, in which the distance between performers and spectators narrows to zero—Artaud pictures his audience as a crowd in the street, a porous, exposed, Nietzschean audience whose ancestor is the Dionysian community: "We are eliminating the stage and the auditorium and replacing them with a kind of single site, without partition or barrier of any kind, which will itself become the theater of the action. A direct communication will be reestablished between the spectator and the spectacle, between the actor and the spectator, because the spectator, by being placed in the middle of the action, is enveloped by it and caught in its crossfire" (OC.114–15/AA.248).

The "Futurist moment," as Marjorie Perloff has shown, is a moment of theatricality whose principal form is the manifesto, "a new literary genre" designed to work like a political intervention rather than as a work of art.[57] The idea is to alter the artworld and not simply to find one's place in it or merely take it over as is. Futurism (whether Italian or Russian) defines the original difference between avant-garde aesthetics in general and the formalist aesthetics of high modernism (as in Greenberg's and Fried's "modernism"): the artist's task is to create a new environment and not just new objects. Indeed, the one is the condition of the other, because the avant-garde environment (the Cabaret Voltaire is the locus classicus) works like an anarchic space in which *any* innovation—indeed, anything at all—can take place. ("Do Whatever" is the rule of Duchampean modernism, according to Thierry de Duve [KD.327].) In *My Futurist Years* Roman Jakobson gives a moving and often funny account of the way he was swept up into just such a space created by Majakovskij and Xlebnikov, whose collection of poems and manifestos, *A Slap in the Face of Public Taste* (1912), was one of the texts that inspired Jakobson to become a linguist specializing in the study of poetic language. Of course Jakobson tried his hand at poetry and at writing manifestos, and he collaborated with Majakovskij and Xlebnikov on many projects, but the moral of his story is that one doesn't have to be an artist to belong to an artworld. The idea is to experience it—and the experience is of social transformation (inhabiting a new world): "The evenings of the Futurists brought together an amazing number of the public: the Large Hall of the Polytechnic Museum was completely packed! The public's reaction to them was various: many came for the sake of scandal, but a broad segment of the student public awaited the new art, wanted the new word (by the way—and this is interesting—they weren't particularly interested in prose. This was a time when readers . . . thought that the main thing was poetry, and that poetry had a genuinely new word to say. Apart from these large public evenings there were many closed groups, circles, and private gatherings, where the main place was allotted to the new word)."[58]

In his study of the poetic communities of North Beach in San Francisco, the poet Michael Davidson gives perhaps the best account we have of how deeply poets like Allen Ginsberg and Jack Spicer invested themselves in the formation of such communities, and how poetic subjectivities (like Davidson's own) took shape within such formations.[59] Imagine an aesthetics whose goal is not so much the creation of the work as the creation of a form of life that produces poets. ("An author who teaches writers nothing, teaches no one," says Walter Benjamin ("The Author as Producer" [GS.2.2:696/SW.2:777]). As Michael Davidson suggests, this would be something like a utopian aesthetics or a political imaginary in which, among other things, poetry and art would no longer be required to justify themselves (before whom?) in order to exist. No apologies, no regrets. Imagine poetry as a given—freed from the Socratic exigency that lovers of poetry must come to its defense. Poetry presupposes a culture of the gift in which responsiveness and acceptance—as well as, to be sure, exposure and risk—are what make reality inhabitable. It presupposes what Nancy calls community: being together or being-in-common in which "we are not a 'being' but a 'happening'" ("Finite History" [BP.157]). The poet David Antin captures something of this in one of his talk-poems, "what it means to be avant-garde":

and i
did the best i could   under the circumstances   of being
there   then   which is my image of what an artist does and
is   somebody who does the best he can   under the
circumstances   without worrying about making it new or
shocking   because the best you can do depends upon what you
have to do and where   and if you have to invent something
new to do the work at hand you will   but not if you have a
ready-made that will work and is close at hand and you want
get on with the rest of the business
then youll pick up
the tool thats there   a tool that somebody else has made
that will work   and youll lean on it and feel grateful
when its good to you   for somebody elses workand youll
think of him as a friend who would borrow as freely from you
if he thought of it or needed to   because there is
a community of artists   who don't recognize copyrights and
patents   or shouldnt   except under unusual circumstances
who send each other tools in the mail or exchange them
in conversation in a bar[60]

Language Writing. Much of the most memorable poetry written in
North America during the past half-century has sometimes gone by
the name of "language poetry," or $L = A = N = G = U = A = G = E$
Poetry, after the journal $L=A=N=G=U=A=G=E$, edited by
Charles Bernstein and Bruce Andrews between 1978 and 1981. Language poetry looks very much like the longest-running literary movement of the twentieth century. Its poets are flourishing thirty years
after the fact. This may be in part because language poetry is not an
aesthetic concept; strictly speaking it is not a concept at all but a family name of poets who trace their lineage to early modernists like
Gertrude Stein and William Carlos Williams, but also to writers like
the Russian poet Osip Mandelstam, whose essay "The Nature of the
Word" (1922) celebrates the rich materiality of his native tongue:
"The Russian language . . . in its totality is a turbulent sea of events,
a continuous incarnation and activation of rational and breathing
flesh. No language resists more strongly than Russian the tendency
toward naming and utilitarian application. Russian nominalism, that
is, the idea of the reality of the word as such, breathes life into the
spirit of our language and connects it with Hellenic philological culture, not etymologically or literally, but through the principle of
inner freedom" (CPL.121).[61] This captures very well the spirit of lan-

guage poetry, with its love of *parataxis*, *anacoluthia*, and *metonymy* — figures of speech (descendents of Hellenic philology) in which language breaks up the integrations of grammatical form. Here, as a random example, is the opening poem of Lyn Hejinian's *The Cell*:

It is the writer's object
    to supply the hollow green
    and yellow life of the
    human I
It rains with rains supplied
    before I learned to type
    along the sides who when
    asked what we have in
    common with nature replied opportunity
    and size
Readers of the practical help
They then reside
And resistance is accurate — it
    rocks and rides the momentum
Words are emitted by the
    rocks to the eye
Motes, parts, genders, sights collide
There are concavities
It is not imperfect to
    have died.[62]

Hejinian thinks of her poetry as "metonymic," that is, organized according to patterns of adjacency, intervals, increments: "The metonymic world," she says, "is unstable. While metonymy maintains the intactness and discreteness of particulars, its paratactic perspective gives it multiple vanishing points. Deduction, induction, and juxtaposition are used to make connections" — but the connections never resolve themselves into a whole, so that the form of the poem is open-ended or, as Hejinian likes to say, "restless."[63] However, putting questions of open form to one side, language poetry is less a formal enterprise than a number of large, diverse, and fluid interactions among poets centered in San Francisco and New York but also embracing Canada and Great Britain, with filiations extending into Eastern Europe and Australia (and translations into, among other languages, Chinese.) Like the surrealists the language poets share practices rather than theories. What makes them a group is their involvement with one another in a variety of activities from poetry readings to literary criticism to publication in a surprising number of journals, anthologies, websites, and thoroughly noncommercial books of poetry published by an array of small presses (Figures, ROOF, Sun and Moon). Individually they do very different things, but they do so within the framework of social relationships highlighted above all by the poetry reading.[64] Charles Bernstein writes:

> Readings are the central social activity of poetry. They rival publishing as the most significant method of distribution of poetic works. They are as important as books and magazines in bringing poets into contact with one another, in forming generational and cross-generational, cultural and cross-cultural, links, affinities, alliances, scenes, networks, exchanges, and the like. . . . The reading is the site in which the audience of poetry constitutes and reconstitutes itself. It makes itself visible to itself. And while most attention has been paid to those moments when the poetry reading has been a means to cross over to a wider audience . . . the fundamental significance of the reading, it seems to me, has to do with infrastructure not spectacle. For this reason I would turn around the familiar criticism that everyone at a poetry reading is a poet to say that this is just what is vital about a reading series, even the essence of a poetry reading. For poetry is constituted dialogically through recognition and exchange with an audience of peers, where the poet is not performing to invisible readers or listeners but actively exchanging work with other performers and participants. . . . The poetry reading is an ongoing convention of poetry, by poetry, for poetry.[65]

Bob Perelman writes: "The performance pieces and talks on poetics that took place frequently during the initial stages of the formation of the language group were communal events, casual, intense interactions that took place in lofts and art spaces. But they were not only addressed to immediate participants: they were also recorded. However contingent and trivial some of the remarks were, those tapes were aimed at entering and redefining literary history."[66] One could also say they were aimed at *appropriating* literary modernism, as if to keep it from coming to an end. Hence their commitment to conceptual innovations in poetics and to formal experimentation as a way of keeping the question of what counts as poetry unsettled and controversial. They understand themselves as belonging to (*and essentially responsible for*) a specific tradition made up of Stein, Ezra Pound, Charles Reznikoff, Louis Zukofsky, Jackson MacLow, the Black

Mountain Poets, Allen Ginsberg and the Beats, as well as the avant-garde groups that San Francisco and New York continue to make possible. If there is a shared idea, it is that poetry is not simply another species of discourse, a particular way of using language that can be contrasted with other discursive genres (philosophy, for example); rather, poetry is an exploration and experience of language in all of its formal, material, and semantic dimensions, including its historical conditions of existence within an array of social and cultural contexts. As Hejinian says in connection with Gertrude Stein, "language is an order of reality itself and not a mere mediating medium," so that one can have a confrontation with a word or phrase that is as significant as one's confrontation with things of the world (LI.90).

The Heteroclite Entity. The preceding helps explain the concentration among language poets upon the idea of poetry as an event as well as a construction, where the emphasis falls, among other places, on how a poem (or how language) makes its appearance.[67] We can think of this emphasis as a modification of the modernist thesis that a poem is made of words but is not a use of them. This is not just an intensification of the thesis but (as in Blanchot's poetics of *désœuvrement*) a bending of it away from the idea of a poem as something made (an artifact). Thus, as we have seen in Gadamer's aesthetics, a performance of the work is not something added to something made; it is the singular thing itself. This is because the temporality of the poem is not of something present but of something that interrupts the present by taking shape there. In one of his talk-poem "durations," David Antin (not one of the language poets but an enormous influence on them) calls attention to the two modes of existence of his "work":

> as a performer im an improviser   so i dont know
>   exactly what im going to say when i begin   though ive
> thought about talking of particular things   and when ive
>   finished talking i may still be interested in something ive
> said and i may want to think about it again   and sometimes
>   i'll want to look at it and transcribe it and maybe even
> publish it   in a more or less extensive form that hangs
>   pretty close to the original talk or the sense of it
>   even when ive extended it   because im much less
> interested in revision and polishing than in the difference
>   between print and performance
>   (wim.65)

The difference between performance and print is, for Antin, analogous to the difference between poetry and works (that is, objects) of art: "most people / in art schools are interested in making objects"—that is, "objects of duration." Such objects don't interest Antin. To say why they don't he recalls a visit of his to the Louvre in which he hunts up mainly the paintings of low-profile artists while trying very hard (but failing) to avoid the Mona Lisa tour. On his way out he passes one of Rembrandt's self-portraits:

> as i passed the rembrandts on the way out i
> stopped for a moment to look once again at the self portrait
> with the pallette in his hand and the turban tied around his
> head   which looks more like a painters cloth to protect his
> hair   and an expression that suggests some kind of comment
> on the object of painting its meaning and perhaps its duration
> a comment that looks to me like the beginning of a very
> rueful jewish grin that expresses something of my own
> disdain for the idea of duration
> (wim.72)

What are "objects of duration"? They are evidently not just things that don't get thrown away—unlike Duchamp's Readymades, which we know of chiefly from photographs or replicas; they are cultural icons like the Mona Lisa, and also of course like Rembrandt's self-portraits. But the Rembrandt that catches Antin's attention is a self-interrupting icon (like the one in John Ashbery's *Self-Portrait in a Convex Mirror*). As a self-portrait it incorporates—one could say, perpetually interrupts—the performance of its composition. The expression on Rembrandt's face is a moment of *désœuvrement*—unworking—inserted into the work, an *entretemps*. Naturally one thinks about whether the same is true of the Mona Lisa's smile. We underestimate the difficulty of such smiles with respect to aesthetic experience as a distinterested event. At any rate Antin reads Rembrandt's face as a "rueful jewish grin that expresses something of my own / disdain for the idea of duration."

I want to say that this disdain of duration expresses the fundamental anarchism (one could call it the antiprinciple principle: the *désœuvrement*) of Antin's poetics (and of the avant-garde, of performance art, and of language poetry). The idea is to produce an event in which the work takes place without taking final form; it materializes without becoming objectified or even finished. The poem in this respect is a singularity, a *haecceity* that can be communicated through a *par-*

tage of voices but which can no longer be identified on its own as a thing set apart from the community that assembles in its company. John Cage remarked on the ability of Robert Rauschenberg's paintings to escape the fixity of painting despite being made of paint, not to mention canvases stretched on a frame and hung on a wall, for all the world objects of art: "Over and over again I've found it impossible to memorize Rauschenberg's paintings. I keep asking, 'Have you changed it?' And then noticing while I'm looking that it changes. I look out the window and see the icicles. There dripping water is frozen into an object. The icicles all go down. Winter more than the others is the season of quiescence."[68] What's the principle here? In " '45' for a Speaker," Cage explains it as follows:

10″

    The principle called mobility-immobility is this:
    every thing is changing
    but while some things
    are changing
    others are not.

20″

    eventually those
    that were
    not

30″

    changing
    begin suddenly
    to change (S.154)

The principle (mobility-immobility: *désœuvrement*) is that the work of art belongs to an unstable environment (historicity is internal to its essence); it cannot be sealed off from this environment because it is, whatever else it is, an event that happens simultaneously with everything else taking place in the ongoing places it traverses and which, indeed, it works to form. (Recall Celan's figure of the poem: *Unterwegssein* ["Der Meridian," GWC.3:186/CP.34].) There are no unaccompanied works of art. Poets and audiences of poetry are clandestine companions of poems that travel from one environment to another. To be sure, we are trained in school to transform works of art into aesthetic phenomena by bracketing them—Gadamer calls this "aesthetic differentiation" (WM.81/TM.85). But the poem cannot be differentiated as a one-time thing that gets picked up now and again by the isolated reader. On the contrary, as Peter Middleton suggests in "The Contemporary Poetry Reading," the concept of the poem needs

to be radically socialized: "Instead of thinking of the poem as something that moves around being variously interpreted, read aloud,
published in different forms, and generally provoking distinct interpretations, we might be better to think of it all as a large heteroclite
entity, that mixes texts, people, performances, memories, and other
possible affinites, in a process that engages many people, perhaps
only briefly, over a long period of time, whose outcomes are usually
hard to see, and which has no clear boundaries, not the page, the
reading, the critical study" (CL.294).

Community without Myth. Thierry de Duve regards modernism as a
utopian project that failed (KD.191). A hundred years of in-your-
face rhetoric has (he thinks) left modernity—the alienated, rationalized world of industrial-technological capitalism—unchanged. (This
is a universal disappointment at the end of the century: art, like politics, is unredemptive.) Says de Duve: the artworld, especially in New
York, is thoroughly commercialized—a market institution if there
ever was one—and painters mostly work alone (KD.191–92). As
a self-professed "man of '68" (KD.288), de Duve longs for community (KD.462). But probably not a poetic community, since such a
community does not fit anywhere along the axis between libertarian-
communitarian or liberal-socialist categories. The poem as a "heteroclite entity" is anarchic on the model of *partage*: as a formal object the
poem is always in excess of itself—ecstatic, journeying outside itself
and absorbing its surroundings into itself as it goes. Why not think
of this as the historical mode of existence of the poem, whose self-
identity is not a logical *ipseity* but entails the multiple communities
that it generates through those whom it fascinates? Nancy points out
that literature is not myth—on a certain romantic, functionalist, na-
tionalist notion of myth as a unitary narrative that gathers a whole
people into a totality. Whereas myth (in this certainly erroneous
sense) produces communion—heterogeneous people united as in one
voice—literature is serial in its production, a sharing or division of
voices. Its unity is not organic, that is, as Nancy puts it, it is "articulated" rather than "organized," where "articulation is only a juncture, or more exactly the play of a juncture: what takes place where
different pieces touch each other without fusing together, where they
slide, pivot, or tumble over one another, one at the limit of the
other—exactly at its limit—where these singular and distinct pieces
fold or stiffen, flex or tense themselves together and through one another, unto one another, without this mutual *play*—which always re-

mains, at the same time, a play *between* them—ever forming into the substance of a higher power of a Whole" (CD.188/IC.76). So one could say that, unlike romantic myth (or ideology, law, or philosophical rationality), what poetry produces is not a totality or a unitary community but a nomadic series of associations whose sociality, if I have it right, is theatrical and performative in the sense that it comes together and disperses, increases or depletes itself, and never settles into place. Its form is as open as the form of its poetry.

Francis Ponge on the Rue de la Chaussée d'Antin

Dear Lorca, I would like to make poems out of real objects. The lemon to be a lemon that the reader could cut and squeeze—a real lemon like a newspaper in a collage is a real newspaper. I would like the moon in my poems to be a real moon, one which could suddenly be covered with a cloud that has nothing to do with the poem, a moon utterly independent of images.
　　　—Jack Spicer, *After Lorca*

Artspace. What becomes of things in art? This is still the question of questions in aesthetic theory, which has understood from the beginning of modernism that the terms "nonrepresentational," "nonmimetic," or "abstract," however much they may capture something of what the experience of nontraditional works of art is like, have little application to twentieth-century art and literature. Modern art is filled with things. A cubist collage is made of real newspaper clippings, and so is a poem by William Carlos Williams. The method of modern poetry is, manifestly, "quotation, commentary, pastische," as if the poem had become a space for language rather than a use of it.[1] What kind of space? When Marcel Duchamp "invented" his Readymades, he altered the relation between works of art and real things in remarkably conservative fashion, as if to argue that the function of the modern work of art is neither to duplicate nor eradicate the world but to find somewhere else for it, which is perhaps all that

Mallarmé had in mind when he said that the world was made to exist in a splendid book.[2]

Call this a law of the conservation of ontology: in art nothing is added to the world, and nothing taken away, but simply moved. The rule of metaphor, after all, has always been to remove something from its usual place and to find another place for it in which, perhaps for no reason at all, or at least after a time, or for a while, it fits; but the thing itself remains what it is. Adorno writes: "Functional forms and cult objects may develop historically into artworks," and so may pieces of prehistoric rubbish—but do we know how?[3] The experience of modern art, perhaps of any art, is comparable to the anthropological experience of arriving somewhere where something apparently recognizable occupies a weird place in the order of things—human body parts get eaten, a specially colored insect is worshipped or feared, noise is music, and an empty canvas is sold at auction. What's an anthropologist to think? Recall Stanley Cavell's essay "Aesthetic Problems of Modern Philosophy," wherein he cites Wittgenstein—"To imagine a language is to imagine a form of life" (*Philosophical Investigations*, §19)—in order to apply this insight to the problem of Schönberg's music: "The language of tonality is part of a particular form of life, one containing the music we are most familiar with; associated with, or consisting of, particular ways of being trained to perform it and to listen to it; involving particular ways of being corrected, particular ways of responding to mistakes, to nuance, above all to recurrence and to variation and modification." Experienced against this background, atonality naturally makes us ask, "Is it music?" But Cavell thinks this question obstructs the real job at hand, which is to accommodate atonality, come what may, and this means (anthropologically) "naturalizing ourselves to a new form of life, a new world"—a world in which Schönberg's *Six Little Piano Pieces* gives the definition of music.[4] As Deleuze and Guattari would say, life with art is nomadic.[5]

Arthur Danto famously argued that every work of art presupposes an "artworld," which is a form of life constituted by narratives, histories, concepts, theories, interpretations, and reasons why something might count as art. Experiencing a thing as art depends on how we inhabit such a world, whether we are in some fashion participants in its practices or merely puzzled onlookers. Danto's exemplary work of art is Andy Warhol's *Brillo Box* which, like one of Duchamp's Readymades, looks very much to be the thing itself, but is not. "What in the end makes the difference between a Brillo Box and a work of art consisting of a Brillo Box," Danto says,

> is a certain theory of art. It is the theory that takes it up into the world of art, and keeps it from collapsing into the real object which it is. . . . Of course, without the theory, one is unlikely to see it as art, and in order to see it as part of the artworld, one must have mastered a good deal of artistic theory as well as a considerable amount of the history of recent New York painting. It could not have been art fifty years ago. But then there could not have been, everything being equal, flight insurance in the Middle Ages, or Etruscan typewriter erasers. The world has to be ready for such things, the artworld no less than the real one. It is the role of artistic theories, these days as always, to make the artworld, and art, possible.[6]

The trick is to understand exactly what sort of transcendental action these theories perform ("take up," "keep from collapsing").[7] Imagine a theory that caused a thing to stop being art. Joseph Kosuth once said: "Actual works of art are little more than historical curiosities. As far as *art* is concerned van Gogh's paintings aren't worth any more than his palette is. They are both 'collector's items.'"[8]

Think about what becomes of words in a poem—for example, a poem by David Antin, who says,

> i don't want to be
> considered a poet if a poet is someone who adds art to
> talking[9]

A poem by David Antin is made of talk, and is, on a certain view, artless (made of improvisations, lots of drift from topic to topic, indifference to triviality, that sort of thing). Unfortunately talk is a species of discourse that has always fallen below thresholds of formal description, so we haven't got a theory of it; but basically what David Antin does is stand up in front of an audience and talk. And since the social space in which he often does such a thing is that of a poetry reading, what one experiences is a sort of category mistake—an *ostranenie*-effect produced not so much by defamiliarization as by a reversal (or reversion) of the aesthetic into the familiar or everyday. Consider "a private occasion in a public place" (tb.211–12):

> i mean if i were to come and read to you from a
> book you would consider it a perfectly reasonable form of behavior
> and its a perfectly respectable form of behavior generally

thought of as a poetry reading   and it would be a little bit like
    taking out a container of frozen peas   warming them up and
serving them to you from the frozen food container   and that
doesn't seem interesting to me because then i turn out to be a cook
    and I dont really want to be a cook   i dont want to cook or
    recook anything for anybody   i came here in order to make a
poem   talking   to talk a poem   which it will be   all
                    other things being equal

What is it to "talk a poem," as against (as one supposes) composing
it on a keyboard and then reciting it? If I understand, Antin would
respond to a question of this sort by urging something like an anal-
ogy between words in a poem and furniture on a stage, where art is
not a *work* of something (a construction or an artifact) but rather, as
he says, "the act of putting it there"[10] — an event rather than (strictly)
an object, which is what characterizes so much of the American art
world since the 1950s, where, in the spirit of Duchamp and John
Cage, performance trumps composition:

                    if vito acconci each day takes one
    object from his apartment near sheridan square to leave it
in a gallery on upper broadway   emptying in the course of
    a conventional thirty day show his spare apartment of most
of the things on which his daily life depends   and he
finds himself riding the subway to make use of his table lamp
    for reading or his kettle to brew himself a cup of tea
        do we when we   walk into the gallery and confront this
    accumulation of used appliances and books and clothing feel
like we're reading a diary looking into an apartment or
    witnessing a dispossession (wim.162)

What is it for works of art and mere things to coincide within the
same space (not to mention within the same physical properties, or
should we say, entities?)?[11] There is an array of unformulated questions here about what happens to things like vito acconci's household
goods when they occupy the space of art. Possibly these questions
fall in among others: the modernist's question of what happens when
material ceases to be a form of mediation (words are treated as
things, a painting is just paint, a wooden cube is a wooden cube); or
the Artaud-like question of what happens to theater when it's removed from the auditorium and staged on the street.[12] To which one
might add a question from performance art: When does an ordinary
event or thing or behavior (two lovers having an argument in a restaurant) become theater? It doesn't seem enough to say that in these

cases the difference between art and non-art becomes difficult to determine or even nonexistent. So what if this is so? One could just as well say that the relationship between art and non-art has become intensely intimate, as if it were a relation of mutual habitation or proximity rather than one of appearance, cognition, representation, meaning, symbolization, or the negation of these things. This seems to be the point of Antin's anecdote about vito acconci, as indeed it is the point of John Cage's aesthetic ("we must bring about a music which is like furniture—a music, that is, which will be part of the noises of the environment").[13] Works and things lose their identity but gain their singularity when they leave or confuse their separate spheres.[14] As Donald Judd once said, we may just not know where to put works of art since there doesn't seem to be any place for them, and so for the sake of economy we convert them into other things:

> I bought a building in New York in 1968, which contains my work and that of others, and two buildings in Texas in 1973, which contain my work. One building in Texas has two large rooms and the other has one. Each of the two took two years of thinking and moving pieces around. The one room took about a year. One of the two rooms was the basis for the installations in the exhibitions of my work for the National Gallery of Canada in 1975, which occupies part of an office building and so has a fairly plain, decent space. Permanent installations and careful maintenance are [as] crucial to the autonomy and integrity of art [as] to its defense, especially now when so many people want to use it for something else.[15]

One could argue (1) that in the space of art things become more thingly, less objective, much in the way as Heidegger's hammer becomes more thingly, less equipmental, when it breaks—that is, it becomes useless and opaque, just like a work of art; and (2) that in the space of things (stacked up against a wall rather than hanging from it) art becomes less a work of spirit, more thing than object, as if materializing without making an appearance.[16] Adorno calls this sort of materialization the "crisis of *semblance* [*Krise des Scheins*]" (AT.100/ AeT.154), where "semblance" is what makes Duchamp's *Fountain* more than just another urinal (it shines out in a way the mere commodity does not). For Adorno, an artwork is its appearance: "Artworks become appearances, in the pregnant sense of the term—that is, as the appearance of an other—when the accent falls on the unreality of their own reality. Artworks have the immanent character of being an act, even if they are carved in stone. This is registered by the feeling of being overwhelmed when faced with an important work. The immanent character of being an act establishes the similarity of all artworks, like that of natural beauty, to music, a similarity once evoked by the term muse. Under patient contemplation artworks begin to move. To this extent they are truly afterimages of the primordial shudder in the age of reification" (AT.79/AeT.123–24). The problem with Duchamp's urinal—and for Adorno this is the failure of the avant-garde if not of all of modernism—is that it produces a shock but not a shudder.[17] Its semblance or unreality—its otherness—is overwhelmed by its self-evident or empirical identity. A modernist work for Adorno is never completely a work of art; its form can never fully emancipate it from "its immanent condition as a thing" (AT.100/AeT.154). For Adorno a philistine is someone who can only experience the work as a mere thing. (So Duchamp makes philistines of us all.) Art for art's sake by contrast wants to purify the work of its thingness the way Mallarmé wanted a language no one ever speaks. Adorno's idea is to be blind to thingness without ever actually losing touch with it (AT.99/AeT.153). As he says, "The difference of artworks from the empirical world, their semblance character, is constituted out of the empirical world and in opposition to it. If for the sake of their own concept artworks wanted absolutely to destroy this reference back to the empirical world [i.e., their own thingness], they would wipe out their own premise" (AT.103/AeT.158–59). Adorno wants the work to show modernity for what it is (a reified thingworld) by being different from it (a nonreified thingworld).

Thingworld. Without abjuring Adorno, let me try to gain some purchase on these paradoxes with the help of the philistine French poet Francis Ponge (1899–1988), whose poetry tries to construct nonpoetic relations among words and things in a way that is symmetrical with David Antin's work. "I have never wanted to 'write poetry,'" Ponge says:

> I write as I write, and I do not want it to be poetry. I do not intend to write poems. I express my feelings about things that move me, or that seem to me to be important to state. I have protested at length against my classification among poets, because lyricism in general disturbs me. That is, it seems to me that there is something too subjective, a display of subjectivity

which appears to me to be unpleasant, slightly immodest. I believe that things—how can I say it?—that emanate from your subjectivity, should not be displayed. Naturally, one never does anything but that. My own resolution was rather to reverse the situation and to try to say things that were generally valuable and pertinent. That is the reason why I have chosen things, objects, so that I would always have a break on my subjectivity, calling back the object as it exists when I write about it.[18]

And so, as Ponge says, when he writes he *takes the side of things* (a kind of French Objectivist). The poems in his first volume, *Le parti pris des choses* (1942), address things that, the odd eighteenth-century ode aside, do not always make it across thresholds of poetic description: a crate, a cigarette, an oyster, a doorknob, a loaf of bread, snails, a piece of meat, a pebble—most famously, a pebble, to which Ponge once wrote an "Introduction au galet" containing this apostrophe: "O ressources infinies de l'épaisseur des choses, *rendues* part le ressources infinies de l'épaisseur des mots!" ("O infinite resources of the thickness of things, *brought out* by the infinite resources of the semantical thickness of words").[19] Thickness here means: the task of poetry is not so much to describe things, rendering them transparent to view, as to relocate them in an environment of ordinary, often random talk, a move whose effect is to scale poetry itself down to the size of things themselves:[20]

LE CAGEOT

A mi-chemin de la cage au cachot la langue française a cageot, simple caissette à claire-voie vouée au transport de ces fruits qui de la moindre suffocation font à coup sûr une maladie.

Agencé de façon qu'au terme de son usage il puisse être brisé sans effort, il ne sert pas deux fois. Ainsi dure-t-il moins encore que les denrées fondantes ou nuageuses qu'il enferme.

A tous les coins de rues qui aboutissent aux halles, il luit alors de l'éclat sans vanité du bois blanc. Tout neuf encore, et légèrement ahuri d'être dans une pose maladroite à la voirie jeté sans retour, cet objet est en somme des plus sympathetiques,—sur le sort duquel il convient toutefois de ne s'appesantir longuement. (PP.38)

THE CRATE

Halfway between *cage* [cage] and *cachot* [prison cell] the French language has *cageot* [crate], a simple openwork case for the transport of those fruits that invariably fall sick over the slightest suffocation.

Put together in such a way that at the end of its use it can be easily wrecked, it does not serve twice. Thus it is even less lasting than the melting or murky produce it encloses.

On all street corners leading to the market, it shines with the modest gleam of whitewood. Still brand new, and somewhat taken aback at being tossed on the trash pile in an awkward pose with no hope of return, this is a most likable object all considered—on whose fate it is perhaps wiser not to dwell. (VT.34–35)

To speak strictly, this is not a prose poem, but a poem in prose.[21] It is not difficult to read Ponge as a language poet, especially because of the way his poems internalize things at hand, as if inhabiting the world and not simply observing it; and also because of the way they internalize words, thickening them by calling attention to their etymological density (Ponge grew up reading an etymological dictionary, and is an obsessive punster). It seems to matter that the crate is a disposable object, or let us say a form of mediation (or transportation) designed to become intransitive or gratuitous, like a poem, which someone once described as leftover language. Of course, in the artworld poems are thought to achieve permanence: their words are used but not used up. However, Ponge thinks of his poems as belonging to a thingworld rather than an artworld.

That is, in Ponge's metaphysics poems and things share the same ontology. Their relation is outside the alternatives of subject and object, or of representational/nonrepresentational art—one could call it (after Emmanuel Levinas) an ethical relation of proximity that reverses subjectivity away from cognition toward contact with things themselves:[22]

LES MÛRES

Aux buissons typographiques constitués par le poème sur une route qui ne mène hors des choses ni à l'esprit, certains fruits sont formés d'une agglomération de sphères qu'une goutte d'encre remplit.

&

Noirs, roses et kakis ensemble sur la grappe, ils offrent plutôt le spectacle d'une famille rogue à ses âges divers, qu'une tentation très vive à la cueillette.

Vue la disproportion des pépins à la pulpe les oiseaux les apprécient peu, si peu de chose au fond leur reste quand du bec à l'anus ils en sont tranverses.

&

Mais le poète au cours de sa promenade professionnelle, en prend de la graine à raison: "Ainsi donc, se dit-il, réussissent en grand nom-

bre les efforts patients d'une fleur très fragile quoique par un rébar-
batif enchevêtrement de ronces défendue. Sans beaucoup d'autres
qualités, —*mûres*, parfaitement elles sont mûres—comme aussi ce
poème est fait." (PP.37)

BLACKBERRIES

On the typographical bushes constituted by the poem, along a road
leading neither away from things nor to the spirit, certain fruits are
formed of an agglomeration of spheres filled by a drop of ink.

↩

Black, pink, khaki all together on the cluster, they offer the spectacle of a haughty family of varying ages rather than a keen temptation
to pick them.
Given the disproportion between seeds and pulp, birds care little for them, since in the
end so little is left once through from beak to anus.

↩

But the poet during his professional stroll is left with something:
"This," he says to himself, "is the way a fragile flower's patient effort
succeeds for the most part, very fragile though protected by a forbidding tangle of thorns. With few other qualities—blackberries [*mûres*],
are perfectly ripe [*mûres*]—just as this poem was made." (VT.34)

Is there a place (between things and the mind) where the poem begins and the blackberries leave off? Ponge wants to say no, rather
there is a space in which different things happen all at once, as in a
pun, and he likes to imagine puns that are made of things as well as
of words. The poem is made of blackberries, even as, being part of
the poem, the blackberries are made of ink, and then one naturally
asks what ink is made of (in antiquity, of pokeberries, whose juice is
black), and in turn what poems are made of, and whether we should
suppress the habit of figuring poets as birds—not birds who sing
about blackberries but birds who eat them, secreting blackberries (or
is it poems?) in the form of ink.
Just so, taking the side of things means siding *with* things, taking
sides against the human world, scaling down the ways in which the
human subject posits itself as a sovereign ego presiding over creation,
perhaps even constructing it. "Notes pour un coquillage," for example, contrasts a seashell with assorted wonders of the world—the
pyramids, the temples of Angkor, and also the Louvre, which (in another thing-pun) Ponge imagines surviving the end of man as a
dwelling place for birds and monkeys, or in other words, as a shell

for larger versions of the hermit crab, which in *Le parti pris des choses* is Ponge's signature thing, creeping from poem to poem. Inverting the scale, a snail's shell is likened to an ideal work of art, not so much because of its form (contrast Valéry's seashell) as for its restraint and acceptance of finitude:

> Et voilà l'example qu'ils nous donnent. Saints, ils font œuvre de leur vie, —œuvre d'art de leur perfectionnement. Leur secrétion même se produit de telle manière qu'elle se met en forme. Rien d'extérieur à eux, à leur necessité, à leur besoin n'est leur œuvre. Rien de disproportionné—d'autre part—à leur être physique. Rien qui ne lui soit nécessaire, obligatoire.(PP.54)

> And that is the lesson they offer us. They are saints, making their life into a work of art—a work of art of their self-perfection. Their very secretion is produced in such a way that that it creates its own form. Nothing exterior to them, to their essence, to their need is of their making. Nothing disproportionate, either, about their physique. Nothing unessential to it, required for it. (VT.45)

We think Michelangelo's *David* a great work of art, but a greater work would be a niche or shell proportioned to fit a human body exactly, with little room left over (PP.76). The problem with monumental works of art, especially since the onset of modernity, is that they are in excess of the world; there is no place for them, and so we house them in artificial rooms like museums, where there is either too much space or too little. As Ponge has it, the task of the poet is to insert poems into the world the way the snail secretes its dribble:

> De ce point de vue j'admire surtout certains écrivains ou musiciens mesurés, Bach, Rameau, Malherbe, Horace, Mallarmé—, les écrivains par-dessus tous les autres parce que leur monument est fait de la véritable sécrétion commune du mollusque homme, de la chose la plus proportionée et conditionnée à son corps, et cependent la plus différante de sa forme que l'on puisse concevoir: je veux dire la PAROLE. (PP.76–77)

> In this sense I most admire a few restrained writers and musicians—Bach, Rameau, Malherbe, Horace, Mallarmé—and writers most of all, because their monument is made of the genuine secretion common to the human mollusk, the thing most

proportioned and suited to his body, yet as utterly different from his form as can be imagined: I mean WORDS. (VT.60–61)

Think of a poem as skin. As if the poem were less a mode of self-expression than a mode of sensibility and therefore less a way of seeing the world than of being touched by it.[23] On this line of thinking our relation with things would not be declarative or possessive but accusative in the way Emmanuel Levinas figures our relation with other people (but also things), where we find ourselves in a condition of sensibility rather than one of cognition and representation. One of Levinas's words for this condition is obsession: others (but one could say things just as well) do not exist for me (*pour soi*), they beset or besiege me (obsession is related etymologically to the ancient and medieval siege); they get under my skin and absorb me—in horror, perhaps, but also in ecstasy or satisfaction. Touching me in this way, or in one way or another, the world materializes itself. It no longer has the spirituality of a concept; it has a thickness to be savored. Levinas writes:

> Savor inasmuch as it satisfies a hunger, savor as quenching, is a breaking up of the form of a phenomenon which becomes amorphous and turns into "prime matter." Matter carries on, "does its job" of being matter, "materializes" in the satisfaction, which fills an emptiness before putting itself into a form and presenting itself to the knowing of this materiality and the possession of it in the form of goods. Tasting is first satisfaction. Matter "materializes" in satisfaction, which, over and beyond any intentional relationship of cognition or possession, of "taking in one's hands," means "biting into." . . . To bite on the bread is the very meaning of tasting. The taste is the way a sensible subject becomes volume, or the irreducible event in which the spatial phenomenon called biting becomes the identification called me.[24]

The movement of Ponge's "Le pain," where observation gives way to biting, captures nicely the scaling down the subject from cognition to sensibility:

> La surface du pain est merveilleuse d'abord à cause de cette impression quasi panoramique qu'elle donne: comme si l'on avait à sa disposition sous la main les Alpes, le Taurus ou la Cordillère des Andes.

Ainsi donc une masse amorphe en train d'éructer fut glissée pour nous dans le four stellaire, où durcissant elle s'est façonnée en vallées, crêtes, ondulations, crevasses. . . . Et tous ces plans dès lors si nettement articulés, ces dalles minces où avec application couche ses feux,—sans un regard pour la mollesse ignoble sous-jacente.

Ce lâche et froid sous-sol que l'on nomme la mie a son tissu pareil à celui des éponges: feuilles ou fleurs y sont comme des sœurs siamoises soudées par tous les coudes à lafois. Lorsque le pain rassit ces fleurs fanent et se rétrécissent: elles se détachent alors les unes de autres, et la masse en devient friable . . .

Mais brisons-la: car le pain doit être dans notre bouche moins objet de respect que de consommation. (PP.46)

The surface of a crusty bread is marvelous, first because of the almost panoramic impression it makes: as though one had the Alps, the Taurus or the Andes at one's fingertips.

It so happened that an amorphous mass about to explode was slid into the celestial oven for us where it hardened and formed valleys, summits, rolling hills, crevasses. . . . And from then on, all those planes so neatly joined, those fine slabs where light carefully beds down its rays—without a thought for the unspeakable mush underneath.

That cold flaccid substratum is made up of sponge-like tissue: leaves or flowers like Siamese twins soldered together elbow to elbow. When bread grows stale, these flowers fade and wither; they fall away from each other and the mass becomes crumbly . . .

But now let's break it up: for in our mouths bread should be less an object of respect than of consumption. (VT.39)

In satisfaction matter materializes—and so do I. I am no longer a consciousness that thinks, a soul beholding the world through looking-glass eyes, but a sequence of openings traversed by the bread that I bite, chew, swallow, digest; and I am nothing without it, a statue by Giacometti at best, but in its wake I am able to maintain a certain density, displace a certain volume of the here and now, before eventually returning, like the bread, to the earth.[25]

Of course it follows that taking the side of things is inevitably comic and satirical in its consequences, since in the thingworld human beings are things (not objects, mind you, but things—unless, Sartre-like, you see someone staring at you).[26] The thingworld is not for sovereign souls. "Les plaisirs de la porte" begins: "Les rois ne touchent pas aux portes" ("Kings do not touch doors"), and so are deprived of "le bonheur d'empoigner au ventre part son nœud de porcelaine l'un de ces hauts obstacles d'une pièce" ("The pleasure of grabbing the midriff of one of these tall obstacles to a room by its porcelain node") (PP.44/VT.38). Presiding over the world deprives one of the experience of it, as if one had to become thinglike in order to know what things are like (one could call this Ponge's Principle).

Meanwhile, on another register, in "Le Gymnaste" the gymnast's density is captured in his letters:

> Comme son **G** l'indique le gymnaste porte le bouc et la moustache que rejoint presque une gross mèche en accroche-cœur sur un front bas.
>
> Moulé dans un maillot qui fait deux plis sur l'aine il porte aussi, comme son **Y**, la queue à gauche. (PP.64)

> Like his **G**, the gymnast wears a goatee and moustache almost reached by the heavy lock on his low forehead.
>
> Molded into a jersey that makes two folds over his groin, he too, like his **Y**, wears his appendage on the left. (VT.52)

(The **Y** should not be printed but handwritten according to the Palmer Method.)

In "R.C. Seine n°," Kafka-like, a stairwell that funnels employees like coffee beans to and from a modern office becomes a window onto filing cabinets, typewriters, ledgers, forms, carbon paper, and the passage of the daily mail across the poet's desk—Ponge is no outsider but is himself a thing in the thingworld:

> Deux ou trois fois par jour, au milieu de ce culte, le courrier multicolore, radieux et bête comme un oiseau des îles, tout frais émoulu des enveloppes marquées de noir par le baiser de la poste, vient tout de go se poser devant moi.
>
> Chaque feuille étrangère est alors adoptée, confiée à une petite colombe de chez nous, qui la guide à des destinations successives jusqu'à son classement.

Certains bijoux servent à ces attelages momentanés: coins dorés, attaches parisiennes, trombones attendent dans des sébiles leur utilisation. (PP.68)

Two or three times a day, in the middle of this ceremony, the mail—multicolored, gleaming, dumb, like tropical birds—suddenly plops down in front of me, fresh from envelopes bearing a black postal kiss.

Each foundling sheet is then adopted, handed over to one of our little carrier pigeons who guides it to successive destinations until its final classification.

Certain jewels are used for these temporary harnessings: gilded corners, glowing clasps, gleaming paper clips all wait in their beggars' cups to be of service. (VT.54)

In Ponge's metaphysics there is no order of things but only a ceaseless flow of traffic in which the poet, one random floating particle among others, accompanies with his rich, colorful language the ongoing large and small career of things—for example, at lunchtime, he flows into a restaurant favored by fellow office workers, Lemeunier's, on the Rue de la Chaussée d'Antin (according to Walter Benjamin, a philistine street):[27]

Des glaces biseautées, des dorures partout. L'on y entre à travers des plantes vertes par une passage plus sombre aux parois duquel quelques dîneurs déjà à l'étroit sont installés, et qui débouche dans une salle aux proportions énormes, à plusieurs balcons de pitchpin formant un seul étage en huit, où vous accueillent à la fois des bouffées d'odeurs tièdes, le tapage des fourchettes et des assiettes choquées, les appels des serveuses et le bruit des conversations. (PP.70)

Bevelled mirrors, gilded moldings everywhere. One enters past green plants through a darker passage, against whose walls a few clients are already tightly installed, which leads to a room of huge proportions with a number of wooden balconies forming the figure eight. There you are assailed by billows of warm odors, clattering cutlery and dishes, shouting waitresses and the din of conversation. (VT.56)

It is, the poet says, a scene worthy of a painting by Veronese or Manet, but since a fixed point of view is impossible, the scene can only form itself in fragments:

Des entremets à plusieurs étages crémeux hardiment super-posés, servis dans des cupules d'un métal mystérieux, hautes de pied mais rapidement lavées et malheureusement toujours tièdes, permettent aux consommateurs qui choisirent qu'on les disposât devant eux, de manifester mieux que par d'autres signes les sentiments profonds qui les animent. Chez l'un, c'est l'enthousiasme que lui procure la présence à ses côtes d'une dactylo magnifiquement ondulée, pour laquelle il n'hésiterait pas à commettre mille autres coûteuses folies du même genre. . . .

Par milliers cependent les miettes blondes et de grandes imprèg-nations roses sont en même temps apparues sur le linge épars ou tendu.

Une peu plus tard, les briquets se saisissent du premier rôle; selon le dispositif qui actionne la molette ou la façon don't ils sont maniés. Tandis qu'élevant les bras dans un mouvement qui découvre à leurs aisselles leur façon personnelle d'arborer les cocardes de la transpiration, les femmes se roiffent ou jouent du tube de fard.

C'est l'heure où, dans un brouhaha recrudescent de chaises repoussés, de torchons claquants, de croûtons écrasés, va s'accomplier le dernier rite de la singulière cérémonie. Succes-sivement, de chacun de leurs hôtes, les serveuses, don't un car-net habite la poche et les cheveux un petit crayon, rapproachent leurs ventres serrés d'une façon si touchante par les cordons du tablier: elles se livrent de mémoire à une rapide estimation. C'est alors que la vanité est punie et la modestie récompensée. Pièces et billets bleus s'échangent sur les tables: il semble que chacun retire son épingle du jeu. (PP.72–73)

Creamy layered desserts piled daringly high—served in bowls of mysterious metal, handsomely footed but rapidly washed and always warm, alas—allow the diners who chose to have them displayed, to manifest more effectively than by other signs their deep feelings. For one, it is enthusiasm generated by the splen-didly curved typist at his side, for whom he would not hesitate to commit a thousand equally costly follies. . . .

Meanwhile, thousands of blond crumbs and pink blotches ap-pear on the scattered or spread linen.

A little later, cigarette lighters take the leading role, according to the striking device or manner of handling; while the ladies, raising their arms in such a way that their armpits reveal each personal style of wearing perspiration's badges, rearrange their hair or toot their lipstick tubes.

This is the moment—amid the increasing tumult of chairs scraping, napkins snapping, crumbs crushing—for the final ritual in this unique ceremony. Moving their sweetly aproned tummies close to each guest in turn, a notebook in their pocket, a pencil stub in their hair, the waitresses apply themselves from memory to a rapid calculation. It is then that vanity is punished and modesty rewarded. Coins and bills change hands across the table, as though everybody were cashing in his chips. (VT.57–58)

Notice how things occupy the grammatical site of agents—"cigarette lighters take the leading role," "[c]oins and bills change hands"—and when humans appear they are (or at least the women are) materialized as perspiring armpits, fingered hair, lipsticked lips, and aproned tummies: figures of one thing touching or being touched by another.

Traditional poetics thinks of language as mediating the space between mind and things, turning things into the mind by means of figures, images, or various propositional attitudes that elevate things to the level of the concept. Ponge's poetics thinks of language as mediating the space between mind and things in the other direction—not elevating things to the category of spirit but turning spirit into things by means of the thingliness of words, emphasizing the way words have histories and so are self-subsistent like things in themselves and thus set apart from the way we try to reduce them to their logical or semantic operations. So words cease to be instruments of the spirit and become instead components of the thingworld, drawing us out of ourselves and into the world, which is where, Ponge seems to think, we are better off. At any rate the point is to think of the word not as a medium for inserting the world into the mind but of inserting the mind into the world. The materiality or, what amounts to the same thing, the historicity of language makes this inhabitation possible. The poet Charles Bernstein reincarnates Ponge's ghost when he writes:

    The thickness of writing,
    far from rivaling that of the world,

is on the contrary the sole
means it has to go to the heart of things
by making itself part of the material world, absorbed
by it.[28]

Realspace. Placing a real thing in the space of art transforms or, to
use Arthur Danto's word, "transfigures" it: the thing is still what it
is and yet at the same time is beside itself, irreducible to what it is
empirically.[29] Remove the chair from the stage and it becomes a chair
again. Meanwhile the musician John Cage shares with Francis
Ponge and David Antin the desire to reinsert works of art into the
everyday world. In an essay on Erik Satie (who once said, "J'em-
merde l'Art," and once composed a piece called "Furniture Music")
Cage writes: "We must bring about a music which is like furniture — a music, that is, which will be part of the noises of the environment, will take them into consideration. I think of it as melodious,
softening the noises of the knives and forks, not dominating them,
not imposing itself."[30] Naturally one thinks again of Adorno to give
this point its definition: "The concept of form marks out art's sharp
antithesis to an empirical world in which art's right to exist is uncertain. Art has precisely the same chance of survival as form does, no
better" (AT.141/AeT.213; cf. AT.252–53/AeT.375). But in Cage's
aesthetic the artwork can no longer be distinguished from real things
by means of formal criteria. The artworld has, so to speak, been
blended into the thingworld and has become, to all appearances, imperceptibly a part of it.

Perhaps all but imperceptibly; perhaps almost but not quite imperceptibly. In "Experimental Music" (1957) Cage says that in his
music "nothing takes place but sounds: those that are notated and
those that are not. Those that are not notated appear in the written
music as silences, opening the doors of the music to the sounds that
happen to be in the environment. This openness exists in the fields
of modern sculpture and architecture. The glass houses of Mies van
der Rohe reflect their environment, presenting to the eye images of
clouds, trees, or grass, according to the situation. And while looking
at the constructions in wire of the sculptor Richard Lippold, it is inevitable that one will see other things, and people too, if they happen
to be there at the same time, through the network of wires" (S.8). Of
course, what is presented to the eye in one of Mies van der Rohe's
glass houses are not the *images* of trees and grass (nor perceptions of
them) but the things themselves; likewise what is presented to the

ear in a performance of one of Cage's compositions are not musical sounds set apart in a world of their own but musical sounds restored to the real space we inhabit. The question for Cage in this event is not how to tell the music from nonmusic but how to inhabit a world in which the two are no longer detachable on the basis of distinctive features; in other words, *how to listen*, not just in the music hall, but in everyday life. Aesthetics has, in effect, been reconceptualized as ethics.

What kind of ethics, then? Not an ethics of rules but (invoking Levinas again) an ethics of proximity, sensibility, and responsiveness ("In the ethical relationship with the real, that is, in the relationship of proximity that the sensible establishes . . . the visible caresses the eye. One sees and hears like one touches" [CPP.118]). Cage imagines a composer with two choices. One is to create new sorts of sound by electronic means (a new technological innovation at the time Cage wrote his essay); the other is to "give up the desire to control sound, clear [one's] mind of music, and set about discovering means to let sounds be themselves rather than vehicles for man-made theories or expressions of human sentiments" (S.10). The idea here is not to elevate mere sound to the status of art but to relocate art at the level of everyday experience. Cage thinks of this as learning to inhabit the world in a new way, learning to acknowledge the world instead of reflecting ourselves out of it as Adorno urges. In an essay on "The Abstract Expressionist Coca-Cola Bottle," Arthur Danto writes:

> Pop redeemed the world in an intoxicating way. I have the most vivid recollection of standing at an intersection in some American city, waiting to be picked up. There were used-car lots on two corners, with swags of plastic pennants fluttering in the breeze and brash signs proclaiming unbeatable deals, crazy prices, insane bargains. There was a huge self-service gas station on a third corner, and a supermarket on the fourth, with signs in the window announcing sales of Del Monte, Cheerios, Land O Lakes butter, Long Island ducklings, Velveeta, Sealtest, Chicken of the Sea. . . . Heavy trucks roared past, with logos on their sides. The sound of raucous music flashed out of the windows of automobiles. I was educated to hate all this. I would have found it intolerably crass and tacky when I was growing up an aesthete. As late as my own times, beauty was, in the words of George Santayana, "a living presence, or an

aching absence, day and night." I think it still is that for someone like Clement Greenberg and Hilton Kramer. But I thought, Good heavens. This is just remarkable! (BBB.139–40)

The Collector. Walter Benjamin says that Eduard Fuchs's achievement as a collector began with his break with "the classicist conception of art."[31] No more masterpieces. "He is not the only great collector to feel an aversion to museums" (GS.2.2:502/SW.3:282). Not a collector, in other words, like Henry James's Adam Verver (Morgan, Carnegie, Rockefeller, Getty), who ransacked Europe's treasures and transported them to the museum of museums in "American City." According to Benjamin, Fuchs's "goal was to restore to the work of art its existence within society" (GS.2.2:503/SW.3:283). He did this by collecting not artworks but the products of mass culture—in particular, caricatures and pornography—as if a true collector collected from below. But, as Benjamin complains, we lack a theory of the collector (GS.2.2:489–90/SW.3:275). Literature gives us no interesting representations of collectors, with the exception of Balzac's Cousin Pons, who gives collecting a kind of precapitalist poetics (GS.2.2:490/SW.3:275).[32] Benjamin would have rejected Henry James's collectors, even though the true collector for James is a woman like Maria Gostrey who gathers small, inexpensive things that are nevertheless exquisite to a sensibility like Lambert Strether's, on whom nothing is lost. Benjamin would have preferred André Breton, or anyhow the narrator of *Nadja*, who goes frequently to the Saint-Ouen flea market in search of "objects that can be found nowhere else: old-fashioned, broken, useless, almost incomprehensible, even perverse."[33] It seems important to him that the objects intimate a principle of nonidentity, "like, for example, that kind of irregular, white, shellacked half-cylinder covered with reliefs and depressions that are meaningless to me, streaked with horizontal and vertical reds and greens, preciously nestled under a legend in Italian, which I brought home and which after careful examination I have finally identified as some kind of statistical device, operating three-dimensionally and recording the population of a city in such and such a year, though this makes it no more comprehensible to me" (N.52). On another day he finds a new copy of Rimbaud's *Œuvres complètes*, "lost in a tiny, wretched bin of rags, yellowed nineteenth-century photographs, worthless books, and iron spoons" (N.52–55), but what is important to him are "two sheets of paper stuck between the pages: one a typewritten copy of a poem in free verse, the other a pencilled series of reflections on Nietzsche" (N.55). As if the true collector were not an art collector or a collector of valuables but simply a keeper of *Wunderkammern*. But what Breton is after may be something like sheer thingness (the nonidentical thing).

Jacques Lacan admitted to being a collector of sorts, like Freud. But Freud liked exotic objects. Lacan's theory, which unfortunately he only sketches, is that the true collector doesn't collect "objects." He recalls visiting his friend the poet Jacques Prévert during the Occupation when of course no one could afford to do much collecting, but Prévert had assembled (of all things) a collection of match boxes:

> Only the match boxes appeared as follows: they were all the same and were laid out in an extremely agreeable way that involved each one being so close to the next one that the little drawer was slightly displaced. As a result they were all threaded together so as to form a continuous ribbon that ran along the mantlepiece, climbed the wall, extended to the molding, and climbed down again next to a door. I don't say it went on to infinity but it was extremely satisfying from an ornamental point of view.[34]

However, the ornamental point of view is not, Lacan thinks, the relevant one: "I believe that the shock of the novelty of the effect realized by this collection of empty boxes—and this is the essential point—was to reveal something that we do not perhaps pay enough attention to, namely, that a box of matches is not simply an object, but that, in the form of an *Erscheinung*, as it appeared in its truly imposing multiplicity, it may be a Thing" (SJL.114). The match box is not an object *pour soi*, that is, it is not (philosophically speaking) an intentional object or even an equipmental being on the order of Heidegger's hammer. In its throwaway condition (these are empty matchboxes, which is to say they no longer serve their function), the match box is like a broken hammer in Heidegger's ontology: it falls out of the world to which it has belonged and so becomes (like the stone in Heidegger's "The Origin of the Work of Art") a merely thingly thing, part of the self-secluding earth. It exists, thinglike, as a nonproductive expenditure of being, a being for nothing or in itself, like Rilke's song ("a breath for nothing").[35] As Lacan formulates it, "This arrangement demonstrated that a match box isn't simply something that has a certain utility, that it isn't even a type in the Platonic sense, an abstract match box, that the match box all by itself is a thing with all of its coherence of being. The wholly gratuitous, proliferating, superfluous, and quasi-absurd character of this collection pointed to its thing-ness as match box. Thus the collector found his motive in this form of apprehension that concerns less the match box than the Thing that subsists in the match box" (SJL.114). Of course, Lacan is allegoriz-ing the match box as a Lacanian *Ding*. The point may be more ele-mentary: the collection of match boxes just bears witness to the match box as a thing in itself, a *singularity* (not a particular vis-à-vis a universal). The collection does not constitute a genus or category; each match box makes its appearance as its own thing and not as a stand-in for something else. Like Meister Eckhart's rose, it is "with-out why."

Naturally thoughts fly to Jacques Prévert: how would he explain his match boxes? Like Ponge (and like the language poets) Prévert was thoroughly at home in the nonpoetical world. And so his poems are occasionally no more than inventories of expressions and some-times of mere things, as if, as a poet, he were still simply a collector of things like match boxes. His first collection of poems, *Paroles*, is a collection of *paroles*. One of the poems in the collection is "Inventaire":

Une pierre	One stone
deux maisons	two houses
trois ruines	three ruins
quatre fossoyeurs	four gravediggers
une jardin	one garden
des fleurs	some flowers
une raton laveur	a racoon
une douzaine d'huîtres un citron un pain	a dozen oysters a lemon a loaf
un rayon du soleil	a ray of sunshine
une lame de fond	a groundswell
six musiciens	six musicians
une porte avec son paillson	a door with doormat
un monsieur décoré de la légion d'honneur	a man decorated with the legion of honor
une autre raton laveur	another racoon
un sculpteur qui sculpte des Napoléon	a sculptor who only sculpts Napoleons
la fleur qu'on appelle aussi	the flower called marigold
deux amoureaux sur un grand lit	two lovers on a big bed
un receveur des contributions une chaise trois dindons	a tax collector three chairs a turkey

ecclésiastique un furoncle	a clergyman a carbuncle
une guêpe	a wasp
un rein flottant	one floating kidney
une écurie de courses	a racing-stable
un fils indigne deux frères	one worthless son two dominican
dominicains trois	brothers
sautereles un strapontin	three twisters one jump-seat
deux filles de joie un oncle	two whores one pederast
Cyprien. . . .	uncle. . . .[36]

And so on. The poem adds some fifty further items to its list, including four or five more racoons. Poetry as kitsch? Or poetry as a *Wund-*
erkammer that collects ordinary things instead of oddities? (A
Pleinkammer? — think of Joseph Cornell's Boxes.) A critical point
would be to see the poem as testimony to the way the poet inhabits
his world. For example, Benjamin distinguishes the collector from
the *flâneur* by saying that the one is in contact with things that the
other merely observes (a Levinasian reversal): "Possessions and having are allied with the tactile, and stand in a certain opposition to the
optical. Collectors are beings with tactile instincts. Moreover, with
the recent turn away from naturalism, the primacy of the optical that
was determinate for the previous century has come to an end"
(GS.5.1:274/AP.206–7). The *flâneur* is a window-shopper in the arcades where things are for sale; the collector constructs an environment in which things are no longer fungible but can now simply
exist, abiding opaquely in themselves (that is, nothing is to be seen by
trying to look through them) — although Benjamin thinks that inside
every collector an allegorist is struggling to get free (GS.5.1:279–80/
AP.211). One can imagine Duchamp as a collector whose desire is
not simply to see the world in a certain way (as an impressionist or
cubist, for example) but simply to relocate things in a kind of free
space (as if following the law of Bataille's general economy). However we imagine him, Duchamp fits Benjamin's definition: "the true
collector detaches the object from its functional relations"
(GS.5.1:274/AP.207). To what end? Perhaps to achieve a kind of
transcendence that Benjamin alone knew how to experience:

> There is in the life of a collector a dialectical tension between
> the poles of order and disorder. Naturally, his existence is tied
> to many other things as well: to a very mysterious relationship
> to ownership . . . ; also, to a relationship to objects which does
> not emphasize their functional, utilitarian value — that is, their

usefulness—but studies and loves them as the scene, the stage, of their fate. The most profound enchantment for the collector is the locking of individual items within a magic circle in which they are fixed as the final thrill, the thrill of acquisition, passes over them. Everything remembered and thought, everything conscious, becomes the pedestal, the frame, the base, the lock of his property. The period, the region, the craftsmanship, the former ownership—for a true collector the whole background of an item adds up to a magic encyclopedia whose quintessence is the fate of his object. In this circumscribed area, then, it may be surmised how the great physiognomists—and collectors are the physiognomists of the world of objects—turn into interpreters of fate. One has only to watch a collector handle the objects in his glass case. As he holds them in his hands, he seems to be seeing through them into their distant past as though inspired. So much for the magical side of the collector—his age-old image, I might call it.[37]

This suggests a question concerning the difference between collected and uncollected things that is perhaps analogous to the question of what happens to things in art. Recall that Ponge's things remain unappropriated: Ponge does not preside over them, has no claim on them—quite the reverse. In Heidegger's lingo, he lets things be things. Benjamin's things are objects, that is, things that have been transformed, although not, strictly, into works of art, as if the collector belonged to a between-world made of "no-longer-things" and "not-quite-artworks": the world of the uncommodified fetish (postcards, children's books).

Transfiguration. Heidegger complains that for philosophers there are no such things as things, only objects held in place by concepts and assertions. Likewise in the *Gestell* of modernity things do not exist; there are only materials that we feed into conversion-systems where they come out as mere objects or products. Left to themselves, however, things produce nothing. They simply *thing*. In the thinging of the thing, nearness comes into play, drawing together earth and sky, gods and mortals. So a world is gathered together in which building and dwelling can occur.[38] A future is possible if we let things be things (*Gelassenheit zu den Dingen*). Likewise for Adorno there are (owing to modernity) no things, only products or fetishes. The task of art is to lift products out of their reified condition and restore them to thingness, that is, to their singularity on the hither side of identity: "In its relation to empirical reality art sublimates the latter's governing principle of *sese conservare* as the ideal of the self-identity of its works; as Schönberg said, one paints a painting, not what it represents. Inherently every artwork desires identity with itself, an identity that in empirical reality is violently forced on all objects as identity with the subject and is thus travestied. Aesthetic identity seeks to aid the nonidentical, which in reality is repressed by reality's compulsion to identify. . . . Artworks are afterimages of empirical life insofar as they help the latter to what is denied them outside their own sphere and thereby free it from that to which they are condemned by reified external experience" (AT.4/AeT.14). Again: "In its relation to its other—whose foreignness it mollifies and yet maintains—form is what is antibarbaric in art: through form art participates in the civilization that it criticizes by its very existence. Form is the law of the transfiguration of the existing, counter to which it represents freedom" (AT.143/AeT.186).

"The transfiguration of the existing": so art is redemptive (thinks Adorno), as in, "The idea of art as the idea of the restoration of nature that has been repressed and drawn into the dynamic of history. Nature, to whose image art is devoted, does not yet in any way exist; what is true in art is something non-existent. What does not exist becomes incumbent upon art in that other for which identity-positing reason, which reduced it to material, uses the word nature. This other is not concept and unity, but rather a multiplicity" (AT.131/AeT.198). That is, what we call "nature" is made of singularities: not things constituted as an order of things but nonidentical things, opaque and self-standing in their reserve.

But what would Adorno accept as an instance of transfiguration? He has his heroes (Beckett, Kafka, Schönberg), but mostly Adorno is impressed by the failure of modernism to bring redemption to term ("what after all is left to do but scream?" [AT.30/AeT.51]). Recall his contrast between impressionism and montage ("the sudden, discontinuous juxtaposition of sequences"): "Impressionism dissolved objects—drawn primarily from the sphere of technical civilization or its amalgams with nature—into their smallest elements in order to synthesize them gaplessly into the dynamic continuum. It wanted aesthetically to redeem the alienated and the heterogeneous in the replica. The conception proved ever less adequate the more intense the superiority of the reified prosaic world over the living subject became. The subjectivization of objective reality relapsed into romanticism. . . . It was against this that montage protested, which developed out of the pasted-in newspaper clippings and the like during the heroic years of cubism" (AT.154–55/AeT.232). By "admitting into itself literal, illusionless ruins of empirical reality," cubism inaugurates modernism as objectivism and fragmentariness. Henceforward, "The artwork wants to make the facts eloquent by letting them speak for themselves. Art thereby begins a process of destroying the artwork as a nexus of meaning. For the first time in the development of art, affixed debris cleaves visible scars in the work's meaning. This brings montage into a much broader context. All modern art after impressionism . . . may be called montage" (AT.155/AeT.232–33). However, this is not to redeem things. "Montage is the inner-aesthetic capitulation of art to what stands heterogeneously opposed to it. The negation of synthesis becomes a principle of form" (AT.155/ AeT.233). But this is a form that dissipates in a twinkling: "The principle of montage was conceived as an act against a surreptitiously achieved organic unity; it was meant to shock. Once this shock is neutralized, the assemblage once more becomes merely indifferent material" (AT.233/AeT.155–56). As in Duchamp, after the initial shock, the form of "the work" is swallowed up by form of the thing itself, semblance gives way to a "barbaric literalism" (AT.158/ AeT.103), so one is left to explain, in the manner of Arthur Danto, how "anything can be a work of art," even though not everything can be one all by itself (TC.65).

Danto's standpoint is much like Adorno's—not surprisingly, since the starting-point for both is Hegel. Like Adorno, Danto believes that art is irreducible to the stuff of which it is made. Like Adorno, he holds the now-canonical idea that modernism just *is* the pressing of art to the material (although maybe not the conceptual) limits of its possibility. Recall Clement Greenberg's famous statement about modernism: "The essential norms or conventions of painting are at the same time the limiting conditions with which a picture must comply in order to be experienced as a picture. Modernism has found that these limits can be pushed back indefinitely before a picture stops being a picture and turns into an arbitrary object; but it has also found that the further back these limits are pushed the more explicitly they have to be observed and indicated."[39] Unlike Greenberg (and Adorno), Danto thinks that the artwork (Warhol's *Brillo Box*, say) can stop looking like a picture and start looking for all the world like an arbitrary object and still be something different from "a mere thing." The difference is what Danto calls transfiguration, after "the

Hegelian ideal in which matter is transfigured into spirit" (TC.111). Danto says that art was invented to give reality something to contrast itself with (TC.78–79). Modernism narrows this contrast to the point of indiscernability, whence the history of art can be said without metaphor to have come to an end in the sense that the artwork (*Fountain*, *Brillo Box*, thingpoem, talkpoem, monochrome) ceases to be an aesthetic object and becomes an object that asks, with thinglike inscrutability, a philosophical question: What is art?[40]—as if the art object were to be defined as an object that raised this question. Of course, if the transfigured thing, as Joseph Margolis points out, is after all still the thing it is, however thoughtful or eloquent, we can imagine it to be asking just as well what a thing is.[41]

Assuming that the form of the question, "What is —?," is adequate to the task. For a thing, at the end of the day, is *matter*. Let me conclude in an open-ended way by citing Jean-François Lyotard. In an essay, "After the Sublime, the State of Aesthetics," Lyotard says, in his characteristically paradoxical fashion, that "matter" is *immaterial*: that is, the mind cannot constitute it as an object of any predicate. Modernism for Lyotard is what gravitates toward this resistant or indifferent "matter" that "can only 'take place' or find its occasion at the price of suspending [the] active powers of the mind."[42] (He mentions John Cage vis-à-vis sounds that are allowed to be themselves.) The "matter" of modernism is a *thing* of pure exteriority:

> The paradox of art "after the sublime" is that it turns toward a thing which does not turn toward the mind, that it wants a thing, or *has it in for* a thing which wants nothing of it. After the sublime, we find ourselves after the will. By matter, I mean *the Thing*. The Thing is not waiting to be destined, it is not waiting for anything, it does not call on the mind. How can the mind situate itself, get in touch with something that withdraws from every relationship?
>
> It is the destiny or destination of the mind to question (as I have just done). And to question is to attempt to establish the relation of something with something. Matter does not question the mind, it has no need of it, it exists, or rather *insists*, it sists "before" questioning and answer, "outside" them. It is presence as unpresentable to the mind, always withdrawn from its grasp. It does not offer itself to dialogue and dialectic. (IR.142)

So a *thing* cannot be thought. It is a limit-experience. Lyotard asks: "Can we find an analogue of matter in the order of thought itself?"—

that is, a quasi-*thing*? I think he gives a good answer: "Perhaps words themselves, in the most secret place of thought, are its matter, its timbre, its nuance, i.e. what it cannot manage to think. Words 'say,' sound, touch, always 'before' thought. . . . Words want nothing. They are the 'un-will,' the 'non-sense' of thought, its mass. . . . But like timbres and nuances, they are always being born. Thought tries to tidy them up, arrange them, control them and manipulate them. But as they are old people and children, words are not obedient. As Gertrude Stein thought, to write is to respect their candor and their age" (IR.142–43).

The Senses of Augustine: On Some of Lyotard's Remains

For Jim Dougherty

Oh Lord, you have stricken my heart.
— *The Confessions,* 10.6

The Pagan. At the time of his death in 1998 the French philosopher Jean-François Lyotard had begun writing what was to have been a substantial work on Augustine's *Confessions.* In the event he has left us only fragments—notes, paragraphs, *envois,* sketches, and two lectures stitched together to form a kind of monograph called "La Confession d'Augustin": *the* confession, referring, as we shall see, to Augustine's confession of his love for God. Like all of Lyotard's productions, this posthumous assembly leaves us guessing as to what kind of writing it is supposed to be. In fact Lyotard was never much more than a writer of fragments (or, in his terms, rudiments, instructions, discussions). Like Sade and Balzac, or Sartre and Derrida, he was someone who could not stop writing even when he wanted to, but he was not monumental—call him a *low* modernist. He thought that writing or thinking should not be the construction of systems, theories, works, or conceptual worlds but simply "an affair of linking phrases [*une affaire d'enchaînment de phrases*]," supposing we know what phrases are (Di.130/D.86).[1] The idea is *not* to assemble phrases into wholes: no more "big talk."[2] *Enchaînment* is rhizomorphous like grass, not arboreal like a tree.[3] Lyotard preferred the address (*l'adresse*) to books, saying that "in the next century there will be no more books," which even now are produced to be sold rather than read (Di.13/D.xv). He said that the "genre" of *Le Différend* (1983) "is that of Observations, Remarks, Thoughts, Studies, and Notes which are relative to an object; in other words, a discontinuous form of the Essay" (Di.12/D.xiv). And he called his most systematic text "lessons," or "a file of notes for the oral explication" of some pages of Kant's *Critique of Judgment*.[4] He invented an original and useful definition of paganism: "When I speak of paganism, I am not using a concept. It is a name, neither better nor worse than others, for the denomination of a situation in which one judges *without criteria*. And one judges not only in matters of truth, but also in matters of beauty (of aesthetic efficacy) and in matters of justice, that is, of politics and ethics, and all without criteria. That's what I mean by paganism" (AJ.33/JG.16).[5] Substitute writing for judging and you can see that Lyotard was in this anarchic sense a pagan writer—and moreover he seems to have thought of himself as encountering in Augustine another pagan writer in just this sense of someone who does not proceed by applying criteria (laws, concepts, methods, rules, categories, distinctions, models, paradigms, master narratives, universals) but who exists in a state of *passibility*: "If we are in a state of passibility, it's that something is happening to us . . . [and] what happens is not at all something we have first controlled, programmed, or grasped by a concept [*Begriff*]. Or else, if what we are passible to has first been plotted conceptually, how can it *seize* us? How can it test us if we already know, or if we can know—of what, with what, for what, it is done?" (In.121–22/I.111). "Passibility" is a neologism that puns on *passivity* and *possibility*, where passivity is not mere passiveness as opposed to activity but an openness to what happens (*se passer*), a disposition free of calculation, being "on guard," plotting, grasping, eyes alert to the main chance. Passability is something like a condition of experience, or at all events experiences of a certain specialty (epiphanies, theophanies, encounters of the third kind). Living without criteria is not a state of privation; anarchy is a condition of possibility. Meanwhile Lyotard also linked up with Augustine as one pagan to another in the more familiar sense of being an ungodly creature, a vagrant of the flesh longing for "I don't know what" (justice, *le tout autre*, the good beyond being). The pagan is a creature caught within the interminability of the *entretemps*, the meanwhile or caesura between the *no longer* and *not yet* in which, most famously, the Messiah is experienced as the imminent one who does not appear, or, as Lyotard says, one of those who can "only come by not arriving [*Ils ne viennent qu'en n'arrivant pas*]" (Di.118/D.77). Lyotard's watchword is: "*Is it happening [Arrive-t-il]?* (the *it* indicating an empty place to be occupied by a referent)" (Di.120/D.79).[6] The pagan is a creature of waiting, suffering, and supplication—a figure of hope rather than of faith, belief, or religious knowledge.[7] These paganisms are where Lyotard's interest in Augustine lies. Without trying to match Lyotard's thought point for point I would like to explore and expand upon this interest, situating it where possible in its various literary and intellectual contexts.

Libidinal Theology. Lyotard had taken up Augustine once before, in *Economie libidinale* (1974), a zany book that, in the spirit of May '68, sought to graft Freud onto Marx in the interest of a more realistic, practical, and (how to say it?) sexier materialism. The main idea of a "libidinal economy" is that desire inhabits social systems in the form of drives or pulsions that bedevil organizations of power and money (not to mention institutions of knowledge). Whereas power and money are productive, at least for those in control, desire is anarchic, an energy that simply wants to spend itself (*jouissance*) and which cannot easily be converted to use, profit, or perhaps even pleasure. Power and money are rational but desire is not. In a libidinal economy return on investment is not guaranteed, and may not even be desired. Libido defeats control. In any case the idea here is that every social institution, practice, discipline, discourse, or relation is libidinal—a wellspring of sexual energies or "intensities"—and not just a logical system that can be justified (or not) in terms of its operations and results. To illustrate how the libidinal economy works Lyotard cites Augustine's polemic against Varro in book 6 of *De civitate Dei*. Varro had distinguished three types or dimensions of theology—natural theology, which is the province of philosophers; mythical philosophy, which is the province of poets; and civic theology, which is the province of the state, or indeed of the whole system of social and domestic administration, from control of the empire to what Foucault has called "care of the self."[8] Augustine accepted the first of these theologies (how could a good Ciceronian do otherwise?) but ridiculed the theatricality of mythical and civic theology as the production of mere simulacra, images of fantastic beings, aphrodisiacs or narcotics for arousing and intoxicating the senses. Special effects (simulacra are not images of things but images in place of things). Pagan theology does not study or even worship the gods; it merely cultivates the pleasure of representing them. Against Augustine, Lyotard has (as I make them out: they are not easy to see) two repostes. One is: What could be more theatrical than the Trinity, in which the Son in his relation to the Father is "the *Simulacrum in itself*," not an image of a being but the incarnation of what is otherwise than being (EL.87/LE.69)? The Son after all does not close down the Roman theater but upstages it (Golgotha), turning his incarnation into the most unforgettable icon of libidinal skin in the abject state of suffering, abandonment, and death. The second reposte is more to the point of Augustine's *Confessions*. In place of Varro's system, in which every human experience gives rise to a divinity, Augustine had appealed to the "omnitemporally real Present" of an invisible God, "the great Zero," as Lyotard plausibly calls him: the No One who, appearances aside, does not abolish or repress the libidinal economy of Roman religion but appropriates it, focusing and intensifying desire, drawing it toward himself (if "himself" is the word) by the sheer force of his transcendence (EL.33–35/LE.8–10). A basic Platonic thesis is that desire exists not in the presence of the good but in its wake. Or, as the theologian Jean-Luc Marion says, our desire for God is coterminous with the infinity of his *distance*: the one is impossible without the other.[9] In any case there is no separating theology from desire as if our relation to God could be merely philosophical or contemplative. The God whom we experience is exactly the one who withholds himself from appearance and apprehension, and who is most absolutely out of reach at precisely the moment when he visits us in the most libidinal way, turning us inside out as subjects exposed to his absence, leaving us to experience the absolute abjection of longing for what is untouchable, unnameable, unimaginable, unknowable, unthinkable, and deathly silent: God as the event of the good (the desirable) beyond being (*hyperousia*). (Lyotard would perhaps prefer: God as the *sublime*.) In this theology, as Marion says, "the intimacy of the divine coincides strictly with withdrawal [*le retrait*]" (IeD.183/ID.139). However we figure it, our relation to such a God is (as in *das Mystische*) outside cognition, outside the alternatives of propositions and negations, *but not outside desire*. Lyotard would say: neither positive nor negative but *libidinal theology*. Our relation to God can only be a relation of prayer (a psalm), which Lyotard describes neatly as "the carnal rhythm of call and abandonment [*rythme charnel d'appels et de derelictions*]" (CdA.111/CA.85).[10]

Augustine, Son of Ovid. *The Libidinal Economy* helps to explain why Lyotard's interest in *The Confessions* is confined almost entirely to book 10, the book of memory and concupiscence in which, before everything else, Augustine finally confesses his love for God—and *to him* (the modality of address, of prayer and praise, tells the whole story of *The Confessions*).[11] And confessing this he asks: "But when I love you, what do I love?"[12] The question sends Augustine on the great introspective journey in which at last he locates God in his memory (that "stomach of the mind" [10.14/C.191]). What does he remember of God? Not a presence but an irrepressible experience of the senses. Lyotard's *The Confession of Augustine* begins here, citing 10.27, which he refers to henceforward as "the syncope" (CdA.33/CA.15):

> Late have I loved you, beauty so old and so new: late have I loved you. And see, you were within and I was in the external world and sought you there, and in my unlovely [*deformis*] state I plunged into those lovely created things which you made. You were with me, and I was not with you. The lovely things kept me far from you, though if they did not have their existence in you, they had no existence at all. You called and cried out loud [*vocasti et clamasti*] and shattered my deafness. You were radiant and resplendent [*coruscasti, splenduisti*], you put flight to my blindness. You were fragrant, and I drew in my breath and now pant after you. I tasted you, and I feel but hunger and thirst for you. You touched me, and I am set on fire to attain the peace which is yours. (10.27/C.201)

A question Augustine does not ask is: With what *kind* of love do I love you, my God? Theologies of various stripes, whose obligation is to save the text according to the rule of faith, have never doubted the answer: *agapē, caritas*.[13] Philosophy meanwhile allegorizes the text by saying that Augustine is just being poetic, after the manner of *The Song of Songs* or Socrates in the *Phædrus*: in reading the point is not to allow the letter to confound the spirit. Remember Augustine on signs. However, Lyotard the pagan reads according to the flesh, libidinously emphasizing the gender switch: "Thus the lover excites the five mouths of the woman, swells her vowels, those of ear, of eye, of nose and tongue, and skin that stridulates [to "stridulate" is to make a shrill grating or chirping sound by rubbing certain body parts together the way crickets do]. At present he is consumed by your fire, impatient for the return to peace that your fivefold ferocity brings him" (CdA.18/CA.2). Not to put too fine a point on it, Lyotard says (addressing God): "you [*tu*] took him as a woman"

(CdA.19/CA.3). And he insists on the image of sexual assault: "The flesh, forced five times, violated in its five senses, does not cry out, but chants, brings to each assault rhythm and rhyme, in a recitative, a *Sprechgesang*" (CdA.19/CA.3). We'll come back to this *Sprechgesang*. One might try to negotiate between spirit and flesh by saying that if the theology of the passage is Christian, the psychology is nevertheless Ovidian—Augustine, after all, is Roman, not Greek or Hebrew. Ovid reposes like a *daimon* in the deep structure of Augustine's theological experience—the allusions are plain enough. Eros in *The Metamorphoses* is violent and traumatic, a demonic invasion of the spirit through the senses—although where Augustine is synaesthetic, Ovid singles out the eye as our most vulnerable portion (cf. *The Confessions*, 10.35, where the eyes are the lustful agents of curiosity). Possessed by Eros, the victim is transformed by desire into an obsessive lover who in a Dionysian frenzy fixes his or her desire on the first creature who comes along—it doesn't matter who: one's father, brother, sister, a passing stranger, oneself (Narcissus). Eros treats all genders equally and is indifferently gay or straight. Anything goes: desire exposes in a twinkling the futility of every taboo, encouraging traffic between gods and mortals, where gods often take the form of animals in order to incarnate (and intensify) their desires. Of course theology's point must be that God in his shrewdness has simply taken Augustine where he is weakest or most vulnerable: there the man sat, absorbed in the beauties of the world, and as he gazed or listened, sniffed or tasted, God entered him through his portals—eyes, ears, tongue; but then how else was he to get in? The main point, on Lyotard's reading, is that he didn't do it secretly, a thief in the night, behind the back the way ideology feeds into the unconscious: "Infatuated [*Engoué*] with earthly delights [this is Lyotard], wallowing in the poverty of satisfaction, the I was sitting idle, smug, like a becalmed boat in a null agitation. Then—but when?—you sweep down upon him and force entrance through his five estuaries. A destructive wind, a typhoon, you draw the closed lips of the flat sea toward you, you open them and turn them, unfurling, inside out" (CdA.18/CA.2). The violence of the invasion is the unmistakably Ovidian signature. Yes, says theology, but the difference between Augustine and Ovid is that now the lover is consumed by a desire for what cannot be seen, or heard, or touched; his fixations have been turned inward. To which the pagan replies, yes, that's all very well, but the point is that, in contrast to modernity's anthropology, with its Cartesian suspicion or evisceration of the body, Augustine's senses have not been shut down or obliterated (contrast Wordsworth's visionary experience, in which "the light of sense goes out" [*Prelude*, 6]); rather Augustine's *sensoria* have been reoriented, turned inward but not disconnected. Remember that flesh is in excess of the mind-body distinction. Unlike Descartes, Augustine in his ecstasy does not become angelic. His experience of God, whatever else it is, is an Ovidian experience — an experience registered or inscribed, however one subsequently allegorizes it, in the flesh:

> But when I love you, what do I love? It is not physical beauty nor temporal glory nor the brightness of light dear to earthly eyes, nor the sweet melodies of all kinds of songs, nor the gentle odour of flowers and ointments and perfumes, nor manna or honey, nor limbs welcoming the embraces of the flesh; it is not these I love when I love my God. Yet there is a light I love, and a food, and a kind of embrace when I love my God [*et tamen amo quandam lucem et quandem vocem et quendam odorem et quendam cibut et quendam amplexum*] — a light, voice, odour, food, embrace of my inner man [*interioris hominis*], where my soul [*animae*] is floodlit by light which space cannot contain, where there is sound that time cannot seize, where there is a perfume which no breeze disperses, where there is a taste of food no amount of eating can lessen, and where there is a bond of union that no satiety can part. That is what I love when I love my God. (10.6/ C.183)

Notice that the passage has the structure of *yes, but*. Spiritualized senses are on display in every Neoplatonic museum, but here they seem to have been more avidly incarnated. In any case the ecstasy of the spirit can only be experienced by the senses; the flesh is not renounced or transcended but appropriated, used more intensely than ever, brought to a pitch. As if only the flesh could be responsive to God's existence (but what else does the doctrine of the Incarnation teach?). As Lyotard says, "The confessing I [*le confessant*] looks for words and, contrary to all expectation, those that come to him are those that make physiology work to the point of pushing the body's sensorial and hence sensual powers [*les puissances sensorielles*] to the infinite. The inhibition that naturally overtakes him is lifted, it is metamorphosed into generosity [*prodigalité*]. To deliver the soul from its misery and death, grace does not demand a humiliated, mortified body; rather, it increases the faculties of the flesh [*le chair*] beyond their limits, and without end" (CdA.11–12/CA.11–12). Recall the syncope: Your call shattered my deafness, your splendor routed my blindness, the taste of you makes me hungry: the senses are not there to be deadened but aroused, intensified.[14] Turning inward, *conversio*, is not a turn away from the flesh but a turning of the flesh itself. The event, as the mystics will later attest, puts the torch to desire.[15]

The Temporality of the Flesh. The spirit is naturally restless, aggressive, omnivorous: it belongs to the temporality of the assertion, the syllogism, the dialectic, the concept (*Begriff*, from *greifen*: to grasp), the narrative, the declarative first person, the active voice, the *cogito*, the system. Its gender is (who needs to be told?) masculine. The natural state of the flesh meanwhile is torpor. Too late did I love you, says Augustine: *Sero te amavi* (10.27). The flesh belongs to the temporality of the meanwhile, in which time does not pass but pauses, meanders, drifts, sits, waits. The present is a hole through which the future drains away; meanwhile the past recedes into oblivion without anything having happened. So there is no story to be told. The rhetorical figure of the flesh is *distentio* (CdA.33–36/CA.15–18), to draw out, prolong, defer, temporize. As Lyotard says, "*Chronos*, at once and in its entirety, consists in delay" (CdA.35/CA.17); time is not logical but sexual, where hurry is pointless: "Upright resolutions, probity and the honest promise—the sexual lets all this go; it will pass" (CdA.38/CA.19). *Consuetudo*, languor, is its form of life (CdA.42/CA.22–23). Who inhabits the flesh? The flesh is outside identity, refractory to categories (hence neither masculine nor feminine but, like Dionysius, heterogynous). The flesh is not *I* but "the other of the I, the *ipse* [*l'autre du je, le soi*]" (CdA.38/CA.20): the *me* who wakes when the *I* sleeps, luxuriating in the concupiscence of an Ovidian theater: "Concupiscence waits for it to be too late, temptation lingers on, pleasure will come in a catastrophic rush, the I will have been able to do nothing to ward off the rout. This future anterior in the negative sets the future upon a powerlessness that is always already accomplished. And the *ipse* comfortably nestles its fatigue into this time of lifeless relapse" (CdA.44/CA.24). The *I* fasts, the *ipse* eats. Flesh is for eating and being eaten. The end of desire is not to be satisfied but to be consumed. "Drunkenness is far from me," says Augustine. "But occasionally gluttony creeps up on your servant" (X.31/C205). Creeping is the modality of the flesh, which is spongelike, permeable, defenseless. Skin might conceal the *I* but it exposes the *ipse* to the world. The flesh is nonviolent in contrast to the *Geist*, whose modality is the *Aufhebung* in which the spirit subsumes everything in its path, converting whatever is not itself (natural things, other people) into the production of the absolute ($I = I$). Flesh's parody of the *Geist* would be Pantagruel with the world in his mouth. The flesh is *passable* and absorptive; it gives itself. ("Passability as the possibility of experiencing [*pathos*] presupposes a donation" [In.121–22/I.110–11].) Hence it is the natural site of suffering, punishment, and (as John Caputo says) sacrifice.[16] Sacrifice for what or for whom? We slit its throat, burn it, consume it in tune with the economy of salvation, which is the model of Hegel's *Geistgeschichte*, whose future (possibly to our good fortune) never arrives. But in itself the flesh is outside of history, incapable of being narrated unless, as Lyotard observes, in a confession that says: "My own life is nothing but this: *distentio*, laxity, procrastination" (CdA.80/CA.56). The spirit moves; the flesh waits. "The *Confessions*," says Lyotard, "are written under the temporal sign of waiting [*l'attente*]" (CdA.96/CA.70).

The Event of Confession. In book 11 Augustine famously asks what time is and confesses his inability to answer. Or he fails insofar as he tries to grasp time conceptually, ontotheologically, which is to say from the standpoint of cognition and representation or according to the propositional attitude (and so he steps back: "I am investigating, Father, not making assertions" [11.17/C.233]). The present (presence) cannot be made visible. The *I* can no more grasp time than it can grasp God or, indeed, other people—or even mere things.[17] As Emmanuel Levinas says, consciousness is called into question by what it seeks to grasp, and this event—this reversal of consciousness—is what he (Levinas) calls *ethics* (TeI.33/T.143). Better to ask: How does the *flesh* experience time? Not as a *mythos* or plot: not as the future receding into the past: not even as the evanescence of the now. Flesh experiences time as a singular event—something outside the routine of coming and going: an event that is not a link in a chain but a break, an interruption, an accident, a swerve, fall, or *Einfall* that causes the flesh to cry out: "What's happening?" (*Arrive-t-il?*) The event is a reversal or displacement of subjectivity. Lyotard here shows (as elsewhere) the influence of Maurice Blanchot, whose essay on "The Limit-Experience" (1962) has these lines: "It is perhaps given to us to 'live' each of the events that is ours by way of a double relation. We live it one time as something we comprehend, grasp, bear, and master (even if we do so painfully and with difficulty) by relating it to some good or to some value, that is to say, finally, by relating it to a Unity; we live it another time as something that escapes all employment and all end, and more, as that which escapes our very capacity to undergo it, but whose trial we cannot escape."[18] A limit-experience is an experience in which we can no longer comport ourselves as cognitive subjects: it is an experience in which the I cannot sustain its self-possession or position as a disengaged punctual ego exercising conceptual control over whatever is presented to it. Experience in this sense is irreducible to cognition. *Le je* is turned into *le soi* (passability). To put it in our terms: here is an event in which the spirit takes flight, leaving the flesh to absorb the blow. Blanchot does not hesitate to call this fleshly experience "the disaster," which is, however, not so much (or necessarily) a catastrophe as it is an event that interrupts both the continuity of the past and the arrival of the future.[19] God's visitation, his breaking and entering, occurs to Augustine in just this way, outside of history: not atemporally but according to the temporality of the event. Lyotard asks: "Where can an absolute event be situated or placed in relation, in a biography? How can it be related?" (CdA.22/CA.6). ("Time is disastrous?" [CdA.53/CA.33].) It cannot be made into a narrative or a memoir; it inscribes itself not in memory but in the flesh:

> Not memory [*le souvenir*], then, but the said inner human [*mais ledit homme intérieur*], who is neither man nor inner, woman and man, an outside inside. This is the only witness of the presence of the Other, of the other of presence. A singular witness, the poem. The inner human does not bear witness to a fact, to a violent event that it would have seen, that it would have heard, tasted, or touched. It does not give testimony, it is the testimony. It is the vision, the scent, the listening, the taste, the contact, each violated and metamorphosed. A wound, an ecchymosis [a blotch or bruise], a scar attests to the fact that a blow has been received, they are its mechanical effect. Signs all the more trustworthy since they do not issue from any intention or any arbitrary inscription: they vouch for the event since they remain after it. Augustine's *Treatises* abound in these analyses of semiotic value: the present object evokes the absent one, in its place. (CdA.23–24/CA.7)

Recall Lyotard's account of the syncope: "The flesh, forced five times, violated in its five senses, does not cry out, but chants, brings to each assault rhythm and rhyme, in a recitative, a *Sprechgesang*" (CdA19/CA3) — "the confessant who is writing here is not a philosopher" (CdA.68/CA.45), nor is he even an autobiographer. He is a *psalmist* (CdA.92–93/CA.66–67). Only the lyric, the apophatic language of the event (which does not know what is happening, can only say what it suffers) rather than the apodictic language of narrative (which knows in advance everything that takes place, sees it all from the standpoint of the end), can bear witness to the experience of the flesh, which interrupts or forestalls the possibility of narration. One could say that memory rather than history registers the event, not as continuity but as a repetition compulsion (what cannot be forgotten).

> As recitatives accompanied by strings, poems in parallel hemistiches whose balance is sometimes broken with the rhythm of the *quînâh*, the short litanies move the body in minimal choreographic figures; one limps in jerks so as to deplore the infirmity of being unable to walk straight, offering this infirmity up. Savors, exhalations of the flesh [*effluves de chair*], touches of sound and gesture that make the blood of the community throb—a whole life astray [*égarée*] comes with the psalmody to beat the holy meditation, the wise argumentation, the upright narrative, to interrupt the clear string of thoughts and tie it to the other, the red and black fiber of the flesh, through which evil holds the creature in its darkness, through which it comes to pass that divine lightning sets him afire." (CdA.110–11/CA.84–85)

As Lyotard observes, Augustine's *Confessions* is filled with echoes of the Psalms: quotations, paraphrases, allusions, plagiarisms: above all, an appropriation of the psalmic voice—the voice of the *cry. Souffrance, suppliance. The Confessions* are written in the (frequently destitute) grammar of the Psalms: the vocative—the call, the groan, the plea, the protest, the prayer, the hymn of anguish or praise. ("Confessing is not only about admitting one's faults, it is also about praising. . . . There is a confession of praise" [CdA.109/CA.83]. As Jean-Luc Marion says, praise is the only discourse that can traverse without abolishing the distance that draws us close to God.[20]

The Essence of Discourse. The vocative deserves some attention. In an essay entitled, "Is Ontology Fundamental?" (1951), Emmanuel Levinas asked "whether language is not based on a relationship that is prior to understanding"—that is, prior to the workings of language studied by logic, linguistics, and various philosophies of language, whose first principle, taken as given, is that the core of language is the proposition: s is p.[21] Is there a region of language prior to cognition or the propositional attitude (a region that is not just prelogical or magical, as if sweeping everything into an undifferentiated whole)? To be sure, it is an indispensable task of language to frame representations and thus to make cognition possible; language grasps the world and objectifies its particulars by means of conceptual determination. "Language," says Levinas, "belongs to the very work of truth, as a thematization and an identification in which being is as it were set, and appears."[22] Henceforward the world is phenomenologically *pour soi* (an object of intentional consciousness). But Levinas insists that prior to the work of truth there is our encounter with other people who cannot be approached by way of cognition and representation (who do not present themselves to me or for myself but require me to leave myself, being open or responsive to the other). "The human being is the only being I cannot meet without my expressing this meeting itself to him or her. This is precisely what distinguishes the meeting from knowledge. In every attitude toward the human being there is a *greeting*—even if it is the refusal of greeting" (En.19/EN.7). And even when I designate something by means of predication, I designate it *for* someone (TeI.231–32/TI.209–10). The proposition implicates the address; the appeal is prior to predication. As Levinas sometimes expresses it: *le Dit*, the Said, presupposes *le Dire*, Saying, which is a movement not of the I but of the "me" (*soi*)— outside myself *toward* and *for* the other, a movement of generosity or of desire that is not reducible to appetite. Saying is exposure.[23] Of course, I can regard the other as if I were invisible, at work behind the other's back, a power of surveillance that sees the other in context rather than face to face. But doing this would mean getting (somehow) out of a prior situation in which the other faces me as a *who*, not a *what*: someone who exposes me to a greeting, to sociality, which is a relationship irreducible to understanding (understood as contextualization, conceptualization, idealization, the reduction of the other to the same). The model of Saying is that of the call and response, not "I speak" but "here I am" (*me voici*), as in the biblical event of election (AE.180/OTB.114: "The word *I* means *here I am* [*me voici*], answering for everything and for everyone"). Recall Lyotard's pun: passability (*se passer* implies, among other things, a passage between myself and another). Levinas characterizes this situation with some audacity: "The relation to the other is therefore not ontology. This bond with the other which is not reducible to the representation of the other, and which invocation is not preceded by an understanding, I call *religion*. The essence of discourse is prayer"

(En.20/EN.7). It is the relation of address, appeal, apostrophe, or summons; it is a prophetic rather than discursive event: an interruption that changes the course of narratives rather than an account or portrayal from a narrative point of view. Levinas is quick to add that his use of the term "religion" here implies neither theology nor mysticism—on a certain view of mysticism as participation in a universal spirit.[24] However, what Levinas calls religion is actually close to what Jean-Luc Marion calls "mysticism," or more accurately "the mystic" (*das Mystiche*), which is a relation to alterity based upon a distance that cognition cannot traverse, *but desire can* (IeD.255–74/ID.198–215). Levinas says: "'Religion' remains the relationship to a being as a being. It does not consist of *conceiving* him as a being, an act in which the *being* is already assimilated" (En.21/EN.8). "Religion" here refers to a relation that is, like mysticism (or like prayer and praise), on the hither side of ontology or ontotheology, doctrine or belief; it is a *movement toward the other*, a relation of one-for-the-other in which the other is not a presence within my horizon but an event of calling or claiming that takes me out of position as a cognitive agent assembling the world before me. It is this region of religion as a relation to irreducible alterity—a relation without relation—that Augustine traverses in his *Confessions*. The modality of the *Confessions* is not that of predication and cognition but of appeal and apostrophe: the *Confessions* cannot instruct God about anything concerning which he does not already know everything. Confession is superfluous with respect to knowledge. Jacques Derrida has made this point in *Sauf le nom*, a dialogue on negative theology (or on negative theology as a kind of language) in which Augustine is identified as someone already speaking the language of Angelus Silesius: "When he [Augustine] asks (himself), when he asks in truth of God and already of his readers why he confesses himself to God when He knows everything, the response makes it appear that what is essential to the avowal or the testimony does not consist in an experience of knowledge. Its act is not reduced to informing, teaching, making known. Stranger to knowing, thus to every determination or to every predicative attribution, confession shares [*partage*] this destiny with the apophatic movement"—an *apophatic movement*, where *apophasis* is the figure of mystic speech, an utterance on the hither side of propositional discourse: speech which denies or disavows every conceptual determination that its use of words might precipitate, and which seeks (against all reason) to remain entirely within the modality of the address—the prayer, the *responsum*, the hymn of desire or praise that is capable of traversing the distance to the other beyond being.[25] The apophatic movement (which corresponds to the Levinasian event of *le Dire*: Saying, the movement of one-for-the-other) is an event that, says Derrida,

> remains at once *in* and *on* language . . . within and at the surface (a surface open, exposed, immediately overflowed, outside of itself). The event remains in and on the mouth, on the tip [*bout*] of the tongue, as is said in English and French, or on the edge of the lips passed over by words that *carry* themselves toward God. They are carried [*portés*], both exported and deported, by a movement of *ference* (transference, reference, difference) toward God. They name God, speak *of* him, speak *him*, speak *to* him, *let him speak in them*, let themselves be carried by him, make (themselves) a reference to just what the name supposes to name beyond itself, the nameable beyond the name, the un-nameable nameable. (SN.60–61/ON.88)

The name of God is, in this event, not the name of a being or an essence but the name of an address: a "vocative name," as Jean-Luc Marion calls it.[26] A name that attaches not to God, who must remain anonymous, but to the lips of the one who is transported by it. I say the name not to identify God but to reach toward him, inaccesible as he is. Recall Paul Celan's poem, "Psalm":

Niemand knetet uns wieder
    aus Erde und Lehm
niemand bespricht unsern Staub.
Niemand.
	No one moulds us again
	    out of earth and clay,
	no one conjures our dust.
	No one.

Gelobt seist du, Niemand. Dir zulieb wollen wir blühn Dir entgegen.[27]	Praised be your name, no one. For your sake we shall flower. Towards You.[28]

Phrasings. Characteristically Lyotard's *The Confession of Augustine* is heteronomous with respect to the rules of any genre. By turns it is, among other things, commentary, parody or mimicry, pastiche, digression, supplementation—*and* confession. What stands out is that in much of his text Lyotard speaks in Augustine's voice or, more accurately, *with* Augustine's voice, citing or reciting Augustine's text (without quotation marks), weaving his own text or voice seamlessly into the original, and above all addressing himself to God, speaking in asides to God as if behind Augustine's back, or sometimes as Augustine's ventriloquist, so that (even when constantly checking one's own copy of Augustine's *Confessions*) the reader of Lyotard's *Confession* cannot always be sure who is speaking, or who signs the confession. In a section of his text entitled, appropriately, "Sendings [*Envois*]," Lyotard asks:

> Of whom are the *Confessions* the work, the *opus*? To put it differently, what are they working at, what are they setting into work, and what are they opening up, to what do they open the work?
>
> The opening [*Confessions*, 1.1–4] gives the tone. This tone is a leitmotif, a guiding thread that relentlessly rivets my tone to the order of your omniscience. The introit of the work opens to your presence. This *invocatio*, the voice through which I call *upon* your voice to come and speak within mine, is repeated throughout the thirteen books, my voice recalls itself to your voice, appeals to it, like a refrain.
>
> My work of confession, of narration and meditation, is only my work because it is yours. The life that it recounts, the conversion and the meditation that it relates are the work of your force, your *virtus*. It is your *sapientia*, your knowledge and wisdom, that grants me what I know thereof, as well as of what I am ignorant. (CdA.89/CA.65–66)

Who speaks? Who am I and who are you? The addressee is indeterminately Augustine, God, No One, while I am an impostor or impersonator who takes up another's voice—the psalmic voice of invocation or apostrophe that Augustine himself impersonates at the outset of (indeed throughout) his *Confessions*—to say things that I have no capacity to speak on my own, *in propria persona*. This is Lyotard:

> Who sings your praise when I sing it? How could the derisory I [*le moi dérisoire*] that I am, weakest of creatures, even muster within it the ability to praise you? How could your incommensurability be put into work, even with regard to a poem, into my finitude, how could your atemporality be put into duration, into the *passage* of melody? The very desire to praise you is already your work, and my disquiet (*inquies*) issues from the fact that what is relative is agitated by the absolute. Besides, how could the *invocatio* operate, be satisfied, while it calls you, you

the infinite, to come and inhabit me, I who am finite. How could I contain you, how could my work lodge you in the miniscule place (*locus*) that I am? (CdA.93–94/CA.67–68)

Who sings your praise when I sing it? In a sense, or in point of fact, no one. *The Confession of Augustine* is *une affaire d'enchaînment de phrases*: the *phrase* being the most beguiling and refractory of Lyotard's terms of art. (*Le Différend*, in which the term is in contant use, is filled with elaborate refusals to define the term [Di.106/D.68–69].) *Phrase* is the French word for "sentence," but in Lyotard's usage it is not a sentence. It is not even a grammatical concept, like the clause. It belongs to the pragmatic order of events rather than to the grammatical order of logical systems. One way to think of the phrase is in terms of Wittgenstein's idea that "to imagine a language is to imagine a form of life." "I confess" is not just a statement; it is a phrase, an *event* of language, that entails various forms of life—confessions of faith or feeling, criminal confessions, extracted confessions, false confessions, personal disclosures of every sort, the sacrament of penance, confessions of failure (I give up!), true confessions (a literary genre), autobiographical narratives, expressions of ignorance, acknowledgement of states of affairs, and so on, perhaps to no definite term. One cannot understand a confession from the outside but only by knowing how to do such a thing, which means understanding the situation that calls for such a thing, or what it is for. On Lyotard's theory a *phrase* is a "universe" that entails (1) something said (2) about something (3) from someone (4) to someone (Di.30–31/D.14). A phrase, Lyotard says, is a move in a language game, not the application of a rule but a piece of strategy or *phronesis* (LR.373). The pagan (from *pagus*, "a border zone" [Di.218/D.151]) is one who inhabits the boundaries of language games, not so much as one who transgresses the rules or regimens of phrases as one who links phrases together in something like an anarchic spirit ("It is necessary to link, but the mode of linkage is never necessary" [Di.52/D.29]). The pagan is someone at home nowhere but rather inhabits the in-between where linkages between phrases, language games, or forms of life are possible. So the pagan's task is the invention of new idioms in order to say what cannot be said within the genres and norms of available discourse. As a pagan writer Lyotard does not interpret Augustine but links his own fragments to fragments from Augustine's text, even as Augustine's text is itself *une affaire d'echaînment*, phrasing and rephrasing the Psalms. Moreover, *The Confession of Augustine* enchains other texts besides—Levinas's ethics of alterity, Jean-Luc Marion's writings on prayer and distance, and, perhaps most interesting, Jacques Derrida's "Circonfession," in which Derrida, a Jew who grew up on *la rue Saint-Augustin* in Algiers, takes up Augustine's position and identity (links himself to Augustine) as a *pied noir*, an alien within the Latin world, vigilant son of a mother more pious than he—and who, like Augustine, confesses, but perhaps no more straightforwardly than does Lyotard:

> No point in going around in circles, for as long as the other does not know, and know in advance, as long as he will not have won back this advance at the moment of the pardon, that unique moment, the great pardon that has not yet happened in my life, indeed I am waiting for it as absolute unicity, basically the only event from now on, no point going round in circles, so long as the other has not won back that advance I shall not be able to avow anything and if avowal cannot consist in declaring, making known, informing, telling the truth, which one can always do, indeed, without confessing anything, without *making* truth, the other must not learn anything that he was not already in a position to know for avowal as such to begin, and this is why I am addressing myself here to God, the only one I take as a witness, without yet knowing what these sublime words mean, and this grammar, and *to*, and *witness*, and *God*, and *take*, take God, and not only do I pray, as I have never stopped doing all my life, but I take him here and take him as my witness, I give myself what he gives me, i.e., the *i.e.* to take the time to take God as a witness to ask him not only, for example, like SA, why do I take pleasure in weeping at the death of a friend, *cur fletus dulcis sit miseris?*, and why I talk to him in Christian French when they expelled me from the Lycée de Ben Aknoun in 1942 a little black and very Arab Jew who understood nothing about it.[29]

Lyotard taught for many years in Algiers after the Liberation. He was one of the founding members of *Socialisme ou barbarie*, a radical group that during the 1950s sought a third way between communism and de Gaulle. Lyotard once confessed that at the age of eleven or twelve he "wanted to become either a monk (especially a Dominican), a painter, or a historian," but was unable to decide and perhaps was still unable long after (p. 1). He added: "There is no monk who does not wonder whether God is turning his face or his back to us"

(p. 3). And again: "I think every writer or thinker carries in him or herself as a particular temptation the weakness or the possibility of ignoring that he or she is committed to an 'I don't know what'" (p. 12). The desire for "I don't know what" is stronger than the religions that seek to give it definition. In the end, it is a desire that probably even God cannot satisfy. Lyotard might be imagined to be saying: the desire is a good in itself (the thesis of libidinal theology).

Deus Absconditus. Lyotard asks (in the voice of Augustine): "How could the *invocatio* operate, be satisfied, while it calls you, you the infinite, to come and inhabit me, I who am finite?" (CdA.94/CA.68). Like the ethical relation in Levinas's philosophy, the psalm or apostrophe is not dialogical but asymmetrical—the other is always incommensurable with me; in the nature of the case, the other cannot answer the call that its very incommensurability has provoked.[30] Nevertheless, against all reason, or according to the law of desire, the other is inside my skin, closer to me than I am to myself, but outside my grasp (AE.181/OTB.114–15). "And if, after all, I wonder, as philosophers are wont, how I can know that it is *you* that I invoke, and not some idol, then I can respond that I do not invoke you because I know you, but *so as* to know you. The invocation is a question and search for you, you who have already found me" (CdA.95/CA.69). But the phrase of cognition is already scrambled by the event that inspires it—"you who have already found me." Found me, he says (who says?), through the work of your preacher (Augustine or Christ): "*Praedicatus* through the ministry of your son, the preacher who has announced you, speaks in advance. You have wrought through him the *advance* of your presence. My work confesses this advance, strains to be acquitted of it. Its inquest disquiets, its restlessness holds in advance its *rest*, it rests upon your announced but still concealed presence, it has as its end the quiet of your direct presence, in the sky of sky, the heaven of heavens" (CdA.95/CA.69–70). Who am I when you are you? Imagine Lyotard, the self-confessed "pagan"—he has said that the pagan is the one who addresses no one when he writes: "We are without interlocutors" (AJ.21/JG.9)— imagine *him*, of all people, speaking in or through the voice of Augustine, putting himself into the phrase of confession to appeal to a God who has "found" him, *but only to abandon him*. To restlessness, *Unheimlichkeit*. As Lyotard says, a "second person" haunts *The Confessions*: the *tu* saturates the book with his silence.

A second person indeed hangs over, surveys the *Confessions*, magnetizes them, filters through them. A you [*toi*], nameless patronym of the Catholic community. You is the addressee [*destinataire*] of the avowal that I write. And yet you is not an interlocutor; you never begins to speak, you never calls me you in turn. I only hear of you from bits of phrases that are reported about your son, about your curses. I invoke you and call you as witness to the purity of my humility: you will never give me quiet, will never acquit me, your jealous dogs love me. My petition leaves you silent. Does it not merit some response? I am only of worth, I exist only through this entreaty, this supplication that is turned toward you, suspended before you. Your silence turns it into a form of torture. (CdA.100–1/CA.75)

In Lyotard's vocabulary, the psalm addressed to God is a transcendental instance of the *différend*, which is the word for a dispute or conflict between parties who speak incommensurable languages; more precisely, it is an impasse between two forms of life where there is no common language or single law that will allow the two to communicate and thus to resolve their differences. One could say that if the confessant's psalm is greeted by silence, it is because I can speak no language in which God could answer. In this sense negative theology would be an interpretation of the *différend* understood as "the unstable state and instant of language wherein something which must be able to be put into phrases cannot be" (Di.29/D.13). There is no "metalanguage" that will overcome the incommensurability of the confessant and God:

In the differend, something "asks" ["*demande*"] to be put into phrases, and suffers from the wrong of not being able to be put into phrases in the right way. This is when the human beings who thought they could use language as an instrument of communication learn through the feeling of pain which accompanies silence (and of pleasure which accompanies the invention of a new idiom), that they are summoned by language, not to augment to their profit the quantity of information communicable through existing idioms, but to recognize that what remains to be phrased exceeds what they can presently phrase, and they must be allowed to institute idioms which do not yet exist. (Di.30/D.13)

So let us (for now) think of *The Confession of Augustine* as an enchainment of phrases across the boundaries or limits of discursive regimes (philosophy, religion, literature) in response to the *différend*. Call it an effort to institute a new idiom for what cannot be said—the peculiar, impertinent, equivocal (above all equivocal) idiom in which a voice that Lyotard shares with Augustine confesses his abandonment, his desire, and for all we know his pagan fidelity to "I don't know what."

> You [*Toi*] the sole object of the writing and its sole content. If it is true that you thus saturate the entries and exits of the con-fession, you who confess and to whom I confess and about which I confess, then I am reduced to receiving nothing but the smallest share. This means little, reduced to nothing, to this nothing which seemed someone, this lure of someone who is no one [*ce leurre d'une personne qui n'était personne*]. I, the apparent subject of the confessive phrase, finds himself, rather loses him-self, undone at all ends. And while he confesses his submission to lures, the desire for which continues to rage, while he dis-avows abject worldliness, he passes under an even more des-potic authority [*un empire encore plus despotique*], he must accept and savor a quite different radical heteronomy under the law of an unknown master of whom he obstinately delights in making himself the subject. (CdA.102–3/CA.75–77)

Put it this way: the desire for God (*Toi*) splits the subject in two—into a first- and third-person singular (*je, il*), as if in the abjection of being abandoned by God, left to oneself, one were lost to oneself just as well. "Why did you abandon him?" (CdA.107/CA.81), Lyotard asks, referring, as everywhere in these pages, to himself as well as to Augustine, all the while knowing full well, as in Jean-Luc Marion's analysis, that God is not God, nor we his lovers, under any other condition: "For God also tempts the soul, as if he was fond of proving its weaknesses rather than kindling its virtue. The imprint that he has stamped into it, almost by surprise, and that leaves it divided within itself, exerts such influence that the soul continues to sigh for the return of ecstasy, henceforth devoted to this visiting and con-demned to repetition. Carry me away, convey me hither, set ablaze, subvert!" (CdA.113/CA.87). God is nothing if not libidinal.

PART III

Anarchist Poetics

Anarchic Temporality: Writing, Friendship, and the Ontology of the Work of Art in Maurice Blanchot's Poetics

Does Literature exist?
    —Stéphane Mallarmé, "La musique et les lettres"

The poem is the truth of the poet, the poet is the possibility of the poem; and yet the poem stays unjustified; even realized, it remains impossible.
    —Maurice Blanchot, "René Char"

Poetry as Unhappy Consciousness. It is well known that in Maurice Blanchot's early criticism writing appears to be less a productive activity than a self-reflexive movement. For example, at the outset of "Littérature et la droit à la mort" (1947–48) he remarks that literature begins when it becomes a question for itself (PF.293/WF.300–301). What sort of question, exactly? Evidently not Jean-Paul Sartre's "What is literature?" which like all "what is . . . ?" questions carries a demand for justification. Inquiring after the nature of a thing is a way of asking why there is such a thing at all, on Leibniz's principle that nothing is without reason (for essences are reasons, and everything is something). Or, again, it is a way of asking literature to identify itself by locating itself in a scheme of things. For example, how does poetry stand in relation to prose, where prose, on Sartre's description, is basically a prosthetic attachment to subjectivity? The writer, Sartre says, "is invested with words. They are prolongations of his meanings, his pincers, his antennae, his eyeglasses. He maneuvers them from within; he feels them as if they were his body; he is surrounded by a verbal body which he is hardly aware of and which extends his action upon the world."[1] As Hegel said, "An individual cannot know what he is until he has made himself a reality through action."[2] Prose is a mode of action. Sartre says: "The word is a certain particular moment of action and has no meaning outside it." Prose is (as it certainly was for Sartre) an alternative to group action. Prose is the way the free individual grasps the world and shapes it into something for others (QL.26/WL.35). Prose knows itself in knowing what it can do: it is a project of world-making in which the writer first of all makes himself real (if himself is the word) by becoming immanent in his effects. Poetry meanwhile does not use words; it contemplates them from the outside as if they were things — but to what purpose? There is a good chance that poetry does not know what it is, much less what it is for. It cannot be traced back to a reason. It is very likely a condition of what Hegel called "unhappy consciousness [*unglückliche Bewußtein*]" (PhG.144–45/PS.126–27): It exists in the form of a question, inaccessible to theory or redemption, divided against itself (without identity), opaque, gratuitous, and *unwirklich*. Whoever enters into this condition enters into an absolutely singular mode of existence, one that cannot be separated into a before and after or subsumed into contexts, categories, or totalities of any kind. So who can call it real?

The Impossibility of Writing. In what follows I want to try to clarify this state of affairs and to extract from it something like Blanchot's conception of the ontology (or perhaps the ontological peculiarity) of the work of art. My thought is that anything that shares this ontology — no matter how trivial or commonplace the thing or however it was materially produced — can claim the status of a work of art. The difficulty is that this excludes very little, almost nothing, not even people. So at the very least we are once more up against the old modernist's question of what counts as art. Blanchot speaks of "the challenge brought against art by the most illustrious works of art in the last thirty years" (PF.294/WF.301). Is Mallarmé's *Un coup de dés*, in which typography replaces syntax as a way of piecing words together, a poem? By what criteria? Modernist works define themselves by the negation of criteria. Blanchot cites "surrealism as a powerful negative movement" that rejects all definitions of what counts as art. This is not just nihilism, however, "because if literature coincides with nothing just for an instant, it is immediately every-thing, and this everything begins to exist" (PF.294/WF.301–2). This is all that modernism means: all criteria are negated and anything is possible; nothing is to be excluded—there is nothing that cannot count as a work of art. Modernism is aesthetic anarchy, a moment of pure negative freedom in which anything can happen. However, for Blanchot, it is precisely here, at what we might think of as modern-ism's conceptual center, that literature calls itself into question: under anarchic conditions in which there *are* no conditions—no stipula-tions, no rules or principles, no models or genres, in short no logical conditions of possibility and therefore no starting point (*archē*)—how is literature possible?

This is the paradoxical question that occupies much of Blanchot's early critical writings, starting with *Comment la littérature est-elle possi-ble?* (Fp.92–101/FP.76–84).[3] Blanchot inherited from Mallarmé the idea that poetic writing is not a mode of lyricism but an exercise of language, where language, however, is *not an instrument under my con-trol* (not, *pace* Sartre, a prosthetic device). As the surrealists became aware, "words have their own spontaneity. For a long time language laid claim to a type of particular existence: it refused simple transpar-ency, it was not just a gaze, an empty means of seeing; it existed, it was a concrete thing and even a colored thing. Surrealists under-stand . . . that language is not an inert thing; it has a life of its own, and a latent power that escapes us" (PF.93/WF.89). So writing for me is not a pure possibility but limited or finite; it is always in some sense or to some extent impossible. The idea here is that language limits my power in the very moment that I try to extend it, and this is what happens in literature: "literature consists in trying to speak when speaking becomes most difficult" (PF.25/W.F17).[4]

It is thus possible to think of poetry as an experience of the *resis-tance* of language to the designs that we place upon it. This was Hei-degger's topic in "Das Wesen der Sprache" (1957): what he calls an "experience *with* language" occurs not when we speak but when words fail us. "In experiences which we undergo *with* language, lan-guage itself brings itself to language. One would think this happens anyway, any time anyone speaks. Yet at whatever time and in what-ever way we speak a language, language itself never has the floor." It is only when language ceases to be a form of mediation that an experience with language is possible: "Language speaks itself as lan-guage . . . when we cannot find the right word for something that concerns us, carries us away, or oppresses us. Then we leave unspoken what we have in mind and, without rightly giving it thought, undergo moments in which language itself has distantly and fleetingly touched us with its essential being." Moreover, having such an experience is what makes the poet. The poet, Heidegger says, "is someone compelled in his own way—poetically—to put into the language the experience he undergoes with language."[5] But if the failure of language is a condition of such experience, how is poetry possible? Or is it that, as Sartre complained, "Poetry is a case of the loser winning"? (QL.43/WL.334). Writing is never a possibility that can be experienced (it is a "limit-experience").[6] This does not mean that my intentions cannot be realized because they exceed my capacity—it is not that they are too grandiose. It does not even mean that I cannot write something. It is rather that in writing I always discover that I cannot be fully myself: my subjectivity is, in a certain sense, not a plenitude; there is something lacking, a weakness where there should be strength, a destitution where there should be power. Sartre will say that it is precisely language that enables me to take up the slack of subjectivity and to make something of it. But Blanchot would answer that in this event when I speak I can no longer say "I" without a bad conscience, since it is not just "I" who speaks but also that part of my subjectivity that belongs to language (and who knows to what more besides?). In writing I experience that part of my subjectivity that does not belong to me; I experience, in other words, the *malheur* of a divided consciousness (I am myself and also another), a state in which, as Hegel showed, I fall short of being in the world (PhG.146–47/PS.129). For Blanchot the locus classicus of this state is to be found in Kafka's *Diaries* where being in the world and writing are incommensurable forms of life—two different orders of existence, two different spatial and temporal registers in which I am nevertheless compelled, simultaneously, to comport myself. We might want to say that to write requires a transition from the one order of being to the other; but this is a movement that no longer belongs to the time of actions that I might undertake (the cross-over time of possibility where one thing follows another for a reason). Rather it is a movement in which the "I" is turned inside out and is no longer in the position of agency. Blanchot says—a statement he repeats again and again in his early criticism—"Kafka grasped the fecundity of literature . . . from the moment that he felt literature was the passage from *Ich* to *Er*, from I to He" (PF.28–29/WF.21). However, to enter into this passage is not at all to travel from one point to another. It is rather to enter into a zone of temporality, a caesura, in which nothing happens. The writer is outside the time of possibility. What once were passages to be traversed are now more like rooms than corridors—rooms, moreover, that are no longer places of habitation ("Poor room, have you ever been lived in?" [AO.13/AwO.4]).

Outside the Subject. It is in Kafka's *Diaries* that Blanchot uncovers the internal link between writing and dying. Both are movements in which I lose the power to say "I"—lose self-possession, mastery, disappear into the event itself. "I am dying" has the grammar of "It is raining" and the mode of being of Levinas's *il y a*. In any case I am turned out of my house. It is never given to me to say "I am dead" or "I am finished."[7] Both writing and existence are interminable—this was, Blanchot says, Kafka's experience: "Existence is interminable, it is nothing but an indeterminacy; we do not know if we are excluded from it (which is why we search vainly in it for something solid to hold on to) or whether we are forever imprisoned in it (and so we turn desperately toward the outside). This existence is an exile in the fullest sense: we are not there, we are elsewhere, and we will never stop being there" (PF.17/WF.9). Interminability is one of the faces of anarchy, where anarchy is to be understood in its etymological sense as that which is on the hither side of beginning, the *an-archē* whence things begin only to begin again, and then again, without possibility of coming to a point. Mallarmé had asked: "Is there a reason for writing? [*Très avant, au moins, quant au point, je le formule:—A savoir s'il y a lieu d'écrire*]."[8] Likewise Blanchot: "What we want to understand is, why write?" (PF.25/WF.17). But the truth is that writing is without why; it is more event than action—as much an interruption of discourse as a species of it, which is why the fragment (which is not a form) becomes for Blanchot the instance or event of writing par excellence.

In "The Paradox of Aytré" (1946) Blanchot asks, "Where does literature begin?" (PF.73/WF.68), and to answer he cites Jean Paulhan's story of a sergeant named Aytré who is asked to keep the logbook of a colonial expedition as it proceeds across Madagascar. "There is nothing extraordinary in this log, we arrive, we leave; chickens cost seven sous; we stock up on medicine; our wives receive magazines, etc." (PF.73/WF.68). But then "the writing changes": "The explanations rendered become longer. Aytré begins to go into his ideas on colonialization; he describes the women's hairstyles, their locks joined together on each side of their ears like a snail; he speaks of strange landscapes; he goes on to the character of the Malagaches; and so on. In short, the log is useless. What has happened?" (PF.73/WF.68). Suddenly writing has become gratuitous, a nonproductive expenditure, an excess of the limits of genre (genre is always purposeful and just; it is writing that is susceptible to formal description and differentiation from an ensemble of alternative possibilities). Writing is at all events no longer under Aytré's control; it now appears of itself, without reason and without end (in principle Aytré could be writing still, like Beckett's Unnamable, of whom Aytré is certainly a prototype). It seems worth remarking that, however gratuitous, Aytré's writing never ceases to be descriptive; it is made of predicates. There is no sign of a schizophrenic's word-salad. One has to say that his writing never ceases to be true of the world. It is only that categories like true and false that define the world's discourse no longer have a coherent application. What categories should one apply to Aytré's writing? It is in fact perfectly ordinary writing but it no longer belongs to the world that it describes with such unexceptional precision. The writing is absolutely singular, refractory to all categories: outside all possible worlds.

Anarchic Temporality. What threshold did Aytré cross? One answer is that he has entered what Blanchot calls "the essential solitude," which is an obscure zone of existence that turns subjectivity inside out—reverses polarities, so to speak, so that the writer who holds the pen is suddenly "gripped" by it, which is why Aytré cannot stop writing:

> The writer seems to be the master of his pen; he can become capable of great mastery over words and over what he wants to make them express. But his mastery only succeeds in putting him, keeping him in contact with the fundamental passivity where the word, no longer anything but its appearance—the shadow of a word—never can be mastered or even grasped. It remains the ungraspable which is also unreleasable; the indecisive moment of fascination.
>
> The writer's mastery is not in the hand that writes, the "sick" hand that never lets the pencil go—that can't let it go because what it holds doesn't really hold; what it holds belongs to the realm of shadows, and it's itself a shade. Mastery always characterizes the other hand, the one that doesn't write and is capable of intervening at the right moment to seize the pencil and put it aside. Thus mastery consists in the power to stop writing, to

interrupt what is being written, thereby restoring to the present instant its rights, its decisive trenchancy. (EL.19/SL.25)

Mastery: the ability to stop writing! Here certainly is what Sartre is reacting against, namely writing that turns the world of freedom and the exigency of tasks upside down. As Blanchot says in one of his texts on Kafka, "It is not a matter of devoting time to the task, of passing one's time writing, but of passing into another time where there is no longer any task; it is a matter of approaching that point where time is lost, where one enters into the fascination and solitude of time's absence" (EL.67/SL.60). What is this other time—this time outside of time? Blanchot explains: "Time's absence is not a purely negative mode. It is the time when nothing begins, when initiative is not possible. . . . Rather than a purely negative mode, it is, on the contrary, a time without negation, without decision, when here is nowhere as well, and each thing withdraws into its image while the 'I' that we are recognizes itself by sinking into the neutrality of a featureless third person. The time of time's absence has no present, no presence" (EL.26/SL.30). A Sartrean would have us imagine a hole in existence through which time drains away instead of progressing toward the future in its usual fashion. Or perhaps time is now passive; it does not cease or come to an end but merely pauses, more or less indefinitely, as in the time of waiting. Time in this event is no longer productive of a future. The trick is to understand that this is not altogether a bad thing.

Let me try to elucidate this temporality with a series of glosses:

1. It may have been Mallarmé who discovered this hiatus in which time ceases to pass (without alluding to any eternity). Recall *Igitur; ou, La folie d'Elbehon*, in which a young man is required (at midnight) to descend into the crypt of his ancestors in order to perform a ritual throw of the dice. But the descent takes him across a threshold into a different order of things. Igitur says: "I have always lived with my soul fixed upon the clock"; "The clock has often done me a great deal of good" (OC.439–40/SPP.97). But midnight on this occasion does not belong to the schedule of clocks. Midnight is "a room of time," not a passage of it (OC.438/SPP.92). As Igitur descends the stairs he enters another temporality, a moment of "pure time or *ennui*," a vigil in which, in the end, nothing was to have taken place. Midnight is a pure present. It disappears into itself, evacuates itself, instead of moving on (the figure is of midnight passing through a mirror). So there is no transition of the future into the past, nor any

Aufhebung of the past into the future (OC.440). There is a similar moment in Mallarmé's "Mimique" in which a mime's performance occurs in an absent present, an absolute caesura between any before or after: "This—'The scene illustrates but the idea, not any actual action, in a hymen (out of which flows Dream), tainted with vice yet sacred, between desire and fulfillment, perpetration and remembrance: here anticipating, there recalling, in the future, in the past, *under the false appearance of a present*. That is how the Mime operates, whose act is confined to a perpetual illusion without breaking the ice or the mirror: he thus sets up a medium, a pure medium, of fiction'" (OC.310/SPP.69). The scene is an interruption of mimesis as a project of bringing something back or anyhow into the present: it is a mimesis without intentionality (it is not *of* something). More exactly, it is a pure performance in which the mime mimes miming: the imitation itself is the thing being imitated. (We'll come back to this.)

2. In a text dating from 1927, this being evidently the unfinished second part of *Sein und Zeit*, Heidegger takes up Aristotle's conception of time, with its focus on the paradoxical temporality of the "now"—paradoxical because the "now" is both foundational for clock-time and uncontainable within it. "The now," says Heidegger, "has a peculiar double visage. . . . Time is held together within itself by the now; time's specific continuity is rooted in the now. But conjointly, with respect to the now, time is divided, articulated into the no-longer now, the earlier, and the not-yet-now, the later." In other words, the now is nothing in itself. It is a fold in time: "the now that we count in following a motion is *in each instance a different now*." That is, "the now is always another, an advance from one place to another. In each now the now is a different one, but still each different now is, as now, always now. The ever different nows are, *as different*, nevertheless always exactly *the same*, namely, now." But this sameness is always a difference in itself: "nowness, being-now, is always *otherness*, *being-other*."[9] One can imagine that the "now" is the time of unhappy consciousness.

3. Emmanuel Levinas, in "Realité et son ombre" (1948), remarks that in conventional phenomenology the image is understood as a form of mediation on the model of the sign, the symbol, or the concept. We suppose it to be a transparent looking glass onto the world of things. But Levinas proposes that the image is simply an event of resemblance, where resemblance is not merely a relation between an image and its original; it is an *event*, "the very movement that engenders the image": "Being is not only itself, it escapes itself. . . . Here

is a familiar everyday thing, perfectly adapted to the hand which is accustomed to it, but its qualities, color, form, and position at the same time remain as it were behind its being, like the 'old garments' of a soul which had withdrawn from that thing, like a 'still life.' And yet all this is . . . is the thing. There is then a duality in . . . this thing, a duality in its being. It is what it is and it is a stranger to itself, and there is a relationship between these two moments. We will say the thing is itself and its image. And that this relationship between the thing and its image is resemblance."[10] A thing is what it is but it also disappears behind its appearance. It has a kind of double ontology: it is "that which is, that which reveals itself in its truth, and, at the same time, it resembles itself, is its own image. The original gives itself as though it were at a distance from itself, as though it were withdrawing from itself" (IH.133/CPP.6). A good example of an image in this sense would be the cadaver. An image is, so to speak, a materialization of being: it is an event in which the essence of the thing withdraws from it, leaving behind a remainder that no longer belongs to the order of things but which, of course, is not just nothing. The cadaver is a being that has, one might say, lost its being. Its existence is gratuitous. Its time has stopped: its past no longer continues into the future because it no longer has a future. But it is not nothing. What Levinas wants to know is: What is this "mere" resemblance, this stoppage of time? A statue appears to belong to this order of things: namely, to a peculiar temporality. "A statue realizes the paradox of an instant that endures without a future. Its duration is not really an instant. It does not give itself out here as an infinitesimal element of duration, the instant of a flash; it has in its own way a quasi-eternal duration. . . . An eternally suspended future floats around the congealed position of a statue like a future forever to come. The imminence of the future lasts before an instant stripped of the essential characteristic of the present, its evanescence. It will never have completed its task as a present, as though reality withdrew from its own reality and left it powerless" (IH.138/CPP.9). The temporality of the statue is like the temporality of dying: "In dying, the horizon of the future is given, but the future as a promise of a new present is refused; one is in the interval, forever an interval." In this temporality, the being of things has been interrupted. It is not that nothing exists; but what exists falls short of being—remains in some fashion on the hither side of being in a between-world that is neither one thing nor the other, in a temporality of the pure *now* that is at once no longer and not yet. Levinas calls this the "meanwhile" (*entre-temps*): "never finished, still enduring—something inhuman and monstrous." This interval in being is what art brings about: the mode of existence of the work of art is this between-time or *now* that the movement of time is unable to traverse (IH.143/CPP.11). The *meanwhile* is the time of vigilance, waiting, dying—and (as we will see in the next chapter) art.

4. The movement of time (that is, clock-time) cannot traverse the interval of being because, as Blanchot says, time in this event is no longer dialectical. It is a "time without negation." This means (among other things) that it is outside the order of conceptual determination in which a merely natural thing is transformed into something essential—an object of consciousness, a thing of the spirit, an identity or universal: an object in the full sense of objectivity (*pour soi*). However, whereas Levinas sees the interval of dying as something "inhuman and monstrous," Blanchot sees it as it as something affirmative or, more exactly, as an affirmation outside the dialectical alternatives of positive and negative, namely an interruption of the "death" in which we make sense of things by objectifying them as this or that theme of predication. In "Littérature et la droit à la mort" Blanchot cites Hegel's line: "'Adam's first act, first act, which made him master of the animals, was to give them names, that is, he annihilated them in their existence (as existing creatures)'" (PF.312/WF.323). Reference, designation, predication: Blanchot doesn't hesitate to call it murder: "I say, 'This woman.' Hölderlin, Mallarmé, and all poets whose theme is the essence of poetry have felt that the act of naming is disquieting. A word may give me its meaning, but first it suppresses it. For me to be able to say, 'This woman,' I must somehow take her flesh and blood reality away from her, cause her to be absent, annihilate her. The word gives me the being, but it gives it to me deprived of being. The word is the absence of that being, its nothingness, what is left of it when it has lost its being—the very fact that it does not exist. Considered in this light, speaking is a curious right" (PF.312/WF.322). To speak—that is, to predicate this of that, to bring things under the rule of identity—is to destroy their singularity or alterity as existing things by integrating them into the order of the same. However, literature, which is to say writing, is not structured on the model of "I speak." The passage from *I* to *He* that makes writing possible is not a dialectical movement: "It is no longer this inspiration at work, this negation asserting itself, this idea inscribed in the world as though it were the absolute perspective of the world in its totality. It is not beyond the world, but neither is it the world itself:

it is the presence of things *before* the world exists, their perseverance after the world has disappeared, the stubbornness of what remains when everything vanishes and the dumbfoundedness of what appears when nothing exists" (PF.317/WF.328). Literature is the refuge of what is singular and irreducible. It "is a concern for the reality of things, for their unknown, free, and silent existence; literature is their innocence and their forbidden presence" (PF.319/WF.330). This is a presence, however, that now belongs to the interval between past and future: it is the time of the nonidentical, the now which, as Heidegger says, "is *always otherness, being other*," irreducible to the traversal of this-as-that.

5. Literature belongs to the temporality of *difference in itself*, that is, the dimension of singularity outside the logic of differentiation that distributes things along the plane of identity and difference. In *Logique du sens* (1969) Gilles Deleuze calls this the temporality of the *Aion*, which in contrast to the chronological progress of "interlocking presents" is an event that breaks ad infinitum into "elongated pasts and futures," that is, dimensions that move apart rather than together into some sort of unity, continuum, or totality. Deleuze writes (and notice that he cites Mallarmé's "Mimique" as an example of what he has in mind):

> The Aion endlessly divides the event and pushes away past as well as future, without ever rendering them less urgent. The event is that no one ever dies, but has always just died or is always going to die, in the empty present of the Aion, that is, in eternity. As he was describing a murder such that it had to be mimed—a pure ideality—Mallarmé said: "Here advancing, there remembering, to the future, to the past, under the false appearance of a present—in such a manner the Mime proceeds, whose game is limited to a perpetual illusion, without breaking the mirror." Each event is the smallest time, smaller than the minimum of continuous thinkable time, because it is divided into proximate past and imminent future. But it is also the longest time, because it is endlessly subdivided by the Aion which renders it equal to its own unlimited line.[11]

The Aion is the pure event, irreducible to a segment in a chain. It is the time of the absolutely singular—what Deleuze and Guattari elsewhere refer to as a *haecceity*, which is never an instance of anything but itself: for example, five o'clock this evening, but one's whole life would do as well so long as one does not imagine such a thing, Aristotle-like, as a totality with a plot. It is rather an absolutely random and contingent event. It is historicity itself. "We are all five o'clock in the evening, or another hour, or rather two hours simultaneously, the optimal and the pessimal, noon-midnight, but distributed in a variable fashion. . . . A *haecceity* has neither beginning nor end, origin nor destination; it is always in the middle. It is not made of points, only of lines. It is a rhizome."[12] So a *haecceity* is always a fragment—not a part broken off from a whole, but something uncontainable within any totality or structure, a testimony to an ontology without integration in which the aleatory—the happening outside of any sequence (or anarchy for short)—gives the definition of reality.

6. In "La double séance" (1970) Jacques Derrida reads Mallarmé's "Mimique" against some passages from Plato's "Philebus" in order to distinguish two orders of *mimesis*: (A) a first order in which *mimesis* is always linked to truth in the sense that *mimesis* is always about "what is"—it is important to stress that *everything* (truth, reason, the order of things) depends on the "discernibility" *between* "what is" and its imitation, where the one comes first in the order of the things and the other second, and where the one is simple and the other is double (multiplies or supervenes upon the one);[13] and (B) a second order, which we might call "*mimesis* in itself," resulting from the fact that (as Derrida reads it) Mallarmé's mime simply mimes. "There is no imitation. The Mime imitates nothing. And to begin with, he doesn't imitate. There is nothing prior to the writing of his gestures. Nothing is prescribed for him. No present has preceded or supervised the tracing of his writing. His movements form a figure that no speech anticipates or accompanies. They are not linked with *logos* in any order of consequence."[14] To be sure, it is not that the mime is actually *doing* something, although of course he is not *not* doing anything, either. Derrida tries to sort out the difficulty as follows: "*There is* mimicry," he says. It is just that in this case "we are faced . . . with mimicry imitating nothing; faced, so to speak, with a double that doubles no simple, a double that nothing anticipates, nothing at least that is not itself already double. There is no simple reference. . . . This speculum reflects no reality; it produces 'reality-effects'" (Di.234/D.206). So what have we got? "In this speculum with no reality, in this mirror of a mirror, a difference or dyad does exist, since there are mimes and phantoms. But it is a difference without a reference [that is, a difference indifferent to any identity, or difference in itself], or rather a reference without a referent, without any first or last unit, a ghost that is the phantom of no flesh, wander-

ing about without a past, without any death, birth, or presence"
(Di.234/D.206). What the mime discloses is a pure *between*, a caesura
in being that interrupts the logic of identity and difference, real
thing and image, single and double, same and other. Derrida notices
that "the word 'between' has no full meaning of its own" (Di.250/
D.221). One thinks of Blanchot's favorite words ("common words,"
he calls them) — "perhaps," "almost," "maybe," "unless," "meanwhile"
(PD.15–16/SNB.7). Derrida tries to locate this *between* with words
like *différance*, *tympan*, *hymen*, *pli* or "fold" — spatial metaphors for
what Blanchot figures temporally when he locates writing in the interval between *archē* and *telos*, design and completion, past and future: the *entre-temps* of dying, suffering, waiting, Igitur's "midnight,"
and so on. This interval is outside the order of reasons in which productions can be accomplished and justified — outside the order of *this*
as *that* (or *this* for *that*, or *this* about *that*): outside any subsumptive
order that places one thing in the service, branch, or business of another. The singular belongs to this *between* or caesura that disengages
the relation of universal and particular. The singular is difference in
itself, the one thing that is unlike anything: the nonidentical, unrepresentable, absolute alterity outside all relations of the one and the two,
the same and the other, this and that.

Ontology of the Snow Shovel. In light of the foregoing, consider (once
more) Marcel Duchamp's Readymades — for example, the mundane
snow shovel, which he buys at a hardware store and then exhibits in
his studio (in a glass case!) under the title, *In Advance of a Broken Arm*.
What is the relation between the snow shovel in the hardware store
and the shovel in the studio? In chapter 5 we tried to resolve this
question in terms of change-of-place: whatever is recontextualized
exhibits itself or places itself between quotation marks. The collector's item, for example, is no longer the mere thing it happens to be
but is, in Benjamin's sense, auratic. Now we have the resources to
think in terms of a change of temporality as well. The shovel is now
both itself and not itself, that is, it lags behind itself in an interval
that will never pass, on the hither side of an imminence (or, indeed,
coincidence) that will no longer take place. Duchamp himself introduced the term "delay" to suggest a work that is refractory, free of
touch, self-identical or, better, nonidentical: Deleuze's difference in
itself or absolute singularity.[15] It is to all appearances your typical
shovel, but it is in excess of what it seems. Levinas would say it is

hypertrophic, thickened to the point where it no longer has the transparency or self-evidence of what Heidegger calls "things-at-hand."

One can put this in a slightly different way. Duchamp's shovel proved to be as ephemeral as any temporal thing. Like his famous urinal and, indeed, like all of his Readymades, it vanished without a trace, or rather with only the trace of a photograph. Nevertheless, Duchamp's shovel remains an original both as an event as well as a "work"; it can be replicated, but there can be no duplicate—no substitute identical with what is missing.[16] As Marjorie Perloff puts it, "The works in [Duchamp's] repertoire are now understood to be completely unique. Not, of course, literally unique in the sense of one of a kind; in almost every case the original has been lost and there are a number of replicas. Rather, their uniqueness, their *aura* is conceptual: the idea, for example, of taking a snow shovel, hanging it by its handle in a glass case—which is hardly the way we normally see shovels—and giving it the witty title, *In Advance of a Broken Arm*."[17] A Readymade, in other words, is a commercial product but also something else: a *conceptual artifact*. The one belongs to the everyday temporality of oblivion (recall Ponge's crate from chapter 5); the other, like any work of art, possesses a history and, indeed, a title that situates it within the temporality of the proper name (which can outlive the one who bears it).[18]

In an essay on "La parole quotidienne" Blanchot makes the argument that the everyday as such falls beneath the threshold of history. The everyday is "existence in its very spontaneity and as it is lived—at the moment when, lived, it escapes every speculative formulation, perhaps all coherence and regularity." Of course, Blanchot, existentialist that he is, is thinking of the everyday subject, that is, one of us—one of Heidegger's "they" (*das Man*): the one who is no longer a subject (no longer says "I," has no proper name, is no longer even a "who"). "The everyday escapes. Why does it escape? Because it is without a subject. When I live the everyday, it is any man, anyone at all who does so; and this anyone, properly speaking, is neither me nor, properly, the other; he is neither the one nor the other and, in their interchangeable presence, their annulled irreciprocity, both one and the other—yet without there being an 'I' or an 'alter ego' able to give rise to a *dialectical recognition*" (EI.364/IC.244). But this only means that at the level of the everyday the subject "does not belong to the objective realm. To live it as what might be lived through a series of technical acts (represented by the vacuum cleaner, the washing machine, the refrigerator, the radio, the car) is to substitute a number of compartmentalized actions for this indefinite presence, this connected movement (which is, however, not a whole) by which we are *continually*, though in the mode of discontinuity, in relation with the *indeterminate* set of possibilities" (EI.364/IC.244). The point would be that Duchamp's shovel is no longer interchangeable with any other once it enters into the conceptual context that Duchamp constructs for it when he places it in his studio.[19] Heidegger would say that it now has the density or materiality of the *thing* rather than the presentness, transparency, and graspability of an object. It is "free of touch."

L'amitié. Here we come upon the boundary that Blanchot shares with Emmanuel Levinas. Can people materialize in the way that the words of writing do? And, if so, how does this happen? As we have seen, they can become cadaverous. Less drastically, or perhaps more, to materialize is to cease to be a thing of the spirit or affair of consciousness; it is to be reinserted into the world as a porous and vulnerable subject rather than as a philosophical subject who, anyhow, only exists on paper. Levinas clarifies this state of affairs by way of sensibility, which is to say my exposure to the other who approaches me outside every context that I have for appropriating the world; in the same stroke the other interrupts my self-relation, turns "I" into "me." I am no longer a cognitive subject; I am my skin ("The ego [*moi*] is not in itself like matter which, perfectly espoused by its form, is what it is; it is in itself like one is in one's skin, that is, already tight, ill at ease in one's own skin. It is as though the identity of matter resting in itself concealed . . . a materiality more material than all matter—a materiality such that irritability, susceptibility or exposedness to wounds and outrage characterizes its passivity, more passive still than the passivity of effects").[20] Levinas calls this condition of exposure, of subjectivity outside the subject, "ethics" (or, more exactly, "the ethical"). Blanchot calls it, among other things, friendship—or, more exactly, the relation of "one for the other" that occurs in the *between* or *entre-temps* between friends (or, for all of that, between lovers).

The crucial thing is to understand that for Blanchot friendship is not an intersubjective relation. It is not a side-by-side relation of collaboration in which we act or exist as one, as if sharing things in common, whether a language, a world, or a sense of identity or purpose. Friendship for Blanchot entails foreignness or separation as one of its conditions. It is an ethical rather than fraternal relation, a face-to-face relation in which I am responsible to and for the other and not just for holding up my end or keeping my side of the bargain. So, in contrast to Aristotle, Blanchot does not think of friendship on the model of logical integration in which the bond between myself and my friend, my sense of oneness with him as if we were interchangeable, can become foundational for a more comprehensive order of things. In other words friendship is not utopian—not an incipient or exemplary community (unless in Bataille's anarchic sense of "a community for those who have no community"). It is on the contrary a relation without terms, a relationship of dissymmetry and nonidentity. One inhabits this relation not as a sovereign "I" but as a "who" or a "me"—a mode of being in the accusative rather than executive or declarative position.

For example, in "L'amitié" (1971), Blanchot says that the "I" of Georges Bataille's writings is

> very different from the ego that those who knew him in the happy and unhappy particularity of life would like to evoke in the light of a memory. Everything leads one to think that the personless presence at stake in such a movement introduces an enigmatic relation into the existence of him who indeed decided to speak of it but not to claim it as his own, still less to make of it an event of his biography (rather, a gap in which the biography disappears). And when we ask ourselves the question "Who was the subject of this experience?", this question is perhaps already an answer if, even to him who led it, the experience asserted itself in this interrogative form, by substituting the openness of a "Who?" without answer for the closed and singular "I"; not that this means that he had simply to ask himself "What is this I that I am?" but much more radically to recover himself without reprieve, no longer as "I" but as a "Who?", the unknown and slippery being of an indefinite "Who?"[21]

In this respect there is an internal coherence between friendship and writing (l'écriture). Like writing, friendship is less an executive performance than a temporality into which one is drawn that deprives one of all the various familiar possessions and initiatives (like the ability to begin or end). Friendship is what Blanchot calls a relation of the third kind, which is neither a relation of cognition nor an "I-Thou" relation of philosophical dialogue but rather "a relation without relation" (EI.104/IC.73)—one can think of it as a kind of ecstatic relation outside the alternatives of identity/difference, same/other, presence/absence, being/nonbeing, past/future. It is "a pure interval" (EI.98/IC.69), "an interruption of being" (EI.109/IC.77), that suspends us together in what Blanchot calls "the infinite conversation"—an example of which prefaces *L'entretien infini*. Two old men, or at any rate two people no longer young who, for who knows how many years, have been talking together much the way Aytré writes:

> *"I asked you to come . . ." He stops an instant: "Do you remember how things happened?" The interlocutor reflects in turn: "I remember it very well." —"Ah, good. I was not very sure, finally, of having initiated the conversation myself." —"But how could I have come otherwise?" —"Friendship would have sent you." He reflects again: "I wrote to you, didn't I?" —"On several occasions." —"But did I not also call you on the telephone?" —"Certainly, several times." —"I see you want to be gentle with me. I am grateful. As a matter of fact it is nothing new; the weariness [fatigue] is not greater, only it has taken another turn." —"It has several, I believe we know them all. It keeps us alive." —"It keeps us speaking. I would like to state precisely when this happened, if only one of the characteristics of the thing did not make precision difficult. I can't help thinking of it." —"Well, then we must think of it together. Is it something that happened to you?" —"Did I say that?" And he adds almost immediately , with a force of decision that might justly be termed moving, so much does it seem to exceed his resources of energy: "Nothing that has happened," yet along with it this reservation: "Nothing that has happened to me." —"Then in my eyes it is nothing serious." —"I didn't say that it was serious." He continues to meditate on this, resuming: "No, it's not serious," as if he perceived at that instant that what is not serious is much more so."* (EI.xiii/IC.xv)[22]

Obviously this is not a philosophical dialogue of the kind Gadamer recommends—namely, two friends, more or less identical, engaged in a disinterested give-and-take that tries to elucidate a subject matter (*die Sache*). Like the dialogue between the lovers (if that is what they are) in *L'attente l'oubli*, Blanchot's "infinite conversation" does not have a logical structure, a *logos*; neither has it an *archē* or a *telos*. It cannot be made intelligible by comparison either with the logical proposition, which is why it does not appear to be about anything, or with the dialectic, since it doesn't go anywhere. It has the structure of waiting. Of the lovers in *L'attente l'oubli* it is said: "There is no real dialogue between them. Only waiting maintains between what they say, a certain relation, words spoken to wait, a waiting of words"

(AO.52/AwO.25). Waiting is how one inhabits the anarchic tempo-rality of friendship (or of writing, suffering, fatigue, dying).

Blanchot emphasizes the opacity of the friend (or lover) who is a presence that cannot be comprehended, who is "radically out of my reach" (EI.98/IC.69) and whose intimacy does not dissipate the strangeness between us. So I am not privy to my friend, about whom I must therefore remain discreet—"discretion" captures in one word the basic idea of Blanchovian ethics: "We must give up trying to know those to whom we are linked by something essential; by this I mean we must greet them in the relation with the unknown in which they greet us as well, in our estrangement. Friendship, this relation-ship without dependence, without episode, yet into which all of the simplicity of life enters, passes by way of the recognition of common strangeness that does not allow us to speak of our friends but only to speak to them" (A.300/F.291). Hence the idea that friendship is an ethical relation on the hither side of or beyond being. It is also a rela-tion that "exposes me to death or finitude" (CI.44/UC.24); that is, friendship belongs with writing to the temporality of dying, or to the interval of art in which my relation with the other is always shad-owed, even constituted, by the imminence of his death (if his is the word). In *La communauté inavouable* Blanchot writes:

> Now, "the basis of communication" is not necessarily speech, or even the silence that is its foundation and punctuation, but the exposure to death, no longer my own exposure, but some-one else's, whose living and closest presence is already the eter-nal and unbearable absence, an absence that the deepest mourning does not diminish. And it is in life itself that that ab-sence of someone else has to be met. It is with that absence—its uncanny presence, always under the prior threat of disappear-ance—that friendship is brought into play and lost at each mo-ment, a relation without relation or without relation other than the incommensurable. (CI.46/UC.25)

This is certainly strange, but it recalls Levinas's reworking of Hei-degger's analysis of Dasein's self-awareness as Being-toward-death. For Heidegger this awareness is (says Levinas) "a supreme lucidity and hence a supreme virility"—Heidegger's notion of authenticity is shaped entirely by the ontology of the Greek hero (as the German romantics imagined him) who confronts his destiny in a history set apart from everyday life. "It [*Sein-zum-Tod*] is," says Levinas, "Da-sein's assumption of the uttermost possibility of existence, which makes possible all other possibilities, and consequently makes possible the very feat of grasping a possibility—that is, it makes possible activity and freedom."[23] For Levinas, by contrast, my death, however much it hovers and looms, is the plain and simple limit of my virility precisely because it is always (like the friend!) outside my reach as a cognitive subject; like the Messiah it is an impossibility, an event in which "something absolutely unknowable appears" (TA.58/TO.71). My death, such as it is, is more Kafkaesque than Homeric: always premature, it will come too late for me to experience it. I am gone in the very instant it arrives. Think of Kafka's K. Everyone will be privy to my death but me. Death is the end of discretion.

It turns out that this is for the most part Levinas's point as well. Before everything else it is the death of the other that stares me in the face, weighs upon me and thus constitutes me as an ethical subject: "In its mortality, the face before me summons me, calls for me, begs for me, as if the invisible death that must be faced by the Other . . . were my business. It is as if that invisible death, ignored by the Other . . . were already 'regarding' me prior to confronting me, and becoming the death that stares me in the face. The other man's death calls me into question, as if, by my possible future indifference, I had become the accomplice of the death to which the other, who cannot see it, is exposed; and as if, even before vowing myself to him, I had to answer for this death of the other, and to accompany the Other in his mortal solitude."[24] Interestingly, it is a condition of roughly this sort that the narrator of Blanchot's *L'arrêt de mort* (1948) inhabits: his love affairs are prolonged, cadaverous experiences of mortality; he himself meanwhile appears to embody the impossibility of dying: "What makes it happen that every time my grave opens, now, I rouse a thought there that is strong enough to bring me back to life? The very derisive laughter of my death."[25] As if exposure to death became a kind of interminable vigil.

In *L'instant de ma mort* Blanchot recalls, or imagines a Blanchot-like narrator recalling, "a young man—a man still young—prevented from dying by death itself."[26] During the Occupation he is hauled out of his château one evening and placed before a firing squad:

> I know—do I know it—that the one at whom the Germans were already aiming, awaiting but the final order, experienced then a feeling of extraordinary lightness, a sort of beatitude (nothing happy, however)—sovereign elation? The encounter of death with death?

In his place, I will not try to analyze. He was perhaps suddenly invincible. Dead—immortal. Perhaps ecstasy. Rather the feeling of compassion for suffering humanity, the happiness of not being immortal or eternal. Henceforward he was bound to death by a surreptitious friendship. (IM.5)

The Concepts of Art and Poetry in Emmanuel Levinas's Writings

Being's essence designates nothing that could be a nameable content, a thing, event, or action; it names this mobility of the immobile, this multiplication of the identical, this diastasis of the punctual, this lapse. This modification without alteration or displacement, being's essence or time, does not await, in addition, an illumination that would allow for an "act of consciousness." This modification is precisely the visibility of the same to the same, which is sometimes called openness. The work of being, essence, time, the lapse of time, is exposition, truth, philosophy. Being's essence is a dissipating of opacity, not only because this "drawing out" of being would have to have been first understood so that truth could be told about things, events and acts that *are*; but because this drawing out is the *original dissipation* of opaqueness.

> —Emmanuel Levinas, *Otherwise than Being,*
> *or Beyond Essence*

Emmanuel Levinas's writings are rich in comments and reflections on art, poetry, and the relations between poetry and ethical theory.[1] Of particular importance is the question of language, because there appears to be a kind of symmetry between language as an ethical relation and the language of poetry, both of which expose us to regions of subjectivity or existence on the hither (anarchic) side of cognition and being. The ethical and the poetic are evidently species of saying (*le Dire*) in contrast to the propositional character of the said (*le Dit*), yet neither one is translatable into the other, and in fact they are in some sense at odds with one another. Unfortunately, Levinas never engaged these matters in any sustained or systematic way, and certainly never without confusion. His friend Maurice Blanchot observed in an early essay that "Levinas mistrusts poems and poetic activity."[2] But it is also clear that Levinas could not get such things out of his mind, for he frequently found in poetry and art conceptual resources for his thinking, which perhaps helps to explain why the ethical in his work is never far removed from the aesthetic. But aesthetic in what sense? My purpose here will be to construct as coherent an account as I can of the place and importance that poetry and art have in Levinas's thinking. This account will have three goals. The first will be to sort out, so far as possible, Levinas's often contradictory statements about art. The second will be to clarify the difference between two conceptions of the aesthetic at work in Levinas's writings, which I will call an "aesthetics of materiality" and an "aesthetics of the visible." The argument here will be that, although Levinas found it difficult to distinguish these two conceptions, or did not want to choose between them, his account of the materiality of the work of art is an important contribution to modernist aesthetics for the way it articulates the ontological significance of modern art and its break with the aesthetics of form and beauty that comes down to us from classical tradition and from Kant. Modernist art is no longer an art of the visible (which is why it is difficult for many people to see it as art). I think we will be able to say that in Levinas both materiality and the beautiful are reinterpreted in terms of the proximity of things, taking proximity to be something like an alternative to visibility. The third aim of this inquiry will be to come to some understanding of the relationship between poetry and the ethical as analogous forms of transcendence in the special sense that Levinas gives to this term. The argument here will be that, if "Being's essence is a dissipating of opacity" (AE.53/OTB.30), poetry is a "darkening of being" (H.140/CPP.9), a thickening, temporalization or desynchronizing of essence that occurs alongside the ethical, if not in advance of it, as "an unheard-of modality of the otherwise than being" (NP.55–56/PN.46).

Poetics Ancient and Modern. In order to make my account precise and meaningful, however, it will be helpful to have a rough sense of where Levinas appears within poetry's conceptual history, starting perhaps with the early years of modernity when German and British romantics pressed the question of what sort of thing poetry might be if it is not (as both ancient and medieval traditions of poetics had taught) a form of mediation in the service of other fields of discourse—namely, the versifying of meanings derived from various contexts of learning, or the rehearsal of traditional themes of religious and erotic experience.[3] Arguably the great achievement of modernity was not only the development of scientific reason but also the invention of a concept of art that, whatever its philosophical difficulties, provided a space for speculation in which such a thing as poetry could become (and remain) a question for itself. For what is distinctive about romantic poetics is that it is no longer concerned simply with the art of composing verses but becomes an inquiry into the nature of poetry and the conditions that make it possible. So Friedrich Schlegel (1772–1829), for example, calls modern poetry a *"Transzendentalpoesie"* that combines the traditional "self-mirroring" of the lyrical poet with "the transcendental raw materials and preliminaries of a theory of poetic creativity [*Dichtungsvermögens*]": "In all its descriptions, this poetry should describe itself, and always be simultaneously poetry and the poetry of poetry."[4] As if modern poetry were now to become the experience of poetry as such, quite apart from the significance or utility it might still have for the church, the court, and the schools.

This is not to say that the classical tradition did not have a profound understanding of the nature (and difficulty) of poetry. For example, the ancients typically regarded poetry as an instance of the dark saying, the *ainigma*, a word that sometimes gets translated as "riddle," but unlike a riddle the enigma's darkness is not something that can be illuminated, or eliminated, by reason or interpretation. It is not a puzzle whose solution justifies its formulation but is opaque in the nature of the case, and to that extent it defines the limits of the discursive regions that we inhabit. Poetry is anarchic in the original sense of the word. In the *Republic* Plato formalized this link between poetry and anarchy (and, in the bargain, instituted the discipline of philosophy) when he charged that poetry is not something that can give itself a reason but is exemplary of all that is incoherent with the just and rational order of things, that is, the order of the λόγος, where ideally everything manifests (from within itself) the reason why it is so and not otherwise. Following Plato—or, in the event, Aristotle, who found a place for poetry in his organon, or rule of discourse, by reconceptualizing it both as a species of cognition (mimesis) and as a kind of consecutive reasoning (plot)—the justification of poetry became the traditional task of allegory, which is a philosophical way of reading nonphilosophical texts by construing them so as to make them coherent with prevailing true beliefs. Henceforward poetry could only justify itself by celebrating or supplementing conceptual worlds already in place. But taken by itself, the poetic text remains exotic in the etymological sense—dense, refractory to the light, not a part of but *a limit of the world and its reasons*—which is perhaps why the classical tradition in poetics has always been concerned to the point of obsession with rules for keeping poetry under rational control.

In the late nineteenth century the French poet Stéphane Mallarmé renewed this enigmatic tradition for modernity with his famous remark, "My dear Degas, one does not make poetry with ideas, but with *words*." Whereas the romantics had conceptualized poetry as a mode of experience or subjectivity, Mallarmé was the first to conceptualize poetry in terms of the materiality of written language (*l'écriture*), so that the basic unit of the poem is no longer the classic alexandrine that had defined French poetry for centuries; rather, the constituents of the poem are the letters of the alphabet—and also the white space of the printed page, the fold in its middle, and the typographical arrangements that the letters inscribe.[5] So poetry is not a form of mediation that brings something other than itself into view (not allegory or symbol). On the contrary, Mallarmé distinguished poetry from informative, descriptive, and symbolic uses of language by claiming for the materiality of poetic language the power to obliterate the world of objects and events: "When I say, 'a flower!' then from that forgetfulness to which my voice consigns all floral form, something different from the usual calyces arises . . . : the flower which is absent from all bouquets" (OC.356). Writing on Mallarmé in 1942 Maurice Blanchot glossed this famous line by explaining that in its propositional form language "destroys the world to make it reborn in a state of meaning, of signified values; but, under its creative form, it fixes only on the negative aspect of its task and becomes the pure power of questioning and transfiguration. That is possible insofar as, taking on a tangible quality, it becomes a thing, a body, an incarnate power. The real presence and material affirmation of language gives it the ability to suspend and dismiss the world."[6] What this means is that poetic language is not just an inert mass, not merely a blank or opaque aesthetic "veil of words"; rather it is a discursive event that interrupts the logical or dialectical movement of signification and thereby opens up a dimension of exteriority or worldlessness—a world without things, or perhaps one should say, things free of the world.

The Ontological Significance of the Materiality of Art. Emmanuel Levinas's earliest writings on art and poetry should be read against the background of the resurgence of interest in Mallarmé that began with the publication of Henri Mondor's *Vie de Mallarmé* in 1941 and Blanchot's critical appropriation of Mallarmé's poetics during this same period, which served to sharpen differences among an array of positions in the controversies about the social significance of art that erupted in Paris following the Liberation.[7] As I have already noted, in a series of essays published in 1947 in *Les temps modernes*, Jean-Paul Sartre elucidated his theory of writing as a form of social action by opposing it to poetry conceived explicitly in Mallarméan terms as the work of "men who refuse to utilize language."[8] The poet, Sartre says, "is outside language," on "the reverse side of words," which he treats as mere things to be assembled the way Picasso constructs a collage (QL.20/WL.30–31). Meanwhile the prose writer is situated "inside of language," which he manipulates as an instrument for grasping the world (QL.19–20/WL.30–31). In prose, words become actions, but poetry for Sartre is the "autodestruction" of language, whose economy is no longer retracted to the exchange of meanings and the production of rhetorical effects but is now an opaque, thing-like thing (QL20–22/WL.35–37).[9]

In 1947 Levinas published *De l'existence à l'existant*, a series of studies of what might be called, after Georges Bataille, "limit-experiences," that is, experiences (fatigue, insomnia, the experience of art) that are irreducible to categories of cognition and whose analyses serve as a way of exploring subjectivity beyond the limits of conventional phenomenology. In the section entitled "Existence sans existant," Levinas takes recourse to Mallarméan aesthetics as a way of introducing the concept of the *il y a*—if "concept" is the word, since the term is meant to suggest the possibility of existence without existents, a pure exteriority of being without appearance, and thus a phenomenology without phenomena. As Levinas figures it, the work of art (by which Levinas, in this context, means the *modernist* artwork) opens up this possibility of existence without being because it makes everyday things present by "extracting [them] from the perspective of the world," where the world is that which comes into being as a correlate of intentionality, cognition, or conceptual determination (DEE.84/EE.52). The idea is that in art our relation to things is no longer one of knowing and making visible. Art does not represent things, it *materializeʃ* them; or, as Levinas would prefer, it presents things in their *materiality* and not as representations. It is clear that Levinas is thinking of the *work* of the work of art as something very different from the work of intentional consciousness, and this is a difference that enables him to formulate in a new way the fundamental question of modernist aesthetics: *What becomeʃ of thingʃ in art?* It is not enough (or even accurate) to say that modern art repudiates mimesis, representation, or realism in order to purify itself of everything that is not art—the so-called doctrine of aesthetic differentiation that figures art as a pure work of the spirit.[10] Levinas speaks rather of "the quest of modern painting and poetry to banish . . . that soul to which the visible forms were subjected, and to remove from represented objects their servile function as expressions" (DEE.89/EE.55). This *baniʃhment of the ʃoul* means, whatever else it means, that the modern work of art cannot be thought of as just another ideal object that consciousness constructs for itself—a nonmimetic or purely formal object, one determined by traditional canons of beauty; on the contrary, the work is now defined precisely as a limit of consciousness: "Its intention is to present reality as it is in itself, after the world has come to an end" (DEE.89/EE.56), as if on the hither side (*en ∂eça*) of the world that consciousness represents to itself. On this analysis modern art can no longer be conceived as an art of the visible. "Paradoxically as it may seem," Levinas says, "painting is a struggle with sight. Sight seeks to draw out the light beings integrated into a whole. To look is to be able to describe curves, to sketch out wholes in which the elements can be integrated, horizons in which the particular comes to appear by abdicating its particularity. In contemporary painting things no longer count as elements in a universal order. . . . The particular stands out in the nakedness of its being" (DEE.90/EE.56). This emancipation of singularity from the reduction to an order of things is the essence of cubism, whose break-up of lines of sight materializes things in a radical way:

> From a space without horizons, things break away and are cast toward us like chunks that have weight in themselves, blocks, cubes, planes, triangles, without transitions between them. They are naked elements, simple and absolute, swellings or abscesses of being. In this falling of things down on us objects attest their power as material objects, even reach a paroxysm of materiality. Despite the rationality and luminosity of these

forms when taken in themselves, a painting makes them exist in themselves [*le tableau accomplit l'en-soi même de leur existence*], brings about an absolute existence in the very fact that there is something which is not in its turn an object or a name, which is unnameable and can only appear in poetry. (DEE.91/ EE.56–57)

The idea is that in cubism the spectator can no longer objectify what he or she sees; the work is no longer visible in the way the world is. For Levinas this means that the materiality of the work of art can no longer be contrasted with form or spirit; it is pure exteriority, uncorrelated with any interior, and therefore it constitutes a kind of transcendence (note that it "can only appear in poetry"). "For here materiality is thickness, coarseness, massiveness, wretchedness. It is what has consistency, weight, is absurd, is a brute but impassive presence; it is also what is humble, bare, and ugly" (DEE.91–92/ EE.57). For Levinas, the materiality of the work of art is just this implacable "materiality of being," where "matter is the very fact of the *il y a*" (DEE.92/EE.57). What Levinas wants to know is (and this is evidently the source of his interest in the work of art): What is "the ontological significance of materiality itself"? (IH.137–38/ CPP.8).

The Experience of Art. Part of this significance emerges when one asks what happens to subjectivity in the encounter with the work of art. What is it to be involved—or, as Levinas prefers, what is it to *participate*—in the moment when the work of art frees things from the conceptual grasp of the subject and returns them to the brute materiality of existence? The point to mark here is that for Levinas the experience of poetry or art is continuous with the experience of the *il y a*, which *De l'existence à l'existant* describes as an experience of a world emptied of its objects. One has to imagine inhabiting a space that is no longer a lifeworld, as though "after the world has come to an end." (In *Totalité et infini* Levinas writes: "When reduced to pure and naked existence, like the existence of the shades Ulysses visits in Hades, life dissolves into a shadow" [TeI.115/TI.112].) Levinas figures this experience of exteriority in terms of insomnia and the interminability of the night, as well as in terms of certain kinds of mystical or magical events in which subjectivity loses itself in an impersonal alterity, but he also compares it to certain kinds of realistic or naturalistic fiction in which "*beings* and things that collapse into their 'materiality' are terrifyingly present in their density, weight and shape" (DEE.97/EE.59–60). Things present in their materiality (like things in the night) are invisible, ungraspable—and horrible, where horror is not just a psychic tremor but a kind of ontological ecstasy, a movement that "turns the subjectivity of the subject, his particularity qua entity, inside out" (DEE.100/EE.61), thus exposing it to "the impersonal, non-substantive event of the night and the *il y a*" (DEE.104/ EE.63). This same ontological ecstasy characterizes the experience of the work of art, which on Levinas's analysis can never be an *aesthetic object*—never just something over and against which we can maintain the disinterested repose of the connoisseur; rather, disturbance and restlessness are the consequences of art. The experience of the modernist work in particular is no longer intelligible from the standpoint of an aesthetics of beauty, with its premium on the integration of discordant elements into a whole. Modernism, with its premium on the fragmentary, is an art of derangement; it does not produce harmony and repose but dissonance and anxiety (think of the noise of the dada drummer).[11] This is part of what it means to say that modern art is no longer an art of the visible. Indeed, Levinas's analysis opens up what one might call the "nonaesthetic" dimension of the work of art; or, put differently, Levinasian aesthetics is an aesthetics of darkness rather than of light, of materiality as against spirit (or, more accurately, an aesthetics of materiality that is prior to the alternatives of matter and spirit).

Darkness is the thesis of "Réalité et son ombre" (1948), which begins by stipulating that the work of art is, contra the Aristotelian tradition, outside all categories of cognition and representation, outside the light and the visible: "It is the very event of obscuring, a descent of the night, an invasion of shadow. To put it in theological terms . . . : art does not belong to the order of revelation" (IH.126/CPP.3). To be sure, a work of art is made of images, but an image is *not* (as in traditional aesthetics, or in Sartre's theory) a form of mediation; on the contrary, it constitutes a limit and, indeed, a *critique* of experience and therefore of subjectivity as such. Levinas writes: "An image does not engender a *conception*, as do scientific cognition and truth. . . . An image marks a hold over us rather than our initiative: a fundamental passivity" (IH.127–28/CPP.3).[12] An image works like a rhythm, which "represents a unique situation where we cannot speak of consent, assumption, initiative or freedom, because the subject is caught up and carried away by it. . . . It is so not even despite itself, for in rhythm there is no longer a oneself, but rather a sort of passage from oneself to anonymity. This is the captivation or incantation of poetry and music. It is a mode of being to which applies neither the form of consciousness, since the I is there stripped of its prerogative to assume, its power, nor the form of unconsciousness, since the whole situation and all its articulations are in a dark light, *present*" (IH.128/CPP.4). This conversion to anonymity means simply that art turns the sovereign ego out of its house in a deposition that anticipates the trauma or obsession of the ethical relation.[13] In the experience of the image, Levinas says, the subject is no longer a "being in the world"—especially since "what is today called 'being-in-the-world' is an existence with concepts" (IH.130/CPP.5), with all that this entails in the metaphor of grasping things and laying them open to view (IH.127/CPP.3). The image implies a reversal of power that turns the subject into a being "among things," wandering "among things as a thing, as part of the spectacle. It is exterior to itself, but with an exterior which is not that of a body, since the pain of the I-actor is felt by the I-spectator, although not through compassion. Here we have really an exteriority of the inward" (IH.129/CPP.4).[14] Here (as in Blanchot's poetics) the subject is no longer an "I" but a "he"—or, as the French more accurately has it, an *il*: he/it, neither one nor the other (neutral, anonymous). The interior of the subject has been evacuated; the subject is no longer correlative with a world but is, so to speak, outside of it—perhaps one should say, exposed to it.[15]

At any rate the experience of the image is not an intentional experience: the image is not an image *of* something, as if it were an extension of consciousness, a light unto the world. Phenomenology is mistaken, Levinas says, when it insists on the "transparency" of images, as if images were signs or symbols, that is, logical expressions of subjectivity—products of "imagination," for example, supposing there to be such a thing (IH.132/CPP.5). But images do not come into being according to a logic of mental operations, say by way of comparisons with an original. On the contrary, *every original is already its own image*:

> Being is not only itself, it escapes itself. Here is a person who is what he is; but he does not make us forget, does not absorb, cover over entirely the objects he holds and the way he holds them, his gestures, limbs, gaze, thought, skin, which escape from under the identity of his substance, which like a torn sack is unable to contain them. Thus a person bears on his face, alongside of its being with which he coincides, its own carica-

ture, its picturesqueness. The picturesque is always to some extent a caricature. Here is a familiar everyday thing, perfectly adapted to the hand which is accustomed to it, but its qualities, color, form, and position at the same time remain as it were behind its being, like the "old garments" of a soul which had withdrawn from that thing, like a "still life." And yet all this is the person and is the thing. There is then a duality in this person, this thing, a duality in being. It is what it is and is a stranger to itself, and there is a relationship between these two moments. We will say the thing is itself and is its image. And that this relationship between the thing and its image is resemblance. (IH.133/CPP.6)

An image is, so to speak, not a piece of consciousness but a piece of the *il y a*: it is a materialization of being, the way a cadaver is the image of the deceased, a remainder or material excess of being, "the remains."[16] Levinas writes: "A being is that which is, that which reveals itself in its truth, and, at the same time, it resembles itself, is its own image. The original gives itself as though it were at a distance from itself, as though it were withdrawing from itself, as though something in a being delayed behind being" (IH.134/CPP.6–7). An image is not a reproduction of a thing but (as in Mallarmé) a withdrawal of it from the world: consciousness is stopped in its tracks by an image and cannot get round behind it to an originating intention that would transform it into a meaning (a symbol or stand-in). Thus a painting is not, *pace* phenomenology, a looking-glass onto another world: "The painting does not lead us beyond the given reality, but somehow to the hither side of it. It is a symbol in reverse" (IH.135/CPP.7). A "symbol in reverse" means: the gaze of the spectator stops at the surface of the painting and is, so to speak, held there, on the hither side of being, suddenly passive, no longer seeing but gripped by what it sees in an ecstasy of fascination. The image no longer belongs to the order of the visible. "It belongs to an ontological dimension that does not extend between us and a reality to be captured, a dimension where commerce with reality is a rhythm" (IH.131/CPP.5).

The Work of Art as a Modality of Transcendence. What is the significance of this dimension—this "irréélité" or materiality of being (IH.137–38/CPP.8)? This question leads in several directions. The work of art is not a mode of revelation but a mode of transcendence, or, as Levinas says (borrowing from Jean Wahl), *transdescendence* (IH.136/CPP.8): in art reality is beside itself, on the hither side of itself, materialized, no longer an object for us but a thing in itself, a pure exteriority. Basically, art is ecstasy. In the third section of "Realité et son ombre" Levinas figures this ecstasy or exteriority temporally as an interruption of being: the *entre-temps*, the meanwhile in which the present is no longer a traversal or evanescence but an interval that separates the past from the future, as in the interminability of the statue, or in the fate of the tragic hero for whom the catastrophe has always already occurred: "Art brings about just this duration in the interval, in that sphere which a being is able to traverse, but in which its shadow is immobilized. The eternal duration of the interval in which a statue is immobilized differs radically from the eternity of the concept; it is the meanwhile, never finished, still enduring — something inhuman and monstrous" (IH.143/CPP.11). To experience art is to enter into this "inhuman or monstrous" *entre-temps*, which is not a "now" but an event that interrupts what is happening in the way insomnia keeps the night from passing in sleep, or the way the messianic vigil defers the end of history, or (as in Blanchot's poetics) the way dying is the impossibility of death: "Death qua nothingness is the death of the other, death for the survivor. The time of *dying* itself cannot give itself the other shore. What is unique and poignant in this instant is due to the fact that it cannot pass. In *dying*, the horizon of the future is given, but the future as a promise of a new present is refused; one is in the interval, forever an interval" (IH.143/CPP.11). It is this interval that explains why, as Levinas says in another context, "incompletion, not completion, [is] paradoxically the fundamental category of modern art" (HS.218/OS.147).

But if art is a passage onto the "inhuman and monstrous," what sort of value, if any, can it have, whatever its ontological significance? Levinas begins his conclusion to "Realité et son ombre" ("Pour une critique philosophique") by saying that the temporality of the work of art "does not have the quality of the living instant which is open to the salvation of becoming. . . . The value of this instant is thus made of its misfortune. This sad value is indeed the beautiful of modern art, opposed to the happy beauty of classical art" (IH.145/CPP.12). Here Levinas is less than clear, but possibly what he means is that it was the good fortune of the classical work to have a place in the human order of things, which it served to illustrate or even complete as a mode of edification. The classical work was part of the economy of redemption. It was at all events a humanist art, whereas the modern work is anarchic—that is, without reason or the mediation of any principle or ideality, informed by the *il y a* and structured according to "the inhuman and monstrous" *entre-temps*. So it is no wonder that the work of art is without any place in the world, which is why modernity sets a special realm aside for it: the museum world of the beautiful or, at any rate, the enigmatic, the eccentric, the strange.

Is this separation a condition of art, or a misreading of it? We may not find a straightforward answer to this question in Levinas's texts, but here are three considerations.

1. It is far from obvious what "the beautiful of modern art" could consist in, or whether any concept of the beautiful could be reconciled with the materiality of art, if one takes seriously the previously noted description of the cubist painting in *De l'existence à l'existant*: "For here materiality is thickness, coarseness, massivity, wretchedness. It is what has consistency, weight, is absurd, is a brute but impassive presence; it is also what is humble, bare, and ugly." Levinas had emphasized that this materiality is outside classical distinctions of letter and spirit or matter and form; it is the materiality of being, outside the visible, whence the experience of art becomes one of dispossession and restlessness, not disinterestedness and repose. Regarding the experience of the modern work of art, recall Kant's account of the experience of the sublime: "In presenting the sublime in nature the mind feels *agitated*, while in an aesthetic judgment about the beautiful in nature it is in *restful* contemplation. This agitation . . . can be compared with a vibration, i.e., with a rapid alternation of repulsion from, and attraction to, one and the same object." Moreover, the experience of the sublime (like the experience of the *il y a*) entails a crisis of subjectivity. The sublime object, Kant says, is "an abyss in which the imagination fears to lose itself."[17] If one follows categories supplied by Kant's third critique, one has to say that Levinasian aesthetics assigns the work of art to the order of the sublime, not to the beautiful.

2. Nevertheless, despite the logic of his analysis, Levinas himself seems to prefer the Sartrean ideology of *Les temps modernes* (in which, after all, "Realité et son ombre" first appeared), namely, as Levinas puts it, that "art, essentially disengaged, constitutes, in a world of initiative and responsibility, a dimension of evasion" (IH.145/CPP.12). Recall the analysis of rhythm in which the subject undergoes a "reversal of power into participation" (IH.129/CPP.4): although earlier the deposition of the sovereign ego had the structure

of critique (emphasizing the "reversal of power"), here it is simply *"la jouissance esthétique,"* or the private escape of subjectivity from cognition and action in the world (an assertion rather than deposition of sovereignty). "Art," says Levinas, "brings into the world the obscurity of fate, but it especially brings the irresponsibility that charms as a lightness and grace. It frees. To make or to appreciate a novel and a picture is to no longer have to conceive, is to renounce the effort of science, philosophy, and action. Do not speak, do not reflect, admire in silence and in peace — such are the counsels of wisdom satisfied before the beautiful. . . . There is something wicked and egoist and cowardly in artistic enjoyment. There are times when one can be ashamed of it, as of feasting during a plague" (IH.146/CPP.12). Such a view clearly appeals to Levinas's iconoclasm, but does it square with his thought?

3. The idea that art "brings into the world the obscurity of fate" summarizes neatly the thesis of the materiality of art (namely that "the artwork [is] an event of darkening of being . . . ; in the general economy of being, art is the falling movement on the hither side of time, into fate" [IH.140/CPP.9–10]). But an argument is missing that would explain how one gets from the "event of darkening" to "lightness and grace." One way to fill the hole would be to isolate the following question: "Is it presumptuous to denounce the hypertrophy of art in our times when, for almost everyone, it is identified with spiritual life?" (IH.146/CPP.12). The question (with its implication of the monstrosity of modern art — "hypertrophy" denotes excessive growth or deformity: a nice anaesthetic concept) suggests that what is really at issue here is not the ontology of the modernist work but the limits of its reception within traditional aesthetics.

Modernism, after all, especially in the various movements of the avant-garde, is a repudiation of the museum, the library, and the concert hall; its rhetoric is that of the outrageous performance that calls into question the distinction between art and non-art, not to say the whole idea of the beautiful. The legacy of Duchamp is nothing if not a critique of the aesthetics of pleasure (what Brecht called "culinary art").[18] Levinas gives little indication of what might constitute a "philosophical criticism" — "that would demand a broadening of the intentionally limited perspective of this study" (IH.148/CPP.13) — but it is clear from what he says that it could not be a spiritualizing criticism that isolates the work of art in a private realm of satisfaction and escape. On the contrary, if anything, Levinas's aesthetics of materiality helps to explain why so much of modern art, poetry, and music has been and continues to be condemned as unintelligible, de-generate, and obscene (and even displayed as such, as in the famous Exhibition of Decadent Art held in Munich in 1937). Thus Levinas says of philosophical criticism that it "integrates the inhuman work of the artist into the human world. . . . It does not attack the artistic event as such, that obscuring of being in images, that stopping of being in the meanwhile" (IH.146/CP.12). The "artistic event as such" would be, following Levinas's analysis, the materialization of things, which is to say "the darkening of being" or retrieval of things from the panoramic world of representation. In this event the task of criticism would evidently be to acknowledge the inhumanness of art, its material link to the *il y a*. This is, as it happens, the import of Maurice Blanchot's writings on poetry and art, which Levinas understood perhaps better than anyone else. Here (as Levinas suggests in the final paragraph of his essay) the experience of art does not result in "artistic idolatry" that makes of art "the supreme value of civilization" (IH.146, 148/CPP.12, 13). It means experiencing the limits of the human, which for Levinas means the limits of the ethical.

A Poetics of Proximity. In the experience of the work of art, Levinas says, we enter into "a mode of being to which applies neither the form of consciousness, since the I is there stripped of its prerogative to assume, its power, nor the form of unconsciousness, since the whole situation and all its articulations are, in a dark light, *present* [*toute le situation et toutes ses articulations, dans une obscure clarté, sont* presenté]" (IH.128/CPP.4). In "Realité et son ombre" Levinas takes recourse to rhythm and participation to elucidate this mode of being. But how to understand this "dark light"? What is it for things to be present in a dark light?

This question is part of the larger problem of how I can enter into a relation with a thing without destroying it, that is, without absorbing it into myself as an object of my consciousness or as part of my grip on existing. The figure of light is a way of formulating the problem, and the figure of "dark light" is a way of resolving it. In *Le temps et l'autre* (1947) Levinas writes: "Light [*Lumière*] is that through which something is other than myself, but already as if it came from me. The illuminated object is something one encounters, but from the very fact that it is illuminated one encounters it as if it came from us. It does not have a fundamental strangeness" (TA.47/TO.64). Art as "an event of the darkening of being" (IH.140/CPP.9) would thus be a way of setting things free of the light in which they exist for me. It would be a way of restoring to things their fundamental strangeness.

Heidegger was perhaps the first philosopher to think of art in this way, that is, not in terms of an aesthetics of the beautiful but in terms of an ontology of freedom. In Paris after the Liberation people were catching up with Heidegger's writings, including "Der Ursprung des Kunstwerke," with its conception of the work of art as an event that "holds open the Open of the world."[19] The *work* of the work of art is the uncovering of ontological difference: "In the midst of beings as a whole an open place occurs. There is a clearing, a lighting [Hofstadter translates one word, *Lichtung*, with two: "clearing" is his interpolation]. Thought of in reference to what is, to beings, this clearing is in a greater degree than are beings. This open center [*Mitte*] is therefore not surrounded by what is; rather, the lighting center itself encircles all that is, like the Nothing which we scarcely know" (G.39–40/PLT.53). In this "lighting" we find ourselves in the midst of things: "Only this clearing [*Lichtung*] grants and guarantees to us humans a passage to those beings that we ourselves are not, and access to the being that we ourselves are. Thanks to this clearing [*Lichtung*], beings are unconcealed in certain changing degrees" (G.40/PLT.53). So *Lichtung* is an ontological metaphor, a figure of Being. Yet this event of disclosure is not to be understood in terms of representation and cognition; the lighting is also *unheimlich*. For "each being we encounter and which encounters us keeps to this curious opposition of presence in that it always withholds itself at the same time in a concealedness. The clearing [*Lichtung*] in which beings stand is in itself at the same time concealment" (G.40/PLT.53). The world in which we find ourselves is not transparent; the world is, as Heidegger says, limned by the earth. Things are present, but not for us—not as objects open to view: "the open place in the midst of beings, the clearing, is never a rigid stage with a permanently raised curtain on which the play of beings runs its course" (G.41/PLT.54). Rather, beings are present *as things*, that is, in their thingly character, which Heidegger had characterized in the opening section of his essay in terms of the resistance of things to the violence of conceptual thinking: "The unpretentious thing evades thought most stubbornly. [Is this a defect in the thing?] Or can it be that this self-refusal of the mere thing, this self-contained independence, belongs precisely to the nature of the thing? Must not this strange and uncommunicative feature of the thing become intimately familiar to thought that tries to think the thing? If so, then we should not force our way to its thingly character" (G.17/PLT.31–32). In contrast to conceptual thinking, the work of the work of art is nonviolent, or rather it disposes us toward things in a nonviolent way (G.54/PLT.66), disclosing them in their strangeness or in their earthliness (G.57/PLT.69). Significantly, Heidegger reserves the term poetry (*Dichtung*) for this disclosure: "It is due to art's poetic nature that, in the midst of what is, art breaks open an open place, in whose openness everything is other than usual" (G.60/PLT.72).

Levinas's objections to Heidegger's phenomenology of disclosure are well known: the world that is opened in Heidegger's analysis has no people in it. Dasein listens for the peal of stillness across a postnuclear landscape. But Levinas becomes implicated in Heidegger's analysis as soon as he asks how any relationship with alterity is possible without reducing alterity to something of mine. He puts this question in an early essay on Blanchot, "Le regarde du poète" (1956): "How can the Other (which Jankélévitch calls the '*absolutely other*' and Blanchot 'eternal streaming of the outside') appear, that is, be for someone, without already losing its alterity and exteriority by way of offering itself to view" (SMB.13–14/PN.130). This question is at the heart of Blanchot's poetics, which is concerned precisely with the alterity of *things*. Already in "Littérature et la droit à la mort" (1947–48) Blanchot had asked about the consequences of intelligibility, given that signification is, as in Hegel, a dialectic of negation that annihilates things in their singularity and replaces them with concepts (PF.313/WF.323–24). The work of the spirit that builds up the world is, paradoxically, "the speech of death" (EI.49/ IC.35). Poetry for Blanchot is a refusal of this speech. By withdrawing into its materiality, poetic language is no longer a form of mediation. Instead it interrupts the dialectical movement in which things are conceptually determined. "The language of literature," Blanchot says, "is a search for [the] moment which precedes literature. Literature usually calls it existence; it wants the cat as it exists, the pebble *taking the side of things*, not man but the pebble, and in this pebble what man rejects by saying it" (PF.316/WF.327). "Literature," Blanchot says, "is a concern for the reality of things, for their unknown, free, and silent existence" (PF.310/WF.330). Poets are what they are, he says, because "they are interested in the reality of language, because they are not interested in the world but in what things and beings would be if there were no world" (PF.321/WF.333) — existence without a world: the *il y a*. But whereas Levinas considers the *il y a* from the standpoint of the subject's experience of it (ecstasy, horror), Blanchot considers it from the standpoint of things in their freedom from subjectivity.

Levinas searches Blanchot's poetics for "an invitation to leave the Heideggerian world" (SMB.20/PN.135). In "Le regard du poète," invoking the figure of the dark light, he writes: "In Blanchot, *the work uncovers, in an uncovering that is not truth, a darkness*" (SMB.21–22/PN.136):

> The literary space to which Blanchot . . . leads us has nothing in common with the Heideggerian world that art renders inhabitable. Art, according to Blanchot, far from elucidating the world, exposes the desolate, lightless substratum underlying it, and restores to our sojourn its exotic essence—and, to the wonders of our architecture their function of makeshift desert shelters. Blanchot and Heidegger agree that art does not lead (contrary to classical aesthetics) to a world behind the world, an ideal world behind the real one. Art is light. Light from on high in Heidegger, making the world, founding place. In Blanchot it is a black light, a night coming from below—a light that undoes the world, leading it back to its origin, to the over and over again, the murmur, ceaseless lapping of waves, a "deep past, never long enough ago." (SMB.23/PN.137)

The contrast that Levinas draws between Heidegger and Blanchot is too broad and misses the strangeness in Heidegger's aesthetics.[20] However, it is true that the Heideggerian world is an opening in which space is a circle or volume to be inhabited, if not altogether familiarly (Heidegger's world is always uncanny), whereas for Blanchot the space of literature is a surface across which one moves endlessly in what Levinas aptly calls "the exteriority of absolute exile" (SMB.17/PN.133). Space here is not open to the light. It is the "Outside," which Levinas approaches guardedly in his conclusion to *L'autrement qu'être*: "the openness of space signifies the outside where nothing covers anything, non-protection, the reverse of a retreat, homelessness [*sans-domicile*], non-world, non-habitation, layout without security" (AE.275–76/OTB.17–18). But Blanchot does not regard exile as a negative condition, a mere deprivation of place; it is rather a region (let us call it a traversal of ontology and ethics) in which subjectivity no longer presides over things from a standpoint or perspective of the whole, certainly not from the perspective of ownership or conceptual possession.[21] Exile is a relation of intimacy (which Blanchot does not hesitate to call responsibility) with what is nevertheless outside my grasp.[22]

In his second essay on Blanchot, "La servant et son maitre" (1966), Levinas writes that "Blanchot's properly literary work brings us primarily a new feeling [*sensation*]: a new 'experience,' or, more precisely, a new prickling sensation of the skin, brushed against by things [*un 'frisson nouveau', ou, plus exactement, une nouvelle démangeaison de l'épiderme, effleuré par les choses'*]" (SMB.34/PN.143). This captures something of what Blanchot, in "Le grand refus" (1959), calls a relation with an "immediate singularity" that cannot be touched—that which refuses "all direct relation, all mystical fusion, and all sensible contact"—but to which the subjectivity of the poet or writer is nevertheless exposed as to "the presence of the non-accessible, presence excluding or exceeding [*débordant*] any present." This amounts to saying that "the immediate, infinitely exceeding any present possibility by its very presence, is the infinite presence of what remains radically absent, a presence in its presence always infinitely other [*autre*], presence of the other in its alterity" (EI.53–53/IC.37–38). The "other" here is neither the Levinasian *Autrui* nor Heidegger's Being but the Outside or foreign, which (philosophy be damned) Blanchot would prefer to think of as neither ethical nor ontological. Neither does Blanchot think of it as the *il y a*; it is simply the singular and irreducible as such. In "Comment découvrir l'obscur" (1959) he calls it simply "the impossible" (EI.68/IC.48).[23] Poetry, he says, is a "response" to this impossibility—"a relation with the obscure and the unknown that would be a relation neither of force [*puissance*], nor of comprehension, nor even of revelation" (EI.68/IC.48).

Poetry in this sense is a relation of proximity, and Levinas appears to pick up on this in "Langage et proximité" (1967), where he distinguishes between two dimensions of language. The first is kerygmatic, which has to do with the power of language to synchronize things in a structure of identity—the "as-structure" of hermeneutics, the logical structure of the proposition, the temporal structure of narrative that proclaims the individual as the same over the course of multiple and heterogeneous transformations. The second, however, concerns the movement of subjectivity outside of itself that Levinas has always regarded as an "original language" on the hither side of discourse (where Blanchot locates poetry). In "L'ontologie est-elle fondamentale?" (1951) Levinas had called it "prayer." In "Langage et proximité" it is called "contact": "there is in speech a relationship with a singularity located outside the theme of speech, a singularity that is not thematized by the speech but is approached" (DHH.224/ CPP.115). Heretofore Levinas had always jealously guarded this "singularity" as a *personal* other, *Autrui*, the face whose "defenseless eyes" constitute "the original language" (BPW.12); whereas, in explicit argument with Levinas, Blanchot had always insisted "that *autrui* is a name that is essentially neutral" (EI.102/IC.72): neither human nor nonhuman but *inhuman* (absolutely without horizon). In *Totalité et infini* things are never singular. They can be enjoyed in sensibility, but sensibility is still an aesthetic (and even economic) concept:[24]

> Things have a form, are seen *in* the light—silhouettes or profiles; the face signifies *itself*. As silhouette and profile a thing owes its nature to a perspective, remains relative to a point of view; a thing's situation thus constitutes its being. Strictly speaking it has no identity; convertible into another thing, it can become money. Things have no face; convertible, 'realizable,' they have a price. . . . The aesthetic orientation man gives to the whole of his world represents a return to enjoyment and to the elemental on a higher plane. The world of things calls for art, in which intellectual accession to being moves into enjoyment, in which the Infinity of the Idea is idolized in the finite, but sufficient, image. (TeI.149/TI.140)

However, in "Langage et proximité" the sensibility of things takes on an ethical significance within the relation of proximity: "The immediacy of the sensible is an event of proximity and not of knowledge" (DHH.225/CPP.116). This means that the sensible no longer belongs to the order of the visible. As Levinas says, "Sensibility must be interpreted first of all as touch" (DHH.227/CPP.118).

Indeed, perception itself is reconceived as "immediacy, contact, and language": "Perception is a proximity with being which intentional analysis does not account for. The sensible is superficial only in its role being cognition. In the ethical relationship with the real, that is, in the relationship of proximity which the sensible establishes, the essential is committed. Life is there. Sight is, to be sure, an openness and a consciousness, and all sensibility, opening as a consciousness, is called vision; but even in its subordination to cognition, sight maintains contact and proximity. The visible caresses the eye. One sees and one hears like one touches" (DHH.228/CPP.118). And whereas since *Le temps et l'autre* the caress had been exclusively human, now "the caress of the sensible" spreads out from the human to the world of things, where it is named "poetry":

> The proximity of things is poetry; in themselves the things are revealed before being approached. In stroking an animal already the hide hardens in the skin. But over the hands that have touched things, places trampled by beings, the things they have held, the images of those things, the fragments of those things, the contexts in which those fragments enter, the inflexions of the voice and the words that are articulated in them, the ever sensible signs of language, the letters traced, the vestiges, the relics—over all things, beginning with the human face and skin, tenderness spreads. Cognition turns into proximity, into the purely sensible. Matter, which is invested as a tool, and a tool in the world, is also, via the human, the matter that obsesses me with its proximity. The poetry of the world is inseparable from proximity par excellence, or the proximity of the neighbor par excellence. (DHH.228/CPP.118–19)

Does it make sense to speak of poetry in this way? It depends on whether one can see the coherence of poetry and the caress as modes of transcendence. In *Le temps et l'autre* the caress is said to be "a mode of the subject's being, where the subject who is in contact with another goes beyond this contact. Contact as sensation is part of the world of light. But what is caressed is not touched, properly speaking. It is not the softness or warmth of the hand given in contact that the caress seeks. The seeking of the caress constitutes its essence by the fact that the caress does not know what it seeks. This 'not knowing,' this fundamental disorder, is essential" (TA.83/TO.89). Compare "Le moi et la totalité," where a "poetic world" is one in which "one thinks without knowing what one thinks" (MT.362/CPP.35), and a "poetic thought" is a "thought which thinks without knowing what it thinks, or thinks as one dreams" (MT.368/CPP.40). The peculiarity is that "not knowing" in the case of the caress carries a positive valence, whereas, in the context of "Le moi et la totalité," the poetic thought that "thinks without knowing what it thinks" is something negative, as if Levinas were simply reciting a line from Plato's *Ion*. But in fact poetry and the ethical occupy the same priority vis-à-vis cognition (both are anarchic). Thus by the time of "Langage et proximité" poetry and the caress are taken up together in a relation of one-for-the-other, no longer part of "the world of light" but characters in "the intrigue of proximity and communication" (AE.82/OTB.48).

The question is whether assimilating poetry to the ethical in this way doesn't just allegorize poetry and therefore reduce it in the usual philosophical style. At the outset of *Totalité et infini* Levinas says that the purpose of his book is to perceive "in discourse a non-allergic relation with alterity" (TeI.38/TI.47). This means reconceptualizing discourse away from intentionality and the proposition toward what is finally termed Saying (*le Dire*), in which "the subject approaches a neighbor in expressing itself, in being expelled, in the literal sense of the term, out of any locus, no longer *dwelling*, not stomping any ground. Saying uncovers, beyond nudity, what dissimulation may be under the exposedness of a skin laid bare. It is the very *respiration* of this skin prior to any intention" (AE.83/OTB.48–49). Meanwhile in his writings since the 1940s Blanchot had been elucidating what looks like much the same thing, namely a theory of poetry as "a non-dialectical experience of speech" (EI.90/IC.63) in which the subject (the poet or writer, but also evidently the reader) enters into a relation with what is outside the grasp of subjectivity, and therefore also outside the grasp of language as conceptual determination (hence the need for writing that occurs "outside discourse, outside language") (EI.vii/IC.xii). But alterity for Levinas is always another human being, whereas Blanchot's argument against Levinas is this: to say that only what is human can be other is already to feature the other within a totality or upon a common ground; it is to assemble with the other a possible (workable) community. Blanchot prefers indeterminate or at least highly abstract terms for alterity, namely the "Outside," the "Neutral," the "Unknown" (*l'inconnu*)—not the beggar, the orphan, or the widow, who are, after all, stock characters out of ancient biblical parables. Thus for Blanchot poetry is in excess of ethical alterity; it is a relation of foreignness or strangeness with what is absolutely singular and irreducible (but, for all of that, a relation of proximity or intimacy in which one is in a condition of exposure rather than cognition). As he says in "René Char et la pensée du neutre" (1963), poetry means that "to speak the unknown, to receive it through speech while leaving it unknown, is precisely not to take hold of it, not to comprehend it; it is rather to refuse to identify it even by sight, that 'objective' hold that seizes, albeit at a distance. To live with the unknown before one (which also means: to live before the unknown, and before oneself as unknown) is to enter into the responsibility of a speech that speaks without exercising any form of power" (EI.445/IC.302). Poetry is thus a species of *le Dire sans le Dit*, but the subject in poetry is exposed to something other than *Autrui*—perhaps it is the *il y a*. Whatever it is, Blanchot leaves it, pointedly, unnamed ("Such is the secret lot, the secret decision of every essential speech in us: naming the *possible*, responding to the *impossible*" [EI.68/IC.48]).

Perhaps in the end the relation of poetry and the ethical comes to this: both are forms of Saying (*le Dire*) on the hither side of thematization and are, therefore, *materializations* of language and so, by the same logic, analogous modes of transcendence. But for Blanchot, poetry is the materiality—the literal "Outside"—of language as such, which he epitomizes with the Mallarméan word *l'écriture*, whereas, by contrast, Levinas figures materiality as the corporeality of the subject: *le Dire* is exposure, "the very respiration of the skin." Levinas thinks of this Saying as "the original language," which is to say a language that is not yet linguistical, "a language without words [*mots*] or propositions" [DHH.228/CPP.119].) Language here is corporeal expression in which "the face speaks" in "the language of the eyes, impossible to dissemble" (TeI.61–62/TI.66).

Owing perhaps to his deep-seated iconoclasm, Levinas restricts the materiality of language as such to the sounds of words, as in "La transcendance des mots: À propos des Biffures" (1949), which begins as if it were to be a review of a volume of Michel Leiris's autobiography, *Biffures* (1948), but which becomes instead an inquiry into the etymology of *biffures*, meaning "crossings-out" or "erasures," where what is erased are things in their temporality or irreducibility to spatial and visual contexts. Levinas construes the word *biffures* as a figure of pure spatiality, or of the simultaneity of things held in place—in other words, a figure of totality. As such it can be traced back to "the visual experience to which Western civilization ultimately reduces all mental life. That experience involves ideas; it is light, it seeks the clarity of the self-evident. It ends up with the unveiled, the phenomenon. All is immanent to it" (HS.218–19/OS.147). In contrast to sight, which is a modality of worldmaking, sound is a modality of transcendence: "There is . . . in sound—and in consciousness understood as hearing—a shattering of the always complete world of vision and art. Sound is all repercussion, outburst, scandal. While in vision a form espouses a content and soothes it, sound is like the sensible quality overflowing its limits, the incapacity of form to hold its content—a true rent in the fabric of the world—that by which the world that is *here* prolongs a dimension inconvertible into vision" (HS.219/OS.147–48). For Levinas, moreover, sound is not simply an empirical sensation; it is phenomenological. That is, not just any noise can achieve the transcendence of sound. "To really hear a sound," he says, "is to hear a word. Pure sound is a word [*Le son pur est verbe*]" (HS.219/OS.149).

It is important to notice that Levinas's word for "word" here is not *mot* but *verbe*, that is, not the word in its spatial and visual fixity as a sign or noun or word-as-image but the word in its temporality, not only in the grammatical sense of the propositional verb but more important as the event of speaking itself, the spoken word as such, where *verbe* entails the power of the word to affect things — to intervene in the world as well as to function in a sentence — as in Rimbaud's *alchemie du verbe* (the writer Michel Leiris, Levinas says, "est chimiste plutôt qu'alchimiste du verbe" [HS.216/OS.145]), that is, more analytical than magical; unlike the surrealists he finds causes for his dreams). The *mot* in its transcendence is always more expression than idea, more *parole* than *langue*, more enigma than phenomenon, more *sens* than *signification*, more *Dire* than *Dit*: an open-ended series of Levinasian distinctions is traceable to his iconoclastic theory of the *verbe*. For Levinas, of course, the priority of sound over semantics is meant to indicate the event of sociality: sound means the *presence* of others making themselves felt in advance of what is said. Sound is not the medium of propositional language but of other people. More than this, however, the sound of words is an ethical event, which Levinas does not hesitate to characterize as *critique*, not only because others interrupt me in making themselves felt, setting limits to my autonomy, but because *even when I myself speak* — even in self-expression — I am no longer an "I," am no longer self-identical, but am now beside myself: "To speak is to interrupt my existence as a subject, a master" (HS.221/OS.149). Of course this is exactly what Blanchot says happens to the subject in the experience of *l'écriture*. Which is why it is most interesting that in Levinas the materiality of language as Blanchot understands it comes into the foreground not as a theme but as an increasingly dominant and controversial dimension of his (Levinas's) own writing.[25] Here, if anywhere, is where poetry and the ethical draw near one another.

Notes

Chapter One

1. *Sein und Zeit* (Tübingen: Max Niemeyer, 1984), p. 8 (*Being and Time*, trans. John Macquarrie and Edward Robinson [New York: Harper and Row, 1962], p. 29).

2. See Arthur Danto, *After the End of Art: Contemporary Art and the Pale of History* (Princeton: Princeton University Press, 1997), who cites this passage from Heidegger and then proposes that we think of modernism in general in Heidegger's terms, namely "as a moment in which it seemed as though things could not continue as they had been, and fresh foundations had to be sought if they were to continue at all. This would explain why modernism so often took the form of issuing manifestos. All the main movements in philosophy of the twentieth century addressed the question of what philosophy itself was: positivism, pragmatism, and phenomenology each undertook radical critiques of philosophy, and each sought to reconstruct philosophy on firm foundations" (pp. 66–67).

It is now customary to distinguish between "modernism" and "modernity," where modernity is understood as the project of enlightenment, or what Max Weber called "the rationalization of the world." See Jürgen Habermas, "Modernity—An Unfinished Project," first published under the title "Modernity versus Postmodernity" in *New German Critique* 22 (Winter 1981): 4–13, in which "aesthetic modernity"—an anarchic revolt against "all that is normative"—is opposed to the authentic modernity of the Enlightenment that tried to develop scientific reason, a morality based on universal principles, and the autonomy of the individual, but which remains "incomplete" precisely because of a preoccupation with the aesthetic dimensions of modernity. See Habermas, *Die Moderne: ein unvollendetes Projekt. Philosophische-politische Aufsätze, 1977–1990* (Leipzig: Reclam, 1990), pp. 32–54, esp. 34–38. Some purchase on these semantic problems can be gained by consulting the journal *Modernism/Modernity*; see, for example, Susan Friedman, "Definitional Excursions: The Meanings of Modern/Modernity/Modernism," *Modernism/Modernity* 8, no.3 (September 2001): 493–513.

3. See Habermas's critique of Heidegger in *Der philosophischen Diskurs der Moderne: zwölf Vorlesungen* (Frankfurt am Main: Suhrkamp, 1985), p. 168 (*The Philosophical Discourse of Modernity*, trans. Frederick Lawrence [Cambridge, MA: MIT Press, 1987], esp. p. 141):

> The language of *Being and Time* had suggested the decisionism of empty resoluteness; the later philosophy suggests the submissiveness of an equally empty readiness for subjugation. To be sure, the empty formula of "thoughtful remembrance" can also be filled in with a different attitudinal syndrome, for example with the anarchist demand for a subversive stance of refusal, which corresponds more to present moods than does blind submission to something superior. But the arbitrariness with which the same thought-figure can be given contemporary actualization remains irritating.

See also *Moralbewußtein und kommunikatives Handlein* (Frankfurt am Main: Suhrkamp, 1983), esp. pp. 16–18 (*Moral Consciousness and Communicative Action*, trans. Christian Lenhardt and Shierry Weber Nicholson [Cambridge, MA: MIT Press, 1990], esp. pp. 17–20), where Habermas argues that philosophy must retain its traditional role as "the guardian of rationality." Rudolf Gasché has an excellent discussion of Habermas in the context of a post-Heideggerian (or "postmodern") critique of subject-centered rationality in "Postmodernism and Rationality," *The Journal of Philosophy* 85, no. 10 (1988): 528–38.

4. See Hans-Georg Gadamer, "The Hermeneutics of Suspicion," in *Hermeneutics: Questions and Prospects*, ed. Gary Shapiro and Alan Sica (Amherst: University of Massachussetts Press, 1984), esp. pp. 63–64:

> Dialectic [the procedure of Greek thinking] does not claim to have a first principle. It is true: Plato as he appeared to Aristotle developed two "principles," the One and the Dyad. The Dyad was an indeterminate Dyad that meant openness for further determination. . . . These "principles" of Plato were not meant to yield an ultimate determinacy. I think Plato was well aware of this position when he said that philosophy is something for human beings, not for gods. Gods *know*, but we are in this ongoing process of approximation and overcoming error by dialectically moving toward truth. In this sense I could present a partial defense of the idea that the oldest heritage of philosophy is exactly its functionality, its giving an account, and that as such it cannot presume to have first principles. This suggests very well what I would

have in place of "foundation." I would call it "participation," because that is what happens in human life.

5. *Philosophische Untersuchungen/Philosophical Investigations*. 3d ed., German text (verso) with revised English version (recto) by G. E. M. Anscombe (Oxford: Basil Blackwell, 2001), p. 33e.

6. (London: Routledge, 1992), pp. 191–96. "Postmodernism" is not a term I've ever found useful, at least not as a period concept. But I find Bauman's conception of the postmodern congenial. A postmodernist is just a late modernist who thinks about where he or she comes from or is located historically and culturally. A postmodernist has a history but not an identity and finds the absence of foundations (in Gadamer's sense, cited in note 5, above) to be a condition of freedom. See note 9, below.

7. "An Anthropological Approach to the Contemporary Significance of Rhetoric," in *After Philosophy: End or Transformation?*, ed. Kenneth Baynes, James Bohman, and Thomas McCarthy (Cambridge, MA: MIT Press, 1967), p. 433.

8. On singularity, see Gilles Deleuze, *Logique du sens* (Paris: Éditions du Minuit, 1969), p. 67 (*The Logique of Sense*, trans. Constantin V. Boundas [New York: Columbia University Press, 1990], p. 52): "The singularity belongs to another dimension than that of denotation, manifestation, or signification. It is essentially pre-individual, non-personal, and a-conceptual. It is quite indifferent to the individual and the collective, the personal and the impersonal, the particular and the general—and to their oppositions. Singularity is *neutral*." For a slightly different view, where the singular is not an isolate and is also a person, see Jean-Luc Nancy, *Être singulier pluriel* (Paris: Éditions Galilée, 1996), pp. 1–131 (*Being Singular Plural* [Stanford: Stanford University Press, 2000], pp. 1–100). The notion of the singular can be traced to Emmanuel Levinas's conception of ethical alterity, where the other is irreducible to the same, that is, refractory to categories. See *Totalité et infini* (The Hague: Martinus Nijhoff, 1961) (*Totality and Infinity: An Essay in Exteriority* [Pittsburgh: Duquesne University Press, 1969]). See also Todd May's useful book, *The Political Philosophy of Poststructuralist Anarchism* (University Park: Pennsylvania State University Press, 1994).

9. See Michel Foucault, *Souveiller et punir: naissance de la prison* (Paris: Èditions Gallimard, 1975) (*Discipline and Punish: The Birth of the Prison*, trans. Alan Sheridan [New York: Vintage Books, 1977]), and esp. an interview from 1976, "Truth and Power," in *Power: Essential Works of Foucault, 1954–1984*, vol. 3, ed. James D. Faubion (New York: The New Press, 1994), pp. 111–33.

10. *The Futurist Moment: Avant-Garde, Avant Guerre, and the Language of Rupture* (Chicago: Chicago University Press, 1986), esp. p. 38: "It is [the] straining of the artwork to assimilate and respond to that which is not art that characterizes the Futurist moment." As such, the futurist moment inau-

gurates the history of modernism, in which the question of what counts as art remains open owing to the openness of the artwork to whatever is not itself. See also Perloff, *21st-Century Modernism: The "New" Poetics* (Oxford: Basil Blackwell, 2002)—a book that links contemporary North American poetry with the work of the early T. S. Eliot, Gertrude Stein, Marcel Duchamp, and the sound-poetry of the Russian futurist Velimir Khlebnikov. For Perloff, a postmodernist is someone who has appropriated or recuperated—brought to life again—the innovations of early modernism. See also Astradur Eysteinnsson's excellent study, *The Concept of Modernism* (Ithaca: Cornell University Press, 1990).

11. *"Allgemeines und Besonderes,"* in *Ästhetische Theorie* (Frankfurt am Main: Suhrkamp Verlag, 1973), pp. 296–334, hereafter cited as AT; "Universal and Particular," in *Aesthetic Theory*, trans. Robert Hullot-Kentor (Minneapolis: University of Minnesota Press, 1997), pp. 199–225, hereafter cited as AeT:

> The nominalistic artwork should become an artwork by being organized from below to above, not by having principles of organization foisted on it. But no artwork left blindly to itself possesses the power of organization that would set up binding boundaries for itself. Investing the work with such power would in fact be fetishistic. Unchecked aesthetic nominalism liquidates . . . all forms as a remnant of a spiritual being-in-itself. It terminates in a literal facticity, and this is irreconcilable with art. . . . The artifactual character of the artwork [i.e., that it is a construction] is incompatible with the postulate of pure relinquishment to the material. By being something made, artworks acquire that element of organization, of being something directed, in the dramaturgical sense, that is anathema to the nominalistic sensibility. (AT.327/AeT.220)

Fredric Jameson gives an excellent account of Adorno's critique of nominalism in *Late Marxism: Adorno, or the Persistence of the Dialectic* (London: Verso Books, 1990), pp. 157–64.

12. See Marjorie Perloff, "The Search for 'Prime Words': Pound, Duchamp, and the Nominalist Ethos," in *Differentials: Poetry, Poetics, Pedagogy* (Tuscaloosa: University of Alabama Press, 2004), pp. 39–59.

13. William Carlos Williams, *Paterson* (New York: New Directions, 1963), pp. 261–62.

14. *Imaginations*, ed. Webster Schott (New York: New Directions, 1970), p. 70. See also Gerald L. Bruns, "'Accomplishments of Inhabitation': Danto, Cavell, and the Argument of American Poetry," in *Tragic Thoughts at the End of Philosophy: Language, Literature, and Ethical Theory* (Evanston: Northwestern University Press, 1999), pp. 133–63.

15. Adorno as I read him—my Adorno—is at bottom an anarchist. A fragment from *Minima Moralia* reads: "Measured by its concept, the individ-

ual [in the modern world] has indeed become as null and void as Hegel's philosophy anticipated: seen *sub specie individuationis*, however, absolute contingency, permitted to persist as a seemingly abnormal state, is itself the essential. The world is systematized horror, but therefore it is to do the world too much honor to think of it entirely as a system." *Gesammelte Schriften* (Frankfurt am Main: Suhrkamp, 1980), Band 4: *Minima Moralia: Reflexionen aus dem beschädigten Leben*, p. 126 (*Minima Moralia: Reflections from a Damaged Life*, trans. Edmund Jephcott [London: Verso, 1978], p. 113).

16. See Thierry de Duve, *Kant after Duchamp* (Cambridge, MA: MIT Press, 1996), who develops this thesis in detail (without, interestingly, mentioning Adorno).

17. *Vorlesungen über die Ästhetik. Werke in zwanzig Bänden.* Band 13.1 (Frankfurt am Main: Suhrkamp, 1970), p. 25 (*Aesthetics: Lectures on Fine Art*, trans. T. M. Knox [Oxford: Clarendon Press, 1975], p. 1:11).

18. Compare Adorno: "If a work opens itself completely, it reveals itself as a question and demands reflection; then the work vanishes into the distance, only to return to those who thought they understood it, overwhelming them for a second time with the question, 'What is it?'" (AT.184/ AeT.121).

19. "The End of Art," in *The Philosophical Disenfranchisement of Art* (New York: Columbia University Press, 1986), pp. 80–115 (emphasis mine). See also Gianni Vattimo, "The Death or Decline of Art," in *The End of Modernity*, trans. Jon R. Snyder (Baltimore: The Johns Hopkins University Press, 1988), pp. 51–64; and Giorgio Agamben, "A Self-Annihilating Nothing," in *The Man without Content*, trans. Georgia Albert (Stanford: Stanford University Press, 1999), pp. 52–58. Jean-Luc Nancy has an interesting variation on this theme in "Le vestige de art," in *Les Muses* (Paris: Éditions Galilée, 1994), pp. 135–59 ("The Vestige of Art," in *The Muses*, trans. Peggy Kamuf [Stanford: Stanford University Press, 1996], pp. 81–100). At the end of art, art ceases to be an image or sensible presentation of the Idea (or of anything at all); rather, it is the *vestige*, no longer a thing itself but only a remainder. Being cannot be predicated of the vestige, which is always in passage, passing away, such that "art is each time radically *another art* [not only another form, another style, but another "essence" of "art"] (p. 143/p. 94). In this sense the vestige is the mode of existence of modernism.

20. One could take this sentence as the paradoxical motto of modernist anarchism. The paradox is that, in defiance of tradition, convention, or the powers of official culture, anything goes within the artworld, but not everything is possible at once, owing to the finitude of historical conditions, as when digital technology makes possible an indefinite array of new forms of poetry and music that were not possible even a few years ago. What is possible in any present moment is open and undetermined but, nevertheless, limited to the present. R. M. Berry formulates this paradox very neatly as an intellectual dilemma in "The Avant-Garde and the Question of Literature,"

Soundings: An Interdisciplinary Journal 88, nos. 1–2 (Spring/Summer 2005): 105–27. See esp. 105–6:

> My background idea is that the continuation into the new millennium of literary experimentation, despite its widespread neglect, is forceful evidence that modernism was not a response to historically circumscribed conflicts and crises, but, on the contrary, arose from necessities internal to literature itself. I will try here to give concreteness to this idea, to indicate how these necessities arise, what they look like, why they are not generally recognized, while attempting some *rapprochement* with the history I am bracketing. After all, what I have situated as internal to literature, counter to history, is simply the necessity for change, that is, for history. Said another way, it is unclear whether I am looking for the necessity of formal experimentation or perhaps for freedom from necessity altogether. These could be the same thing.

Whatever else an anarchist might want, "freedom from necessity" would be the main thing. Meanwhile, on the restrictions of chance, randomness, or arbitrary decisions in art, see Holger Schulze, "Hand-Luggage: For a Generative Theory of Artifacts," *Leonardo Music Journal* 13 (2003): 61–65, esp. 62: "the limitations of our work are already established before we set out. These are natural restrictions, from which there is no escape: preferences for certain materials, the organization of workflow and movements, antipathies against certain tools or environments. There is no pure chance." To which he adds: "Also, there is absolutely no 'Anything goes!' Even if we work randomly—or by destructing, disorganizing, decomposing, deconstructing—we cannot possibly transcend these limits. We can only use sources, which are also artifacts in themselves and thus products designed very much on purpose. By choosing certain materials or products we automatically choose their underlying intentions." But of course, as Duchamp shows with his snow shovel, we also bracket these intentions.

21. See *Marcel Duchamp*, ed. Anne d'Harnoncourt and Kynaston Mc-Schine (Prestel, Germany: The Museum of Modern Art and Philadelphia Museum of Art, 1989), p. 212.

22. See Wittgenstein's *Philosophical Investigations*, §211: "How can he *know* how he is to continue a pattern by himself—whatever instructions you give him?—Well, how do I know?—If that means 'Have I reasons?' the answer is: my reasons will soon give out. And then I shall act, without reasons" (p. 84e). And §217: "'How am I able to obey a rule?'—if this is not a question about causes, then it is about the justification for my following the rule in the way I do. If I have exhausted the justifications I have reached bedrock, and my spade is turned. Then I am inclined to say: 'This is simply what I do.'" (p. 85e).

23. See Cavell's discussion (of Wittgenstein's critique) of criteria in *The Claim of Reason: Wittgenstein, Skepticism, Morality, and Tragedy* (Oxford: Ox-

ford University Press, 1979), pp. 3–48, and esp. p. 45, where the shortfall of criteria is said to "affirm" the thesis of skepticism, namely: "Our relation to the world as a whole, or to others in general, is not one of knowing, where knowing construes itself as being certain."

24. Already in 1937, in a talk entitled "The Future of Music: Credo," Cage had said: "Whereas, in the past, the point of disagreement has been between dissonance and consonance, it will be, in the immediate future, between noise and so-called musical sounds. The present methods of writing music, principally those which employ harmony and its reference to particular steps in the field of sound, will be inadequate for the composer, who will be faced with the entire field of sound." *Silence: Lectures and Writings by John Cage* (Middletown, CT: Wesleyan University Press, 1961), p. 4, hereafter cited as S. Like Duchamp, Cage was anarchic. In a text called "'45' for a Speaker" (S.160), Cage wrote:

> Very frequently no one knows that
> contemporary music is or could be
> art.
> He simply thinks it was irritating.
> Irritating one way or another
> that is to say
> keeping us from ossifying.
> It may be objected that from this point
> of view anything goes. Actually
> anything *does* go—but only when
> nothing is taken as the basis. In an utter emptiness
> anything can take place.

Anything goes, because nothing can be traced back to (or held back by) a principle or foundation. For Cage, "utter emptiness" is not a void but an open field of possibilities.

25. *Must We Mean What We Say? A Book of Essays* (Cambridge: Cambridge University Press, 1987), pp. 188–89, hereafter cited as MW.

26. On "living with a concept," see Cora Diamond, "Losing Your Concepts," *Ethics* 98, no. 2 (1988): 255–57.

27. Compare John Cage, "Experimental Music" (1957), on the use of magnetic tape "not simply to record performances but to make new music that [is] possible only because of it. . . . But advantage can be taken of these possibilities only if one is willing to change one's musical habits radically" (S.9).

28. Thus, for example, when it comes to literature, Arthur Danto turns away from Andy Warhol and back into an Aristotelian for whom literature is nothing if not about the world, or at least a possible world. See his essay, "Philosophy / as / and / of Literature," in *The Philosophical Disenfranchisement of Art*, pp. 135–61.

29. Jameson's essay, "Postmodernism, or the Cultural Logic of Late Capitalism," first appeared in the *New Left Review* 146 (1984): 53–92, hereafter cited as PM. See his discussion of a passage from Bob Perelman's poem, "China," pp. 73–75.

30. *A Poetics* (Cambridge: Harvard University Press, 1992), p. 93.

31. *Dark City* (Los Angeles: Sun and Moon Press, 1994), pp. 9–10.

32. See Bakhtin's "Discourse in the Novel," in *The Dialogic Imagination: Four Essays by M. M. Bakhtin*, ed. Michael Holquist, trans. Caryl Emerson and Michael Holquist (Austin: University of Texas Press, 1981), pp. 270–71.

33. "today's not opposite date," from *With Strings: Poems* (Chicago: University of Chicago Press, 2001), pp. 72–73.

34. *Republics of Reality: 1975–1995* (Los Angeles: Sun and Moon Press, 2000), p. 309. Marjorie Perloff gives a close reading of this passage as social commentary as well as Duchampean wordplay in *21st Century Modernism*, pp. 174–77.

35. On visual poetry, see Johanna Drucker, *The Visible Word: Experimental Typography and Modern Art* (Chicago: University of Chicago Press, 1994); and idem, *Figuring the Word: Essays on Books, Writing, and Visual Poetics* (New York: Granary Books, 1998). See also Craig Dworkin, *Reading the Illegible* (Evanston, IL: Northwestern University Press, 2003); and Ferdinand Kriwet, "Decomposition of the Literary Unity: Notes on Visually Perceptible Literature," *Triquarterly* 20 (Winter 1971): 209–51; and Marjorie Perloff, "The Invention of Concrete Prose: Haroldo de Campos's *Galaxias* and After," in *Differentials: Poetry, Poetics, Pedagogy*, pp. 175–205.

36. See Kenner, "Pound Typing," in *The Mechanic Muse* (Oxford: Oxford University Press, 1987), esp. pp. 37–59.

37. See Gerald L. Bruns, *The Material of Poetry: Sketches toward a Philosophical Poetics* (Athens: University of Georgia Press, 2005), pp. 61–62, 66–75.

38. "Parole de fragment," in *L'entretien infini* (Paris: Éditions Gallimard, 1969), p. 453, hereafter EI; "The Fragment Word," in *The Infinite Conversation*, trans. Susan Hanson (Minneapolis: University of Minnesota Press, 1993), p. 308, hereafter IC.

39. *Gesammelte Werke* (Frankfurt am Main: Suhrkamp Verlag, 1986), 1, p. 226, hereafter GWC; *Selected Poems and Prose of Paul Celan*, trans. John Felstiner (New York: W. W. Norton, 2001), p. 159, hereafter SPP.

40. See Silke-Maria Weineck, "Logos and Pallaksch: The Loss of Madness and the Survival of Poetry in Paul Celan's 'Tübingen, Jänner,'" *Orbis Litterarum: International Review of Literary Studies* 54, no. 4 (1999): 262–75.

41. See chapter 2. This is the conundrum that Hans-Georg Gadamer takes up in his commentary on "Atemkristall," the first section of Celan's *Atemwende*, "Wer bin Ich und wer bist Du?" See Gadamer, *Gesammelte Werke* (Tübingen: J. C. B. Mohr [Paul Siebeck], 1986–93), 9:383–451, hereafter cited as GW; *Gadamer on Celan: Who Am I and Who Are You? And Other Essays*,

trans. Richard Heinemann and Bruce Krajewski (Albany: State University of New York Press, 1997), pp. 67–147, hereafter cited as GC. For Gadamer, it is enough to know that the dialogical structure of I-Thou shapes almost all of Celan's lyrics, and is consistent with what Celan himself has to say (in "Der Meridian," for example), namely, that poems are "encounters, paths from a voice to a listening You" (GWC.3:201). Shifters, as the linguists say, can be filled with anyone, and so Celan's pronouns preserve the condition of nonidentity. See "The Meridian," *Paul Celan: Collected Prose*, trans. Rosmarie Waldrop (River-on-Hudson, NY: Sheep Meadow Press, 1986), p. 53.

42. Quoted by Israel Chalfen, *Paul Celan: A Biography of His Youth*, trans. Maximilian Bleyleben (New York: Persea Books, 1991), p. 4.

43. See Joris's introduction to his translation of *Atemwende* (*Breathturn*) (Los Angeles: Sun and Moon Press, 1995), p. 38. However, perhaps "invented German" is an overstatement. In an unpublished essay, "'Speech Scraps, Vision Scraps': Paul Celan's Poetic Practice," Marjorie Perloff, who was born in Vienna, finds Celan's German, for all of the strangeness of his writing, "familiar enough, especially to an Austrian ear like mine": "Celan's German was never that of Berlin or Frankfurt but the German of Vienna, which was the center and magnet of the Austro-Hungarian empire, into which Celan was belatedly born in 1920 two years after its dissolution. For his parents, the 'official' German of Vienna was the necessary language of the educated classes: Paul's mother Fritzi always spoke German to her son and taught him the German classics."

44. Gilles Deleuze and Felix Guattari, *Kafka: pour une littérature mineure* (Paris: Éditions du Minuit), p. 48 (*Kafka: Toward a Minor Literature*, trans. Dana Polan [Minneapolis: University of Minnesota Press, 1986], p. 26).

45. See *Gilles Deleuze and the Boundaries of Philosophy*, ed. Constantin V. Boundas and Dorothea Olkowski (London: Routledge, 1994), pp. 25–26.

46. See Blanchot, *L'espace littéraire* (Paris: Éditions Gallimard, 1955), p. 221, hereafter cited as EL; *The Space of Literature*, trans. Ann Smock (Lincoln: University of Nebraska Press, 1982), pp. 163–70, hereafter cited as SL. See esp. 167–68, where the day of the Enlightenment appropriates the night in order to rest from "work at its empire," whereas the *other* night is the one suffered by the beast in Kafka's *The Burrow*, for whom there is no longer any shelter or security, only an endless, indeterminate noise.

47. *Gesammelte Schriften*, ed. Rolf Tiedemann and Hermann Schweppenhäuser (Frankfurt am Main: Suhrkamp Verlag, 1991), 2.1:140–56, hereafter cited as GS; *Selected Writings*, ed. Marcus Bullock and Michael Jennings (Cambridge, MA: Harvard University Press, 1996), pp. 68–70, hereafter cited as SW.

48. The term "protosemantic" is the poet Steve McCaffery's invention. See his *Prior to Meaning: The Protosemantic and Poetics* (Evanston, IL: Northwestern University Press, 2001).

49. See "Langage et proximité," in *En découvrant l'existence avec Husserl et Heidegger*, 2d ed. (Paris: Librairie philosophique, 1967), pp. 217–36 ("Lan-

guage and Proximity," in *Collected Philosophical Papers*, trans. Alphonso Lingis [The Hague: Martinus Nijhoff, 1987], pp. 109–26).

50. "L'instant, Newman," in *L'inhumain: Causeries sur le temps* (Paris: Éditions Galilée, 1988), p. 95, hereafter cited as In; "Newman: The Instant," in *The Inhuman: Reflections on Time*, trans. Geoffrey Bennington and Rachel Bowlby (Stanford: Stanford University Press, 1991), p. 84, hereafter cited as IR.

51. *Le Différend* (Paris: Éditions du Minuit), "Gertrude Stein Notice," pp. 104–5, hereafter cited as Di; *The Differend: Phrases in Dispute*, trans. Georges Van Den Abbeele (Minneapolis: University of Minnesota Press, 1983), pp. 67–68, hereafter cited as D.

52. *Selected Writings of Gertrude Stein*, ed. Carl Van Vechten (New York: Vintage Books, 1972), p. 463.

53. Auerbach's "modernist" is Augustine, whose "paratactic" style in describing his friend Alypius's experience at the games (*Confessions*, 6.8) is, Auerbach says, "manifestly unclassical." *Mimesis: The Representation of Reality in Western Literature*, trans. Willard Trask (New York: Doubleday, 1953), p. 61.

54. Apropos of *and*: in an essay entitled "Language and 'Paradise,'" in *The Language of Inquiry* (Berkeley: University of California Press, 2000), the American poet Lyn Hejinian, commenting on her own poem, *The Guard* (1984), writes:

> Meanwhile, in the seventh part of the poem, I was becoming increasingly aware that, wherever there is a fragility of sequence, the particular character of diverse individual things becomes prominent; their heterogeneity increases the palpability of things.
>
> This palpability has both metaphysical and aesthetic force, which is to say that these particulars are not isolated, but to understand their relations under conditions in which sequential logic is in disarray, one must examine other connections. The most basic and resilient is that of the simple conjunction, *and*. It is fundamental to all paratactic presentations, it is the signal component of collage, and it is the first instrument through which children begin to offer accounts of the world. All relations begin with *and*. (pp. 67–68)

55. "The Death of the Novel," in *The Death of the Novel and Other Stories* (New York: The Dial Press, 1969 [Tallahassee, FL: FC2, 2003]), p. 53.

56. See Bakhtin, "Discourse and the Novel," in *The Dialogic Imagination: Four Essays*, p. 282.

57. "The Death of the Novel" is a constant allusion to Samuel Beckett's famous double bind, in which the writer rejects "the art of the feasible," preferring instead "the expression that there is nothing to express, nothing with which to express, no desire to express, together with the obligation to express." See "Three Dialogues," in *Disjecta: Miscellaneous Writings*, ed. Ruby

Cohn (London: John Calder, 1983), p. 139. This impasse is most fully developed in Beckett's *The Unnamable* in which a disembodied voice speaks under an invisible compulsion, concluding (or not) as follows: "I can't go on. I go on."

58. Ashbery is usually identified with the "New York School" of poets that included Frank O'Hara and Kenneth Koch, and began flourishing in the 1950s; but, Ashbery says, he and his contemporaries identified themselves not as a school or group but simply as poets committed to experimentation. He was one of the first serious readers of Gertrude Stein's work. See his interview with Jack Tranter dating from April 1985 in *Jacket 2* (January 1998); *Jacket 2*, edited by Jack Tranter, is a free online literary magazine available at http://www.jacketmagazine.com. See also Ashbery, "The Invisible Avant-Garde" (1968): "Things were very different twenty years ago when I was a student and was beginning to experiment with poetry. At that time it was the art and literature of the Establishment that were traditional. There was in fact almost no experimental poetry being written in this country, unless you counted the rather pale attempts of a handful of poets who were trying to imitate some of the effects of the French Surrealists. The situation was a little different in the other arts." John Ashbery, *Reported Sightings: Art Chronicles, 1957–1987*, ed. David Bergman (Cambridge, MA: Harvard University Press, 1991), p. 390.

59. *Houseboat Days* (New York: Penguin Books, 1977), p. 45, hereafter cited as HD.

60. Interview with Jack Tranter, May 1988, *Jacket 2* (January 1998), available at http://www.jacketmagazine.com.

61. Of course, "Lecture on Nothing" is a performance piece in which words are composed as columns of sounds organized into rhythmic structures of different durations, so that the work is simultaneously a lecture, a poem, and a piece of music—what Cage thinks of as "theater": "all the various things / going on at the same time" (S.149).

62. See Fredman's analysis of Ashbery's *Three Poems* (New York: Penguin Books, 1972) in *Poet's Prose: The Crisis in American Verse*, 2d ed. (Cambridge: Cambridge University Press, 1991), esp. p. 106 (on "not-understanding" as a "positive experience").

63. See Marjorie Perloff's discussion of Ashbery's "discontinuities," "'The Mysteries of Construction': The Dream Songs of John Ashbery," in *The Poetics of Indeterminacy: Rimbaud to Cage* (Princeton: Princeton University Press, 1981), pp. 248–87. See also Angus Fletcher, "Ashbery Meditates Complexity," *Annals of Scholarship* 15, nos. 2–3 (2004): 69–80.

Chapter Two

1. Gadamer goes so far as to say that "however much [the work] is transformed or distorted in being presented, it still remains itself. . . . Every repetition is as original as the work itself" (WM.116/TM.122).

2. In "The Relevance of the Beautiful," Gadamer writes:

What is it that is so distinctive about form? The answer is that we must trace it out as we see it actively—something required by every composition, graphic or musical, in drama or in reading. There is constant co-operative activity here. And obviously, it is precisely the identity of the work that invites us to this activity. . . . A synthetic act is required in which we must unite and bring together many different aspects. We "read" a picture, as we say, like a text. We start to "decipher" a picture like a text. It was not Cubist painting that first set us this task, though it did so in a drastically radical manner by demanding that we successively superimpose upon one another the various facets or aspects of the same thing, to produce finally on the canvas the thing depicted in all its facets and thus in a new colorful plasticity. (GW.8:117–18/RB.27)

3. See Danto, *The Transfiguration of the Commonplace: A Philosophy of Art* (Cambridge, MA: Harvard University Press, 1981), esp. pp. 1–32.

4. *Must We Mean What We Say? A Book of Essays* (Cambridge: Cambridge University Press, 1987), p. 84, hereafter cited as MW.

5. See Diane P. Michelfelder, "Gadamer on Heidegger on Art," in *The Philosophy of Hans-Georg Gadamer*, ed. Lewis Edwin Hahn (Chicago: Open Court Press, 1997), pp. 451–52.

6. "Le vestige de l'art," in *Les Muses* (Paris: Éditions Galilée, 1994), p. 140 ("The Vestige of Art," in *The Muses*, trans. Peggy Kamuf [Stanford: Stanford University Press, 1996], p. 85).

7. See Adorno, "Valéry Proust Museum," where Valéry takes the objectivist view that the work of art, in virtue of its formal integrity, is what it is in itself apart from anyone's experience of it, in contrast to Proust, for whom "works of art are from the outset something more than their specific aesthetic qualities. They are part of the life of the person who observes them; they become an element of his consciousness. He thus perceives a level in them very different from the formal laws of the work. It is a level set free only by the historical development of the work, a level which has as its premise the death of the living intention of the work." *Gesammelte Schriften* (Frankfurt am Main, 1980), Band 10.1: *Kulturkritik und Gesellschaft, I: Prismen*, p. 189 (*Prisms*, trans. Samuel and Shierry Weber [Cambridge, MA: MIT Press, 1981], p. 181). Like Adorno, Gadamer seeks an account of the experience of the work that embraces both Valéry's formalism ("transformation into structure") and Proust's aestheticism, which is a mode of performance that one might think of calling "being-with the work."

8. See Paul Ricoeur, "Appropriation," *Hermeneutics and the Human Sciences*, trans. John B. Thompson (Cambridge, MA: MIT Press, 1981), pp. 182–93.

9. In "A Matter of Meaning It" Stanley Cavell describes his experience of Anthony Caro's sculptures, which he cannot simply dismiss as absurd,

but which he cannot integrate into his prior experiences of what sculpture (or, indeed, art) is. "The problem is that I am, so to speak, struck with the knowledge that this is sculpture, in the same sense that any object is. The problem is that I no longer know what sculpture is, why I call *any* object, the most central or traditional, a piece of sculpture. How *can* objects made this way elicit the experience I had thought confined to objects made so differently? And that this is a matter of experience is what needs constant attention" (MW.218).

10. See *Truth and Method* (WM.285/TM.301–2):

Consciousness of being affected by history (*wirkungsgeschichtliches Bewußtein*) is primarily consciousness of the hermeneutical *situation.* To acquire awareness of a situation is, however, always a task of peculiar difficulty. The very idea of a situation means that we are not standing outside it and hence are unable to have any objective knowledge of it. We always find ourselves within a situation, and throwing light on it is a task that is never entirely finished. This is also true of the hermeneutic situation—i.e., the situation in which we find ourselves with regard to the tradition that we are trying to understand. The illumination of this situation—reflection on effective history—can never be completely achieved; yet the fact that it cannot be completed is not due to a deficiency in reflection but to the essence of the historical being that we are. *To be historically means that knowledge of oneself can never be complete.*

11. *Nietzsche: Der Wille zur Macht als Kunst* (Frankfurt am Main: Vittorio Klostermann, 1985), pp. 89–108 (*Nietzsche: The Will to Power as Art*, trans. David Farrell Krell [New York: Harper and Row, 1979], pp. 77–91). See Robert Bernasconi, "The Greatness of the Work of Art," in *Heidegger in Question: The Art of Existing* (Atlantic Highlands, NJ: Humanities Press, 1993), pp. 99–116.

12. *Atemkristall* is a small sheaf of poems first published in a large folio edition that included remarkable artwork by Celan's wife, Gisèle Celan-Lestrange (Paris: Brunidor, 1965) and later included as the first section of *Atemwende* (Frankfurt am Main: Suhrkamp Verlag, 1967). See Celan, *Gesammelte Werke* (Frankfurt am Main: Suhrkamp Verlag, 1983), 2:11–31, hereafter cited as GWC.

13. See Szondi, "Lecture de Strette. Essai sur la poésie de Paul Celan," *Critique* 27, no. 288 (1971): 387–420. And Pöggeler, "Mystische Elemente im Denken Heideggers und im Dichten Celans," *Zeitwende* 53 (1982): 65–92; "Mystical Elements in Heidegger's Thought and Celan's Poetry," trans. Henry Pickford, in *Word Traces: Readings of Paul Celan*, ed. Aris Fioretos (Baltimore: Johns Hopkins University Press, 1994), pp. 75–109.

14. *Schibboleth pour Paul Celan* (Paris: Éditions Galilée, 1986), pp. 59–60 ("Shibboleth: For Paul Celan," trans. Joshua Wilner, in *Word Traces*, pp. 34–35).

15. See Blanchot on "Nietzsche et l'écriture fragmentaire," *L'entretien in-fini* (Paris: Éditions Gallimard, 1969), p. 231, hereafter cited as EI. "Nietzsche and Fragmentary Writing," in *The Infinite Conversation*, trans. Susan Hanson (Minneapolis: University of Minnesota Press, 1993), p. 154, hereafter cited as IC. In Nietzsche, Blanchot says, one discovers two kinds of speech. There is the speech of the "higher man"—"an integral discourse, the logos that says the whole, the seriousness of philosophic speech . . . : a speech that is discontinuous, without intermittence and without blanks, the speech of logical completion that knows nothing of chance, play, or laughter" (EI.233/IC.155). And then there is "plural speech":

> The plurality of plural speech: a speech that is intermittent, discontinuous; a speech that, without being insignificant, does not speak by reason of its power to represent, or even to signify. What speaks in this speech is not signification, not the possibility of either giving meaning or withdrawing meaning, even a meaning that is multiple. From which we are led to claim, perhaps with too much haste, that this plurality designates itself on the basis of the between [*l'entre-deux*], that it stands as a sort of sentry duty around a site of divergence, a space of dis-location that it seeks to close in on, but that always dis-closes it, separating it from itself and identifying it with this margin or separation, this imperceptible divergence where it always returns to itself: identical, non-identical. (EI.234–35/IC.156)

16. From *The Autobiography of Alice B. Toklas* (1933). See *Selected Writings of Gertrude Stein*, ed. Carl Van Vechten (New York: Vintage Books, 1962), p. 112.

17. Hugo Huppert, "('In the Prayer Mill's Rattling'): A Visit with Paul Celan," trans. James Phillips, in *Translating Tradition: Paul Celan in France*, ed. Benjamin Hollander, special ed. of *Acts: A Journal of New Writing* 8–9 (1988): 158.

18. Celan, "Edgar Jené und der Traum vom Traume" (1948), (GWC.3:160) ("Edgar Jené and the Dream about the Dream," in *Collected Prose*, trans. Rosmarie Waldrop [Riverdale-on-Hudson: The Sheep Meadow Press, 1986], pp. 8–9).

19. See Maurice Blanchot, "L'expérience-limite" (EI.300–22/IC.202–17), where the limit-experience means just what it says: an experience that sets a limit to the possibility of experience itself:

> [It] must be understood that possibility is not the sole dimension of our existence, and that it is perhaps given to us to "live" each of the events that is ours by way of a double relation. We live it one time as something we comprehend, grasp, bear, and master (even if we do so painfully and with difficulty) by relating it to some good or to some value, that is to say, finally, by relating it to Unity; we live it another time as something that escapes all employ and all end, and more, as

that which escapes our very capacity to undergo it, but whose trial we cannot escape. (EI.306–7/IC.207)

20. "Celan's Folds and Veils," *Textual Practice* 18, no. 2 (2004): 200.

21. "The Saturated Phenomenon," trans. Thomas Carlson, in Dominique Janicaud, Jean-François Courtine, Jean-Louis Chrétien, Michel Henry, Jean-Luc Marion, and Paul Ricoeur, *Phenomenology and the "Theological Turn": The French Debate* (New York: Fordham University Press, 2000), pp. 196–97.

22. Jean-Luc Marion, "Introduction: What Do We Mean by 'Mystic'?" in *Mystics: Presence and Aporia*, ed. Michael Kessler and Christian Sheppard (Chicago: University of Chicago Press, 2003), pp. 3–4. See also Kevin Hart, "The Experience of Nonexperience," in ibid., pp. 188–206.

23. *De surcroît: Études sur les phénomènes satur* (Paris: Presses Universitaires de France, 2001), p. 84; (*In Excess: Studies of Saturated Phenomena*, trans. Robyn Horner and Vincent Berraud [New York: Fordham University Press, 2002], p. 70).

24. See Lucy Lippard, *The Dematerialization of the Art Object, 1966–1972* (Berkeley: University of California Press, 1997).

25. *La croisée du visible* (Paris: Presses Universitaires de France, 1996), p. 37 (*The Crossing of the Visible and the Invisible*, trans. James. K. A. Smith [Stanford: Stanford University Press, 2004], p. 17).

26. Ian Fairley provides us with an alternative translation:

The sighted isle's heartscript moraine
at midnight, by the little light
of the ignition key.

There are too many
powers enthralled of an end
in even this
to all appearance starpierced
ether.

The suspired free mile
hurtles upon us.

See Paul Celan, *Fathomsuns and Benighted: Fadensonnen & Eingedunkelt* (Riverdale-on-Hudson, NY: The Sheep Meadow Press, 2001), p. 147.

27. *The Language of Inquiry* (Berkeley: University of California Press, 2000), pp. 42–43.

Chapter Three

1. Fredric Jameson, *A Singular Modernity: Essay on the Ontology of the Present* (London: Verso, 2002), pp. 119–21.

2. On the formal kinship between Wittgenstein and Gertrude Stein, see Marjorie Perloff, *Wittgenstein's Ladder: Poetic Language and the Strangeness of the Ordinary* (Chicago: University of Chicago Press, 1996).

3. See Artaud, "En finir avec les chefs-d'œuvre," in *Le théâtre et son double* (Paris: Èditions Gallimard, 1964), p. 128 ("An End to Masterpieces," in *Antonin Artaud: Selected Writings*, ed. Susan Sontag, trans. Helen Weaver [Berkeley: University of California Press, 1976], p. 259): "I propose then a theater in which violent physical images pound and hypnotize the sensibility of the spectator, who is caught by the theater as if in a whirlwind of higher forces. . . . A theater that produces trances."

4. For Heidegger, works that hang in exhibitions or collections are mere art objects, not works—that is, they no longer *work* as events that open up time and history: "Whenever art happens—that is, whenever there is a beginning—a thrust enters history, history either begins or starts over again." A museum is a place where nothing can happen. Heidegger's monumental Greek temple tends to disguise the fact that "Der Ursprung des Kunstwerkes" is *the* classic work of modernist aesthetic theory. See Heidegger, *Gesamtausgabe*, Band V: *Holzwege* (Frankfurt am Main: Vittorio Klosterman, 1977), p. 65 (*Poetry, Language, Thought*, trans. Albert Hofstadter [New York: Harper and Row, 1971], p. 77).

5. Heidegger, for example, speaks of "undergoing an experience with language [*mit der Sprache eine Erfahrung zu machen*]" which is not an event that occurs in the speaking of it. See "Der Wesen zur Sprache," *Unterwegs zur Sprache* (Pfullingen: Gunther Neske, 1959), p. 61. *Erfahrung* entails the sense of undergoing a journey, trial, or transformation. It is not a term of agency but, if anything, one of suffering.

6. See the final chapter of *Folie et déraison*, in which Artaud's madness is characterized as "the *absence* of the work of art," but this absence is not a negation but paradoxically (and obscurely) a kind of reversal or exchange: "Artaud's *œuvre* experiences its own absence in madness, but that experience, the fresh courage of that ordeal, all those words hurled against a fundamental absence of language, all that space of physical suffering and terror which surrounds or rather coincides with the void—that is the work of art itself: the sheer cliff over the abyss of the work's absence" (FD.662/ MC.287). See Foucault's "Le 'non' du père" (DE.1:201/AME.17) and "La folie, l'absence d'œuvre" (DE.1:412–20).

7. See Blanchot, *L'espace littéraire* (Paris: Éditions Gallimard, 1955), pp. 48–49, hereafter cited as EL; *The Space of Literature*, trans. Ann Smock (Lincoln: University of Nebraska Press, 1982), p. 46, hereafter cited as SL.

8. Baudelaire, *Œuvres complètes*, 2, ed. Claude Pichois (Paris: Éditions Gallimard, 1976), p. 695, hereafter cited as Œ.II. "The Painter of Modern Life," *Selected Writings on Art and Literature*, trans. P. E. Charvet (London: Penguin Books, 1972), p. 403, hereafter cited as SWA.

9. A presumption is that modernist art is an art of the beautiful like any other, but in Baudelaire's analysis this is less clear in fact than it is in principle. Beauty, to be sure, "is always and inevitably compounded of two elements," one "eternal and invariable, "the other "circumstantial," but the one

seems effaced by the other in Baudelaire's paradoxical formulation: "Beauty is made up, on the one hand, of an element that is eternal and invariable, though to determine how much of it there is is extremely difficult, and, on the other, of a relative circumstantial element, which we may like to call, successively or at one and the same time, contemporaneity, fashion, morality, passion. Without this second element, which is like the amusing, teasing, appetite-whetting coating of the divine cake, the first element would be indigestible, tasteless, unadapted and inappropriate to human nature" (Œ.2:695/SWA.392). As if the eternal dimension of beauty were, in itself, ugly. At any rate there is little attention paid to the eternal and variable in Baudelaire's essay; it is not really a dimension in which he has any interest. The idea is rather to discover in the ephemeral a new source of aesthetic interest.

10. Benjamin, *Gesammelte Schriften*, 1.2, ed. Rolf Tiedemann and Hermann Schweppenhäuser (Frankfurt am Main: Suhrkamp, 1974), p. 558, hereafter cited as GS. *Selected Writings*, ed. Howard Eiland and Michael W. Jennings, trans. Edmund Jephcott et al. (Cambridge, MA: Harvard University Press, 1996–2003), pp. 31–32, hereafter cited as SW.

11. *The Concept of Irony, with Continual Reference to Socrates*, trans. Howard V. Hong and Edna H. Hong (Princeton, NJ: Princeton University Press, 1989), p. 281.

12. Recall the opening lines of Foucault's inaugural address: "I would really liked to have slipped imperceptibly into this lecture, as into all the others I shall be delivering, perhaps over the years ahead. I would have preferred to be enveloped in words, borne away beyond all possible beginnings. At the moment of speaking, I would like to have perceived a nameless voice long preceding me, leaving me entirely to enmesh myself in it, taking up its cadence, and to lodge myself, when no one was looking, in its interstices as if it had paused an instant, in suspense, to beckon me" (OD.7/AK.215).

13. See Mallarmé, *Correspondance*, I (Paris: Éditions Gallimard, 1959), p. 259. Leo Bersani provides a very interesting commentary on Mallarmé's account of his experience in *The Death of Stéphane Mallarmé* (Cambridge: Cambridge University Press, 1982).

14. *Œuvres complètes*, ed. Henri Mondor et G. Jean-Aubry (Paris: Éditions Gallimard, 1945), p. 366, hereafter cited as ŒM.

15. See Bruns, "Mallarmé: The Transcendence of Language and the Aesthetics of the Book," in *Modern Poetry and the Idea of Language: A Critical and Historical Study* (New Haven: Yale University Press, 1974), pp. 101–38.

16. See Jean-Jacques Lecercle, *Philosophy through the Looking-Glass: Language, Nonsense, Desire* (LaSalle, IL: Open Court Press, 1985), p. 80. Lecercle's idea (following Jacques Lacan, but also an assortment of eccentric writers on language like Lewis Carroll, Jacques Brisset, and Louis Wolfson) is that language is a formal system (*la langue*), but it is pervaded by a

remainder or surplus (*lalangue*) that makes possible wordplay, poetry, logophilia or the language of schizophrenics, glossolalia—or speaking in tongues—and other "infelicities" of speech. "The main characteristic of language is *excess*: more meaning creeps into the sentence than the author intended, echoes and involuntary repetitions disturb the careful ordering of linguistic units. Phrases are analysed, and re-analysed, symptoms and word plays proliferate. But to this excess there corresponds a *lack*: the absence of the central all-mastering subject who means what he says and says what he means. . . . The utterance is full of involuntary admissions, echoes of other voices, traces imposed by the structure itself, distortion and displacement which irretrievably conceal the truth." See also idem, *The Violence of Language* (London: Routledge, 1990).

17. Adorno, *Ästhetische Theorie* (Frankfurt am Main: Suhrkamp, 1973), pp. 334–38 (*Aesthetic Theory*, trans. Robert Hullot-Kentor [Minneapolis: University of Minnesota Press, 1997], pp. 225–29).

18. See *The L=A=N=G=U=A=G=E Book*, ed. Bruce Andrews and Charles Bernstein (Carbondale: Southern Illinois University Press, 1984). See also Charles Bernstein's ars poetica, "Artifice of Absorption," in *A Poetics* (Cambridge, MA: Harvard University Press, 1992), and Steve McCaffery, "Writing as a General Economy," in *North of Intention: Critical Writings, 1973–1986* (New York: Roof Books, 1986), pp. 201–21, esp. pp. 214–15: "Sound poetry is a poetry of complete expenditure in which nothing is recoverable and useable as 'meaning.' Involved is a decomposition of both an operative subject and the historical constraints of a semantic order." For a concise history of twentieth-century sound poetry, see McCaffery, "Voice in Extremis," in *Prior to Meaning: The Protosemantic and Poetics* (Evanston, IL: Northwestern University Press, 2001), pp. 161–86.

19. See Douglas Kahn, *Noise, Water, Meat: A History of Sound in the Arts* (Cambridge, MA: MIT Press, 2001).

20. See Julia Kristeva, *La revolution du langage poétique: L'avant-garde à la fin du XIX siècle* (Paris: Éditions du Seuil, 1974); available in English in an abridged version as *Revolution in Poetic Language*, trans. Margaret Waller (New York: Columbia University Press, 1984).

21. See Habermas, *Der philosophischen Diskurs der Moderne: zwölf Vorlesungen* (Frankfurt am Mein, 1985), p. 366 (*The Philosophical Discourse of Modernity*, trans. Frederick G. Lawrence [Cambridge, MA: MIT Press, 1987], p. 314).

22. In an alternative preface to volume 2 of *The History of Sexuality*, Foucault writes: "in *Madness and Civilization* I was trying . . . to describe a locus of experience from the viewpoint of the history of thought, even if my usage of the word 'experience' was very floating" (DE.4:581/EWI.202). How the "eighteenth century" experiences madness is continuous with how it constructs it. But experience also means how the mad experience their madness, which Foucault takes up in the final chapter of *Madness and Civilization*, and which, as he says, forms a threshold for future work.

23. See Heidegger, "Hegels Begriff der Erfahrung, *"Gesamtausgabe* Band V: *Holzwege* (Frankfurt am Main: Vittorio Klosterman, 1977), p. 180 (*Hegel's Concept of Experience* [New York: Harper and Row, 1970], pp. 113–14): "Experience is now no longer the term for a kind of knowledge. . . . Experience designates the subject's subjectness."

24. See Hegel's introduction to the *Phenomenologie des Geistes*, ed. Hans-Friedrich Wessels und Heinrich Clairmont (Hamburg: Felix Meiner, 1988), 1:62 (*Hegel's Phenomenology of Spirit*, trans. A. V. Miller [Oxford: Oxford University Press, 1977], p. 51).

25. See Levinas, *De l'existence à l'existant* (Paris: Éditions de la revue fontaine, 1947), pp. 80–92 (*Existence and Existents*, trans. Alphonso Lingis [The Hague: Martinus Nijhoff, 1978], esp. pp. 52–67); and also idem, "Reality and Its Shadow" (1948), in *Collected Philosophical Papers*, trans. Alphonso Lingis (The Hague: Martinus Nijhoff, 1987), esp. pp. 3–4.

26. In "Foucault as I Imagine Him," Maurice Blanchot recalls Roger Callois' allergic reaction to Foucault's early prose: "Foucault's style, in its splendor and precision, perplexed him. He was not sure whether this grand baroque style didn't ultimately ruin the singular knowledge whose multiple facets—philosophical, sociological, and historical—irritated and exalted him. Perhaps he saw in Foucault an alter ego who would have made off with his heritage." *Foucault/Blanchot*, trans. Jeffrey Mehlman (New York: Zone Books, 1987), p. 64.

27. "Sacrifices" (1933), in *Œuvres complètes* (Paris: Èditions Gallimard, 1970), 1:91–92, 94; *Visions of Excess: Selected Writings, 1927–1939*, trans. Allan Stoekl (Minneapolis: University of Minnesota Press, 1985), pp. 132, 133–34, hereafter cited as VE.

28. See Bataille, *L'Expérience intérieure* (Paris: Éditions Gallimard, 1943), p. 67 (*Inner Experience*, trans. Leslie Anne Boldt [Albany: State University of New York Press, 1988], p. 39): "The extreme limit of the 'possible' assumes laughter, ecstasy, terrified approach towards death; assumes error, nausea, unceasing agitation of the 'possible' and the impossible and, to conclude . . . the state of supplication, its absorption into despair." The best commentary on Bataille's concept of experience is Blanchot's, "The Limit-Experience," from which the citation above is taken, and which includes the following: "It must be understood that possibility is not the sole dimension of existence, and that it is perhaps given to us to 'live' each of the events that is ours by way of a double relation. We live it one time as something we comprehend, grasp, bear, and master (even if we do so painfully and with difficulty) by relating it to some good or to some value, that is to say, finally, by relating it to a Unity; we live it another time as something that escapes all employ and all end, and more, as that which escapes our very capacity to undergo it, but whose trial we cannot escape." *L'entretien infini* (Paris: Éditions Gallimard, 1969), pp. 307–8, hereafter cited as EI. *The Infinite Conversation*, trans. Susan Hanson (Minneapolis: University of Minnesota Press, 1993), p. 207, hereafter cited as IC.

29. See "La folie, l'absence d'œuvre" (1964): "Hence . . . that strange proximity between madness and literature, which ought not to be taken in the sense of a relation of common psychological parentage now finally exposed. Once uncovered as a language silenced by its superposition upon itself, madness neither manifests nor narrates the birth of a work (or of something which, by genius or by chance, could have become a work); it outlines an empty form from where this work comes, in other words, the place from where it never ceases to be absent, where it will never be found because it had never been located there to begin with. There, in that pale region, in that essential hiding place, the twinlike incompatibility of the work and of madness becomes unveiled; this is the blind spot of the possibility of each to become the other and of their mutual exclusion" (DE.1:419). This English translation by Peter Stastny and Deniz Sengel appears in *Critical Inquiry* 21, no. 2 (Winter 1995): 296–97.

30. *La part maudite, precede de La notion de dépense* (Paris: Éditions du Minuit, 1967), pp. 30–31; VE.120.

31. See "Littérature et la droit à la mort" (1948), *La part du feu* (Paris: Éditions Gallimard, 1949), pp. 312–17 ("Literature and the Right to Death, in *The Work of Fire*, trans. Charlotte Mandell [Stanford: Stanford University Press, 1995], pp. 322–28).

32. The figure, or structure, of parentheses deserves more attention than it has received. It is a kind of pure middle into which additional middles can be endlessly inserted, and so constitutes the basic form of the holotext. An especially interesting use of this form is to be found in Raymond Roussel's poem, *Nouvelle Impressions d'Africa*, a poem in four cantos, each of which is made of a series of parenthetical interruptions—four or sometimes five parentheses within parenthesis ((((()))))—so that the first lines of each canto are suspended until last lines. To read the poem as a semantic construction one has to work back and forth from end to beginning, until one arrives at a middle made, for example, of lists that theoretically could have been allowed to lengthen indefinitely. See Foucault's discussion of this poem in *Raymond Roussel* (Paris: Éditions Gallimard, 1963), chap. 3; *Death and the Labyrinth: The World of Raymond Roussel*, trans. Charles Ruas (New York: Doubleday, 1986), pp. 29–47.

33. See Ian Hacking, "Making Up People," in *Reconstructing Individualism: Autonomy, Individuality, and the Self in Western Thought*, ed. Thomas C. Heller, Morton Sosna, and David E. Wellbery (Stanford: Stanford University Press, 1986), p. 223.

34. Levinas, *Autrement qu'être ou au-dela de l'essence* (The Hague: Martinus Nijhoff, 1974), p. 198 (*Otherwise than Being or Beyond Essence*, trans. Alphonso Lingis [The Hague: Martinus Nijhoff, 1981], p. 124).

Chapter Four

1. Werner Jaeger says: "Hesiod is a poet because he is a teacher." *Paideia: The Ideals of Greek Culture*, trans. Gilbert Highet (New York: Oxford

University Press, 1939, 1:74. See also Eric Havelock, *Preface to Plato* (Cambridge, MA: Harvard University Press, 1963), pp. 105–6, hereafter cited as PP. In Hesiod we see "the oral poet as priest, prophet, and teacher of his community and . . . oral poetry as an overall source book of history and morality."

2. "Vox Clamans in Deserto," in *The Birth to Presence*, trans. Brian Holmes et al. (Stanford: Stanford University Press, 1993), p. 239, hereafter cited as BP.

3. *Autrement qu'être ou au-delà de l'essence* (The Hague: 1974), p. 221 (*Otherwise than Being or Beyond Essence*, trans. Alphonso Lingis [The Hague: Martinus Nijhoff, 1971], pp. 141).

4. *Ion*, 533d–34e. It is worth noting that Socrates identifies lyric poets as particularly Dionysian: "So it is with the good lyric poets: as the worshipping Corybantes are not in their senses when they dance, so the lyric poets are not in their senses when they make these lovely lyrics. No, when once they launch into harmony and rhythm, they are seized with the Bacchic transport, and are possessed [*katexomenai*]—as the bacchants, when possessed, draw milk and honey from the rivers, but not when in their senses" (534a; trans. Lane Cooper). Interestingly, Havelock thinks the ecstatic theory of poetry begins with philosophers (preeminently Plato) "who were intent upon constructing a new type of discourse which we can roughly characterize as conceptual rather than poetic—[and who] were driven to relegate poetic experience to a category which was non-conceptual and therefore non-rational and non-reflective. Thus was invented the notion that poetry must be simply a product of ecstatic possession, for which the Greek animistic term was 'enthusiasm'" (PP.156). I think there is no doubt that the ecstatic theory of poetry is originally a philosophical construction, but this construction seems already in place with Hesiod, and the interesting question has to do with how this construction is put into play in the history of poetry, where it seems to capture something essential.

5. Maurice Blanchot, *L'espace littéraire* (Paris: Éditions Gallimard, 1955), p. 28 (*The Space of Literature*, trans. Ann Smock [Lincoln: University of Nebraska Press, 1982], p. 32).

6. Of poets like Demodocos and Phemios in the *Odyssey* George Walsh writes: "The singer is a public figure, a *dêmioergos* like a seer or a physician, and as such he does not belong to the household for which he sings. He seems always to be an outsider (*xeinos*), less attached to his patrons than even a seer, for the gods are his audience as well as the source of his skill." *The Varieties of Enchantment: Early Greek Views of the Nature and Function of Poetry* (Chapel Hill, NC: University of North Carolina Press, 1984), p. 15. Later poets like Hesiod are wanderers. See also Bruno Gentili, *Poetry and Its Public in Ancient Greece: From Homer to the Fifth Century*, trans. A. Thomas Cole (Baltimore: Johns Hopkins University Press, 1988), pp. 155–76, on the poet's "Intellectual Activity and Socioeconomic Situation." See, too,

Gregory Nagy, *Poetry as Performance: Homer and Beyond* (Cambridge: Cambridge University Press, 1996).

7. Jean-Luc Nancy, *Le partage de voix* (Paris: Éditions Galilée, 1982), pp. 62–65, hereafter cited as PV; "Sharing Voices," trans. Gayle Ormiston, in *Transforming the Hermeneutic Context: From Nietzsche to Nancy*, ed. Gayle Ormiston and Alan D. Schrift (Albany: State University of New York Press, 1990), pp. 234–35, hereafter cited as SV. See also George Walsh, *The Varieties of Enchantment: Early Greek Views of the Nature and Function of Poetry* (Chapel Hill, NC: University of North Carolina Press, 1984), pp. 3–36; and especially Eric Havelock, "The Psychology of Poetic Performance," pp. 145–64.

8. See Maurice Blanchot, *La communauté inavouable* (Paris: Éditions Minuit, 1983), pp. 18–19, hereafter cited as CI); *The Unavowable Community*, trans. Pierre Joris (Barrytown, NY: Station Hill Press, 1988), p. 7, hereafter cited as UC: "It is striking that Georges Bataille, whose name for so many of his readers signifies the mystique of an ecstasy or the non-religious quest for an ecstatic experience, *excludes* . . . 'fusional fulfillment in some collective hypostasis' (Jean-Luc Nancy). It is something he is deeply averse to. One must never forget that what counts for him is less the state of ravishment where one forgets everything (oneself included) than the demanding process that realizes itself by bringing into play and carrying outside itself an existence that is insufficient [unto itself], a movement that ruins immanence as well as the usual forms of transcendence." Blanchot's text is a response to Nancy's "La communauté desœuvrée," *Alea* 4 (1983). Nancy's *La communauté désœuvrée* (Paris: Christian Bourgois Editeur, 1986), responding to Blanchot, contains a revised and enlarged version of "La communauté désœuvrée" plus two additional essays, "De l'être-en-commun" and "L'histoire finie." The English translation, *The Inoperative Community*, cited below, adds two more, "L'amour en éclats," or "Shattered Love," and "Des lieux divins," or "Divine Places." See note 10, below.

9. Maurice Blanchot, "La question la plus profonde," in *L'entretien infini* (Paris: Éditions Gallimard, 1969), p. 28, hereafter cited as EI; "The Most Profound Question," in *The Infinite Conversation*, trans. Susan Hanson (Minneapolis: University of Minnesota Press, 1993), pp. 21, hereafter cited as IC.

10. *La communauté désœuvrée*. Nouvelle édition revue et augmentée (Paris: Christian Bourgois, 1990), p. 22, hereafter cited as CD; *The Inoperative Community*, trans. Peter Connor, Lisa Garbus, Michael Holland, and Simona Sawhney (Minneapolis: University of Minnesota Press, 1991), p. 6, hereafter InC.

11. In *The Unavowable Community* Blanchot writes:

May '68 has shown that without project, without conjuration, in the suddenness of a happy meeting, like a feast that breached the admitted and expected social norms, *explosive communication* could affirm itself. . . .

"Without project": that was the characteristic, all at once distressing and fortunate, of an incomparable form of society that remained elusive, that was not meant to survive, to set itself up, not even via the multiple "committees" simulating a disordered order, an imprecise specialization. Contrary to "traditional revolutions," it was not a question of simply taking power to replace it with some other power. . . . [What] mattered was to let a possibility manifest itself, the possibility—beyond any utilitarian gain—of a *being-together* that gave back to all the right to equality in fraternity through a freedom of speech that elated everyone." (IC.60/UC.29–30)

12. See also Giorgio Agamben, "The Most Uncanny Thing," in *The Man Without Content*, trans. Georgia Albert (Stanford: Stanford University Press, 1999), pp. 4–5, hereafter MwC:

Plato, and Greek classical antiquity in general, had a very different experience of art [from our modern conception], an experience having little to do with disinterest and aesthetic enjoyment. The power of art over the soul seemed to him so great that he thought it could by itself destroy the very foundations of his city; but nonetheless, while he was forced to banish it, he did so reluctantly, "since we ourselves are very conscious of her spell." The term he uses when he wants to define the effects of inspired imagination is θειος φοβος, "divine terror," a term that we, benevolent spectators, no doubt find inappropriate to define our reactions, but that nevertheless is found with increasing frequency, after a certain time, in the notes in which modern artists attempt to capture their experience of art.

13. *Nietzsche Werke: Kritische Ausgabe*, heraus. Giorgio Colli und Mazzino Montinari (Berlin: Walter de Gruyter, 1972), 3.1:57 (*The Birth of Tragedy*, trans. Francis Golffing [New York: Anchor Books, 1956], pp. 55–56). See Martin Heidegger, "Der Rausch as ästhetischer Zustand," in *Nietzsche* (Pfullingen: Neske, 1961), 1:109–11 ("Rapture as Aesthetic State," in *Nietzsche: The Will to Power as Art*, trans. David Farrell Krell [New York: Harper and Row, 1979], 1:92–106).

14. "One-way Street," in *Gesammelte Schriften* (Frankfurt: Suhrkamp, 1972), 4.1:146–47, hereafter cited as GS; *Selected Writings*, ed. Marcus Bullock, Howard Eiland, and Michael W. Jennings, trans. Edmund Jephcott et al. (Cambridge, MA: Harvard University Press, 1996–2003), 1:486–87, hereafter cited as SW.

15. Benjamin, GS.5.1:369; Walter Benjamin, *The Arcades Project*, trans. Howard Eiland and Kevin McLaughlin (Cambridge, MA: Harvard University Press, 1999), p. 290, hereafter cited as AP.

16. See *Wahrheit und Methode: Grundzüge einer philosophischen Hermeneutik*. 4th Auflage. (Tübingen: J. C. B. Mohr [Paul Siebeck] 1975), pp. 119, hereafter cited as WM; *Truth and Method*, 2d rev. ed., trans. Joel Weinsheimer and Donald G. Marshall (New York: Crossroad Publishing, 1989), pp. 125–26, hereafter cited as TM:

> The true being of the spectator, who belongs to the play of art, cannot be adequately understood in terms of subjectivity [i.e., as a disengaged cognitive subject], as a way that aesthetic consciousness conducts itself. But this does not mean that the nature of the spectator cannot be described in terms of being present at something. . . . Considered as a subjective accomplishment of human conduct, being present has the character of being outside oneself [*Außersichseins*]. In the *Phaedrus* Plato already described the blunder of those who take the viewpoint of rational reasonableness and tend to misinterpret the ecstatic condition of being outside oneself, seeing it as a mere negation of being composed within oneself and hence as a kind of madness [*Verrücktheit*]. In fact, being outside oneself is the positive possibility of being wholly with something else. This kind of being present is a self-forgetfulness, and to be a spectator consists in giving oneself in self-forgetfulness to what one is watching. Here self-forgetfulness is anything but a privative condition, for it arises from devoting one's full attention to the matter at hand, and this is the spectator's own positive accomplishment.

17. This distancing factor by which an audience is constituted is already conceptualized ironically in the *Ion* when Socrates gets Ion to confess that he (Ion) watches the Dionysian effects that his recital of Homer produces in his audience (535d–e). In Plato, poetry is already integrated into a culture of rhetoric. George Walsh, however, thinks of Odysseus as the first disenchanted spectator (*Varieties of Enchantment*, pp. 16–17). Cf. Havelock, "Psyche or the Separation of the Knower from the Known," pp. 197–214.

18. See Foucault, *L'order du discourse* (Paris: Éditions Gallimard, 1971), pp. 41–42 ("Discourse on Language," trans. Rupert Sawyer, appended to *The Archeology of Knowledge*, trans. A. M. Sheridan Smith [New York: Pantheon Books, 1972], pp. 225–26):

> A rather different function is filled by "fellowships of discourse," whose function is to preserve or to reproduce discourse, but in order that it should circulate within a closed community, according to strict regulations, without those in possession being dispossessed by this very distribution. An archaic model of this would be those groups of Rhapsodes, possessing knowledge of poems to recite, or, even, upon which to work variations and transformations. But though the ultimate object of this knowledge was ritual recitation, it was protected and preserved within a determinate group by the often extremely

complex exercises of memory implied by such a process. Apprentice-ship gained access both to a group and to a secret which recitation made manifest, but did not divulge. The roles of speaking and listening were not interchangeable.

19. Trans. Willard R. Trask (Princeton: Princeton University Press, 1953), p. 468. See also Max Weber, "The Chinese Literati," in *Sociological Writings*, ed. Wolf Heydebrand (New York: Continuum, 1994), pp. 122–50, esp. pp. 135–36.

20. See the "Gespräche vom Poesie," in *Kritische Schriften* (München: Carl Hanser Verlag, 1956), p. 285, hereafter cited as KS ("Dialogue on Poesy," in *Theory as Practice: A Critical Anthology of Early German Romantic Writers*, ed. and trans. Jochen Schulte-Sasse et al. [Minneapolis: University of Minnesota Press, 1997], p. 181). In *The Inoperative Community* Nancy remarks that "the myth of the literary community was outlined for the first time (although in reality it was perhaps not the first time) by the Jena romantics, and it has filtered down to us in various different ways through everything resembling the idea of a 'republic of artists' or, again, the idea of communism (of a certain kind of Maoism, for example) and revolution inherent, *tel quels*, in writing itself" (CD.90/InC.64).

21. KS.37–38, 50–51. *Philosophical Fragments*, trans. Peter Firchow (Minneapolis: University of Minnesota Press, 1991), pp. 31–32, 50–51. Compare Hegel: "The *philosophy* of art is therefore a greater need in our day than it was when art by itself as art yielded full satisfaction. Art invites us to intellectual consideration, and that not for the purpose of creating art again, but for knowing philosophically what art is." *Vorlesungen über die Ästhetik* (Frankfurt am Main: Suhrkamp, 1970), 1:25–26 (*Aesthetics: Lectures on Fine Art*, trans. T. M. Knox [Oxford: Clarendon Press, 1975], 1:13).

22. See Charles Bernstein, "Optimism and Critical Excess (Process)," in *A Poetics* (Cambridge, MA: Harvard University Press, 1992), p. 151, hereafter cited as P.

23. See Blanchot, "The Athenaeum" (EI.515–27/IC.351–59), and also his essay on René Char, "The Fragment Word" (EI.439–50/IC.307–13). *Désœuvrement* is not an easy term to translate, since it is a word for an event in which something does not take place. "Unworking," "worklessness," "uneventfulness" are some of the possibilities. For Blanchot *désœuvrement* means that writing is not a mode of production but an experience of the interminability of writing: writing without *archē* or *telos*. It belongs to the family of Bataille's *dépense*, or nonproductive expenditure. See note 25, below.

24. The break-out of painting is arguably earlier—perhaps, as Giorgio Agamben suggests, when people begin collecting paintings and hanging them in galleries. See his "The Cabinet of Wonders" (MwC.28–39). Agamben's interest is in that moment when the artist or poet is no longer simply a craftsman working with his material but becomes a unique subjectivity, a

special mode of inwardness in whose work the spectator can no longer see a reflection of himself but rather experiences an alienation, a "being-outside-himself" (MwC.37).

25. Philippe Lacoue-Labarthe and Jean-Luc Nancy, "L'exigence fragmentaire," in *L'absolu littéraire: Théorie de la littérature du romanticisme allemande* (Paris: Éditions du Seuil, 1985), pp. 58–59 ("The Fragmentary Exigency," in *The Literary Absolute: The Theory of Literature in German Romanticism*, trans. by Phillip Barnard and Cheryl Lester [Albany: State University of New York Press, 1988], p. 40).

26. See Georges Bataille, *The College of Sociology*, ed. Dennis Hollier, trans. Betsy Wing (Minneapolis: University of Minnesota Press, 1988), hereafter cited as CS. See also Blanchot, *The Unavowable Community* (CI.27–30/UC.12–16), on Bataille's experiments in community during the 1930s, starting with his experience of surrealism as a group project. Later Bataille would write: "The force of conviction animating [André Breton] allowed him to bring together a number of people whose names today are known everywhere—not by external ties of action, but by more intimate ties of passion. It was André Breton who rightly recognized that a poet or painter does not have the power to say what is in his heart, but that an organization or a collective body could. This 'body' can speak in different terms from an individual. If painters and poets together took consciousness of what weighed on poetry and painting, anyone who speaks in their name must plead that it is the vehicle of impersonal necessity." "L'surréalisme et sa differance avec l'existentialisme," *Œuvres complètes* (Paris: Éditions Gallimard, 1988), 11:73–74, hereafter cited as OC; "Surrealism and How It Differs from Existentialism" (1947), in *The Absence of Myth: Writings on Surrealism*, trans. Michael Richardson (London: Verso, 1994), p. 60, hereafter cited as AM. See also Bataille's essay therein, "La sens moral de la sociologie" ("The Moral Meaning of Sociology"):

> Until about 1930, the influence of Durkheim's sociological doctrine had barely gone beyond the university domain. It had no influence in the arena of intellectual fever. Durkheim had been dead for a long time when young writers emerging from surrealism (Caillois, Leiris, Monnerot) began following the lectures of Marcel Mauss, whose remarkable teaching was fully in accord with the founder of the school. It is difficult to define exactly what they sought. . . . There was only a vague orientation, independent of the personal interests which explain it. Detachment from a society that was disintegrating because of individualism and the malaise resulting from the limited possibilities of the individual domain was combined there. Although we cannot assume the same value for every one of them, there was possibly a great attraction to realities which, as they establish social bonds, are considered sacred. These young writers felt more or less clearly that society

had lost the secret of its cohesion, and this was precisely what the obscure, uneasy and sterile efforts of poetic fever sought to address. (OC.11.58/ΛM.104–5)

27. *The Guilty*, trans. Bruce Boone (Venice, CA: Lapis Press, 1988).

28. See *La part maudite, précédé de la notion de dépense* (Paris: Éditions du Minuit, 1967), p. 28, hereafter cited as PM; "The Notion of Expenditure," *Visions of Excess: Selected Writings, 1927–1939*, trans. Allan Stoekl (Minneapolis: University of Minnesota Press, 1985), pp. 118, hereafter cited as VE. To be sure, all ecstatic communities have an ambiguous relation to the social order in which they are contained—armies are the most emphatic example. But one should think of armies not so much as disciplined orders in which everything is regulated by command but as packs or bands that a state cannot finally keep under control. See Gilles Deleuze and Felix Guattari, "1227: Treatise on Nomadology—The War Machine," in *Milles plateaux: capitalisme et schizophrénie* (Paris: Éditions du Minuit, 1980), pp. 434–527, hereafter cited as MP; *A Thousand Plateaus*, trans. Brian Massumi (Minneapolis: University of Minnesota Press, 1987), pp. 351–415, hereafter cited as TP.

29. See Steve McCaffery, "Writing as a General Economy," in *North of Intention: Critical Writings, 1973–86* (New York: Roof Books, 1986), pp. 201–21.

30. See Georges Bataille, *L'expérience intérieure* (Paris: Éditions Gallimard, 1943), p. 147 (*Inner Experience*, trans. Leslie Anne Boldt [Albany: State University of New York Press, 1988], p. 94).

31. "Projective Verse," in *The Human Universe*, ed. Donald Allen (New York: Grove Press, 1967), p. 59, hereafter cited as PV.

32. Compare Louis Zukofsky, "A Statement for Poetry [1950]," in *Prepositions: The Collected Critical Essays* (Hanover, NH: Wesleyan University Press, 2000), p. 23: "The best way to find out about poetry is to read poems. That way the reader becomes something of a poet himself: not because he 'contributes' to the poetry, but because he finds himself subject of its energy."

33. Adorno, *Gesammelte Schriften* (Frankfurt am Main, 1977), Band 10.1: *Kulturkritik und Gesellschaft, 1: Prismen*, pp. 155–56 (*Prisms*, trans. Samuel and Shierry Weber [Cambridge, MA: MIT Press, 1981], p. 152):

Schoenberg's instinctive mode of reaction is melodic; everything in him is actually "sung," including the instrumental lines. This endows his music with its articulate character, free-moving and yet structural down to the last tone. The primacy of breathing over the beat of abstract time contrasts Schoenberg to Stravinsky and to all those who, having adjusted better to contemporary existence, fancy themselves more modern than Schoenberg. The reified mind is allergic to the elaboration and fulfilment of melody, for which it substitutes the docile repetition of mutilated melodic fragments. The ability to follow the breath of the music unafraid had already distinguished Schoenberg from older, post-Wagnerian composers like Strauss and Wolf, in whom the music seems unable to develop its substance according to its intrinsic impulses and requires literary and programmatic support, even in the songs.

34. *Olson's Push: Origin, Black Mountain, and Recent American Poetry* (Baton Rouge: Louisiana University Press, 1978), p. 39.

35. Stephen Fredman, *Grounding American Poetry: Charles Olson and the Emersonian Tradition* (Cambridge: Cambridge University Press, 1993), p. 55:

> The Black Mountain poets functioned as a kind of mystery sect, particularly between the years 1950, when Olson and Creeley began corresponding and Cid Corman started *Origin*, and 1970, when Olson died. As the leader, Olson encouraged a host of others to join this community of resistant poets. Thus, a group of writers formed around such centers as Black Mountain College, *Origin*, and *The Black Mountain Review*: Olson, Creeley, Duncan, Corman, Denise Levertov, Edward Dorn, Paul Blackburn, Joel Oppenheimer, Fielding Dawson, Michael Rumaker, Hilda Morley, John Wieners, Larry Eigner, Jonathan Williams, Le Roi Jones, Gilbert Sorrentino, and others. In the course of this twenty-year period, a second wave of projectivist writers appeared and intermingled with the first; of a larger number that could be mentioned, the following writers maintained a more or less strict adherence to the projectivist doctrine during at least some of this time: Robert Kelly, Theodore Enslin, Kenneth Irby, Jerome Rothenberg, Clayton Eshleman, Edward Sanders, David Bromige, Richard Grossinger, Ronald Johnson, and Armand Schwerner.

36. Quoted by RoseLee Goldberg, *Performance: Live Art 1909 to the Present* (New York: Harry N. Abrams, 1979), p. 79, hereafter cited as PLA.

37. *Black Mountain: An Exploration in Community* (New York: E. P. Dutton, 1972), pp. 344–67, hereafter cited as BM.

38. In *Olson's Push* Sherman Paul writes: "Seen in the context of Black Mountain College, 'Apollonius at Tyana' is a demonstration of the 'Theater Exercises' Olson initiated there in the summer of 1949. Art had always been important in the curriculum of the college, and at this time, as Olson explained in a letter, dance, because of the presence of Katherine Litz and Merce Cunningham, was 'the most forward of the disciplines' and hence the core of the performing arts. Olson himself was acquainted with dance. . . . As a young man he had had some training at the Gloucester School of the Little Theatre and had even danced—motionless—in a Massine production of *Bacchanale* in Boston." *Olson's Push: Origin, Black Mountain, and Recent American Poetry* (Baton Rouge: Louisiana State University Press, 1978), p. 88.

39. *The Black Mountain Book: A New Edition* (Rocky Mount, NC: North Carolina Wesleyan Press, 1991), pp. 178–79.

40. See Thierry de Duve, *Kant after Duchamp* (Cambridge, MA: MIT Press, 1996), p. 375, hereafter cited as KD: "Something unprecedented in the whole history of art surfaced in the sixties: it had become legitimate to be an artist without being either a painter, or a poet, or a musician, or a sculptor, novelist, architect, choreographer, filmmaker, etc. A new 'category' of art appeared—art in general, or art at large—that was no longer absorbed in traditional disciplines." In "Why Are There Several Arts?" Jean-Luc Nancy seems to contest de Duve. See *Les Muses* (Paris: Èditions Gallilée, 1994), pp. 11–70 (*The Muses*, trans. Peggy Kamuf [Stanford: Stanford University Press, 1994], pp. 1–39). Cf. Stanley Cavell, "A Matter of Meaning It" (1967), in *Must We Mean What We Say? A Book of Essays* (Cambridge: Cambridge University Press, 1969), pp. 188–90, on the work of Anthony Caro, whose sculpture is no longer sculptured, thus depriving us of criteria for determining what we are looking at. This is the modernist project, which leaves us in the dilemma of always having to discover anew the conditions that enable us to accept something as a work of art.

41. *Der philosophische Diskurs der Moderne: zwölf Vorlesungen.* Frankfurt am Main: Suhrkamp, 1985), p. 243–45 (*The Philosophical Discourse of Modernity: Twelve Lectures*, trans. Frederick G. Lawrence [Cambridge: MIT Press, 1987], pp. 205–7.

42. "Art and Objecthood" (1967), in *Minimal Art: A Critical Anthology*, ed. Gregory Battcock (Berkeley: University of California Press, 1995), p. 120, hereafter cited as AO.

43. *Ästhetische Theorie* (Frankfurt: Suhrkamp, 1973), p. 212, hereafter cited as AT; *Aesthetic Theory*, trans. Robert Hullot-Kentor (Minneapolis: University of Minnesota Press, 1997), p. 141, hereafter cited as AeT.

44. See Greenberg, "Modernist Painting," in *The New Art*, ed. Gregory Battock (New York: Dutton, 1973), pp. 72–73. See also Arthur Danto, "Works of Art and Mere Real Things," in *The Transfiguration of the Commonplace: A Philosophy of Art* (Cambridge, MA: Harvard University Press, 1981), pp. 1–32. Thierry de Duve has a good chapter on this matter in *Kant After Duchamp*, "The Monochrome and the Blank Canvas" (KD.199–279).

45. "Experimental Music," in *Silence* (Middletown, CT: Wesleyan University Press, 1961), p. 12, hereafter cited as S.

46. Perhaps not so new. In an important footnote Fried remarks on "the deep affinity between literalists and Surrealist sensibility. . . . This affinity can be summed up by saying that Surrealist sensibility . . . and literalist sensibility are both *theatrical*" (AO.145).

47. See Marjorie Perloff on Fried's separation of art from theater, *The Futurist Moment: Avant-Guerre, Avant-Garde, and the Language of Rupture* (Chicago: University of Chicago Press, 1986), pp. 109–11.

48. See Artaud, *Le théâtre et son double* (Paris: Éditions Gallimard, 1964): "La mise en scène et la métaphysique," pp. 49–72, and "En finir avec les

chefs-d'œuvre," pp. 115–30, hereafter cited as TD; *Antonin Artaud: Selected Writings*, ed. Susan Sontag (Berkeley: University of California Press, 1988): "Mise en scène and Metaphysics," pp. 227–39, and "An End to Masterpieces," pp. 252–59, hereafter cited as AA. Interestingly, Fried describes the encounter with the minimalist "object" as if it were a not-altogether-friendly encounter with another person. The minimalist work does not just sit there; it is aggressive. It *confronts* the beholder, who is warned not to come any closer but to stand back or give ground. The experience is "not entirely unlike being distanced, or crowded, by the silent presence of another *person*; the experience of coming upon literalist objects unexpectedly—for example, in somewhat darkened rooms—is disquieting in just this way" (AO.128). As if minimalist art were not just theater but "theater of cruelty."

49. "1730: Becoming-Intense, Becoming-Animal, Becoming-Imperceptible . . .": "There is a mode of individuation very different from that of a person, subject, thing, or substance. We reserve the name *haecceity* for it. A season, a winter, a summer, an hour, a date have a perfect individuality lacking nothing, even though this individuality is different from that of a thing or a subject. They are haecceities in the sense that they consist entirely of relations of movement and rest between molecules or particles, capacities to affect and be affected" (MP.318–19 / TP.261).

50. See Arthur Danto, "The End of Art," in *The Philosophical Disenfranchisement of Art* (New York: Columbia University Press, 1986), pp. 81–115. For Danto, as we saw earlier, art comes to an end, not when it turns into theater, but when it is "transmuted into philosophy," that is, when the work just is the theory that constitutes it (conceptual art): "Now if we look at the art of our recent past . . . what we see is something which depends more and more upon theory for its existence as art, so that theory is not something external to a world it seeks to understand, so that in understanding its object it has to understand itself. But there is another feature exhibited by these late productions which is that the objects approach zero as their theory approaches infinity, so that virtually all there is at the end *is* theory, art having finally become vaporized in a dazzle of pure thought about itself, and remaining, as it were, solely as the object of its own theoretical consciousness" (p. 111).

51. See Henry Sayre, *The Object of Performance: The American Avant-Garde Since 1970* (Chicago: University of Chicago Press, 1989), pp. 1–34; and Lucy Lippard, *Six Years: The Dematerialization of the Art Object from 1966 to 1972* (New York: Praeger, 1973).

52. An indispensable chronicle of New York performance art is to be found in Cynthia Carr's *On Edge: Performance at the End of the Twentieth Century* (Middletown, CT: Wesleyan University Press, 1993), a collection of reviews written mainly for the *Village Voice*.

53. See Chris Burden and Jan Butterfield, "Through the Night Softly," in *The Art of Performance: A Critical Anthology*, ed. Gregory Battcock and Rob-

ert Nickas (New York: E. P. Dutton, 1984), pp. 222–39; and Parveen Adams, "Operation Orlan," in *The Emptiness of the Image* (London: Routledge, 1991), esp. p. 145.

54. The surrealists were always a plurality in which, in Nancy's words, "different pieces touch each other without fusing" (CD.188 / InC.76). In *The Unavowable Community* Blanchot remarks on the aleatory character of André Breton's group: "There it is: something had taken place which, for a few moments and due to the misunderstandings peculiar to singular existences, gave permission to recognize the possibility of a community established previously though at the same time already posthumous: nothing of it would remain, which saddened the heart while also exalting it, like the very ordeal of effacement that writing demands" (IC.41 / UC.21).

55. A "war machine" is like a pack, band, or gang: "it seems to be irreducible to the State apparatus, to be outside its sovereignty and prior to its law: it comes from elsewhere" (MP.435/TP.352).

56. Robert Creeley, *Was That a Real Poem & Other Essays*, ed. Donald Allen (Bolinas, CA: Four Seasons Foundation, 1979), p. 17.

57. "Violence and Precision: The Manifesto as Art Form," in *The Futurist Moment*, pp. 80–115.

58. *My Futurist Years*, ed. Bengt Jangfeldt, trans. Stephen Rudy (New York: Marsilio Publishers, 1992), pp. 4–5. Interestingly, Osip Mandelstam gives an account of Jakobson's poetic scene from the outside. In "An Army of Poets" (1923) (in Osip Mandelstam, *Critical Prose and Letters*, trans. Jane Gary Harris and Constance Link [Ann Arbor, MI: Ardis Publishers, 1979], hereafter CPL), he contrasts poetry writing in France from what is happening in Russia following the Revolution. In France poetry is a school subject in which students learn to compose alexandrines; when they graduate they happily forget all about it. (Perhaps this helps to explain why the history of French poetry in the twentieth century is so thin.) In Russia by contrast poetry is a Dionysian epidemic:

> In Russia the writing of poetry among young people is so widespread that it should be treated as a major social phenomenon and should be studied like any mass-scale operation which, although useless, has profound cultural and physiological causes.
>
> Being acquainted, if only superficially, with the circle of those who write poetry, draws one into a sick, pathological world, a world of eccentrics, of people whose central nerve of both will and brain is diseased, of outright failures who are incapable of adapting in the struggle for existence and who frequently suffer not only from intellectual, but also physical cachexia. . . .
>
> In the exceptionally difficult struggle for existence, tens of thousands of Russian youths manage to take time off from their studies and daily work to write poetry which they cannot sell and which wins approval, at best, from only a few acquaintances.

This, of course, is a disease and the disease is not accidental. It is not surprising that it attacks the age group of approximately seventeen to twenty-five. . . .

After our difficult transitional years, the quantity of poets greatly increased. Because of widespread malnutrition there was an increase in the number of people whose intellectual awakening had a sickly character and had no outlet in any healthy activity.

The concurrence of the famine years, rations, and physical deprivations with the highest peak of mass poetry writing is not a coincidence. During those years when cafes such as the Domino, the Coffeehouse of Poets, and the various Stables thrived, the younger generation, especially in the capital cities, was by necessity alienated from normal work and professional knowledge since only a professional education offers a antidote to the disease of poetry, a real and serious disease because it deforms the personality, deprives a youth of a solid foundation, makes him the butt of jokes and poorly concealed disgust, and deprives him of the social respect given others of his own age. (CPL.191–93)

This is a polemic aimed against Majakovskij, who thought that everyone should be a poet. Mandelstam by contrast thinks that poetry is a species of learning. It must be rooted in philology and must resonate with poetic tradition. "Modern Russian poetry did not just fall from the skies; it was foreshadowed by our nation's entire poetic past" (*Critical Prose and Letters*, p. 165).

59. See Michael Davidson, *The San Francisco Renaissance: Poetics and Community at Mid-century*. Cambridge: Cambridge University Press, 1989). In *New York Modern: The Arts and the City* (Baltimore: The Johns Hopkins University Press, 1999), William B. Scott and Peter M. Rutkoff have an interesting chapter on the abstract expressionists who flourished in New York after World War II. The "participants refused to agree that they constituted a school or that they could be grouped under a common name. Instead, they concluded that they belonged to an 'ideal society' inherently at odds with the 'goals that most people accept.'" Nevertheless, "New York abstract expressionists craved artistic community. In the fall of 1949 some twenty painters and sculptors . . . gathered at the studio of Ibram Lassaw on the corner of Sixth Avenue and 12th Street to form the Club. 'We always wanted a loft, like the Greek and Italian social clubs on Eighth Avenue, instead of sitting in one of those goddamned cafeterias,' recalled one of the artists. 'One night we decided to do it—we got up twenty charter members who each gave ten dollars.' The Club, also called, because of its location at 39 West Eighth Avenue, the Eighth Street Club, served as an artists' hangout where members could face each other 'with curses mixed with affection, smiling and evil eyed each week for years'" (p. 311). See also David Leh-

man's *The Last Avant-Garde: The Making of the New York School of Poets* (New York: Doubleday, 1999), which treats the intersection of Frank O'Hara, Kenneth Koch, and John Ashbery with the artworld of the New York expressionists during the 1950s.

60. *What it means to be avant-garde* (New York: New Directions, 1993), pp. 46–47.

61. See Marjorie Perloff, "The Word as Such: $L=A=N=G=U=A=G=E$ Poetry in the Eighties," in *The Dance of the Intellect: Studies in the Poetry of the Pound Tradition* (Cambridge: Cambridge University Press, 1985), pp. 215–38.

62. Lyn Hejinian, *The Cell* (Los Angeles: Sun and Moon Press, 1992), p. 7.

63. "Strangeness," in *The Language of Inquiry* (Berkeley: University of California Press, 2000), pp. 148–49, hereafter cited as LI. See also Hejinian's "The Rejection of Closure" (LI.40–58). Compare Ron Silliman's description of the "new sentence," which is a sentence that resists the syllogistic movement that would integrate it into larger semantic units (and so made to disappear); on the contrary, the new sentence is characterized by the removal of context that allows each sentence its own integrity. *The New Sentence* (New York: ROOF Books, 1989), pp. 63–93.

64. See Hejinian, "Who is Speaking?," on the formation of the poetic community as a context in which the individual work is not so much a formal object as a public event (LI.31–39).

65. "Introduction" to *Close Listening: Poetry and the Performed Word*, ed. Charles Bernstein (New York: Oxford University Press, 1998), p. 24, hereafter cited as CL. See also Ron Silliman, "The Political Economy of Poetry," in *The New Sentence*, pp. 20–31; and Charles Bernstein, "I Don't Take Voice Mail: The Object of Art in the Age of Electronic Technology," in *My Way: Speeches and Poems* (Chicago: University of Chicago Press, 1999), pp. 73–80, esp. p. 76.

66. *The Marginalization of Poetry: Language Writing and Literary History* (Princeton: Princeton University Press, 1996), p. 14.

67. See, for example, Steve McCaffery, "Voice in Extremis," in *Close Listening*, pp. 162–77. See Marjorie Perloff, "'No More Margins': John Cage, David Antin, and the Poetry of Performance," in *The Poetics of Indeterminacy: Rimbaud to Cage* (Princeton: Princeton University Press, 1981), pp. 288–339; and Stephen Fredman, "The Crisis at Present: Talk Poems and the New Poet's Prose," in *Poet's Prose: The Crisis in American Verse*, 2d ed. (Cambridge: Cambridge University Press, 1990), pp. 136–49.

68. "On Robert Rauschenberg, Artist, and His Work" (S.102).

Chapter Five

1. See John Matthias, "The Stefan Batory Poems" ("Five: the library"), *Crossing* (Chicago: Swallow Press, 1979), pp. 81–82. *Crossing* has

this bibliographical note appended to it: "I am indebted, as in *Turns* and *Bucyrus* [Matthias's earlier volumes], to an odd assortment of books and authors for facts, fancies, passages of verse or of prose, translations, information, scholarship and scandal which I have had occasion in these poems to quote, plagiarize, willfully ignore, tactfully modify, stupidly misconstrue, or intentionally travesty" (p. 121).

2. *Œuvres complètes de Stéphane Mallarmé*, ed. Henri Mondor (Paris: Éditions Gallimard, 1945), p. 378.

3. *Ästhetische Theorie* (Frankfurt: Suhrkamp, 1973), p. 272, hereafter cited as AT. *Aesthetic Theory*, trans. Robert Hullot-Kentor (Minneapolis: University of Minnesota Press, 1997), p. 182, hereafter cited as AeT.

4. See Cavell, *Must We Mean What We Say?* (Cambridge: Cambridge University Press, 1969), p. 84.

5. *Milles plateaux: capitalisme et schizophrénie* (Paris: Éditions le Minuit), pp. 614–25 (*A Thousand Plateaus*, trans. Brian Massumi [Minneapolis: University of Minnesota Press, 1987], pp. 492–500).

6. See Danto, "The Artworld," *Journal of Philosophy* 61, no. 19 (October 1964): 581. See also idem, "The Art World Revisited: Comedies of Similarity," in *Beyond the Brillo Box: The Visual Arts in Post-historical Perspective* (New York: Noonday Press, 1992), pp. 33–53, hereafter cited as BBB. See esp. pp. 38–40, where Danto distinguishes his (historical) conception of the artworld from George Dickie's Institutional Theory of Art, where a thing is art if it is said to be so by experts.

7. Joseph Margolis thinks that Danto "confuses artworks with ordinary material objects," since the difference between the work and the stuff of which it is made may be imperceptible. Artworks, Margolis says, are not made of materials but of "Intentional properties" which attach to artworks as "historied objects." But it's hard to see much difference between Margolis's historicism and Danto's. For Danto, the perception of anything as a work of art is conceptually mediated, but concepts do not fall from the sky. They emerge culturally in just the way Margolis says they do. See Margolis, *What Is, After All, a Work of Art? Lectures on the Philosophy of Art* (University Park: Pennsylvania State University Press, 1999), p. 27. See esp. p. 94: "The truth is, we cannot understand any sentence, thought, or Intentional structure [e.g., a work of art] apart from the *lebensformlich* 'world' in which it is so discerned."

8. Joseph Kosuth, "Art after Philosophy," *Art in Theory, 1900–1990*, ed. Charles Harrison and Paul Wood (Oxford: Basil Blackwell, 1992), p. 845. Kosuth imagines the artworld as a conceptual realm in which real objects — paintings, shoes — can come and go without altering the logical form of the landscape ("This is art"); but such a realm would still be subject to the constraints that govern Danto's "artworld," which is a world in which anything is possible but not at every moment. We need a theory to help us pick a thing out as art, but theory is always historically mediated. Or, to put it

another way, the hermeneutical circle is always historical, and we are always inside of it.

9. "what am i doing here?," *talking at the boundaries* (New York: New Directions, 1976), p. 3, hereafter cited as tb.

10. "the structuralist," *what it means to be avant-garde* (New York: New Directions, 1990), pp. 159–60, hereafter cited as wim.

11. Joseph Margolis would say that this question begs the question about cultural entities. See *What, After All, Is a Work of Art?*, p. 89:

> The individuation and identity of artworks are hardly the same as the individuation and identity of the natural and linguistic entities upon which they depend (and which they incorporate). If, for instance, a block of marble, however cut, lacks Intentional properties, whereas a sculpture — say, Michelangelo's *Moses*, which incorporates the marble — intrinsically possesses Intentional properties, then the two *denotata* cannot be numerically the same. So far, so good. It goes some distance toward explaining why so many theorists speak of artworks as a way of *using* natural or physical objects or the like, or of transfiguring them rhetorically, by imputing all sorts of Intentional properties, which, on the argument, these physical objects could not logically possess.

12. See Heidrun Friese, "Literal Letters. On the Materiality of Words," *Paragraph* 21, no. 2 (July 1998): 167–99; Donald Judd, "Specific Objects," in *Art in Theory, 1900–1990: An Anthology of Changing Ideas*, ed. Charles Harrison and Paul Wood (Oxford: Blackwell, 1992), pp. 809–13; and Antonin Artaud, "Le théâtre de la cruauté (Premier manifeste), *Le théâtre et son double* (Paris: Éditions Gallimard, 1964), pp. 137–56 ("The Theater of Cruelty (First Manifesto)," in *Antonin Artaud: Selected Writings*, ed. Susan Sontag [Berkeley: University of California Press, 1976], pp. 248–49). As for paintings made of paint — or, more exactly, of drips of paint ("drips acquired a kind of mystical exaltation of status in the 1950s") — see Arthur Danto, *Transfigurations of the Commonplace* (Cambridge, MA: Harvard University Press, 1981), pp. 107–9, hereafter cited as TC. See esp. p. 108: "The drip . . . calls attention insistently to paint as paint."

13. "Erik Satie," in *Silence* (Middletown, CT: Wesleyan University Press, 1961), p. 76.

14. Thierry de Duve thinks that Duchamp's Readymades, for example, are neither paintings nor sculptures but works of art in general. "The readymades . . . are 'art' and 'nothing but art'. . . . You call Malevich an artist through the same judgment that makes you call him a painter. Logically, if not chronologically, he is a painter first. With the legitimation of Duchamp's readymades, a very different situation was seemingly made legitimate, a situation about which, I believe, one should never stop wondering and perhaps worrying: you can now be an artist without being either a painter, or

a sculptor, or a composer, or a writer, or an architect—an artist at large." *Kant after Duchamp* (Cambridge, MA: MIT Press, 1996), p. 153, hereafter cited as KD. But, to speak strictly, an "artist at large" would produce works of art that were singular, that is, irreducible to any category (not answerable to any concept, hence nonidentical). Interestingly, de Duve redeems Duchamp by reassimilating him to the history of painting (KD.154–72).

15. "On Installation," in *Complete Writings, 1975–1986* (Eindhoven: van Abbemuseum, 1987), p. 94.

16. Adorno says: "That through which artworks, by becoming appearance (*Erscheinung*), are more than they are: This is their spirit. . . . It makes artworks, things among things, something other than thing" (AT.134/AeT.86).

17. See Adorno, "Rückblickend auf den Surrealismus," in *Noten zur Literature* (Frankfurt am Main, 1970), 1:153–60, esp. pp. 158–59 ("Looking Back on Surrealism," in *Notes to Literature*, trans. Shierry Weber Nicholsen [New York: Columbia University Press, 1991], pp. 86–90, esp. pp. 88–89).

18. Interview with Serge Gavronsky, in *Poems & Texts*, trans. Serge Gavronsky (New York: October House, 1969), p. 37.

19. *Le parti pris des choses, suive de Proêmes* (Paris: Éditions Gallimard, 1948), p. 176, hereafter cited as PP; *The Voice of Things*, trans. Beth Archer (New York: McGraw-Hill, 1972), p. 79, hereafter cited as VT.

20. See Jean-Paul Sartre's essay on Ponge, "L'homme et choses," in *Situations, 1* (Paris: Éditions Gallimard, 1947), pp. 226–70, hereafter cited as Si. See esp. pp. 242–43: "It is not a question of *describing* things. . . . [Ponge] talks about a cigarette without saying a word about the white paper in which it is rolled, about a butterfly without hardly a mention of the patterns adorning its wings: he is not concerned with the qualities of things but with *being*." Perhaps not with *being* as such but with things in their singularity and proximity in which our relation to them is not one of observing, knowing, asserting, describing, or any of the other acts of a cognitive subject.

21. See Stephen Fredman, *Poet's Prose: The Crisis in American Verse*, 2d ed. (Cambridge: Cambridge University Press, 1990). A poem in prose is a poem that has migrated, Antin-like, from its proper formal category to the category of how people ordinarily talk. Gadamer would say that the aesthetic in this event is no longer differentiated.

22. See Emmanuel Levinas, "Langage et proximité," in *En découvrant l'existence avec Husserl et Heidegger*, 2nd ed. (Paris: Librairie philosophique, 1967), p. 222, hereafter cited as EDL; "Language and Proximity," in *Collected Philosophical Papers*, trans. Alphonso Lingis (The Hague: Martinus Nijhoff, 1987), p. 116, hereafter cited as CPP:

> The *ethical* does not designate an inoffensive attenuation of passionate particularisms, which would introduce the human subject into a universal order and unite all rational beings, like ideas, in a kingdom of

ends. It indicates a reversal of the subjectivity which is *open upon* beings and always in some measure represents them to itself, positing them and taking them to be such or such . . . into a subjectivity that enters *into contact* with a singularity, excluding identification in the ideal, excluding thematization and representation—an absolute singularity, as such unrepresentable. This is the original language, the foundation of the other one. The precise point at which this mutation of the intentional into the ethical occurs, and occurs continually, at which the approach *breaks through* consciousness, is the human skin and face. Contact is tenderness and responsibility.

23. See Ponge, *Nouveau Recueil* (Paris: Éditions Gallimard, 1967), p. 143.

24. E. Levinas, *Autrement qu'etre ou au-dela de l'essence* (The Hague: Martinus Nijhoff, 1974), p. 118 (*Otherwise than Being or Beyond Essence*, trans. Alphonso Lingis [The Hague: Martinus Nijhoff, 1981], p. 73).

25. Arthur Danto, celebrating Andy Wahrhol's *Hammer and Sickle* paintings, in which hammers and sickles are, like Duchamp's shovel, hardware items, still retaining their manufacturers' insignia, writes:

Think of someone who drinks the wine and takes the bread on his tongue as a religious act, but not in the spirit so much of transubstantiation as of transfiguration; who ingests these substances as themselves and *self*-symbolizing, in Feuerbach's expression, "in sacramental celebration of their earthly truth"—the bread symbolizing bread, the wine wine, rather than flesh and blood respectively. That would be exactly the spirit of Warhol: his soups are in sacramental celebration of their earthly reality, simply as what one might call one's daily soup, as what one eats day after day, as he said he himself did. If this sacramental return of the thing to itself through art is the energy which drove him as an artist to bring into the center of his work what had never really been celebrated before—what would have been aesthetically despised and rejected, impugned as commercial, in a limbo outside the redemptive reach of art—then it would have been the most ordinary of *vin ordinaire*, the most daily of daily bread, not fine vintages or gourmet loaves baked in special ovens which would be the sacramental stuff of the Feuerbachian ritual. (BBB.136)

26. In "L'homme et choses" Sartre gives a provocative reading of the events of "dehumanization" in Ponge's poetry. These events are not entirely negative but consist in a relocation of subjectivity, as in the attempt to see the world through the eyes of mere things (Si.266). There is a good discussion of Sartre's essay by Natascha Heather Lancaster, "Freedom at Work: Sartre on Ponge," in *Situating Sartre in Twentieth-Century Thought and Culture*, ed. Jean-François Fourny and Charles D. Minahan (New York: St. Martin's Press, 1997), pp. 53–70.

27. In his *Arcades Project*, in the section on "The Streets of Paris," Benjamin cites the following: "Around 1830: 'The Chaussée d'Antin is the neighborhood of the nouveaux riches of the financial world. All these districts in the western part of town have been discredited: the city planners of the period believed that Paris was going to develop in the direction of the saltpeter works, an opinion that ought to instill prudence in today's developers. . . . A lot on the Chaussée d'Antin had trouble finding a buyer at 20,000 to 25,000 francs.' Lucien Dubech and Pierre d'Espezel, *Histoire de Paris* (Paris, 1926), p. 364." *Gesammelte Schriften* (Frankfurt: Suhrkamp, 1982), 1:648, hereafter cited as GS; *The Arcades Project*, trans. Howard Eiland and Kevin McLaughlin (Cambridge, MA: Harvard University Press, 1999), p. 520, hereafter cited as AP.

28. "Artifice of Absorption," in *A Poetics* (Cambridge, MA: Harvard University Press, 1992), p. 87.

29. "Works of Art and Mere Real Things" (TC.1–32). See also p. 46: "Picasso was famous for transfigurations of the commonplace. He had made the head of a chimpanzee out of a child's toy; a goat's thorax out of an old wicker basket; a bull's head out of bicycle parts; a Venus out of a gasjet — and so why not the ultimate transfiguration, an artwork out of a mere thing?"

30. *Silence: Lectures and Writings by John Cage* (Middletown, CT: Wesleyan University Press, 1961), p. 76, hereafter cited as S.

31. GS.2.2:478; *Selected Writings*, ed. Marcus Bullock, Howard Eiland, and Michael W. Jennings, trans. Edmund Jephcott et al. (Cambridge, MA: Harvard University Press, 1996–2003), 3:268, hereafter cited as SW.

32. Pons's principle secures the work of art against the ostentation of capital by inverting the ratio of price and value: "This old musician applied as axiomatic the claim made by Chenavard, that expert collector of priceless engravings: that a work by Ruysdael, Hobbema, Holbein, Raphael, Murillo, Greuze, Sebastian del Piombo, Giorgione or Albrecht Dürer, is only pleasurable to look at when it has not cost more than fifty francs. Pons ruled out all purchases above the sum of a hundred francs. An object had to be worth three thousand francs before he would pay fifty francs for it. The loveliest thing in the world, if it cost three hundred francs, ceased to exist for him." *Cousin Pons*, trans. Herbert J. Hunt (London: Penguin Books, 1968), pp. 25–26.

33. *Nadja*, trans. Richard Howard (New York: Grove Press, 1960), p. 52.

34. *The Seminar of Jacques Lacan: Book VII: The Ethics of Psychoanalysis, 1959–60*, trans. Dennis Porter (New York: W. W. Norton, 1992), p. 114, hereafter SJL.

35. In Georges Bataille's theory of *dépense*, such a thing would no longer inhabit a restricted economy of production and consumption but would belong, along with works of art, to an economy of pure expenditure, or expenditure without return. "La notion de dépense," in *La part maudite, precede de*

la notion de dépense (Paris: Éditions du Minuit, 1967), pp. 28–29 ("The Notion of Expenditure," in *Visions of Excess: Selected Writings, 1927–1939*, trans. Allan Stoekl [Minneapolis: University of Minnesota Press, 1985], pp. 118–20).

36. *Paroles* (Paris: Éditions Gallimard, 1949), p. 208, hereafter cited as P (Jacques Prévert, *Words for All Seasons*, trans. Teo Savory [Greensboro, NC: Unicorn Press, 1979], p. 15).

37. "Unpacking My Library: A Talk about Book Collecting" (GS.4.1:389) (*Selected Writings*, trans. Rodney Livingstone et al., ed. Michael Jennings, Howard Eiland, and Gary Smith [Cambridge, MA: Harvard University Press, 1999], p. 487).

38. Heidegger writes: "The jug is a thing neither in the sense of the Roman *ens*, nor in the sense of the medieval *ens*, let alone in the modern sense of object. The jug is a thing insofar as it things. The presence of something present such as the jug comes into its own, appropriatively manifests and determines itself, only from the thinging of the thing." "Das Ding," in *Vorträge unde Aufsätze* (Tübingen: Günther Neske Pfullingen, 1954), p. 170 ("The Thing," in *Poetry, Language, Thought*, trans. Albert Hofstadter [New York: Harper and Row, 1971], p. 177).

39. "Modernist Painting," in *The Collected Essays and Criticism*, vol. 4 (Chicago: University of Chicago Press, 1993), 4:89–90.

40. "The End of Art," in *The Philosophical Disenfranchisement of Art* (New York: Columbia University Press, 1986), esp. pp. 84–86. See also idem, *After the End of Art: Contemporary Art and the Pale of History* (Princeton: Princeton University Press, 1997), esp. pp. 83–86.

41. See Margolis, *What, After All, Is a Work of Art?*, p. 35. Transfiguration is not transformation.

42. *L'Inhuman: Causeries sur le temps* (Paris: Éditions Galilée, 1988), p. 154, hereafter cited as In; *The Inhuman: Reflections on Time*, trans. Geoffrey Bennington and Rachel Bowlby (Stanford: Stanford University Press, 1991), p. 140, hereafter cited as IR.

Chapter Six

1. See "Discussions, or Phrasing after Auschwitz" (LR.372–73). "I confess" is a phrase, which is not a grammatical unit but one of a number of "language games" or "forms of life" in Wittgenstein's sense of these terms. Lyotard likes to think of phrases as events: "A wink, a shrugging of the shoulder, a tapping of the foot, a fleeting blush, or an attack of tachycardia can be phrases.—And the wagging of a dog's tail, the perked ears of a cat?" (Di.108/D.70).

2. Lyotard, "Presentations," *Philosophy in France Today*, ed. Alan Montefiore (Cambridge: Cambridge University Press, 1983), p. 124.

3. Deleuze and Guattari write: "A rhizome as subterranean stem is absolutely different from roots and radicles. Bulbs and tubers are rhizomes.

Plants with roots or radicles may be rhizomorphic in other respects altogether: the question is whether plant life in its specificity is not entirely rhizomatic. Even some animals are, in their pack form. Rats are rhizomes. Burrows are too, in all of their functions of shelter, supply, movement, evasion, and breakout. The rhizome itself assumes very diverse forms, from ramified surface extension in all directions to concretion into bulbs and tubers. When rats swarm over each other. The rhizome includes the best and the worst: potato and couchgrass, or the weed. Animal and plant, couchgrass is crabgrass [*le chiendent, c'est le crab-grass*]." *Mille plateaux: capitalisme et schizophrenie* (Paris: Éditions de Minuit, 1980), p. 13; *A Thousand Plateaus: Capitalism and Schizophrenia*, trans. Brian Massumi (Minneapolis: University of Minnesota Press, 1987), pp. 6–7. Some pages later they write: "We're tired of trees. We should stop believing in trees, roots, and radicles. They've made us suffer too much. All of arborescent culture is founded on them, from biology to linguistics. Nothing is beautiful or loving or political aside from underground stems and aerial roots, adventitious growths and rhizomes" (MP24/TP15).

4. *Leçons sur l'analytique du sublime* (Paris: Éditions Gallimard, 1991) (*Lessons on the Analytic of the Sublime* [*Kant's 'Critique of Judgment,'* §§ 23–29]), trans. Elizabeth Rottenberg (Stanford: Stanford University Press, 1991), p. viii.

5. Lyotard repeatedly stresses the etymology of the word "pagan," *pagus*, meaning "boundary," "frontier," or "edge." A pagan is someone who lives on the outskirts: "I think that the relation between gods and humans is to be thought of in terms of boundaries. And *pagus* always indicates the country, the region. It is the opposite of *Heim*, of 'home,' that is, of the village. It is quite a beautiful word since it gave us *pax*, 'companion,' etc. It is the place where one *compacts* with something else. (It is the same root. From time to time, let us allow ourselves some parodic etymologies; this one happens to be 'true' in any case.) It is a place of boundaries. Boundaries are not borders" (AJ.82/JG.42–43). Augustine would be a pagan in this sense, namely one living (on the coast of Africa) on the open boundary between Roman and Christian cultures.

6. See also Di.14/D.xv: "Reflection requires that you watch out for occurrences, that you don't already know what's happening. It leaves open the question: *Is it happening*? (*Arrive-t-il*?)"

7. Compare Jacques Derrida's "absolutely undetermined messianic hope"; *Spectres de Marx: l'état de la dette, le travail du deuil et la nouvelle Internationale* (Paris: Éditions Galilée, 1993), p. 111 (*Specters of Marx: The State of Debt, the Work of Mourning, and the New International*, trans. Peggy Kamuf [London: Routledge, 1994], pp. 65–66).

8. *Histoire de la sexualité III: Le souci de soi* (Paris: Éditions Gallimard, 1984), esp. pp. 53–94 (*The History of Sexuality, 3: The Care of the Self*, trans. Robert Hurley [New York: Vintage Books, 1988], esp. pp. 39–68).

9. *L'Idole et la distance* (Paris: Éditions Bernard Grasset, 1977), pp. 255–56, hereafter cited as IeD; *The Idol and Distance*, trans. Thomas A. Carlson (New York: Fordham University Press, 2001), p. 198, hereafter cited as ID. The idea is that God is outside "ontotheology," that is, outside of metaphysics, without or beyond being (*sans ou au-delà l'être*), outside the alternatives of presence and absence, and therefore inaccessible (dead) to conceptual representation as such. In other words, in Marion's term of art, *distant*: "Neither a subject of discourse, nor an object of science, distance removes itself from definition by definition. Indeed, it ensures communion only between terms whose separation it provokes. Now, among these terms, one interests us directly, since we ensure it, we who are speaking here. As for the other, we can approach it only within a communion that is traversed by separation all the more in that it is a matter of distance. The definition of distance defines us as one of its terms, and therefore removes us from the other, *at the very moment when it exerts its attraction*. The other, infinitely foreign, disappears in his very apparition, is defined by the indefinite itself" (IeD.256/ID.199).

10. See Jean-Luc Marion, *Dieu sans l'être: Hors-texte* (Paris: Librairie Arthème Fayard, 1982) (*God without Being*, trans. Thomas Carlson [Chicago: University of Chicago Press, 1991], p. 46): "Concerning God, let us admit clearly that we can think him only under the figure of the unthinkable, but of an unthinkable that exceeds as much what we cannot think as what we can; for that which I may not think is still the concern of *my* thought, and hence to *me* remains thinkable. On the contrary, the unthinkable taken as such is the concern of God himself, and characterizes him as the *aura* of his advent, the glory of his insistence, the brilliance of his retreat." So we can speak *of* God only by crossing him out: GØD. Leaving us with nothing to do but pray."

11. See Jean-Luc Marion on "The Discourse of Praise" (IeD.227–50/ID.180–95). See also idem, "In the Name: How to Avoid Speaking of 'Negative Theology,'" in *God, the Gift, and Postmodernism*, ed. John D. Caputo and Michael J. Scanlon (Bloomington: Indiana University Press, 1999), pp. 20–42. Hereafter cited as GG. For Marion, a theology of prayer and praise constitutes a third way between dogmatic and negative theologies—"no longer predicative [this is or is not that] but purely pragmatic. It is no longer a matter of naming or attributing something to something, but of aiming in the direction of . . . , of relating to . . . , of comporting oneself toward . . . , of reckoning with . . .—in short of dealing with. . . . By invoking the unattainable as . . . and inasmuch as . . . , prayer definitively marks the transgression of the predicative, nominative, and therefore metaphysical sense of language" (p. 30). This text is part of an ongoing dialogue with Jacques Derrida—a response to Derrida's essay on negative theology, "Comment ne pas parler: *Dénégations*," *Psyché: Inventions de l'autre* (Paris: Éditions Galilée, 1987), pp. 535–95 ("How to Avoid Speaking: Denials," trans. Ken Frieden,

in *Languages of the Unsayable: The Play of Negativity in Literature and Literary Theory*, ed. Sanford Budick and Wolfgang Iser [New York: Columbia University Press, 1989], pp. 3–70), which in turn is a response to Marion's *God without Being* and *Idol and Distance*, cited above.

12. Lyotard's English translator, Richard Breadworth, cites the Loeb Classical Library translation of Augustine, which dates from 1912 and sounds like it. I've used the translation by Henry Chadwick (Oxford: Oxford University Press, 1992), p. 183, hereafter cited as C.

13. In fact, Augustine confounds the distinction between eros and agape. See Henri de Lubac, "Eros and Agape," *Theological Fragments*, trans. Rebecca Howell Balinski (San Francisco: Ignatius Press, 1984), pp. 85–90.

14. One could argue that God's "assault" upon Augustine's senses is not Ovidian but is an instance of what Jean-Luc Marion calls "the saturated phenomenon." In Husserl's phenomenology our intentions, concepts, or significations are either fulfilled or left deficient by intuition, but in certain kinds of experience—that of the lover's face would be one, that of the theophany would be another—there is a surplus or excess of intuition that overwhelms us, but leaves us grasping the air. A "saturated phenomenon" is (i) invisible, (ii) unbearable, (iii) uncontainable within any horizon, and (iv) irreducible to consciousness. God reveals himself, not as a presence (*pour soi*), but as a "saturated phenomenon." The point of such an idea is to salvage the possibility of a philosophy of religion, or at least a phenomenology of religious experience. See Marion, "The Saturated Phenomenon," trans. Thomas A. Carlson, in Dominique Janicaud, et al., *Phenomenology and the "Theological Turn": The French Debate* (New York: Fordham University Press, 2000), pp. 176–216. However, whereas Augustine is set afire in his experience, Marion imagines that such an experience would freeze us, as if seeing the Medusa: "Access to the divine phenomenonality is not forbidden to man; in contrast, it is precisely when he becomes entirely open to it that man finds himself forbidden from it—frozen, submerged, he is by himself forbidden from advancing and likewise from resting. In the mode of interdiction, terror attests to the insistent and unbearable excess in the intuition of God." See Marion, "In the Name" (GG.41). Augustine's experience is surely ecstasy rather than terror.

15. See Richard Kearney, "Desire of God" (GG.112–30). Kearney agrees that the distinction between *eros* and *agapē* is purely theoretical and loses its application at the level of our experience of God, as we know from the mystics—and, before everyone else, from Augustine. Meanwhile Kearney, following Emmanuel Levinas, makes a distinction between two kinds of desire: an ontotheological desire based on lack (a lack of presence, a lack of conceptual identity, a failure of consciousness to produce what it wants to see), and desire as a movement of one-for-the other, or eschatological desire, where the other is always outside cognition and representation: the unknowable as such. See *Totalité et infini; essai sur l'extériorité* (The Hague:

Martinus Nijhoff, 1961), p. 57, hereafter cited as TeI; *Totality and Infinity: An Essay on Exteriority*, trans. Alphonso Lingis (Pittsburgh: Duquesne University Press, 1969), p. 34, hereafter cited as TI.

16. *Against Ethics: Contributions to a Poetics of Obligation with Constant Reference to Deconstruction* (Bloomington: Indiana University Press, 1993), p. 197. In "D'un trait d'union [On a Hyphen]" (1992) Lyotard has an interesting paragraph on the Incarnation:

> The incarnation is a mystery. It exceeds the secret meaning, the *sod*, of the letter left by the invisible Voice [of the Hebrew Bible]. It is the voiced Voice, the Voice made flesh, made of another flesh. In the *Miqra* [the Hebrew Bible], the Voice can perform miracles. And miracles are signs. The people picked out by the Lord need signs. But the Incarnation is not a miracle; it is a mystery, a mystery that destroys the regimen of every reading. The mystery offers nothing to be understood or interpreted. With Jesus, the purpose of the covenant is made manifest, for Jesus *is* the covenant made flesh. The Voice is no longer deposited in traces; it no longer marks itself in absence; it is no longer deciphered through signs. The Voice speaks the flesh, it speaks flesh. And the mystery has to do only with this—not with what the Voice says. The whole content of the new covenant is the result of its mode of assertion. That is why Paul can unite the new covenant to the old one with a single trait—with a hyphen. But the new mode breaks with the old. It breaks with it simply because the Voice is vocalized, because it offers itself up to be partitioned out, far from paradise, in the abjection of suffering, abandonment, and death. So that reading is in vain.

Lyotard's argument (against Paul) is that the relation between Judaism and Christianity cannot be inscribed as Judaeo-Christian because the hyphen is a mark of the *différend*, not one of union, not one of old and new versions of the same. See Lyotard and Eberhard Gruber, *The Hyphen: Between Judaism and Christianity*, trans. Pascale-Anne Brault and Michael Naas (Amherst, New York: The Humanity Press, 1999), pp. 22–23.

17. Actually Lyotard thinks that Augustine's dissertation on time is quite successful and anticipates Edmund Husserl's phenomenology of internal time: "The past is no longer, the future is not yet, the present passes by, but as things (*opera*). And yet, I am aware of their nothingness, since I can think them in their absence. There is therefore a present of the past, and this present, as long as I think it, does not pass. It is this present that Husserl will call the *Living Present*, oddly. In Augustine, this present, immanent to internal consciousness, this umbilic, from which signs become readable to me, this present, then, is like the echo in temporality of the divine Present, of his eternal today" (CdA.99–100/CA.73–74). But contrast what Lyotard says in *The Différend*: "God is for later, 'in a moment'; the Living Present is to come.

These only come by not arriving. Which is what Beckett signifies. Time is not what is lacking to consciousness, time makes consciousness lack itself" (Di.118/D.77).

18. *L'Entretien infini* (Paris: Éditions Gallimard, 1969), pp. 307–8 (*The Infinite Conversation*, trans. Susan Hanson [Minneapolis: University of Minnesota Press, 1993], p. 207).

19. *L'Écriture du désastre* (Paris: Éditions Gallimard, 1980), p. 1 (*The writing of the Disaster*, trans. Ann Smock [Lincoln: University of Nebraska Press, 1986], p. 1): "We are on the edge of disaster without being able to situate it in the future: it is rather always already past, and yet we are on the edge or under the threat, all formulations which would imply the future—that which is yet to come—if the disaster were not that which does not come, that which has put a stop to every arrival."

20. See Marion, "The Discourse of Praise" (IeD.232–39/ID.184–91). Marion makes the interesting point that as a speech act praise is neither (exactly) a proposition, *s* is *p*, nor a performative in which language causes something to exist. Unlike "I now pronounce you man and wife" or "Strike three!," "I praise you" institutes nothing; rather, words are given as gifts: "Praise indeed functions as a performative ('I praise you . . .'), but as a performative that, instead of making things with words, elaborates with words gifts ('I praise you as *y*, *y'*, *y"*,' etc.). Praise plays as a performative all the more in that it more radically sets the statement outside of the one stating. On this condition alone, the statement assumes enough consistency to merit the dignity of a gift—to traverse distance" (IeD.239/ID.190–91).

21. *Entre Nous: Essais sur le penser-à-l'autre* (Paris: Editions Grasset and Fasquelle, 1991), p. 17, hereafter cited as En; *Entre Nous: On Thinking-of-the-Other*, trans. Michael B. Smith and Barbara Harshav (New York: Columbia University Press, 1998), p. 6, hereafter cited as EN.

22. "Langage et proximité," *En découvrant l'existence avec Husserl et Heidegger*. 2d ed. (Paris: Librairie Philosophique, 1967), pp. 223–24 ("Language and Proximity," in *Collected Philosophical Papers*, trans. Alphonso Lingis [The Hague: Martinus Nijhoff, 1987], p. 115).

23. See Levinas, *Autrement qu'être; ou, Au-delà de l'essence* (The Hague: Martinus Nijhoff, 1978), p. 81, hereafter cited as AE; *Otherwise than Being; or, Beyond Essence*, trans. Alphonso Lingis (The Hague: Martinus Nijhoff, 1981), p. 48, hereafter cited as OTB.

24. Levinas's conception of mysticism was shaped by his reading of Lucien Lévy-Bruhl's theories of primitive mentalities, and accordingly he thinks of mysticism as an experience of participation in an all-enveloping spirit, in contrast to a more theological view of mysticism that emphasizes the experience of *le tout autre* that traverses a relation of incommensurability or an insurmountable gap. In fact Levinas is closer to this second view than he is to the first insofar as he sees our relation to other people and to God as a relation of separation: outside cognition, which is to say outside the

relation of essence, identity, categories, concepts, horizons, and totalities of every sort. See Levinas, "Lévy Bruhl and Contemporary Philosophy" (En.53–68/EN.39–51).

25. Jacques Derrida, *Sauf le nom* (Paris: Éditions Galilée, 1993), pp. 22–23, hereafter cited as SN; *On the Name*, trans. Thomas Dutoit (Stanford: Stanford University Press, 1995), pp. 38–39, hereafter cited as ON.

26. See "In the Name" (GG.41–42). See also Marion's discussion of the Name of God in *Idol and Distance* (IeD.186–92/ID.141–45).

27. *Gesammelte Werke* (Frankfurt am Main: Suhrkamp Verlag, 1986), 1:225.

28. *Poems of Paul Celan*, trans. Michael Hamburger (New York: Persea Books, 1989), pp. 174–75.

29. "Circonfession," in Geoffrey Bennington and Jacques Derrida, *Jacques Derrida* (Paris: Éditions du Seuil, 1991) ("Circumfession," in *Jacques Derrida*, trans. Geoffrey Bennington [Chicago: University of Chicago Press, 1993], pp. 55–58). For a discussion of "Circumfession," see John D. Caputo, *The Prayers and Tears of Jacques Derrida: Religion without Religion* (Bloomington: Indiana University Press, 1997), pp. 281–329.

30. See Levinas, "Transcendence et hauteur," *Bulletin de la Société Française de Philosophie* 56, no. 3 (1962): 89–101 ("Transcendence and Height," in *Basic Philosophical Writings*, ed. Adriaan Peperzak, Simon Critchley, and Robert Bernasconi [Bloomington: Indiana University Press, 1996], pp. 16–20); and also *Totality and Infinity*: "Transcendence designates a relation with reality infinitely distant from my own reality, yet without this distance destroying this relation and without this relation destroying this distance, as would happen with relations within the same [or identity: I = I]; this relation . . . is prior to the negative or affirmative proposition; it first institutes language [prayer], where neither the no nor the yes is the first word" (TeI.31–32/TI.41–42).

Chapter Seven

1. Jean-Paul Sartre, *Qu'est-ce que la littérature?* (Paris: Éditions Gallimard, 1948), pp. 19–20, hereafter cited as QL; *What Is Literature & Other Essays* (Cambridge, MA: Harvard University Press, 1988), p. 30, hereafter cited as WL.

2. *Phänomenologie des Geist*, heraus. Hans-Friedrich Wessels und Heinrich Clairmont (Hamburg: Felix Meiner, 1988), p. 264, hereafter cited as PhG; *Hegel's Phenomenology of Spirit*, trans. A. V. Miller (Oxford: Oxford University Press, 1977), p. 238, hereafter cited as PS.

3. The essay dates from 1941, and is a review of Jean Paulhan's *Les fleurs de Tarbes*, which examines the poetics of the "Terrorists," the name of a hypothetical group of writers who believe that the writer's task is to reject the rules and conventions, the forms and commonplaces, indeed the conditions of language that make literature possible: in other words, *modernists* — whose critique is in fact the formation of an impasse:

It is a fact; literature exists. It continues to exist despite the inherent absurdity that lives in it, divides it, and makes it actually inconceivable. In the heart of every writer there is a demon who pushes him to strike dead all literary forms, to become aware of his dignity as a writer insofar as he breaks with language and with literature; in a word, to call into question in an expressible way what he is and what he does [*il rompt avec le langage et avec la littérature, en un mot, à mettre en question d'une manière indicible ce qu'il est et ce qu'il fait*]. How, in these conditions, can literature exist? How can the writer, the one who distinguishes himself from other men by the single fact that he questions the validity of language, the one whose work should be to prevent the formation of a written work, end up creating a literary work? How is literature possible? (Fp.97/FP.80–81)

Paulhan's book is, Blanchot says, a discovery that the struggle against literary forms can only take place by the very means (that is, language) that engender these forms: "There is in this discovery enough to cause the silence of Rimbaud to fall upon everyone" (Fp.99/FP.82).

4. And not just literature. Much of Blanchot's work is an exploration of the strange ontological condition in which speech becomes an impossible exigency. *L'attente l'oubli* (Paris: Éditions Gallimard, 1962, hereafter cited as AO; *Awaiting Oblivion*, trans. John Gregg (Lincoln: University of Nebraska Press, 1997), hereafter cited as AwO, is a text made up of narrative fragments and pieces of conversation that deal obsessively (not to say tortuously) with this condition:

Express only what cannot be expressed. Leave it unexpressed. (AO.35/AwO.6)

"Yes, speak to me now."—"I cannot."—"Speak without the ability to do so."—"You ask me so calmly to do the impossible." (AO.86/AwO.44)

Wanting to and not being able to speak; not wanting to and not being able to evade speech; thus speaking—not speaking, in an identical movement her interlocutor had the duty to maintain. (AO93/AwO48)

Speaking, not wanting to; wanting to, not being able to. (AO.93/AwO.48)

5. *Unterwegs zur Sprache* (Pfullingen: Günther Neske, 1959), pp. 161–62 (*On the Way to Language*, trans. Peter Hertz [New York: Harper and Row, 1971], p. 59).

6. See "L'expérience-limite" (1962), where Blanchot glosses Bataille's idea that "possibility is not the sole dimension of our existence": "It is perhaps given to us to 'live' each of the events that is ours by way of a double relation. We live it one time as something we comprehend, grasp, bear, and

master . . . by relating it to some good or to some value, that is to say, finally, by relating it to Unity; we live it at another time as something that escapes all employment [*emploi*] and all end, and more, as that which escapes our very capacity to undergo it, but whose trial we cannot escape. Yes, as though impossibility, that by which we are no longer able to be able, were waiting for us behind all that we live, think, and say" (EI.307–8/IC.207). It is this division of time into two temporalities that I'm trying to clarify in what follows.

7. See "La mort possible" (1952): "You cannot write unless you remain your own master before death; you must have established with death a relation of sovereign equals. If you lose face before death, if death is the limit of your self-possession, then it slips the words out from under the pen, it cuts in and interrupts" (EL.110/SL.91).

8. *Œuvres complètes*, ed. Henri Mondor (Paris: Éditions Gallimard, 1945), p. 645.

9. *Gesamtausgabe* (Frankfurt am Main: Vittorio Klostermann, 1975), Band 24: *Der Grundprobleme der Phänomenologie*, pp. 349–50 (*The Basic Problems of Phenomenology*, trans. Albert Hofstadter [Bloomington: Indiana University Press, 1982], pp. 247–48).

10. *Les imprévus de l'histoire* (Montpelier: Éditions Fata Morgana, 1994), p. 133, hereafter cited as IH; *Collected Philosophical Papers*, trans. Alphonso Lingis (The Hague: Martinus Nijhoff, 1987), p. 6, hereafter cited as CPP.

11. *Logique du sens* (Éditions du Minuit, 1969), p. 80 (*The Logic of Sense*, trans. Mark Lester [New York: Columbia University Press, 1990], p.63).

12. *Milles plateaux: capitalisme et schizophrénie* (Paris: Éditions du Minuit, 1980), p. 321 (*A Thousand Plateaus: Capitalism and Schizophrenia*, trans. Brian Massumi [Minneapolis: University of Minnesota Press, 1993], p. 263).

13. On indiscernibility as a philosophical difficulty, see Arthur Danto, "Works of Art and Mere Real Things," in *The Transfiguration of the Commonplace: A Philosophy of Art* (Cambridge, MA: Harvard University Press, 1981), pp. 1–32.

14. *La dissemination* (Paris: Éditions du Seuil, 1972), p. 221, hereafter cited as Di; *Disseminations*, trans. Barbara Johnson (Chicago: University of Chicago Press, 1981), pp. 194–95, hereafter cited as D.

15. "The Green Box" (1912), in *The Writings of Marcel Duchamp*, ed. Michael Sanouillet and Elmer Peterson (New York: Da Capo Press, 1973), p. 26.

16. A replica, to be precise, makes no effort to reproduce an original or to serve, as in the case of a duplicate, as a replacement. It is frequently smaller and highly mediated. The postcard one buys in the shop of an art museum *replicates* one of its holdings; it is not a copy like the reproduction that the art student on the third floor, sitting with paint and easel before a Picasso, is meticulously imitating.

17. "The Conceptual Poetics of Marcel Duchamp," in Perloff, *21st-Century Modernism: The "New" Poetics* (Oxford: Blackwell, 2002), p. 86.

18. Adorno has an interesting passage in his *Aesthetic Theory* that bears upon this matter:

> The processual character of artworks [their mode of existence as an event, process, or material object] is nothing other than their temporal nucleus. If duration becomes their intention in such fashion that they expel what they deem ephemeral and by their own hand eternalize themselves in pure impregnable forms or, worse, by the ominous claim to the universally human, they cut short their lives and assimilate themselves into the concept that—as the fixed circumference of shifting contents—by its form pursues precisely that temporal stasis against which the drawn tension of the artwork defends itself. Artworks, mortal human objects, pass away all the more rapidly the more doggedly they stave it off. Although permanence cannot be excluded from the concept of their form, it is not their essence. . . . Today it is conceivable and perhaps requisite that artworks immolate themselves through their temporal nucleus, devote their own life to the instant of the appearance of truth, and tracelessly vanish without thereby diminishing themselves in the slightest. . . . The idea of the permanence of works is modeled on the category of property and is thus ephemeral in the bourgeois sense; it was alien to many periods and important productions. . . . Stockhausen's concept of electronic works—which, since they are not notated in the traditional sense but immediately "realized" in their material, could be extinguished along with this material—is a splendid one of an art that makes an emphatic claim yet is prepared to throw itself away. (AT.265/AeT.177–78)

19. Alternatively one could argue that, by conceptualizing the snow shovel as a work of art, Duchamp reconceptualizes the everyday, which is no longer beneath the threshold of recognition but has acquired a visibility it never before possessed.

20. *Autrement qu'être pi au-dela de l'essence* (La Haye: Martinus Nijhoff, 1974), p. 170 (*Otherwise than Being or Beyond Essence*, trans. Alphonso Lingis [The Hague: Martinus Nijhoff, 1981], p. 108).

21. *L'amitié* (Paris: Éditions Gallimard, 1971), pp. 328–29 (*Friendship*, trans. Elizabeth Rottenberg [Stanford: Stanford University Press, 1997], pp. 290–91).

22. Fragments of a similar conversation punctuate *Le pas au-delà*: "*We speak, we speak, two immobile men whom immobility maintains facing one another, the only ones to speak, the last to speak*" (PD.127/SNB.91–92).

23. *Le temps et l'autre* (Montpellier: Éditions Fata Morgana, 1979 [1947]), p. 57, hereafter cited as TA; *Time and the Other*, trans. Richard A. Cohen (Pittsburgh: Duquesne University Press, 1987), p. 70, hereafter cited as TO.

24. "Éthique comme philosophie première," in *Justifications de l'éthique* (Bruxelles: Éditions de l'Université de Bruxelles, 1984), p. 48 ("Ethics as First Philosophy," trans. Seán Hand and Michael Temple, in *The Levinas Reader*, ed. Seán Hand [Oxford: Blackwell, 1989], p. 83).

25. *L'arrêt de mort* (Paris: Éditions Gallimard, 1948), p. 99, hereafter cited as AM; *Death Sentence*, trans. Lydia Davis (Barrytown: Station Hill Press, 1978), p. 52, hereafter cited as DS.

26. Maurice Blanchot and Jacques Derrida, *The Instant of My Death/Demeure: Fiction and Testimony*, trans. Elizabeth Rottenberg (Stanford: Stanford University Press, 1999), p. 3, hereafter cited as IM.

Chapter Eight

1. Readers should consult Jill Robbins, *Altered Reading: Levinas and Literature* (Chicago: University of Chicago Press, 1999), and Steve McCaffery, "The Scandal of Sincerity: Towards a Levinasian Poetics," in *Prior to Meaning: Protosemantics and Poetics* (Evanston: Northwestern University Press, 2001).

2. "Connaissance de l'inconnu," *L'entretien infini* (Paris: Éditions Gallimard, 1969), p. 76, hereafter cited as EI; "Knowledge of the Unknown," in *The Infinite Conversation*, trans. Susan Hanson (Minneapolis: University of Minnesota Press, 1993), p. 53, hereafter cited as IC.

3. The most detailed and authoritative study of antique poetics remains that of Ernst Robert Curtius, *European Literature and the Latin Middle Ages* (1948), trans. Willard Trask (New York: Harper and Row, 1953), esp. pp. 145–227, 468–86. Curtius remarks that a "history of the theory of poetry" remains to be written (p. 468). The statement is as true today as it was a half-century ago.

4. Athenäum Fragment 238, *Kritische Schriften* (München: Carl Hauser Verlag), pp. 50–51. See Friedrich Schlegel, *Philosophical Fragments*, trans. Peter Firchow (Minneapolis: University of Minnesota Press, 1991), pp. 50–51.

5. See "Le mystère dans les lettres," *Œuvres complètes*, ed. Henri Mondor (Paris: Éditions Gallimard, 1945), pp. 385–87, hereafter cited as OC. See Maurice Blanchot, "La poésie de Mallarmé est-elle obscure?" in *Faux pas* (Paris: Éditions Gallimard, 1943), pp. 126–31, esp. p. 129 ("Is Mallarmé's Poetry Obscure?" in *Faux Pas*, trans. Charlotte Mandell [Stanford: Stanford University Press, 2002], pp. 107–11).

6. "Le mythe de Mallarmé," in *La part du feu* (Paris: Éditions Gallimard, 1949), p. 44, hereafter cited as PF; "The Myth of Mallarmé," in *The Work of Fire*, trans. Charlotte Mandell (Stanford: Stanford University Press, 1995), p. 37, hereafter cited as WF.

7. See Michael Holland on Blanchot's reception of Mallarmé, "From Crisis to Critique: Mallarmé for Blanchot," *Meetings with Mallarmé in Contemporary French Culture*, ed. Michael Temple (Exeter: University of Exeter Press, 1998), pp. 81–106.

8. *Qu'est-ce que la littérature* (Paris: Éditions Gallimard, 1948), p. 7, here-after cited as QL; *"What is Literature?" and Other Essays*, trans. Steven Ungar (Cambridge, MA: Harvard University Press, 1988), p. 29, hereafter cited as WL.

9. Sartre's writings on Mallarmé, which stress the idea of poetry as self-annihilating discourse, have been collected in *Mallarmé; or, The Poet of Nothingness*, trans. Ernest Sturm (University Park: Pennsylvania State University Press, 1988). See Dominic LaCapra's discussion of Sartre's changing conceptions of language and writing, *A Preface to Sartre: A Critical Introduction to Sartre's Literary and Philosophical Writings* (Ithaca: Cornell University Press, 1978), pp. 63–91.

10. The term "aesthetic differentiation" derives from Hans-Georg Gadamer's discussion (and critique) of idealist aesthetics in *Wahrheit und Methode: Grundzüge einer philosophischen Hermeneutik*. 4th Auflage. (Tübingen: J. C. B. Mohr [Paul Siebeck], 1975), pp. 77–96, hereafter cited as WM; *Truth and Method*, 2d rev. ed., trans. Joel Weinsheimer and Donald G. Marshall (New York: Crossroad, 1989), pp. 81–100, hereafter cited as TM. Gadamer writes: "What we call a work of art . . . aesthetically depends on a process of abstraction. By disregarding everything in which a work of art is rooted (its original context of life, and the religious or secular function that gave it significance), it becomes visible as the 'pure work of art.' In performing this abstraction, aesthetic consciousness performs a task that is positive in itself. It shows what a pure work of art is, and allows it to exist in its own right. I call this 'aesthetic differentiation'" (WM.81/TM.85).

11. See Arthur Danto, "Art and Disturbation," in *The Philosophical Disenfranchisement of Art*, pp. 117–33. See also Levinas on "disturbance" (*le dérangement*) —in contrast to rational discourse—in "Enigme et phénomènon" (DHH.202–5/CPP.61–63).

12. Compare Blanchot on fascination and the image in *L'espace littéraire* (Paris: Éditions Gallimard, 1955), pp. 28–31 (*The Space of Literature*, trans. Ann Smock [Lincoln: University of Nebraska Press, 1982], pp. 32–33).

13. In his interviews with Philippe Nemo, Levinas refers to the deposition of the sovereign ego as the mode of escape from the *il y a*, but it is hard to make sense of this statement, since this deposition already occurs in the experience of the work of art, which is to say the experience of materiality, irreality, or the *il y a* itself. See *Ethics and Infinity: Conversations with Philippe Nemo*, trans. Richard A. Cohen (Pittsburgh: Duquesne University Press, 1985), p. 52. The symmetry between the aesthetic and the ethical in this regard has yet to be studied but has been noted by Edith Wyschogrod in "The Art in Ethics: Aesthetics, Objectivity, and Alterity in the Philosophy of Emmanuel Levinas," in *Ethics as First Philosophy: The Significance of Emmanuel Levinas for Philosophy, Literature, and Religion*, ed. Adriaan Peperzak (London: Routledge, 1995), pp. 138–39.

14. The "exteriority which is not that of a body" perhaps means that in this event one's body is materialized in such a way that one experiences it

from the outside—hence the somewhat incoherent metaphor of the "I-actor" becoming the "I-spectator"; but it is no longer obvious that it makes sense to speak of "experience," since the "I" is no longer an experiencing subject in the sense of witnessing a spectacle. Indeed, in the next sentence Levinas complains that phenomenology has yet to produce a concept of experience that would do justice to "this fundamental paradox of rhythm and dreams, which describes a sphere situated outside of the conscious and the unconscious" (IH.129/CPP.4). Blanchot's poetics might be called a phenomenology of this sphere of exteriority.

15. The question is whether there is any important difference between exposure to the world and the exposure to others that constitutes the ethical relation. See Jean-Luc Marion on this question, "A Note Concerning the Ontological Difference," *Graduate Faculty Philosophy Journal* 20–21 (1998): 25–50, esp. 32–37.

16. Already in *De l'existence à l'existant* Levinas had invoked the figure of the cadaver: "A corpse is horrible; it already bears in itself its own phantom, it presages its return. The haunting spectre, the phantom, constitutes the very element of horror" (DEE.100/EE.61). See Blanchot's "Les deux versions de l'imaginaire," in *L'espace littéraire*, pp. 346–49 ("Two Versions of the Imaginary," in *The Space of Literature*, pp. 256–60).

17. *Critique of Judgment*, trans. Werner S. Pluhar (Indianapolis: Hackett Publishing, 1987), p. 115.

18. See Bertold Brecht, "Modern Theatre is Epic Theatre," in *Brecht on Theatre: The Development of an Aesthetic*, trans. John Willett (New York: Hill and Wang, 1964), p. 35. Levinas's conception of *jouissance* in *Totalité et infini* is distinctly culinary—"Nourishment, as a means of invigoration, is the transmutation of the other into the same, which is in the essence of enjoyment [*jouissance*]" (TeI.113/TI.111). It might be possible, nevertheless, to link Levinas's conception of "*jouissance l'esthétique*" to conceptions of *jouissance* that derive from the experience of aesthetic modernity. See Paul-Laurent Assoun, "The Subject and the Other in Levinas and Lacan," trans. Diana Jackson and Denise Merkle, in *Levinas and Lacan: The Missed Encounter*, ed. Sarah Harasym (Albany: State University of New York Press, 1998), pp. 79–101, esp. pp. 93–97.

19. *Gesamtausgabe* (Frankfurt: Vittorio Klostermann, 1977), 5: *Holzwege*, p. 31, hereafter cited as G; *Poetry, Language, Thought*, trans. Albert Hofstadter (New York: Harper, 1971), p. 45, hereafter cited as PLT.

20. This point is well made by Jean Greisch in "Ethics and Ontology: Some 'Hypocritical' Considerations," trans. Leonard Lawler, *Graduate Faculty Philosophy Journal* 20–21 (1998): 41–69, esp. 62–64, where Greisch speculates that art can mediate the breach between ethics and ontology.

21. In "Etre juif" (1962) Blanchot writes: "The words exodus and exile indicate a positive relation with exteriority, whose exigency invites us not to be content with what is proper to us (that is, with our power to assimilate

everything, to identify everything, to bring everything back to our 'I'" (EI.186/IC.127).

22. Blanchot develops this idea most fully in "Comment découvrir l'obscur?" (1959), where speech (now called "poetry") is no longer the expression of sovereignty, power, or conceptual control but is a mode of responsiveness to what is singular and refractory to consciousness. This essay is reprinted in *L'entretien infini* as the second part of "La grand refus" (EI.57–69/IC.40–48).

23. In defiance of contradiction, Blanchot says, it is possible to characterize impossibility in terms of three traits:

> First this one: in impossibility time changes direction, no longer offering itself out of the future as what gathers by going beyond; time, here, is rather the dispersion of a present that, even while being only passage does not pass, never fixes itself in a present, refers to no past and goes toward no future: *the incessant* [or "meanwhile"]. A second trait: in impossibility, the immediate is a present to which one cannot be present, but from which one cannot separate; or, again, it is what escapes by the very fact that there is no escaping it: the *ungraspable that one cannot let go of*. Third trait: what reigns in the experience of impossibility is not the unique's immobile collecting unto itself, but the infinite shifting of dispersal, a non-dialectical movement where contrariety has nothing to do with opposition or with reconciliation, and where the *other* never comes back to the same. (EI.64–65.IC.45–46)

24. Interestingly, in "Realité et son ombre" the sensible was figured as the shadow of being: "The notion of shadow . . . enables us to situate the economy of resemblance within the general economy of being. Resemblance is not a participation of a being in an idea . . . ; it is the very structure of the sensible as such. The sensible is being insofar as it resembles itself, insofar as, outside of its triumphal work of being, it casts a shadow, emits that obscure and elusive essence, that phantom essence which cannot be identified with the essence revealed in truth" (IH.136/CPP.7–8).

25. Paul Ricoeur calls this dimension Levinas's "hyperbole"—the "systematic practice of *excess* in philosophical argumentation"—which in *Autrement qu'être*, Ricoeur says, is carried to "the point of paroxysm." *Oneself as Another*, trans. Kathleen Blamey (Chicago: University of Chicago Press, 1992), p. 337. See D. H. Brody, "Emmanuel Levinas: The Logic of Ethical Ambiguity," in *Otherwise than Being or beyond Essence*," *Research in Phenomenology* 25 (1994): 177–203.

Bibliography

Adams, Parveen. *The Emptiness of the Image*. London: Routledge, 1991.

Adorno, Theodor W. *Aesthetic Theory*. Trans. Robert Hullot-Kentor. Minneapolis: University of Minnesota Press, 1997.

———. *Ästhetische Theorie*. Frankfurt am Main: Suhrkamp, 1973.

———. *Gesammelte Schriften*. Frankfurt am Main: Suhrkamp, 1980. Band 4: *Minima Moralia: Reflexionen aus dem beschädigten Leben*.

———. *Gesammelte Schriften*. Frankfurt am Main, 1977. Band 10.1: *Kulturkritik und Gesellschaft,1: Prismen*.

———. *Minima Moralia: Reflections from a Damaged Life*. Trans. Edmund Jephcott. London: Verso, 1978.

———. *Noten zur Literatur,1*. Frankfurt am Main, 1963.

———. *Notes to Literature*. Trans. Shierry Weber Nicholsen. New York: Columbia University Press, 1991.

———. *Prisms*. Trans. Samuel and Shierry Weber. Cambridge, MA: MIT Press, 1981.

Agamben Giorgio. *The Man without Content*. Trans. Georgia Albert. Stanford: Stanford University Press, 1999.

Antin, David. "language," in *Marcel Duchamp*, ed. Anne d'Harnoncourt and Kynaston McSchine, p. 212. Prestel, Germany: The Museum of Modern Art and Philadelphia Museum of Art, 1989.

———. *talking at the boundaries*. New York: New Directions, 1976.

————. *what does it mean to be avant garde?* New York: New Directions, 1990.

Artaud, Antonin. *Œuvres complètes*. Paris: Éditions Gallimard, 1956.

————. *Selected Writings*. Ed. Susan Sontag. Berkeley: Berkeley University Press, 1988.

————. *Le théâtre et son double*. Paris: Éditions Gallimard, 1964.

Ashbery, John. *Houseboat Days*. New York: Penguin Books, 1977.

————. *Reported Sightings: Art Chronicles, 1957–1987*. Ed. David Bergman. Cambridge, MA: Harvard University Press, 1989.

Assoun, Paul Laurent. "The Subject and the Other in Levinas and Lacan." Trans. Diana Jackson and Denise Merkle. In *Levinas and Lacan: The Missed Encounter*, 79–101. Albany: State University of New York Press, 1998.

Bataille, Georges. *The Absence of Myth: Writings on Surrealism*. Trans. Michael Richardson. London: Verso, 1994.

————. *The Accursed Share: An Essay on General Economy*. Trans. Robert Hurley. New York: Zone Books, 1988.

————. *The College of Sociology*. Ed. Denis Hollier. Trans. Betsy Wing. Minneapolis: University of Minnesota Press, 1988.

————. *L'expérience intérieure*. Paris: Éditions Gallimard, 1943.

————. *Guilty*. Trans. Bruce Boone. Venice, CA: Lapis Press, 1988.

————. *The Impossible*. Trans. Robert Hurley. San Francisco: City Lights Books, 1991.

————. *Inner Experience*. Trans. Leslie Anne Boldt. Albany: State University of New York Press, 1988.

————. *Œuvres complètes*. 12v. Paris: Éditions Gallimard, 1970–1988.

————. *La part maudite, precede de la notion de dépense*. Paris: Editions du Minuit, 1967.

————. *Visions of Excess: Selected Writings, 1927–1939*. Trans. Allan Stoekl. Minneapolis: University of Minnesota Press, 1985.

Battock, Gregory. Ed. *The Art of Performance: A Critical Anthology*. New York: E. P. Dutton, 1984.

————. Ed. *The New Art*. New York: E. P. Dutton, 1973.

Baudelaire, Charles. *Œuvres complètes*, 2. Ed. Claude Pichois. Paris: Éditions Gallimard, 1976.

————. "The Painter of Modern Life." In *Selected Writings on Art and Literature*. Trans. P. E. Charvet. London: Penguin Books, 1972.

Benjamin, Walter. *The Arcades Project*. Trans. Howard Eiland and Kevin McLaughlin. Cambridge, MA: Harvard University Press, 1999.

————. *Charles Baudelaire: A Lyric Poet in the Era of High Capitalism.* Trans. Harry Zohn. London: Verso, 1973.

————. *Gesammelte Schriften.* 7v. Frankfurt am Main: Suhrkamp, 1972.

————. *Selected Writings, 1: 1913–1926.* Ed. Marcus Bullock and Michael W. Jennings. Trans. Edmund Jephcott et al. Cambridge, MA: Harvard University Press, 1996.

————. *Selected Writings, 2: 1927–1934.* Ed. Marcus Bullock and Michael W. Jennings. Trans. Edmund Jephcott et al. Cambridge, MA: Harvard University Press, 1999.

————. *Selected Writings, 3: 1935–1938.* Ed. Howard Eiland and Michael W. Jennings. Trans. Edmund Jephcott et al. Cambridge, MA: Harvard University Press, 2002.

————. *Selected Writings, 4: 1938–1940.* Ed. Howard Eiland and Michael W. Jennings. Trans. Edmund Jephcott et al. Cambridge, MA: Harvard University Press, 2003.

Bernstein, Charles. *A Poetics*, Cambridge, MA: Harvard University Press, 1992.

————. *Dark City.* Los Angeles: Sun and Moon Press. 1994.

————. *Republics of Reality: 1975–1995.* Los Angeles: Sun and Moon Press, 2000.

————. *With Strings: Poems.* Chicago: University of Chicago Press, 2001.

Bernstein, Charles, and Bruce Andrews, eds. *The L=A=N=G=U=A=G=E Book.* Carbondale, IL: Southern Illinois University Press, 1984.

Berry, R. M., Jr. "The Avant-Garde and the Question of Literature" *Soundings: An Interdisciplinary Journal* 88, no. 1–2 (Spring/Summer 2005): 105–27.

Bersani, Leo. *The Death of Stéphane Mallarmé.* Cambridge: Cambridge University Press, 1982.

Blanchot, Maurice. *L'amité.* Paris: Éditions Gallimard, 1971.

————. *L'attente, l'oubli.* Paris: Éditions Gallimard, 1962.

————. *L'arrêt de mort.* Paris: Éditions Gallimard, 1948.

————. *Awaiting Oblivion.* Trans. John Gregg. Lincoln: University of Nebraska Press, 1997.

————. *The Book to Come.* Trans. Charlotte Mandel. Stanford: Stanford University Press, 2003.

————. *La communauté inavouable.* Paris: Éditions du Minuit, 1983.

————. *Death Sentence.* Trans. Lydia Davis. Barrytown, NY: Station Hill Press, 1978.

————. *L'écriture du désastre*. Paris: Éditions Gallimard, 1980.

————. *L'entretien infini*. Paris: Éditions Gallimard, 1969.

————. *L'espace littéraire* Paris: Éditions Gallimard, 1955.

————. *Faux pas*. Paris: Éditions Gallimard, 1943.

————. *Faux pas*. Trans. Charlotte Mandel. Stanford University Press, 2001.

————. *Friendship*. Trans. Elizabeth Rottenberg. Stanford: Stanford University Press, 1997.

————. *The Gaze of Orpheus and Other Literary Essays*. Trans. Lydia Davis. Barrytown, NY: Station Hill Press, 1981.

————. *The Infinite Conversation*. Trans. Susan Hanson. Minneapolis: University of Minnesota Press, 1993.

————. *Le livre à venir*. Paris: Éditions Gallimard, 1959.

————. *La part du feu*. Paris: Éditions Gallimard, 1949.

————. *Le pas au-delà*. Paris: Éditions Gallimard, 1973.

————. "Michel Foucault as I Imagine Him." In *Foucault/Blanchot*. Trans. Geoffrey Mehlman. New York: Zone Books, 1987.

————. *The Space of Literature*. Trans. Ann Smock. Lincoln: University of Nebraska Press, 1982.

————. *The Step Not Beyond*. Trans. Lycette Nelson. Albany: State University of New York Press, 1992.

————. *The Unavowable Community*. Trans. Pierre Joris. Barrytown, NY: Station Hill Press, 1988.

————. *The Work of Fire*. Trans. Charlotte Mandell. Stanford: Stanford University Press, 1995.

Blanchot, Maurice, and Jacques Derrida. *The Instant of My Death/Demeure: Fiction and Testimony*. Trans. Elizabeth Rottenberg. Stanford: Stanford University Press, 1999.

Blumenberg, Hans. "An Anthropological Approach to the Contemporary Significance of Rhetoric." In *After Philosophy: End or Transformation?* ed. Kenneth Baynes, James Bohman, and Thomas McCarthy, 429–58. Cambridge, MA: MIT Press, 1967.

Brecht, Bertold. *Brecht on Theater: The Development of an Aesthetic*. Trans. John Willett. New York: Hill and Wang, 1964.

Breton, André. *Nadja*. Trans. Richard Howard. New York: Grove Press, 1966.

Bruns, Gerald L. *Heidegger's Estrangements: Language, Truth, and Poetry in the Later Writings*. New Haven: Yale University Press, 1989.

————. *The Material of Poetry: Sketches for a Philosophical Poetics*. Athens: University of Georgia Press, 2005.

————. *Maurice Blanchot: The Refusal of Philosophy*. Baltimore: The Johns Hopkins University Press, 1992.

————. *Modern Poetry and the Idea of Language: A Critical and Historical Study*. New Haven: Yale University Press, 1974.

————. *Tragic Thoughts at the End of Philosophy: Language, Literature, and Ethical Theory*. Evanston, IL: Northwestern University Press, 1999.

Cage, John. *Anarchy*. Middletown, CT: Wesleyan University Press, 2001.

————. *Empty Words: Writings, '73–'78*. Middletown, CT: Wesleyan University Press, 2001.

————. *M: Writings, '67–'72*. Middletown, CT: Wesleyan University Press, 1973.

————. *Silence: Lectures and Writings by John Cage*. Middletown, CT: Wesleyan University Press, 1961.

————. *X: Writings, '79–'82*. Middletown, CT: Wesleyan University Press, 1983.

————. *A Year from Monday: New Lectures and Writings*. Middletown, CT: Wesleyan University Press, 1967.

Caputo, John. *Against Ethics: Contributions to a Poetics of Obligation with Constant Reference to Deconstruction*. Bloomington: Indiana University Press, 1993.

————. *The Prayers and Tears of Jacques Derrida*. Bloomington: Indiana University Press, 1997.

Caputo, John, and Michael J. Scanlon, eds. *God, the Gift, and Postmodernism*. Bloomington: Indiana University Press, 1999.

Carr, Cynthia: *On Edge: Performance at the End of the Twentieth Century*. Middletown, CT: Wesleyan University Press, 1993.

Cavell, Stanley. *The Claim of Reason: Wittgenstein, Skepticism, Morality, and Tragedy*. New York: Oxford University Press, 1979.

————. *In Quest of the Ordinary: Lines of Skepticism and Romanticism*. Chicago: University of Chicago Press, 1988.

————. *Must We Mean What We Say? A Book of Essays*. New York: Scribner, 1969.

————. *The Senses of Walden*. San Francisco: North Point Press, 1981.

Celan, Paul. *Atemkristall*. Paris: Brunidor, 1965.

————. *Breathturn*. Trans. Pierre Joris. Los Angeles: Sun and Moon Press, 1995.

————. *Collected Prose*. Tran. Rosemarie Waldrop. Riverdale–on–Hudson, NY: Sheep Meadow Press, 1986.

———. *Fathomsuns and Benighted: Fadensonnen and Eingedunkelt*. Riverdale-on-Hudson, NY: The Sheep Meadow Press, 2001.

———. *Poems of Paul Celan*. Trans. Michael Hamburger. New York: Persea Books, 1988.

———. *Gesammelte Werke*. 5v. Frankfurt am Main: Suhrkamp, 1986.

———. *Threadsuns*. Trans. Pierre Joris. Los Angeles: Sun and Moon Press, 2000.

Creeley, Robert. *Was That a Real Poem? And Other Essays*. Ed. Donald Allen. Bolinas, CA: Four Seasons Foundation, 1979.

Curtius, Ernst. *European Literature in the Latin Middle Ages*. Trans. Willard R. Trask. Princeton: Princeton University Press, 1953.

Danto, Arthur. *After the End of Art: Contemporary Art and the Pale of History*. Princeton: Princeton University Press, 1997.

———. "The Artworld." *Journal of Philosophy* 61, no. 19 (October 1964): 571–84.

———. *Beyond the Brillo Box: The Visual Arts in Post-historical Perspective*. New York: Farrar Straus Giroux, 1992.

———. *The Philosophical Disenfranchisement of Art*. New York: Columbia University Press, 1986.

———. *The Transfiguration of the Commonplace: A Philosophy of Art*. Cambridge, MA: Harvard University Press, 1981.

Dawson, Fielding. *The Black Mountain Book: A New Edition*. Rocky Mount, NC: North Carolina Wesleyan Press, 1991.

Deleuze, Gilles. *The Logic of Sense*. Trans. Mark Lester and Charles Stivale. New York: Columbia University Press, 1990.

———. *Logique du sens*. Paris: Éditions du Minuit, 1969.

Deleuze, Gilles, and Felix Guattari. *Milles plateaux: capitalisme et schizophrenie*. Paris: Éditions du Minuit, 1980.

———. *A Thousand Plateaus: Capitalism and Schizophrenia*. Trans. Brian Massumi. Minneapolis: University of Minnesota Press, 1987.

Derrida, Jacques. *La dissemination*. Paris: Éditions du Seuil, 1972.

———. *Disseminations*. Trans. Barbara Johnson. Chicago: University of Chicago Press, 1981.

———. "How to Avoid Speaking: Denials." Trans. Ken Frieden. In *Languages of the Unsayable: The Play of Negativity in Literature*, ed. Sanford Budick and Wolfgang Iser, 3–70. New York: Columbia University Press, 1989. Pp. 3–70.

———. *On the Name*. Trans. Thomas Dutoit. Stanford: Stanford University Press, 1995.

———. *Psyché: Inventions d l'autre*. Paris: Éditions Galilée, 1987.

————. *Sauf le nom*. Paris: Éditions Galilée, 1993.

————. *Schibboleth pour Paul Celan*. Paris: Éditions Galilée, 1986.

————. *Signéponge: Signsponge*. Trans. Richard Rand. New York: Columbia University Press, 1984.

————. *Specters of Marx: The State of the Debt, the Work of Mourning, and the New International*. Trans. Peggy Kamuf. London: Routledge, 1994.

————. *Spectres de Marx: l'état de la dette, le travail du deuil et la nouvelle Internationale*. Paris: Éditions Galilée, 1993.

Diamond, Cora. "Losing Your Concepts." *Ethics* 98, no. 2 (1988): 255–77.

Drucker, Johanna. *The Visible Word: Experimental Typography and Modern Art, 1909–1923*. Chicago: University of Chicago Press, 1994.

Duberman, Martin. *Black Mountain: An Exploration in Community*. New York: E. P. Dutton, 1972.

Duchamp, Marcel. *The Writings of Marcel Duchamp*. Ed. Michael Sanouillet and Elmer Peterson. New York: Da Capo Press, 1973.

Duve, Thierry de. *Kant after Duchamp*. Cambridge, MA: MIT Press, 1996.

Eysteinnsson, Astradur. *The Concept of Modernism*. Ithaca: Cornell University Press, 1990.

Fioretos, Aris, ed. *Word Traces: Readings of Paul Celan*. Baltimore: The Johns Hopkins University Press, 1994.

Foucault, Michel. *L'Archéologie du savoir*. Paris: Éditions Gallimard, 1969.

————. *The Archeology of Knowledge*. Trans. A. M. Sheridan Smith. New York: Pantheon Books, 1972.

————. *Aesthetics, Method, and Epistemology: Essential Works of Foucault, 1954–1984*. Vol. 2. Ed. James D. Faubion. New York: The New Press, 1998.

————. *Death and the Labyrinth: The World of Raymond Roussel*. Trans. Charles Ruas. New York: Doubleday, 1986.

————. *Discipline and Punish: The Birth of the Prison*, trans. Alan Sheridan. New York: Vintage Books, 1977.

————. *Dits et écrits*. 4 vols. Ed. Daniel Defert et al. Paris: Éditions Gallimard, 1994.

————. *Ethics, Subjectivity, and Truth: Essential Works of Foucault, 1954–84*. Vol. 1. Ed. Paul Rabinow. New York: The New Press, 1997.

————. *Folie et déraison: Histoire de la folie à l'âge classique*. Paris: Plon, 1961.

———. *Histoire de la sexualité*. Paris: Éditions Gallimard, 1976. 1: *La volonté de savoir*; 2: *L'usage des plaisirs*; 3: *Le souci de soi*.

———. *The History of Sexuality*. Trans. Robert Hurley. New York: Vintage Books, 1990. 1: *Introduction*; 2: *The Use of Pleasure*; 3: *The Care of the Self*.

———. *Madness and Civilization: A History of Insanity in the Age of Reason*. Trans. Richard Howard. New York, Vintage Books, 1965.

———. *Les mots et les choses*. Paris: Éditions Gallimard, 1996.

———. *The Order of Things: An Archeology of the Human Sciences*. New York: Vintage Books, 1970.

———. *L'ordre du discours*. Paris: Éditions Gallimard, 1971.

———. *Power: Essential Works of Foucault, 1954–1984*. Vol. 3. Ed. James D. Faubion. New York: The New Press, 2000.

———. *Raymond Roussel*. Paris: Éditions Gallimard, 1963.

———. *Surveiller et punir: naissance de la prison*. Paris: Éditions Gallimard, 1975.

Fredman, Stephen. *The Grounding of American Poetry: Charles Olson and the Emersonian Tradition*. Cambridge: Cambridge University Press, 1993.

———. *Poet's Prose: The Crisis in American Verse*. 2d ed. Cambridge: Cambridge University Press, 1990.

Fried, Michael. "Art and Objecthood." In *Minimal Art: A Critical Anthology*, ed. Gregory Battock, 115–25. Berkeley: University of California Press, 1995.

Friedman, Susan. "Definitional Excursions: The Meanings of Modern." *Modernity/Modernism* 8, no. 3 (September 2001): 493–513.

Friese, Heidrun. "Literal Letters: On the Materiality of Words." *Paragraph* 21, no. 2 (July 1998): 167–99.

Gadamer, Hans–Georg. *Dialogue and Dialectic: Eight Hermeneutical Studies on Plato*. Trans. P. Christopher Smith. New Haven: Yale University Press, 1980.

———. *Gadamer on Education, Poetry, and History: Applied Hermeneutics*. Trans. Lawrence Schmidt and Monica Reuss. Albany: State University of New York Press, 1992.

———. *Gesammelte Werke*. 10 vols. Tübingen: J. C. B. Mohr (Paul Siebeck), 1986–1993.

———. "The Hermeneutics of Suspicion." In *Hermeneutics: Questions and Prospects*, ed. Gary Shapiro and Alan Sica, 54–65. Amherst: University of Massachusetts Press, 1984.

———. *Philosophical Hermeneutics*. Trans. David E. Linge. Berkeley: University of California Press, 1976.

————. *Reason in the Age of Science*. Trans. Frederick G. Lawrence. Cambridge, MA: MIT Press, 1981.

————. *The Relevance of the Beautiful and Other Essays*. Ed. Robert Bernasconi. Trans. Nicholas Walker. Cambridge: Cambridge University Press, 1986.

————. *Truth and Method*. 2d rev. ed. Trans. Donald G. Marshall and Joel Weinsheimer. New York: Crossroad Publishing, 1989.

————. *Wahrheit und Methode: Grundzüge einer philosophischen Hermeneutik*. 4th Auflage. Tübingen: J. C. B. Mohr (Paul Siebeck), 1975.

Gasché, Rudolf. "Postmodernism and Rationality." *The Journal of Philosophy* 85, no. 10 (1988): 528–38.

Gentili, Bruno. *Poetry and Its Public in Ancient Greece: From Homer to the Fifth Century*. Trans. A. Thomas Cole. Baltimore: The Johns Hopkins University Press, 1988.

Giddens, Anthony. *The Consequences of Modernity*. Stanford: Stanford University Press, 1990.

Goffman, Erving. *Forms of Talk*. Philadelphia: University of Pennsylvania Press, 1981.

Goldberg, RoseLee. *Performance: Live Art 1909 to the Present*. New York: Harry N. Abrams, 1979.

Greenberg, Clement. *The Collected Essays and Criticism*. Chicago: University of Chicago Press, 1993.

Greisch, Jean. "Ethics and Ontology: Some 'Hypocritical' Considerations." *Graduate Faculty Philosophy Journal* 20–21 (1998): 41–69.

Habermas, Jürgen. *Die Moderne: ein unvollendetes Projekt. Philosophische-politische Aufsätze, 1977–1990*. Leipzig: Reclam, 1990.

————. "Modernity versus Postmodernity." *New German Critique* 22 (Winter 1981): 4–13.

————. *Moralbewußtein und kommunikatives Handeln*. Frankfurt am Main: Suhrkamp, 1983.

————. *Moral Consciousness and Communicative Action*. Trans. Christian Lenhardt and Shierry Weber Nicholsen. Cambridge, MA: MIT Press, 1990.

————. *The Philosophical Discourse of Modernity: Twelve Lectures*. Trans. Frederick G. Lawrence. Cambridge, MA: MIT Press, 1987.

————. *Der philosophischen Diskurs der Moderne: zwölf Vorlesungen*. Frankfurt am Main: Suhrkamp, 1985.

Hacking, Ian. "Making Up People." In *Reconstructing Individualism: Autonomy, Individuality, and the Self in Western Thought*. Ed. Thomas C. Heller, Morton Sosna, and David E. Wellbery. Stanford: Stanford University Press, 1986.

d'Harnoncourt, Anne, and Kynaston McSchine, *Marcel Duchamp*. Prestel, Germany: The Museum of Modern Art and Philadelphia Museum of Art, 1989.

Havelock, Eric. *Preface to Plato*. Cambridge, MA: Harvard University Press, 1963.

Hegel, Friedrich. *Aesthetics: Lectures on Fine Art*. Trans. T. M. Knox. Oxford: Clarendon Press, 1975.

———. *Phänomenologie des Geist*. Zweiter Band. Ed. Hans–Friedrich Wessels und Heinrich Clairmont. Hamburg: Felix Meiner, 1988.

———. *Phenomenology of Spirit*. Trans. A. V. Miller. Oxford: Oxford University Press, 1977.

———. *Vorlesungen über die Ästhetik. Werke in zwanzig Bänden*. Band 13.1. Frankfurt am Main: Suhrkamp, 1970.

Heidegger, Martin. *Basic Problems in Phenomenology*. Trans. Albert Hofstadter. Bloomington: Indiana University Press, 1982.

———. *Being and Time*. Trans. Edward Robinson and John McQuarrie. New York: Harper and Row, 1962.

———. *Gesamtausgabe*. 5: *Holzwege*. Frankfurt: Vittorio Klostermann, 1977.

———. *Die Grundprobleme der Phänomenologie*. Ed. Friedrich-Wilhelm von Hermann. Frankfurt am Main: Vittorio Klostermann, 1975.

———. "Hegels Begriff der Experience." *Gesamtausgabe*. 5: *Holzwege*. Frankfurt am Main: Vittorio Klostermann, 1977.

———. *Hegel's Concept of Experience*. New York: Harper and Row, 1970.

———. *Nietzsche: The Will to Power as Art*. Trans. David Farrell Krell. New York: Harper and Row, 1979.

———. *Nietzsche: Der Wille zur Macht als Kunst*. Frankfurt am Main: Vittorio Klostermann, 1985.

———. *On the Way to Language*. Trans. Peter Hertz. New York: Harper and Row, 1971.

———. *Poetry, Language, Thought*. Trans. Albert Hofstadter. New York: Harper and Row, 1971.

———. *Sein und Zeit*. Tübingen: Max Niemeyer Verlag, 1993.

———. *Unterwegs zur Sprache*. Pfullingen: Gunther Neske, 1959.

———. "Der Ursprung des Kunstwerk." *Gesamtausgabe*, Band 5: *Holzwege*. Frankfurt am Main. Vittorio Klostermann, 1977.

———. *Vorträge und Aufsätze*. Tübingen: Günther Neske Pfullingen.

Harrison, Charles, and Paul Wood, eds. *Art in Theory, 1900–1990: An Anthology of Changing Ideas*. Oxford: Basil Blackwell, 1992.

Hejinian, Lyn. *The Cell*. Los Angeles, CA: Sun and Moon Press, 1992.

————. *The Language of Inquiry*. Berkeley: University of California Press, 2000.

Holland, Michael. "From Crisis to Critique: Mallarmé for Blanchot." In *Meetings with Mallarmé in Contemporary French Culture*, ed. Michael Temple, 81–106. Exeter: University of Exeter Press, 1998.

Hollander, Benjamin, ed. *Translating Tradition: Paul Celan in France*. Special ed. of *Acts: A Journal of New Writing* 8/9 (1988).

Jaeger, Werner. *Paideia: The Ideals of Greek Culture*. 2 vols. Trans. Gilbert Highet. New York: Oxford University Press, 1948.

Jakobson, Roman. *My Futurist Years*. Ed. Bengt Jangfeldt. Trans. Stephen Rudy. New York: Marsilio Publishers, 1992.

Fredric Jameson. "Postmodernism, or the Cultural Logic of Late Capitalism." *New Left Review* 146 (1984): 53–92.

————. *A Singular Modernity: Essay on the Ontology of the Present*. London: Verso, 2002.

Janicaud, Dominique, ed. *Phenomenology and the "Theological Turn": The French Debate*. New York: Fordham University Press, 2000.

Judd, Donald. *Complete Writings, 1975–1986*. Eindhoven: van Abbemuseum, 1987.

————. "Specific Objects." In *Art in Theory, 1900–1990: An Anthology of Changing Ideas*, ed. Charles Harrison and Paul Wood, 809–13. Oxford: Basil Blackwell, 1992.

Kahn, Douglas. *Noise, Water, Meat: A History of Sound in the Arts*. Cambridge, MA: MIT Press, 2001.

Kenner, Hugh. *The Mechanic Muse*. Oxford: Oxford University Press, 1987.

Kierkegaard, Søren. *The Concept of Irony, with Continual Reference to Socrates*. Trans. Howard V. Hong and Edna H. Hong. Princeton: Princeton University Press, 1989.

Kojève, Alexandre. *Introduction to the Reading of Hegel: Lectures on* The Phenomenology of the Spirit *Assembled by Raymond Queneau*. Trans. James H. Nichols, Jr. New York: Basic Books, 1969.

Kosuth, Joseph. "Art after Philosophy." In *Art in Theory, 1900–1990: An Anthology of Changing Ideas*, ed. Charles Harrison and Paul Wood, 840–50. Oxford: Blackwell, 1993.

Kristeva, Julia. *La revolution du langage poétique: L'avant-garde à la fin du XIX siècle*. Paris: Éditions du Seuil, 1974.

————. *Revolution in Poetic Language*. Trans. Margaret Waller. New York: Columbia University Press, 1984.

Lacan, Jacques. *The Seminar of Jacques Lacan: Book 7: The Ethics of Psychoanalysis, 1959–60*. Trans. Dennis Porter. New York: W. W. Norton, 1992.

Lacoue–Labarthe, Philippe, and Jean-Luc Nancy. *L'absolu littéraire: Théorie de la littérature du romanticisme allemande*. Paris: Èditions du Seuil, 1985.

———. *The Literary Absolute: The Theory of Literature in German Romanticism*. Trans. Philip Barnard and Cheryl Lester. Albany: State University of New York Press, 1988.

Lecercle, Jean–Jacques. *Philosophy through the Looking–Glass: Language, Nonsense, Desire*. LaSalle, IL: Open Court Press, 1985.

———. *The Violence of Language*. London: Routledge, 1990.

Levinas, Emmanuel. *Autrement qu'être ou au–delà l'essence*. The Hague: Martinus Nijhoff, 1974.

———. *Basic Philosophical Writings*. Ed. Adriaan T. Peperzak, Simon Critchley, and Robert Bernasconi. Bloomington: Indiana University Press, 1996.

———. *Collected Philosophical Papers*. Trans. Alphonso Lingis. The Hague: Martinus Nijhoff, 1987.

———. *De l'existence à l'existant* Paris: Éditions de la revue fontaine, 1947.

———. *En découvrant l'existence avec Husserl at Heidegger*. 3d ed. Paris: Vrin, 1974.

———. *Entre nous: Essais sur le penser–à–l'autre*. Paris: Éditions Grasset and Fasquelle, 1991.

———. "Éthique comme philosophie première." In *Justifications de l'éthique*, 41–51. Bruxelles: Éditions de l'Université de Bruxelles, 1984.

———. *Existence and Existents*. Trans. Alphonso Lingis. Dordrecht: Kluwer Academic Publishers, 1978.

———. *Humanisme de l'autre homme*. Montpellier: Éditions Fata Morgana, 1976.

———. *Les imprevus de l'histoire*. Montpellier: Éditions Fata Morgana, 1994.

———. "Le moi et la totalité." *Revue de métaphysique e de morale* 59, no. 4 (1954): 353–73.

———. *The Levinas Reader*. Ed. Sean Hand. Oxford: Basil Blackwell, 1989.

———. *Nine Talmudic Readings*. Trans. Annette Aronowicz. Bloomington: Indiana University Press, 1990.

———. *Noms propres*. Montpellier: Éditions Fata Morgana, 1976.

———. *Otherwise Than Being, or Beyond Essence*. Trans. Alphonso Lingis. The Hague: Martinus Nijhoff, 1981.

————. *Proper Names*. Trans. Michael B. Smith. Stanford: Stanford University Press, 1996.

————. *Sur Maurice Blanchot*. Montpellier: Éditions Fata Morgana, 1975.

————. *Le temps et l'autre*. Paris: Montpellier: Éditions Fata Morgana, 1979.

————. *Time and the Other*. Trans. Richard Cohen. Pittsburgh: Duquesne University Press, 1987.

————. *Totality and Infinity: An Essay on Exteriority*. Trans. Alphonso Lingis. Pittsburgh: Duquesne University Press, 1969.

————. *Totalité et infini. Essai sur l'extériorité*. The Hague: Martinus Nijhoff, 1961.

————. "The Trace of the Other." In *Deconstruction in Context*, ed. Mark Taylor, 345–59. Chicago: University of Chicago Press, 1986.

————. "Transcendence et hauteur." *Bulletin de la Société Française de Philosophie* 56, no. 3 (1962): 89–101.

Lippard, Lucy. *The Dematerialization of the Art Object, 1966–1972*. Berkeley: University of California Press, 2002.

Lubac, Henri de. *Theological Fragments*. Trans. Rebecca Howell Balinski. San Francisco: Ignatius Press, 1984.

Lyotard, François. *La confession d'Augustin*. Paris: Éditions Galilée, 1998.

————. *The Confessions of Augustine*. Trans. Richard Beardsworth. Stanford: Stanford University Press, 2000.

————. *Le différend*. Paris: Éditions du Minuit, 1983.

————. *The Differend: Phrases in Dispute*, trans. Georges Van Den Abbeele. Minneapolis: University of Minnesota Press, 1988.

————. *Économie libidinale*. Paris: Éditions du Minuit, 1974.

————. *L'Inhuman: Causeries sur le temps*. Paris: Éditions Galilée, 1988.

————. *The Inhuman: Reflections on Time*. Trans. Geoffrey Bennington and Rachel Bowlby. Stanford: Stanford University Press, 1991.

————. *Just Gaming*. Trans. Wlad Godzich. Minneapolis: University of Minnesota Press, 1985.

————. *Leçons sur l'analytique du sublime*. Paris: Éditions Gallimard, 1991.

————. *Lessons on the Analytic of the Sublime (Kant's 'Critique of Judgment,' §§ 23–29)*. Trans. Elizabeth Rottenberg. Stanford: Stanford University Press, 1991.

————. *Libidinal Economy*. Trans. Iain Hamilton Grant. Bloomington: Indiana University Press, 1993.

————. *The Lyotard Reader*. Ed. Andrew Benjamin. Oxford: Basil Blackwell, 1989.

————. *Peregrinations: Law, Form, Event*. New York: Columbia University Press, 1988.

————. "Presentations." In *Philosophy in France Today*, ed. Alan Montefiore, p. 124. Cambridge: Cambridge University Press, 1983.

Lyotard, Jean–François, and Jean-Loup Thébaud. *Au Juste*. Paris: Christian Bourgois, 1979.

Mallarmé, Stéphane. *Œuvres complètes*. Ed. Henri Mondor. Paris: Éditions Gallimard, 1945.

Mandelstam, Osip. *Critical Prose and Letters*. Trans. Jane Gary Harris and Constance Link. Ann Arbor, MI: Ardis Publishers, 1979.

Margolis, Joseph. *What Is, After All, a Work of Art? Lectures on the Philosophy of Art*. University Park: Pennsylvania State University Press, 1999.

Marion, Jean–Luc. *Dieu sans l'être: Hors–texte*. Paris: Librairie Arthème Fayard, 1982.

————. *God without Being*. Trans. Thomas Carlson. Chicago: University of Chicago Press, 1991.

————. *The Idol and Distance*. Trans. Thomas A. Carlson. New York: Fordham University Press, 2001.

————. *L'Idole et la distance*. Paris: Éditions Bernard Grasset, 1977.

————. "In the Name: How to Avoid Speaking of 'Negative Theology.'" In *God, the Gift, and Postmodernism*, ed. John D. Caputo and Michael J. Scanlon, 20–42. Bloomington: Indiana University Press, 1999.

————. "A Note Concerning the Ontological Difference." *Graduate Faculty Philosophy Journal* 20–21 (1998): 25–50.

————. "The Saturated Phenomenon." Trans. Thomas A. Carlson, Dominique Janicaud et al. In *Phenomenology and the "Theological Turn": The French Debate*, 176–216. New York: Fordham University Press, 2000.

Matthias, John. *Crossing*. Chicago: Swallow Press, 1976.

May, Todd. *The Political Philosophy of Poststructuralist Anarchism*. University Park: Pennsylvania State University Press, 1994.

McCaffery, Steve. *North of Intention: Critical Writings, 1973–1986*. New York: ROOF Books, 1986.

————. *Prior to Meaning: The Protosemantic and Poetics*. Evanston, IL: Northwestern University Press, 2001.

Michelfelder, Diane P. "Gadamer on Heidegger on Art." In *The Philosophy of Hans–Georg Gadamer*, ed. Lewis Edwin Hahn, 437–56. Chicago: Open Court Press, 1997.

Nagy, Gregory. *Poetry as Performance: Homer and Beyond*. Cambridge: Cambridge University Press, 1996.

Nancy, Jean–Luc. *Being Singular Plural*. Trans. Robert D. Richardson and Anne E. O'Byne. Stanford: Stanford University Press, 2000.

———. *The Birth to Presence*. Trans. Brian Holmes. Stanford: Stanford University Press, 1993.

———. *La communauté désœuvrée*. Paris: Christian Bourgois, 1990.

———. *Être singulier pluriel*. Paris: Éditions Galilée, 1996.

———. *L'expérience de la liberté*. Paris: Éditions Galilée, 1988.

———. *The Experience of Freedom*. Trans. Bridget McDonald. Stanford: Stanford University Press, 1993.

———. *The Inoperative Community*. Trans. Peter Connor et al. Minneapolis: University of Minnesota Press, 1991.

———. *Les Muses*. Paris: Éditions Gallilée, 1994.

———. *The Muses*. Trans. Peggy Kamuf. Stanford: Stanford University Press, 1996.

———. *Le partage de voix*. Paris: Éditions Galilée, 1982.

———. "Sharing Voices." In *Transforming the Hermeneutic Context: Nietzsche to Nancy*. Ed. Gayle L. Ormiston and Alan D. Schrift. Albany: State University of New York Press, 1990.

Nietzsche, Friedrich. *Nietzsche Werke: Kritische Ausgabe*. Heraus. Giorgio Colli und Mazzino Montinari. Berlin: Walter de Gruyter, 1972.

Olson, Charles. *The Human Universe*. Ed. Donald Allen. New York: Grove Press, 1967.

Paul, Sherman. *Olson's Push: Origin, Black Mountain, and Recent American Poetry*. Baton Rouge: Louisiana University Press, 1978.

Peperzak, Adriaan. *Ethics as First Philosophy: The Significance of Emmanuel Levinas for Philosophy, Literature, and Religion*. London: Routledge, 1995.

Perloff, Marjorie. *Differentials: Poetry, Poetics, Pedagogy*. Tuscaloosa: University of Alabama Press, 2005.

———. *The Futurist Moment: Avant-garde, Avant Guerre, and the Language of Rupture*. Chicago: University of Chicago Press, 1986.

———. *The Poetics of Indeterminacy: Rimbaud to Cage*. Princeton: Princeton University Press, 1983.

————. *21st-Century Modernism: The "New" Poetics*. Oxford: Basil Blackwell, 2002.

————. *Wittgenstein's Ladder: Poetic Language and the Strangeness of the Ordinary*. Chicago: University of Chicago Press, 1996.

Pöggeler, Otto. "Mystische Elemente im Denken Heideggers und im Dichten Paul Celans." *Zeitwende* 53 (1982): 65–92.

Ponge, Francis. Interview with Serge Gavronsky. In *Poems and Texts*, trans. Serge Gavronsky, p. 37. New York: October House, 1969.

————. *Nouveau Recueil*. Paris: Éditions Gallimard, 1967.

————. *Le parti pris des choses, suive de Proêmes*. Paris: Éditions Gallimard, 1948.

————. *The Voice of Things*. Trans. Beth Archer. New York: McGraw-Hill, 1972.

Prévert, Jacques. *Paroles*. Paris: Éditions Gallimard, 1949.

————. *Words for All Seasons*. Trans. Teo Savory. Greensboro, NC: Unicorn Press, 1979.

Ricoeur, Paul. *Hermeneutics and the Human Sciences*. Trans. John B. Thompson. Cambridge, MA: MIT Press, 1981.

————. *Oneself as Another*. Trans. Kathleen Blamey. Chicago: University of Chicago Press, 1992.

Robbins, Jill. *Altered Reading: Levinas and Literature*. Chicago: University of Chicago Press, 1999.

Sartre, Jean–Paul. *Mallarmé; or, The Poet of Nothingness*. Trans. Ernest Sturm. University Park: Pennsylvania State University Press, 1988.

————. *Qu'est–ce que la littérature?* Paris: Éditions Gallimard, 1948.

————. *Situations, 1*. Paris: Éditions Gallimard, 1947.

————. *Situations, 2*. Paris: Éditions Gallimard, 1948.

————. *"What Is Literature?" and Other Essays*. Trans. Steven Ungar. Cambridge, MA: Harvard University Press, 1988.

Sayre, Henry. *The Object of Performance: The American Avant-Garde Since 1970*. Chicago: Chicago University Press, 1989.

Schlegel, Friedrich. *Kritische Ausgabe*. München: Verlag Ferdinand Schöningh, 1967.

————. *Kritische Schriften*. München: Carl Hanser Verlag, 1956.

————. *Philosophical Fragments*. Trans. Peter Firchow. Minneapolis: University of Minnesota Press, 1991.

Schulz, Holger. "Hand-Luggage: For a Generative Theory of Artifacts." *Leonardo Music Journal* 13 (2003), 61–65.

Schute–Sasse, Jochen, ed. and trans. *Theory as Practice: A Critical Anthology of Early German Romantic Writers*. Minneapolis: University of Minnesota Press, 1997.

Stein, Gertrude. *Selected Writings of Gertrude Stein*. Ed. Carl Van Vechten. New York: Vintage Books, 1962.

Szondi, Peter. "Lecture de Strette: Essai sur la poésie de Paul Celan." *Critique* 27, no. 288 (1971): 387–420.

Vattimo, Gianni. *The End of Modernity*. Trans. Jon R. Snyder. Baltimore: The Johns Hopkins University Press, 1988.

Walsh, George. *The Varieties of Enchantment: Early Greek Views of the Nature and Function of Poetry*. Chapel Hill: University of North Carolina Press, 1984.

Zukofsky, Louis. *Complete Short Poetry*. Baltimore: The Johns Hopkins University Press, 1997.

———. *Prepositions: The Collected Critical Essays*. Hanover, NH: Wesleyan University Press, 2000.

Index

Adams, Parveen, 229n53

Adorno, Theodor, 216n17, 234n17; as anarchist, 202–3n15; art as critique of modernity, 39, 41, 54; Celan's inorganic language, 22; on form, 7–8, 10, 17–18, 34, 65, 92, 122, 128–30, 210n7; nominalism, 5–8, 202n11; "processual character of artworks," 246n18; on Schönberg, 89, 225–26n33; semblance (*Erscheinung*), 110–11, 234n16

aesthetics: Adorno's, 7–8, 17, 110–11, 128–30; formalist, 92–93; Gadamer's, 34–42, 50–54; of the sublime, 51–53, 131–32, 186–87; Levinas's, 179–90, 210n7, 248n10

Agamben, Giorgio, 86, 203n19, 221n12, 223n24

anarchy (*an-archē*), 4–5, 10, 81 159, 203–4n15

Antin, David: "language," 10; "talking at the boundaries," 108–9; "what it means to be avant-garde," 97–98, 101–2, 108–9

art theory, 9–10, 50–51, 108–9, 228n50, 232n8

Artaud, Antonin, 58, 68, 69, 76, 109, 214n3, 214n6, 227n48, 233n12; theater of cruelty, 93–96

artworks: aesthetic differentiation of, 248n10; appropriation of, 39–43; and duration, 102–3, 184–85, 246n18; experience of, 35–39; and form, 7–10, 92–93, 202n11, 233n11, 234n16; materiality of, 179–82, 187–88; performance of, 34–35; sublime, 50–52; and things, 92–93, 106–11, 122, 128–32, 189–90, 232n7, 236n29

Ashbery, John, 209n58, 209n62, 209n63, 231n59; "And *Ut Pictura Poesis* Was Her Name," 29–31; "Ice-Cream Wars," 31

Assoun, Paul Laurent, 249n18

Bataille, Georges, 225n30; Artaud's performance, 95; community, 87, 85–86,170, 224–25n26; expenditure (*dépense*), 74–75, 85–86, 236–37n35; "inner experience," 71–73, 217n28; upturned eye, 74–75

Baudelaire, Charles, 9, 73, 82, 96, 214n8, 214n9; as *flaneur*, 86–88; modernism (*modernité*), 59–62

Matthias, John, 231n1
May, Todd, 201n8
McCaffery, Steve, 225n29, 231n67, 247n1; protosemantic, 207n48; sound poetry, 216n18
Michelfelder, Diane, 210n4
Middleton, Peter, 103–4

Nagy, Gregory, 220n6
names, vs. signs, 22–24
Nancy, Jean-Luc, 203n19, 224n25, 227n40; anarchic community, 81, 95, 97, 220n8, 223n20, 229n54; fragment, 84–85; literature (vs. myth), 104–5; *partage*, 81, 85–86; voice, 80–81, 88–89; singularity, 39, 201n8
Nietzsche, Friedrich, 40, 68, 69, 82, 96, 125, 211n11, 212n15, 220n7, 221n13
noise, 20, 65–68, 93, 110, 196–97, 205n24
nominalism. 5–9, 98, 156–57, 202n11

Olson, Charles, 30, 88–90, 200n3, 226n34, 226n38

paganism, 134–35; etymology of, 148, 238n5
Paul, Sherman, 89, 226n38
Peperzak, Adriaan, 243n30
performance, 34–35, 89–90, 92–95, 100–2, 162, 209n61, 210n7, 225n32
Perloff, Marjorie, 202n12, 206n34, 206n35, 207n43, 209n63, 213n2, 227n47, 231n67, 245n17; futurist moment, 5, 96–97; modernist manifesto, 8–9; on Duchamp, 168–69
philosophy of art, 9–12, 33–36, 50–54, 307–8, 130–31, 180–88, 223n21, 232n7
phrasing, 24–27, 31, 133–34, 146–48, 237n1
play, 33–38, 46–47, 51, 104–5, 222n16
poetry: as *dépense*, 72–73, 85–86; as ecstasy, 79–83, 219n4; experience with language, 157–58; hermetic, 45–46; as language, 12–17, 62–63;

98–101, 155–56, 178–79; and madness, 48–49, 72; as performance, 100–2, 225n32; as Saying (*le Dire*), 175–76, 195–96; a short history of, 83–85; sound-, 65, 216n18; and the sublime, 25–26; and things, 111–22, 165–66, 190–94; *Transzendentalpoesie*, 177
Ponge, Francis, 25, 111–21, 122, 126, 128, 234n19, 235n23, 235n26; "Le cageot," 112–13; "Le gymnaste," 118; Les mures," 113–14; "Notes pour un coquillage," 114–16; "Le pain," 116–17; "R. C. Seine n°," 118–21
Prévert, Jacques, "Inventaire," 125–27, 237n36

rhizome, 237–38n3
Ricoeur, Paul, 39, 210n8, 213n21, 250n25
Roussel, Raymond, 218n32

Sartre, Jean-Paul, 70, 75, 118, 133, 161, 179, 182, 243n1, 248n9; on Ponge, 234n20, 235n26; prose (vs. poetry), 155–58, 179
Sayre, Henry, 228n51
Schlegel, Friedrich, 61, 84–85, 177, 247n4
Schulz, Holger, 204n20
singularity, 35, 81, 94, 102, 110, 126, 129, 164–65, 167, 180, 190, 192–93, 201n8, 234–35n22
sound, 19–21, 45–46, 63, 122–23, 196–97, 216n18
Stein, Gertrude: English language, 46; paratactic writing, 26–27; *Tender Buttons*, 26, 57; and Wittgenstein, 213n2
subjectivity, 57–58, 70, 76, 83; reversal of, 60–61, 111–13, 141, 158, 160, 169, 178–83, 192, 234–35n22; writing, 64–65
sublime, the, 23, 25–27, 37, 51–53, 131–32, 186–87
Szondi, Peter, 44, 211n3